"I believe *Authentic Love* should be required reading for all therapists and a mandate for all Christian counselors.... Of particular benefit is Brennan Mullaney's synthesis of myriad therapeutic approaches into one, simple and comprehensive whole. He reaches perhaps the highest level of abstraction in his discussion of love, with the result being the simplification of heretofore complex reality.... This groundbreaking work makes it abundantly clear that the fundamental cause and the ultimate cure lies in our ability or lack thereof to love and be loved. How utterly simple! How utterly difficult! How utterly true!"
— John Runda, Ph.D., Professor of Sociology, University of Mobile

"To whom would I recommend this book, *Authentic Love*? To everyone in the field of mental health, counselors of all kinds, anyone who works with others: teachers, pastors, Boy Scouts, Girl Scouts, *et alia*.... I am already blessed for having read it."
— Rev. Monsignor Theodore H. Hay, S.T.L.
(Who served as a mental health chaplain for twenty-five years).

"With impeccable logic and a crystalline simplification of human complexities, Brennan Mullaney's *Authentic Love* has revolutionized the mental health system. His explication of love as the basic drive of life and the root reason for our every emotion, action and thought, provides a hopeful new way for both lay people and professional caregivers to understand others, and themselves, too. Love therapy engulfs and subsumes, but also respects, utilizes and makes sense out of the hundreds of disparate theories floating around the therapeutic marketplace."
— Mark Wiegand, P.T., Ph.D., Chairman,
Physical Therapy Department, Bellarmine University

AUTHENTIC LOVE: THEORY AND THERAPY

Visit our web site at
www.albahouse.org
(for orders www.stpauls.us)

or call 1-800-343-2522 (ALBA)
and request current catalog

AUTHENTIC LOVE:
Theory and Therapy

J. Brennan Mullaney, MSSW

ST PAULS

Library of Congress Cataloging-in-Publication Data

Mullaney, J. Brennan.
  Authentic love: theory and therapy / by J. Brennan Mullaney.
    p. cm.
  Includes bibliographical references and index.
  ISBN 978-0-8189-1264-1
  1. Love. 2. Psychotherapy. I. Title.

BF575.L8M85 2008
152.4'1—dc22

                          2007047085

Care has been taken to protect the confidentiality of clients by making
multiple changes in details so as to disguise their identity.

Produced and designed in the United States of America by the
Fathers and Brothers of the Society of St. Paul,
2187 Victory Boulevard, Staten Island, New York 10314-6603
as part of their communications apostolate.

ISBN-10: 0-8189-1264-2
ISBN-13: 978-0-8189-1264-1

Printing Information:

Current Printing - first digit   1   2   3   4   5   6   7   8   9   10

Year of Current Printing - first year shown

2008   2009   2010   2011   2012   2013   2014   2015   2016   2017

DEDICATION

To Joyce
John, Danny and Laurie
Mom and Dad
Family
Friends
Clients
And all who taught me
to love and be loved

Contents

PART THREE: LOVE THERAPY WITH THE
MAJOR EMOTIONAL DISORDERS

Acknowledgments

Love is everywhere. Love is in the air. Love is the ground of our being. Love is in all the people I have passed on the street, and maybe some of their love rubbed off — so maybe I should thank each of them for their contribution to this writing. Sadly but surely, I cannot acknowledge everyone who has loved me, allowed me to love them, and thereby taught me enough to write *Authentic Love*. Here, though, are a few.

Three great friends, all brilliant, all great teachers and huge lovers, each wrote incisive critiques and beautiful reviews of the manuscript. They are: John Runda, Ph.D., Chairman of the Sociology Department of Mobile University; Rev. Monsignor Theodore Hay, S.T.L, now partially retired after twenty-five years as chaplain in mental hospitals; and Mark Wiegand, P.T., Ph.D., Chairman of the Physical Therapy Department, Bellarmine University.

Twenty years ago, when the first draft of *Authentic Love* was written, Emmanuel (Joe) Willett, Ph.D., then President of the Kentucky Psychological Association, critiqued the manuscript and offered valuable criticisms. A decade later, psychologist, editor, and Christian leader Doug Schoeninger, Ph.D., president-elect ('09) of my own (international) Association of Christian Therapists provided such incisive and wisdom-filled tough-love in his review that it allowed me to reconstruct the entire work into its final form.

The first draft of the manuscript was typed by a great friend, Margie (Mrs. Charlie) Boyd, using an old manual typewriter. During that time the work was also reviewed by my dear friends, Norman and Sheila Linton, Susan (Mrs. Louie) Spratt, Donald Feldkamp, and Kathy (Mrs. Joseph) Schmidlin, each of whom

ix

made valuable contributions. More recently, Ms. Joyce Hayes, P.T., reviewed the manuscript not once but twice and helped with both form and substance.

As a computer dunce, I am enormously grateful to Bill Farnsley, graphic artist and computer whiz, who was able to decipher my scribbled drawings and convert them into beautiful diagrams and charts. So, too, I am most appreciative of the computer assistance of Marian (Mrs. Joe) Cotton, Ms. Jane Kelley and Dale Erny.

The beginnings of the thought process for *Authentic Love*, over forty years ago, are described in the Introduction. The actual writing took twenty years. Throughout that time, I was constantly encouraged by friends, clients, and especially my children, John, Danny and Laurie. They are now thriving, loving adults, but those poor kids grew up hearing about the love book before learning nursery rhymes. I am deeply grateful for their unwavering confidence and support.

With a full heart, I am grateful to the beautiful girl I loved from the first instant I laid eyes on her, Joyce, my wife of forty-three years. The crazy story of our becoming engaged within four hours of meeting is contained in the book. What is not told is how she patiently responded the thousands of times I turned to her after jotting a new idea and asked, "What do you think?" She was the one who not only loved me enough to remain constantly supportive, she was the one who was honest enough to sometimes answer warmly, "That's stupid, dear."

Finally, how can I possibly thank the Author of Love, God Himself? I can only guess He would want me to simply acknowledge His patience during the many decades that *Authentic Love* has been in the works. Thus, I am reminded of the amazing stories that are told of the saints and mystics — that as they enter the silence of contemplation, some of these holy people actually hear God breathe. I think I finally understand a tiny bit of what the mystics experience. When this book was finally finished, I really think I heard God breathe — a sigh of relief.

J. Brennan Mullaney

Introduction

If love... be not the law of our being,
the whole of my argument falls to pieces.
— *Mahatma Gandhi*[1]

Love begins shyly, so there is surely no graceful way to begin a book on love. Authentic love is always a little reticent at first, a little awkward, and love at its best is a mystical experience that leaves us in awe, dumb-stuck, mouths agape — silent. Indeed, love is an unfathomable mystery. Yet, it is the ambitious goal of this book to reach for its ethereal heights and to bring love down to earth. We must do that, I believe, if we are ever going to understand ourselves, much less obtain healing. Love alone heals. That is the fundamental premise of love therapy, a new model of psychotherapy introduced here.

The word "love" has been romanticized, sentimentalized, sugar-coated, sing-songed, pulpiteered, hypersexualized, hawked, valentined, prostituted and slandered. Love has been written about till its pages are yellowed and brittle. Yet, sailing into the

---

[1] Mahatma Gandhi, *Non-violence in Peace and War* (Navajivan Publishing House: Ahmedabad, India, 1948), Vol. 1, p. 121, in Thomas Merton, Ed., *Gandhi on Non-Violence* (New York: New Directions, 1964), p. 25. The words which I omitted from this quote, indicated by ellipses, are "...or non-violence." Much as I believe in non-violence, I cannot equate it with love, as Gandhi seems to do in this sentence. Non-violence is not necessarily love any more than non-jealousy or non-hatred are love. Authentic love is a positive reality, not merely the absence of a negative. However, I am wholly in accord with Gandhi in saying that if the law of our being is not love, then the whole of my argument falls to pieces.

face of all that misuse, I must adopt that same pitiful old bag lady of a word as the name of a new model of psychotherapy. Love therapy boldly promises new insights into mental and emotional disorders, and even — imagine! — an understanding of what authentic love is all about.

But all of us use the word "love" repeatedly every day, so is a new exploration of the subject really needed? Don't we all understand what love is? I trust that many will agree when I dare answer unequivocally and emphatically, but sadly: No! A quick glance at the latest statistics on divorce — is it now fifty percent of marriages that fail? — provides the first hint that at least that many people made one of the biggest decisions of their lives without knowing what they were doing. Look at the crime rate, at wars throughout the world, at the discrimination in all its forms, at the injustices of poverty, the abuse and neglect of millions of our children, at the desperation of the homeless and the criminality of hunger in a land of plenty, and then decide if you believe that most people know what love is — authentic love, that is. Adjust your vision to a panoramic view of the huge numbers of sexually abused women and men, at the devastation of the worldwide drug epidemic, at the rampant promiscuity proved by the spread of herpes alone, at the huge numbers of battered wives and children, at the inhumanity of slavery that still exists in a dozen countries, not to mention the worldwide scourge of mental illness and emotional disorders, and then answer, "Does the world seem to know what authentic love is all about?"

Love, the ultimate mystery, offers astounding answers to the perplexities that every human being grapples with from birth to death — Who am I? Indeed, what am I? What is the fundamental drive and purpose of my life? How can I explain my feelings, my thoughts, my deepest yearnings? This volume is intended to ease the inevitable and normal pain of wrestling with those inescapable perplexities of daily life. But life can become rough sometimes, so painful that some of us — maybe all of us at some time or another — will admit to periods of suffering a mental or emotional disorder. This in-depth exploration offers a personality theory grounded in love, and a model of psychotherapy which integrates that theory: Love Therapy. Together, the theory and therapy are contained in eighteen principles.

In Part One on love theory our human personality is described through nine principles which collectively define day-to-day life in terms of normalcy, to wit, only love is normal. Immediately, that equation, love and normalcy, presents a challenge that is best handled, I would suggest, with a good sense of humor. Thus, as normal as I like to consider myself, I must honestly admit that there are times when I am not at all loving and thus "abnormal," and thus "a little bit crazy." Hey, we need to be able to laugh at ourselves because love's logic insists that even the sanest, most "normal" among us is sometimes a little bit daffy.

Love theory, though, is intended to teach us how love works. Then, knowing how it works should make it a little easier to bring love down to earth and into practice. Thence we will be able to love both others and ourselves a little more, and that, per love theory, is all that any of us really want, to love and to be loved.

It is only in Part Two on love therapy that we address the extremes of the abnormal, the mental and emotional disorders. Herein, the new model of psychotherapy is contained in a second set of nine principles. Love theory and therapy both are founded on Principle One, which I preview here in abbreviated form. *Love is simultaneously the fundamental drive and goal of human life and the basic motivation for every human act.* Before this book ends, every emotion will be reinterpreted as a product and expression of that universal need, to love and be loved. Then, all mental and emotional disorders will be understood as distinct love disorders. Thence, after showing why love and only love heals emotional disorders, a new approach to psychotherapy will be presented. This new theory of personality reinterprets and then subsumes many earlier, respected schools and methods of therapy. That is a bold statement, so let me hasten to add that love therapy does not pretend to wholly replace, and would surely never denigrate, any earlier form of therapy. There is a collective wealth of wisdom in those methods, and love therapy gratefully incorporates and utilizes many of them. But there is a distinct difference in the way love therapy incorporates many therapies and the way the widely used "eclectic therapy" does. Eclectic therapy utilizes "this theory, that method — whatever works." In contrast, in love therapy, it is love that guides and infuses every theory and method that it incorporates.

It sounds as if I am saying that love can virtually revolutionize psychotherapy and the entire mental health system. Precisely! And that every emotion is somehow explained in terms of love. Exactly! And that love is the bottom-line explanation for every thought, every feeling, every decision, and every human act. Righto! And that love is simply a panacea for every human problem. Forsooth! — except, I must add, there is absolutely nothing simple about love.

And with that, the response of some professional cohorts has often been, "Love?"! Why, that's not even a professional word. If you want people to seriously consider such revolutionary ideas, why not use *"agape"* or *"philia"* or some other Greek word that sounds scientific? Why "love" therapy? Why even try to explain or reinterpret such a hackneyed old term? Why not just find another word?

Believe me, I tried. For forty years I tried. Yet, I could never find another word that conveyed what I became convinced was the "heart of the matter" of not just emotional disorders, but of life itself. More importantly, while counseling thousands of people with panic disorders, psychoses, phobias, sexual disorders, depression — the whole wide scope of human misery — I never met a person who did not know what love meant. Even those who had sustained horrible inner damage because love had been so terribly absent in their lives, somehow knew what the word meant, albeit vaguely. Even when I tried to damn and discard the word, as I did many times, a suffering client would open her/his heart wide, show me an open wound, and tell me what caused it — love that had been battered, rejected or betrayed — and then teach me what would be required to heal that wound — yes, love.

Early Struggles With Love, as a Freudian Heretic

By sharing with you my personal story of how it all began, we can begin looking at the logic of love in comparison with the hundreds of other personality theories that are floating around the psychotherapeutic marketplace. In 1962-64, I was in a graduate school of psychiatric social work which required that I do field work in a mental hospital and in a children's mental health clinic. In both the school and in clinical supervision, there was only one theory of human personality that was advanced or accepted: Freudian. And only one diagnostic method that was approved: psychoanalytic. Sigmund in those days was still recognized as "Father Freud," and heaven help the student who tried to buck his system of thought.

For the Freudians — all my teachers and supervisors — there was one and only one cause of all human behavior, emotion, and thought — sex. Of course, sex was wrapped up in "scientific" terms like id, libido, instincts, Oedipus and Electra complexes and such. Yet, if sex wasn't the overt explanation of behavior, it was the symbolic answer for *everything*. Thus, students and teachers alike would have serious classroom discussions in which penises were seen *everywhere*. In every telephone pole, broomstick and tall building, my colleagues would see a penis. (Always erect. I kept wondering why Freud didn't find symbols for the ordinary shriveled kind.) Similarly, every cavity, every body of water, every room, was interpreted as symbolizing a vagina or a womb. The bottom line was that all human behavior and every mental and emotional disorder had to be fundamentally explained in terms of the single rudimentary instinct — sex. From day one, that struck me as a kooky idea.

Then on day two, I made a terrible mistake: I started to think for myself. Immediately, intuitively somehow, it struck me that, much as I liked sex, love seemed much more fundamental. That's when the trouble began. A professor presented the case history of a young woman who had been having anxiety attacks, and then asked, "Now, class, what is the etiology, the cause, the basic explanation of this patient's symptoms?" One classmate answered in terms of "libidinal instincts," and the teacher smiled approvingly. Another added that "penis envy" was evident; the teacher smiled. A third classmate elicited a broader smile by waxing eloquent on the Electra complex, plumbing to the depths of the patient's problem — frustration over not being able to have sex with her father. Midst unanimous agreement that sex explained the case, I interjected, "Excuse me, but it seems to me that this patient had a love problem. The history shows she was emotionally deprived, love-starved. So she had to have a lot of fear in her. She felt unprotected; that's the anxiety. I can't see how sex had anything to do with this case. Her problem was love. That's the etiology." The professor didn't smile.

For the next several weeks, the same scenario was repeated time and again. A case history would be presented. Teachers and classmates would unanimously concur that the etiology was sex — and I would apologetically insist, "No. Love is the answer."

The result should have been predictable, but little did I know that my opinions had created a big debate in the back rooms of the university. I was notified that a special faculty meeting had been called at the insistence of several professors, a meeting that would decide whether I would be kicked out of graduate school. The word wasn't used, but I was basically charged with "heresy" because I kept challenging Freudian doctrine by insisting that love, not sex, was the basic drive in life.

While the faculty meeting went on — and on, and on — I waited nervously in the school lobby. Two hours later, two teachers emerged from the meeting, delegated to negotiate terms. By a narrow vote of the faculty, it had been agreed that I could remain in the school on one condition: that I promised to stop "promoting love" until I graduated. Prophetically, one teacher added, "You've made some friends on the faculty who believe that some day you'll be writing about your 'love' ideas. For now, though, if you want to stay in this *Freudian* school, what you must do with that love stuff is this: stop mouthing off about it!"

At the time, I felt I had to agree to the faculty's terms, not just to avoid being excommunicated and expelled, but because I could not "prove" that love was the fundamental drive of human life any more than Freud had "proven" that the id-libido-sexual instinct was basic. It took a while for the logic to dawn on me that one cannot prove a truth that is rock-bottom fundamental. The most basic truths, called "first principles" by philosophers, are either self-evident or a matter of faith.

Love Logic Midst The Madness Called Mental Health

So what is the basic truth about human beings, the fundamental dynamic that makes us tick?

Depending on how you count, the "Table of Schools of Psychiatry" in *The American Psychiatric Association's Psychiatric Glossary*[2] lists twenty-six officially recognized schools of psychotherapy. That means that there are, if not twenty-six, at least a dozen or more "fundamental" premises to explain how human beings operate. Each theorist starts with one fundamental "truth," a first premise, and then builds his/her theory on that first statement.

A more exhaustive listing is provided in *The Psychotherapy Handbook*,[3] which listed two hundred-fifty different therapies that were in use in 1980. We can guess that there may be another fifty that have been developed since that listing. Are there that many "basic" premises about what makes human beings tick represented in those hundreds?

Look at the logic! There certainly cannot be hundreds of "basic" truths, first premises, nor a dozen, or even two. Yet, those hurting people looking for help might unwittingly find themselves facing anything from Active Analytic Psychotherapy, to Aikido, to Behavioral, to Cognitive, to Gestalt, to Mandala Therapy, or from

---

[2] *The American Psychiatric Association's Psychiatric Glossary* (Washington, DC: American Psychiatric Press, Inc.,1984).

[3] Richie Herink, ed., *The Psychotherapy Handbook* (New York: Meridian, 1980).

Mythosynthesis to Poetry Therapy or Vita-Erg Therapy, and on to the Zanaleya Psychoenergetic Technique, or any of *hundreds* of other "schools," all of which purport to offer suffering people the one groundwork of truth that will help them. This is a logical shambles! Am I being unkind when I conclude that the logic of the mental heath field is a cruel joke? Truth is one! The idea that academic or professional "freedom" can abide twenty or two hundred versions of "fundamental" truth and still say that it is logical and sane enough to help the mentally ill is insane!

A Dozen Therapies, a Dozen First Principles?

Over the past century or so, a virtual multitude of so-called fundamental drives and goals have been named and defended, many with so-called scientific arguments. Philosophically, each drive or goal named would be considered by the theorist to be his "first premise." He may not call it that, but when a personality theory is presented, the writer starts with a "fundamental idea" which he claims as the rock-bottom truth about human beings; that is his first premise. Following is a list of a dozen well-known models of psychotherapy, with the fundamental or first principle of each. The question is: can there possibly be a dozen principles, each and all of them "first"?

Model	First Premise, Basic Principle
Sigmund Freud (Psychoanalysis)	Sex (id, libido)
Carl Jung (Analytical Psychology)	Both sex and power, plus archetypes
Alfred Adler (Adlerian Psychotherapy)	Striving for completion, significance
Otto Rank (Will Therapy)	Will
Albert Ellis (Rational-Emotive Therapy)	Belief systems
Harry Stack Sullivan (Sullivanism)	Social experience
Viktor Frankl (Logotherapy)	Meaning
Aaron Beck (Cognitive Therapy)	Automatic, hidden thoughts

Behavioral Therapy	Stimulus-response conditioning
Fritz Perls (Gestalt Therapy)	Whole (gestalt) present awareness
Psychopharmacology	Brain chemicals
Eclectic Therapy	This, that, whatever might work

Logic insists that all of these theorists cannot all be correct; they are contradicting one another. There simply cannot be a dozen fundamental human drives. There can be only one. It is love. Of course, I cannot debate even a dozen theories here, much less hundreds, so allow me to present the logic of love with just three comparisons.

Viktor Frankl's logotherapy (*logos* means "meaning") is subsumed as an integral approach of love therapy. Frankl's contribution to psychotherapy is beyond measure, so it is certainly not meant to diminish the value of his thought when I take issue with his fundamental tenet, that finding "meaning" is the most fundamental task of therapy. The love therapy position can be stated quite succinctly: people need to find meaning in their lives, certainly; but without love, life has no meaning at all. Psychologically, no less than ontologically, love means everything.

Cognitive therapy is based on the theory that cognition — conscious thinking and conscious memories — is more important than the unconscious. Rather than probe subterranean depths looking for libidinal instincts, as Freud did, cognitive therapists help people find their "hidden, automatic" thoughts, conscious cognitive errors, habitual and mistaken ideas that are causing their emotional problems.

Love therapy frequently incorporates cognitive therapy. It has great validity, so in no way do I wish to demean it when I say that it is incomplete. Cognitive errors accompany many emotional problems, true, but they *fundamentally* cause none. Nor has knowledge, thought analysis, nor correcting erroneous ideas ever healed a serious emotional problem. Emotional and mental disorders are caused only by love damage, love that is twisted, sliced, rejected or absent, and they are healed only by authentic love. Love heals — only love.

A third comparison: ironically, behavior therapy is effective for some emotional problems, even though it seems that behavior theorists have not understood why it works. The behaviorists saw that if you change a stimulus (S), you can effect a changed behavioral response (R). Reward or punishment, a stimulus, can change responses — anxiety, a child's school behavior, phobias, sexual dysfunction, or whatever. This reductionist S-R philosophy views human beings as organisms that operate no differently than Pavlov's dog. Here we need take only a tiny conceptual step toward rewriting the underlying philosophical construct of behavior therapy. Thus: using the broadest possible view — ontologically — love is a movement toward the good. Therefore, if any reward (S) is perceived as *good*, it will automatically be seen as love, so *of course* a reward can change behavior (R) — because love heals. That reward, that stimulus, is love. Contrariwise, punishment, or negative conditioning, may be seen as non-love, just as the dysfunctional behavior that needs to be changed always involves a pseudo-love.

We could continue arguing the fundamentality of love versus two hundred more therapies and their hundreds of "first" principles, and that does indeed need to be done. There are valuable gems of truth in almost all theories, and love therapy honors them all. At the same time, both love and logic demand that the sheer madness of the theory-sated mental health field be brought to an end. Allow me, therefore, to say this as gently as possible (though it may have the impact of a sledgehammer): in terms of fundamental truth, all prior models of therapy and all personality theories are either incomplete, partial truths, or simply wrong. There can be only one basic truth.

Love in Science, Poetry and Ontology

The little research that has been done on love-related subjects does strongly support the principles and methods of love therapy. Here I would suggest only one convincing line of inquiry — the research of Charles Truax, who began by looking hard at the approach of one of the giants of psychotherapy, Carl Rogers. Truax's mountain of research alone, I would assert, goes further in providing support for love therapy than any research in support of psychoanalysis, behavioral, cognitive, or any other model.

Carl Rogers grounded his client-centered therapy[4] on the key concept, "unconditional positive regard." That "regard," he said, was the essence of effective counseling. When I first read that phrase, my immediate response was, "Why didn't Rogers just say 'love'?" Truax, too, must have wanted a more precise understanding because he began years of research to identify the key factors that marked effective psychotherapy. His *Toward Effective Counseling and Psychotherapy*[5] sums up his conclusions: Effective counseling, above all, is the product of the therapist's "accurate empathy, non-possessive warmth, and genuineness."[6] Again, after reading Truax's research and his conclusion, my response was, "Why didn't Truax just say 'love'?"

In research terms, the major hypothesis of love therapy is that "Effectiveness in counseling is a product of and proportionate to the counselor's love." A second hypothesis of love therapy is that "Regardless of the model or methodology followed — whether Rogerian, psychoanalytic, cognitive, transactional, gestalt, or any other — if any counseling is effective, it is primarily because the client was authentically, accurately, and skillfully loved by the therapist." Once stated, we immediately recognize that we are again faced with the task of defining terms. What is love?

My definition(s) of love are proffered below, and this entire book continues to unfold its meanings, but let's pause to see where we have arrived. Rogers' "unconditional positive regard"

---

[4] Carl R. Rogers, *Client-Centered Therapy: Its Current Practice, Implications, and Theory* (Boston, MA: Houghton Mifflin, 1951).

[5] Charles B. Truax and Robert R. Carkhuff, *Toward Effective Counseling and Psychotherapy* (Chicago, IL: Aldine Publishing Company, 1967).

[6] *Ibid.*, pp. 80, 141.

and Truax's "accurate empathy, non-possessive warmth, and genuineness" would certainly be marks of therapeutic love, but those phrases certainly do not capture the totality of love, do they? Suppose we were to add these qualities:

> Love is patient and kind; it is not jealous or conceited or proud; love is not ill-mannered or selfish or irritable; love does not keep a record of wrongs; love is not happy with evil, but is happy with truth. Love never gives up; and its faith, hope and patience never fail.[7]

Now who would argue that these qualities are not essential to effective psychotherapy? Adding those biblical qualities to those of Rogers and Truax, though, barely begins to describe the surface of what love is. Even this early in the Introduction, it is clear that we will never define love with any final precision. Yet, there is great benefit in struggling to find words befitting it. That is what poets of all ages have tried to do.

Glancing through the index of Bartlett's *Familiar Quotations*,[8] one finds over one thousand references to "love," far more than of any other subject. Why is it so difficult? Why does love so deftly evade capture by language? One poet, Edward Estlin Cummings, summed it up: "Love is the whole and more than all."[9] But it was Emily Dickinson who said it most succinctly: "Love is all there is."[10] Those are ontological definitions. Yes, difficult to grasp. Let me hazard this promise, though: in this book, beginning below, we will begin to bring love down to earth, beginning with what I call a "quadruplex definition" of love, i.e., four definitions that can be read as one, definitions that will satisfy not just your mind, but your heart and soul.

---

[7] 1 Corinthians 13:4-8, *The Bible in Today's English* (New York: United Bible Societies).

[8] John Bartlett, *Familiar Quotations* (Boston, Toronto: Little, Brown and Company, 1968), pp. 1460-1466.

[9] *Ibid.*, p. 1031 b.

[10] *Ibid.*, p. 739 a.

So What Is Love?

Can we define it? In order to set the stage for the huge definitional leap that love therapy takes, let's begin with several definitions proffered by some respected others. There are valuable facets of the huge gem of love to be found in each definition.

> I define love as that which satisfies our need to receive and bestow affection and nurturance; to give and be given assurance of value, respect, acceptance, and appreciation; and to feel secure in our unity with, and belonging to, a particular family, as well as the human family. (Walsh) [11]

> Love is "the relationship between persons in which they confer mutual benefits upon each other." (Montagu) [12]

> I define love thus: the will to extend one's self for the purpose of nurturing one's own or another's spiritual growth. (Peck) [13]

> Love is a response to a generalized hope signal, a grand expectancy. The love object, be it a thing or a person, is a generalized, secondary, positive reinforcer. (Miller and Siegel) [14]

Although neither seems to provide a per se definition of love, Arthur Janov's *The Biology of Love*,[15] and *A General Theory of Love*[16]

---

[11] Anthony Walsh, Ph.D., *The Science of Love* (Buffalo, NY: Prometheus Books, 1991), p. 24.

[12] Montagu, cited in *ibid.*, p. 7.

[13] Peck, cited in *ibid.*, p. 81.

[14] H.L. Miller and P.S. Siegal, *Loving: A Psychological Approach* (New York: Wiley, 1972).

[15] Arthur Janov, *The Biology of Love* (Amherst, NY: Prometheus Books, 2000).

[16] Thomas Lewis, *et al*, *A General Theory of Love* (New York: Vintage Books, 2000).

by Lewis, Amini and Lannon, both magnificent works, present examinations of love that are heavily focused on physiology and neurology. Thus, Janov says, "love is not an abstraction but a literal neurochemical event."[17] In the same vein, Lewis says, "Love emanates from the brain; the brain is physical, and thus is as fit a subject for scientific discourse as cucumbers or chemistry."[18] And my response is: is it that simple?

After providing a most thoughtful analysis of love and struggling with many definitions, Bernard Murstein arrives at a conclusion which I hope was tongue in cheek; in any case, I laughed, whether Bernard meant me to do so or not. His definition serves well in capturing the complexity:

> Love is an Austro-Hungarian empire uniting all sorts of feelings, behaviors, and attitudes, some having little in common, under the rubric 'love'.... Love can manifest itself as a feeling, as behavior, or as a judgment (decision). A definition that attempts to unify these diverse phenomena results in a simplistic tautological definition that love is what one decides it is.[19]

Given even more definitions that scholars could dig out of the literature on love, the question is whether we must conclude with Murstein that love can be any willy-nilly thing we decide it is, or is it conceivable that we can eliminate the confusion and define love in a way that comes close to capturing the whole Austro-Hungarian empire, the complete elephant, the entire infinitely faceted diamond? Indeed, what is love?

---

[17] Janov, *op. cit.*, p. 272.

[18] Lewis, *et al, op. cit.*, p. 12.

[19] Bernard I. Murstein, "A Taxonomy of Love," in Robert J. Sternberg and Michael L. Barnes, Eds., *The Psychology of Love* (New Haven and London: Yale University Press, 1988), p. 33.

Love Theory's Definition of Love

The love theory definition of love is quadripartic: four definitions can be read as one sentence. I have alluded to three of these earlier. The fourth, given below, will surely be the most controversial, but it can best be understood in relation to the other three. Following, therefore, is the love theory general definition of love:

Part One — Theologically: Love is God (and vice versa).

Part Two — Metaphysically: Love is a movement of the will toward that which is perceived as good.[20]

Part Three — Psychologically: Love is simultaneously the fundamental drive and goal of human life, the push and pull of every human act, the raw force from which is derived and toward which is aimed, all emotion, all thought, all volition (will), and all behavior.

Part Four — Materially, physically: Love is the fundamental "spiritual substance" from which the atom, the building block of all material reality, was created; as such, love remains in the atom as the elemental dynamic force, flux, medium, ether or energy that binds together and governs the functioning of every electron, proton, neutrino, quark and yet-to-be-found subatomic microparticle and of every movement of the macrocosmic physical universe. In short: Love is reality.

This quadruplex definition obviously moves love a quantum leap beyond the romance-, emotion-, biological and relationship-centered ways in which it has been typically defined. Yet, it refutes no one. Love is all the things that all the theorists, all the scientists, all the poets, all that thousands of other writers have said it is. It is just more — far, far more.

So does this definition of love satisfy that task of describing the whole elephant, the entire empire, or on the contrary, does

---

[20] This is my paraphrase of a concept which I attribute to Avery R. Dulles, S.J., James M. Demske, S.J., and Robert J. O'Connell, S.J., *Introductory Metaphysics* (New York: Sheed and Ward, 1955), p. 263.

this four-dimensional definition, sweeping as it obviously is, still capture only a few facets of love, something less than the entire diamond? It has taken me forty years to write that definition of love; it's a start.

A Personal Touch

Now the question is, do my forty-odd years of professional experience, and that many years of thought invested in the subject, qualify me as an expert on love? Certainly not. No one has enough professional credentials or experience to present themselves as an "authority" on the subject. The more we study it, the more we understand that love is humbling. Humility is simply the acceptance of the truth about ourselves, the realization that we do not create our own being, we do not sustain ourselves in existence, nor do we make ourselves what we are. Humility is the recognition that our lives, our every breath, all that we are and all that we have, including our capacity to love, are gifts. We are gifts from God and gifts from other people, and every gift is an act of love, a gift that we can be proud of, a gift we can celebrate.

It is in that spirit that love therapy is presented — with inexpressible gratitude for the love I have received from God, wife, family, clients, and from oh-so-many people. And the love I have been able to give, for that, too, I am very grateful. It's the kind of gratitude that makes me laugh because I always think what a funny gift love is: love is the clown who keeps pulling scarves out of his sleeve, and keeps finding more scarves. The only way you can keep the gift of love is to give it away. So you do; you give it away. But when you look in your sleeve again, you've still got the same love you gave away.

Given an inexhaustible supply of the stuff, there would seem to be no excuse for not loving, consistently and exquisitely. Love, after all, is all there is. Now if only we can figure out what that means....

Part One

LOVE THEORY –
Love as The Measure of Normalcy

CHAPTER ONE

The Basic Love Principle

Principle One: The Basic Principle of Love Theory

Love is simultaneously the fundamental drive and highest goal of human life, the basic motivation and purpose, the push and the pull, the Alpha and Omega of every human act. Love is the most elemental human need, the raw force of the psychospiritual heart from which is derived all emotion, all thought, all volition and all behavior. The self-evident first principle of human life is, "I am loved and I love; thus do I know that I am, and thence do I know that what is, is."

(As each principle in the book is stated, it will be followed by several follow-up statements — corollaries and explanations that support or derive from the principle. A principle is by definition an extremely condensed statement of truth, so the explanations are intended to flesh out and to make the case for the principle in as succinct fashion as possible.)

Explanations

• The first convincing proof that love is the most essential need to sustain life is seen in physiological form, in the evidence presented by marasmus babies (in present-day language, these infants usually are diagnosed as "failure to thrive"). Despite wholly adequate physical care, these infants are not given the first essential, elementary form of love — touching, cuddling, kissing and stroking. Without this crucial early form of love, these babies rapidly wither and die.

• The psychological proof that love is the basic drive and goal of life is intellectually and experientially self-evident. This self-evidence of love's essentiality, and its primacy in relation to all other needs and desires, is provided by a form of knowledge that is far deeper than abstract reasoning; this is *raison de cœur*, reason of the heart, the psychospiritual power that enables us to unify knowledge, goodness, beauty and love so as to intuit and embrace truth that is ordinarily beyond the ken of the intellect. Pascal said it beautifully: "The heart has its reasons, which reason does not know."[1]

• Every Psychology begins with a Philosophy, whether stated or unstated. In turn, every Philosophy begins with "first principles," which are supreme principles of reality and of thought. A first principle is a self-evident truth, i.e., a truth unto itself which the mind and heart immediately affirm, and which needs no other proof. Thus, Thomas Aquinas, following Aristotle, began with the first principle, "What is, is."[2] René Descartes' first principle was the well-known *"Cogito ergo sum"*: "I think, therefore I am." Reflecting on Aquinas' and Descartes' first principles, many will affirm Aquinas as true, and most dispute Descartes, but surely we will all agree that they are both "heady," i.e., their principles

---

[1] Blaise Pascal, *Pensées* [1670] trans. by W. F. Trotter (New York: Random House, 1941), no. 277, p. 95. One sees slight variations of this translation. Thus, in the Introduction to this edition, the Saxe Commins translation is, "The heart has reasons of which reason itself knows nothing." *Ibid.*, p. xv. For purists and linguists, the original French is given in John Bartlett, *Familiar Quotations* (Boston: Little, Brown, 1968), p. 363b: *"Le coeur a ses raisons que la raison ne conait point."* By highlighting the value of the heart's reasoning, there is certainly no intent to denigrate the value of intellectual reason nor science. Nor can *raison de cœur* be used as an excuse for bad logic. Balance is always imperative. Pascal is again helpful in this regard: "If we submit everything to reason, our religion will have no mysterious and supernatural element. If we offend the precepts of reason, our religion will be absurd and ridiculous." Pascal, *Ibid.*, p. 94.

[2] Dulles, *et al, op. cit.*, p. 11.

begin and end as abstract thoughts that reflect only the intellect. Consider: a first principle that is truly first, it would seem, must ring true at the deepest level of being and reflect the whole of my being. Pascal said it well: "We know truth, not only by reason, but by the heart, and it is this last way that we know first principles; and reason, which has no part of it, tries in vain to impugn them."[3] Thus, in love theory, we begin with a first principle which is self-evident both intellectually and existentially, i.e., the most fundamental truth that is affirmed at the deepest level of my being. The first of first principles is this: "I love and I am loved; thus do I know that I am, and thence do I know that what is, is."

• Psychologically, love is the first natural law. This universal yearning and striving, the need to receive and to give love, corresponds to the subsistence of love in all created reality (Discussed at length in Principle Seven).

• Thought, volition (will), emotion and behavior are all powers of love; without love they would not exist at all, and when love is deficient, or when it is twisted, betrayed, perverted or otherwise damaged, then thought, decisions, feelings and behavior are all damaged accordingly, i.e., to the same quantitative and qualitative degree.

• In response to the age-old question as to which is more important, heredity or environment, genes or child-rearing, the answer, in a word, is love. Love is the fundamental biopsycho-spiritual energy, the basic creational and formational "substance" of both nurturing and genetics. The abundance or deficiency of love changes, for good or ill, brain chemistry and endocrine functioning, which in turn influence the complex interactions of the brain's synaptic connections through such love-sensitive biochemicals as GABA, MAO, dopamine, serotonin, AcH, THP, and norepinephrine.[4] The estimate in love therapy is that functional love deficits directly cause ninety percent of mental and

---

[3] Pascal, *op. cit.*, no. 282, p. 95.
[4] Cf., Michael Liebowitz, *The Chemistry of Love* (New York: Berkley Books, 1983), p. 45.

emotional disorders. Some of the remaining percentage is caused by brain damage, certainly, but all that remaining ten percent of organically-related disorders cannot be said to be solely caused by genetics and chemical imbalances. Rather, love deficits indirectly caused many of those biological disorders also. Consider: if a love deficit is capable of negatively impacting *any* brain or endocrine chemical at all, then reason suggests that over time, generation to generation, love and love-deficits accrue systematically so as to progressively change genetic make-up positively or negatively. In sum, love molds genes.

• Love damage is expressed through symptoms and defenses, distortions of thought, emotions, volition and behavior which the heart designs to compensate for the same quality of love that was damaged or lost, and/or to protect the threatened but undamaged love that remains in the heart. (Qualitatively, the primary diagnostic question of psychotherapy is always, "What is this painful emotional symptom, this irrational decision, this odd behavior saying about the damaged love and the precise kind of love needed by this psychospiritual heart?")

• Only love is "normal" according to the love theory standard, i.e., love alone is the criterion according to which an individual's, a family's, or a society's mental health can be adequately evaluated. Physical medicine's standard of normalcy is "free from disease," but mental health, because it has had no singular accepted personality theory, nor indeed an accepted definition of a human being, has had no clear standard of what mental health is. As a result, Psychology has compromised, defining "normal" in terms of a "range" of behavior established by finding the average of what people report, or by averaging what can be observed about them. Such averaging of normalcy compromises human dignity. Human beings have a right to mental health education which teaches that "normal" means to love and be loved; that *any* amount of love deprivation causes degrees of both emotional and physical illnesses; that no one needs to be ashamed to openly proclaim the personal need for love; that children need to learn about love in school far *more* than they need to learn reading and math; that love damage and love deprivation cause more pain and death than cancer, heart disease, crime and all other causes put together; and that the most fundamental meaning of being normal is that none of us will accept anything less, in this life or beyond, than being loved and loving. "Mental health" and "normal" are both precise synonyms for loving and being loved.

Love theory issues in very new and different ways of thinking about the mind, emotions, behavior, and indeed the whole of Psychology. Seventeen remaining love principles support and explicate the general principle above. Love changes our basic understanding of how we are made (the subject of Principle Three, on personality structure), and of each of our emotions, not just how they operate, but what they are (Principle Five addresses the emotions). Love theory provides a new and simpler way of understanding all, and each particular mental and emotional disorder. As the eighteen principles unfold, a new understanding of these disorders will emerge, and with it, a comprehensive new approach to treatment which unifies many of the theories and techniques of the past.

Here, we need only cite the general support that study after study has provided for the love principle.

Marasmus babies, noted in the first Explanation, provide the most dramatic, poignant and undeniable evidence that love is crucial to our bare survival, not "just as important as" food, water, and the air we breathe, but more so. Two tragic experiences of modern history provide the absolute proof of the basic love principle.

In 1945, a famous study by René Spitz[5] compared two groups

---

[5] René Spitz, "Hospitalism. An Inquiry into the Genesis of Psychiatric Conditions in Early Childhood," *The Psychoanalytic Study of the Child*, Vol. 1 (New York: International Universities Press, 1945).

of infants, one group from a foundling home where the babies were provided care by professional nurses, the other from the nursery of an institution for delinquent girls where the babies were cared for by the girl-mothers. The hygiene, nutrition and medical care of the foundling home were far superior to the girl's institution. Yet, over a two year period, the developmental quotients (D.Q.s) of the professionally-tended foundling home babies went *down*, while the D.Q.s of the delinquent girls' babies went *up*. Worse, though, during the two-year study, thirty-seven percent of the foundling home babies died. None of the babies of the delinquent girls died.

The crucial difference Spitz found was that the girl-mothers cuddled, kissed, rocked, stroked and played with their babies — in other words, they loved them — whereas the busy professional nurses, though they had provided far better hygiene and nutrition, had failed to provide the fundamental necessity for the babies' survival — adequate love. Photographs of marasmus babies show tiny creatures who have shriveled, wrinkled, and appear to be two hundred years old. The lesson of marasmus babies is precisely as Dr. Smiley Blanton's title warns: *Love or Perish*.[6]

In Romania, following the fall of communist rule, the world discovered that thousands of children had been warehoused in that country's overcrowded and understaffed orphanages, in the same profound love-starved conditions as the babies in Spitz's England — except that Romania's children's plight was infinitely worse. Day in, day out, for years on end, those children lay in their cribs alone, grossly neglected. We will never know how many of these marasmus babies withered away and died, but it was surely thousands. Studies conducted on some of the Romanian survivors are demonstrating in a quantitative way just how crucial the love quotient is for human development. Dr. Mary Carlson, a Harvard neuroscientist, reports that many of the Romanian

---

6 Smiley Blanton, M.D., *Love or Perish* (New York/Greenwich, CT: Simon and Schuster/Fawcett Publications, 1955, 1956).

orphans are below the third percentile in weight and height. Her studies show that the absence of maternal interaction produces profound failure to thrive that has lasting effects. At age ten, some of these children are the size of three-year-olds. Indisputably, the effects of lovelessness are devastating. There are, nevertheless, a few rays of love's hope emerging even from these ruins. In British Columbia, forty-four of the Romanian orphans who were adopted are being studied on an ongoing basis. Early indications are that love given late can still save children's lives, though permanent damage from the early gross love deficit is likely.[7]

The evidence of how absolutely essential love is to both physical and mental health is overwhelming. Harry Harlow's famous 1958 monkey studies[8] showed that early love deprivation caused by separating young monkeys from their mothers results in rocking, withdrawal, posturing, and other behaviors which in humans would be called catatonic schizophrenia. Less than a decade later, Powell, *et al*, conducted studies on hypopituitary dwarfism which could be attributed only to "emotional deprivation"[9, 10] — not enough love.

Several studies have shown that love-deprived children are far more inclined to suicide. Rosenthal and Rosenthal found that abused and neglected children were significantly more likely to attempt suicide than non-abused and non-neglected children.[11]

---

[7] Dr. Mary Carlson's work and other studies of the Romanian orphans are beautifully summarized in Sandra Blakeslee, "A toddler's experiences may shape nerve cell connections," in "Science Times," *The New York Times*, August 29, 1995, pp. B5, B8.

[8] Harry Harlow, "The Nature of Love," *American Psychologist*, 13 (1958), pp. 673-675.

[9] G. Powell, J. Brasel, and R. Blizzard, "Emotional Deprivation and Growth Retardation Simulating Ideopathic Hypopituitary Dwarfism. I. Clinical Evaluation of the Syndrome," New *England Journal of Medicine*, 276 (1967a), pp. 1271-1278.

[10] G. Powell, S. Raid, and R. Blizzard, "Emotional Deprivation and Growth Retardation Simulating Ideopathic Hypopituitary Dwarfism. II. Endocrinologic Evaluation of the Syndrome," *New England Journal of Medicine* (1967b), pp. 1279-1283.

[11] R. Rosenthal and S. Rosenthal, "Suicidal Behavior by Preschool Children," *American Journal of Psychiatry*, 141 (1984), pp. 520-524.

Walsh and Beyer compared delinquents who had attempted suicide with delinquents who had not. They found that those who had attempted suicide had been significantly more love-deprived than those who had not.[12] Deykin, *et al* found that abused and neglected girls were over six times more likely, and abused and neglected boys nearly four times more likely to attempt suicide than control groups of non-abused children.[13]

It requires no huge logical leap to extrapolate from those love deprivation/suicide studies to conclude that love-starvation might well be fundamental to depression also. Indeed, in a review of research through 1975, Akiskal and McKinney concluded that depression is triggered most severely and most frequently by the loss of a loved one through death, separation, or breakups, and that depression is to some degree constant among the emotionally unattached and lonely. They linked love losses, like rejection and lack of relatedness, to reduced brain catecholamines, which are chemicals known to be associated with behavioral experiences such as loss of appetite, insomnia, and slowing or agitation of psychomotor functioning — all symptoms of depression.[14]

Love-deprivation studies have convincingly linked it to elevated blood pressure[15, 16, 17] and lymphocyte function.[18]

---

12 Anthony Walsh and J. Arthur Beyer, unpublished data, described in Walsh, *op. cit.*, p. 128.

13 E. Deykin, J. Alpert, and J. McNamara, "A Pilot Study of the Effect of Exposure to Child Abuse and Neglect on Adolescent Suicidal Behavior," *American Journal of Psychiatry* 142 (1985), pp. 1299-1303.

14 H. Akiskal and W. McKinney, "Overview of Recent Research in Depression," *Archives of General Psychiatry*, 32 (1975), pp. 285-303.

15 Anthony Walsh and Patricia Walsh, "Social Support, Assimilation, and Biological Effective Blood Pressure Levels," *International Migration Review* 21 (1987), pp. 577-591.

16 Anthony Walsh, "The Prophylactic Effect of Religion on Blood Pressure Levels among a Sample of Immigrants," *Social Science and Medicine*, 148 (1980), pp. 59-63.

17 Sam Sisca, Anthony Walsh and Patricia Walsh, "Love Deprivation and Blood Pressure Levels among a College Population, A Preliminary Investigation," *Psychology* 22 (1985), pp. 63-70.

18 Walsh, *The Science of Love, op. cit.*, p. 108.

Now, beginning with the evidence that lovelessness can kill us before we even emerge from infancy, and reviewing all its devastating impacts on both mind and body in later life, including the fact that it can lead to suicide, can there be any doubt that love-lessness is also the cause of most severe mental disorders — the bipolar and depressive psychoses and schizophrenias? Surprisingly, for some professionals there is considerable doubt. In fact, it is probably a fair statement to say that the majority of mental health practitioners believe that most psychoses are induced by chemical imbalances in the brain. That majority seems to discount the evidence suggested by Harlow's little monkeys who became catatonic schizophrenics because they were deprived of the love of their mothers. Yet, in a long-term study of children identified at genetic risk for schizophrenia, Mednick discovered that the children who eventually did have a psychotic breakdown were those who suffered significantly more maternal deprivation, loss of mother love.[19]

There is far more evidence of the crucial central role that love plays in our lives, but the studies mentioned above are surely enough to substantiate the first General Love Principle. At this point I will defer to Anthony Walsh's *The Science of Love*[20] for additional scientific evidence that mental health and love are so intimately linked that they might well be considered synonymous terms. Alongside Walsh, there are two other equally magnificent books that must be given special recognition for their investigations into the biological and neurological operations of love, both appearing in the year 2000. They are Lewis, Amini and Lannon's *A General Theory of Love*,[21] and Arthur Janov's *The Biology of Love*.[22]

---

[19] Mednick is a Danish researcher. His long-term child study is described by Walsh, *op. cit.*, p. 125, and R. Trotter, "Schizophrenia: A Cruel Chain of Events," *Psychology*, 9/80: Annual Editions, ed., C. Borg (Guilford, CT, 1979).

[20] Anthony Walsh, *The Science of Love, op. cit.*

[21] Thomas Lewis, M.D., Fari Amini, M.D., Richard Lannon, M.D., *A General Theory of Love* (New York: Vintage, 2000).

[22] Arthur Janov, *The Biology of Love* (Amherst, NY: Prometheus, 2000).

It is especially on the shoulders of these three works that I stand scientifically, in order to show that we can move beyond science so as to include the ontology and spirituality of love, and thereby find a solid foundation for the eighteen principles of love theory and therapy.

The general assertion of Principle One is that, like the roads to Rome, all the scientific evidence leads to love as the answer to *every* psychogenic (i.e., non-organic) mental and emotional disorder, including most psychoses, plus a huge number of medical conditions which heretofore have been thought to have physical causes. Science, however, can never offer final proof for any *ultimate* question. Love theory, therefore, relies first upon a much more convincing proof of the love principle: it is self-evident.

Perhaps the most startling words in the basic love principle are those that describe love as the "raw force of the psychospiritual heart." Most professional psychotherapists do not use the word "heart." Neither is the word "psychospiritual" in their lexicon. Twenty years ago, they rarely used the word "love" either, but given a rationale and evidence, they began to accept the word. "Love," at least now, has a chance of gaining professional respectability. Such is my hope for the psychospiritual heart.

Clearly, the "heart" we are talking about is not the blood pump. The psychospiritual heart has an ancient, honorable and popular history which we need not fully recount because hardly a day goes by that we do not speak of it. We all recognize that some hearts are warm, others are cold. Hearts come in all sizes, temperatures, and degrees of health. Hearts are described as big, burning, bleeding, broken, faint, full, flying, whole, half, hard, soft, down, wild, gold, black, stony, stout, sinking, sick, pure, light, lonely, leaping, and oh woe, achy-breaky. The brave among us are said to have hearts of lions, but the cowardly are chicken-hearted. Hearts are sometimes found in odd places — mouths, throats, and stomachs, or even worn on sleeves. And when the singer Tony Bennett crooned that he lost his heart in San Francisco, not one of us thought he was talking about a physical heart transplant.

We could even bet that, in their tender and intimate moments, not even the most hard-boiled scientist whispers to his beloved, "I love you with my whole id and ego." No, we all have hearts. But where are they exactly? That question is answered in Principle Three where we will show that the psychospiritual heart is the central personality structure of love therapy.

The Basic Love Principle offers a global view of how omnipresent love is in our lives, and it provides the fundamental truth that will help us develop a new understanding of emotional disorders. As this principle was presented, though, it was necessary to rely heavily on scientific evidence. Beyond science, there remains in us a hunger to understand human love from a more down-to-earth, experiential viewpoint. That is the subject of Principle Two, next, on Defining Human Love.

CHAPTER TWO

Defining Human Love

Principle Two: An Operational Definition of Human Love

Human love is a fusion of psychospiritual hearts, an experience of intersubjectivity, a communion of uniques in their uniqueness, an interpenetration of beings,[1] a dynamic mutuality of subjective selves given, received, and so fully united that even some of the otherwise unknowable spiritual mysteries of the heart become known. Love is the power that enables us to risk a leap into mystery — believing, trusting, and hoping in the unseen and unproved goodness of others, ourselves and God, risking that we will not be hurt. Existentially, i.e. in the actual living, love, faith, trust and hope are one phenomenon, a quadruplex integer, one act; none can be separated from the others except as an intellectual abstraction.

Explanations

• Human love exists on a continuum of fullness or intensity that includes countless degrees and levels — degrees of intersubjectivity, types of communion, amounts of sharing — and a

---

[1] Karl Stern, *The Third Revolution. A Study of Psychiatry and Religion* (Garden City, NY: Image, Doubleday, 1961), p. 193. "Interpenetration of being," which I gratefully adopt as one of the basic descriptions of human love, was described by Stern in his final chapter, which was entitled "Beyond Psychology" to wit: "In the world of the natural sciences no two objects can be in the same place at the same time. In the relationship of I and Thou, there is an interpenetration of being.... [This is] related to love.... The 'I and Thou ' contains an implicitly metaphysical quality."

vast array of differentiated types: liking, fondness, infatuation, compassionate, romantic, friendly, brotherly, sexual, parental, spiritual, consummate, bonded, caring, ecstatic, sacrificial, etc.[2] The operational definition is an attempt to provide a standard that names the essential qualities and actions that are common to all forms, levels and nuances of human love.

• Faith is the power and act of love that risks the affirmation of truth and goodness existing in the mystery of another.

• Trust is the love that risks vulnerability when goodness is affirmed by faith. Trust is the act of opening the psychospiritual heart to another with the confidence that the other would never deliberately hurt me.

• Hope is the love that risks cleaving to the future goodness of a mystery that is believed and trusted.

• Faith, trust and hope are essential constituents and pre-conditions of love, and to the degree that any one of the three constituents does not exist, love and its other constituents are diminished.

• Human love is inherently a risk: human beings are by nature imperfect, finite, and bound to err, so the risk of being hurt by love being rejected, damaged or unfulfilled is an inescapable counterpart of loving.

• Love is a free choice, so it is possible to avoid being hurt altogether by never loving, thus staying "safe." Yet, life is love, so it follows that the only way to stay perfectly safe is by staying away from life, viewing life as an objective observer, never as a subjective participant, and thus never as one who is truly living.

• Fusion of hearts, intersubjectivity, the communion of uniques, and the interpenetration of beings, all describe love in terms of relationship, thus mandating interdependence. Apart from interdependence, until we have received love from others, self-

---

[2] Many of these types of love, and more, are discussed by Robert J. Sternberg, "Triangulating Love," pp. 119-138, and by Bernard I. Murstein, "A Taxonomy of Love," pp. 13-37, both of which are in Robert J. Sternberg and Michael L. Barnes, Eds., *The Psychology of Love* (New Haven and London, 1988).

love is impossible; thus, there is no safety in aloneness, and on the contrary, the avoidance, rejection or deprivation of love is the source of all functional mental illness.

• Love heals. Healing is an integral component of human love; where love is, healing is constantly occurring. (This intrinsic healing property of love is the focus of all the principles of Part II, which addresses psychotherapy and emotional problems directly.)

Even as we define human love, the mystery of it cannot be escaped; the mystery is integral to the definition. Logically, one might argue that the mystery still renders human love undefined and indefinable. In the absolute sense, that is perfectly true. The best we will ever do is to *try* to define it, operationally define it. Paradoxically, though, even the faintest glimmer of actual love casts more light and provides more understanding than our most brilliant intellectual insight. Why? Because we *experience* love, and that experience speaks louder than a thousand words of definition.

The definition of human love is worded entirely in terms of subjectivity. There is absolutely nothing objective about it. This means that if human love, per se, is to be studied, there is no object to study. Thus, natural science, which demands an object that can be somehow measured and quantified, is utterly useless when it comes to studying what human love and relationships are really all about. Love therapy, therefore, will necessarily be a scandal to behaviorism, psychoanalysis, experimental psychology and other fields that strive to be "objective" and "scientific." Conversely, offering only Science to an emotionally suffering people needing love is as scandalous as distributing cookbooks to a starving nation.

The intersubjectivity and non-objectivity of love insist that there is no such thing as an "I and it" nor an "I and they" relationship. There is only the mystery of I and Thou, thee and me. It is within the context of this intersubjectivity that love therapy explains how love heals mental and emotional disorders. Here, as we move toward understanding healing, the first task is to try to capture what intersubjectivity means. Obviously, "intersubjectivity" means being as personal as we can be, so let me do that. Following is my own subjective experience of what happens within me as I love you.

When I love you, my heart, the center of the center of me, the spirit of me, leaves the confines of my body and I move into you. If you are lost, even unto yourself, I go in search of you. It is strange, this power of love, for sometimes I find you even before you have found yourself, and finding you, I will never let you go. Finding you, I stand inside you, in your shoes, inside your skin, looking out at the world through your eyes, seeing what you see, hearing what you hear, feeling what you feel, not just understanding your hurts (empathy), but suffering the pain of your hurts right along with you. When there is grief yet unwept, buried in your heart, my heart grows heavy as I fight away tears with you. You want to cry, but cannot, so my throat hurts. When you recount the agony of childhood rejection, my chest hurts. When you are unjustly treated, I rage even when you cannot. And when you remain bewildered, still lost, I speak to you with my eyes, silently saying, "Here you are — right here! See? You are the one I am loving." Sadly, though, as you discover yourself, you rediscover the wounds that sent you into hiding, and with those wounds comes pain, boiling up from the deep, and my heart suffers right along with you. Finally, then, you cry, and I taste salt.[3] But when you sing, my heart hums along in harmony. Inside you, I can see clearly the beauty, the courage, the honesty, all your virtues — the unique goodness that you are. Here, inside

---

[3] This beautiful image of the closeness of love, one person crying, the other tasting salt, belongs to Rosalie Ingram and Joan Kirsten, "Loving One Another," *Passage* (Catholic Charities/Parish Outreach of the Diocese of Rockville Centre, July-August, 1986), p. 4.

you, I can see, absorb and unite with the spirit of you that may not have been apparent at all from the outside. Here, within, I can see unique value, strengths, and wonderful yearnings that no one could see from the outside — goodness buried beneath pain and pain's obnoxious symptoms and defenses that may have pushed people away. Loving you, I experience you from outside-in and inside-out simultaneously; I remain me while growing in oneness with you, uniting with you, and in a very real way, albeit mysteriously, becoming you.

How is it that I can "see" this innermost part of you, this heart level essence of you that even you yourself may not see? This is one of the wondrous powers of love, a subtle, humble, quiet power that has not been identified nor explored. Traditional thinking would call this mere faith in a person, or even blind optimism. It is far more than that. This is knowledge; no faith is required. I begin with love that says, "I believe in you," but once I have penetrated your heart, I know with all my own heart that a pool of unique value and beauty rests hidden in your heart. Let me call this, simply enough, "heart-knowledge": I know that I know that I know, even though it may contradict all external evidence and even reason itself. An existential analyst might say that I "know-with-love."

Still, how can I reach your heart, the center of your being, even before you yourself may be aware that you have one? Here, again, is a power of love that has been barely explored. Some mystics were known to be able to "read hearts," and this was seen as an extraordinary, God-given gift. Now we see that heart-reading is an ordinary power of love. Mystics may be better at it because they love more, but this is simply a matter of degree. Lovers, close friends, husbands and wives, often know what the other is thinking and feeling without a word being said. They read hearts. How? That answer lies in the intersubjective unity that love allows. Through love comes oneness; two hearts become one. At other, shallower psychological levels, the two might be totally different. They may even be engaged in angry battles. At the heart level, though, they beat together as one, sharing one and the same psychospiritual blood.

Listening to a familiar biblical story, it began to dawn on me what love's "oneness" actually means.... Abel was killed, God confronted Cain asking where his brother was. Cain answered, "Am I my brother's keeper?" For years I thought I was better than Cain when I answered, "Yes, I am indeed my brother's keeper." After hearing this story for the umpteenth time, it finally occurred to me that my answer was as shallow as Cain's question. It is not enough to be a keeper. When we become aware of the oneness that love is, the only adequate answer is "I am my brother."

Granted, that sounds a little weird. I am my brother. I am my father, my mother, wife, children, friends, and I am a couple thousand people I have seen in psychotherapy. Now there's an identity crisis for you! At least it would seem so until we consider: is it not true that all the people I have loved are an integral part of me? This is the power of love that brings oneness. Let's call it "heart fusion."

The client-therapist relationship, as defined in love therapy, is just this close. It is fused. It is a love relationship. At heart level, there is little that is "professional" about it. In the therapist-client relationship — let me say this unequivocally — it is the therapist's primary responsibility to love that client. His or her prime role is not analyzer, teacher, dream interpreter, behavior modifier, unconscious prober, role model, patient listener, nor reality-finder, though a counselor may be all of these; the therapist's primary function is to love. At the outset, therapeutic love is almost totally unrequited; it's all give and no get, and that's tough precisely because it is not yet the fullness of authentic love; that always requires receiving as well as giving. But it is only love that heals, and neither semblance, nor reasonable facsimile of love will do; it's got to be the genuine article. Mere ingredients of love that have traditionally been accepted by professionals to describe the therapeutic relationship — care, respect, acceptance and empathy — are not enough to heal.

The Unity of the Love-Faith-Trust-Hope Experience

If I love you, I believe in you, I trust in you, and I place my hope in you. When we say, "I love him but I don't trust him," we mean that our love has been diminished in exact proportion to our distrust. Similarly, if we greatly believe in someone, we love that person to the extent of our faith, and our hope and trust are proportionately great. This existential unity of love-faith-trust-hope is essential to the understanding of ourselves or others at the heart level.

Earlier, we discussed understanding at heart level, *raison de coeur*. It is the existential unity of love-faith-trust-hope that explains why reaching heart-level understanding, the very essence and hallmark of love therapy, can be so difficult to obtain for both counselee and counselor. It is difficult because the ordinary day-to-day act of thinking, abstraction, is largely saturated with defenses designed to protect our hearts from both the agonies and ecstasies of the experience of loving. Simply put, it is a lot easier to think, to abstract, than it is to undergo the experience of our total beings that is required when our hearts are allowed to be open.

Given the understanding of the existential unity of the love experience, in love therapy, abstract meandering about secondary questions involving hope, faith or trust often can be rendered moot, unnecessary, by keeping the focus on what those secondary questions mean to love. Look, for example, at these three statements: "He lies all the time! (so I can have no *faith* in him)"; "She actually spies on me! (so she doesn't *trust* me)"; "I don't think I'll ever get well (so I have no *hope*)." The therapist's responses to all three statements in love therapy would be translated in terms of the deeper experience of love-hurt that lies beneath the faith, trust, or hope problems.

Love's Trust

The existential unity that love provides can be seen more clearly perhaps in relation to trust, a frequent topic in counseling. In fact, love precedes and is the mother of trust, but in our experience, we are much more likely to say that we trust someone before we love them. We need not debate the chicken-and- egg question, however, because we are talking about a single existential reality, love-trust or trust-love.

Trust is an indispensable pre-condition and an integral dynamic component of love. To the degree that trust does not exist, vulnerability cannot reasonably be risked, and to that same degree love cannot exist.

Yet, love must be rational and balanced. One cannot rationally love someone who cannot be trusted without becoming irrationally vulnerable, exposing one's self to hurt, which is not to love one's self, or, without rationally deciding to risk noble self-sacrifice. Thus, love always requires the assessment of risk, which in turn requires wisdom. Self-sacrificial love, if it is not to be masochistic or simply foolish requires the wisdom and self-knowledge to accurately determine that sufficient self-love is available to withstand the high risk of hurt.

The case of a woman suffering battered wife syndrome is a pitiful but classic example of love-trust gone awry. With spirit broken, and self-love shattered, the battered wife continues to be trapped in a complex web of pseudo-trust in her brutal husband's pseudo-love. Her suffering is best understood and treated as a love-trust disorder. As counseling progresses, given authentic love that enables her to explore her feelings in the light of truth, a battered wife invariably discovers that neither her trust nor her love were real. Her "trust" of an untrustworthy husband was in fact a sick dependence born of a broken spirit that crushed her capacity to love or trust herself.

Love's Faith

Faith, too, is an utterly essential pre-condition and an in-separable element of love. To the degree that love is authentic and full, faith says of the person loved, "I believe in you just as you are — not as I want you to be (which would be simply a reflection of myself and therefore self-love), but just as you are." The essential fact that must be noted about faith is that (especially at first) we never fully know the person we have faith in and love. Were we to fully know (as if we could), we would not need faith. So too, were we to wait until we *knew* the person in the scientific sense, we would never love. Faith demands a leap into the unknown, the affirmation of the mystery that a person fundamentally is. Faith always says, therefore, "I believe in you just as you are — mysterious."

But authentic faith is not foolhardy and authentic love, contrary to popular wisdom, is not blind at all. On the contrary, authentic faith-love sees with extraordinary clarity. Faith is a leap into the unknown, yes, but it begins with reason, and it is built upon reason. I see goodness, goodness, and more goodness in you, and as my vision deepens, I have good reason to have faith in you. When I risk the leap of faith in you, it is reason that provides the springboard.

Having leapt to believing in you, and loving you, something uncanny happens: I discover that more and more of the mystery which my faith and love affirmed becomes knowledge. In some remarkable way, I know the mystery that you are.

Yet, just as love-trust can be misplaced, a person's entire capacity for faith-love can be distorted, twisted. When I do *not* have faith in you, or you, or you, or in *anyone*, then I am left without faith in reality, and that is called serious mental illness, psychosis. Psychosis is too often described in abstract terms like "losing contact with reality"; the descriptions are depersonalized. In fact, the crucial reality that is lost in psychosis begins with loss of faith in persons, the inability to believe in the mystery of other people or of self.

Were it not for faith, our ordinary everyday capacity to love just about everyone at least a little, and to have faith in the goodness and mystery of strangers, all of us would be psychotic. When we stop to think about it, no one *proves* who they are or what they are. All of us, all our days, are mysteries wrapped in skin.

Love's Hope

Love-hope, too, can find expression in unrealistically positive, unrealistically negative, or heroically positive, realistic forms. Realistic love-hope can be seen every day. She hopes for job advancement, loves in advance the increased status, pay, personal fulfillment and appropriate self-love the advancement will bring, and by hard work realizes the hope: she is awarded with a new position and a raise; then she celebrates hope realized.

Heroic love-hope is not often seen, precisely because there are not so many heroes. Heroic love-hope is seen best perhaps in the emaciated forms of concentration camp prisoners who, despite the torments of hell, despite years of humiliation, starvation and torture which have reduced them to pitiful, stick-like caricatures of human beings, courageously hold on to the "impossible dream" of freedom and return to normal life and love in the future.[4] But when love-hope is damaged, then the balance that love provides to life is lost and emotional disturbance of two extreme forms (actually two sides of one coin, love-hope) can be seen — depression or mania.

We discuss depression at length in a later chapter. It is important to note here that the existential unity of love-hope is essential to understanding how (bipolar) mania and depression flow out of an identical wound. The depressive sees hope *nowhere*. The manic

---

[4]   See Viktor Frankl, *Man's Search for Meaning* (Boston, MA: Beacon Press, 1959). Frankl's description of his experience in a Nazi concentration camp is a beautiful example of "heroic love-hope." I recommend it to many clients, especially those who are struggling with the meaninglessness that depression often induces.

sees hope *everywhere*, far beyond the constraints of reality. In a manic phase, a patient may spend money as if the hope of obtaining more money has no limits in reality, or voice a hopeful plan for creating universal world peace within the week. As later chapters will show, however, heavy focus in counseling on realistic versus unrealistic hope misses the mark and betrays understanding of what the manic-depressive's suffering is about. As with all mental and emotional disorders, it is only love that is hurt. The existential unity of love-hope can be expressed as a principle: there is only one hope that counts — to love and be loved.

Love's Oneness

The love-hope-trust-faith principle emphasizes that any of the four acts invariably involve leaps into mystery. We sometimes make the mistake of thinking of any of the four as a "state," as static reality. Thus, we speak of "having" faith or trust, or of "being" in love or being hopeful, as if they were accomplished facts, *fait accompli*, whereas, as the principle emphasizes, love is a dynamic act, and it exists in real life (beyond abstraction) in constant action. In turn, the actual living of faith, hope, trust and love are endless acts of risking leaps into the unknown. Indeed, the simple act of living, constantly risking, takes courage.

The acts of leaping to say "Yes" to the goodness of other human beings, of God and of myself, none of whom I will ever know in an absolute sense, forces us to embrace the fact that we live in the arms of mystery all our days.

It bears repeating that neither psychoanalysis nor analysis of any kind has ever healed anybody. Only love heals, and that is a *synthesizing* experience which is a product of the oneness developed between two people. This is not to say that there is never a place for analysis. On the contrary, healing love must be accurate, targeted to the heart wound. Hence, love therapy does require some amount of analysis, but this is enormously simplified by focus on love as a quadruplex integer. Faith, trust, and hope are analyzed as "parts" of love that are by definition inseparable from the singular integrating and synthesizing experience that love is.

Many therapists have done a lot of dancing around the idea of love for decades, using some impressive professional jargon as defenses against the vulnerability and plain old hard work that love demands. Thus, for example, we speak of "caring." Indeed, caring is a kind of love. The word "care" comes from the Gothic word, *kara*, which means "to lament." It is being with a person in sorrow, just being with them in silence. "Care" is a very good word, and a good thing to do, especially when dealing with grief. It is far too restrictive a concept to meet the general needs in counseling, though.

Other popular professional substitutes for love are "acceptance," "support," "accurate empathy," and the best of all, the one that tickles me most, "unconditional positive regard." Again, nice words, useful concepts, good to do — but not love. Before going further in the effort to explicate love, perhaps I should again answer the question as to why I insist on that particular word.

A common differentiation of types of love is the familiar Greek breakdown of *eros, philia* and *agape*.[5] When giving talks on love, someone in the audience will invariably ask which of these kinds of love I'm referring to. Even more embarrassing, a philosopher in the crowd may ask if I'm discussing love as *amor concupiscentiae* or *amor amicitiae*.[6] To both questions, I can

---

[5] Very generally — *Eros* is erotic, physical, or any of our more earthy loves. *Philia* is brotherly love, friendship. *Agape* is altruistic, unconditional, God-like love. A collection of readings addresses the philosophies in Alan Soble, Ed., *Eros, Agape and Philia* (St. Paul, MN: Paragon House, 1989).

[6] See Robert Johann, S.J., *The Meaning of Love. An Essay Towards a Metaphysics of Intersubjectivity* (Glen Rock, NJ: Paulist Press, 1966), pp. 17-18. This double tendency of love is the differentiation of St. Thomas Aquinas. *Amor concupiscentiae* involves love of a relative good. *Amor amicitiae* is love of an absolute good. I owe to Johann a large measure of gratitude for triggering in me several of the major concepts of love therapy. Very briefly: the psychology of love, intersubjectivity, flows into, mixes with, and eventually becomes one with the metaphysics of intersubjectivity, but transcends both. Hence the concept, "psychospirituality." Johann's influence is also seen in the beginning of my Introduction, wherein I

only answer, "Uh-huh." People laugh, but I try to explain that that answer, whether it is judged clever or smart-aleck, is based on my firm conviction that my own heart never knows the difference as to whether I am loving my wife sexually, my brother fraternally, or God spiritually. When I love, I just experience my heart moving, and whether I am *eros*-ing, *philia*-ing, or *agape*-ing, that heart movement seems always the same except in terms of degree. When I tried to examine what my heart was doing, I found nuances of love that I could express in not just three ways, but at least ten or twenty. For awhile, I considered the possibility that I just had a dumb heart that didn't know its *agape* from its *eros*. But then I read a line about love in India, and I took heart about my heart: the Hindu language "differentiates," as we learn from Coomaraswamy, "three hundred and sixty kinds of the fine emotions of a lover's heart."[7]

That did it. The Hindus convinced me that the complexity of love could easily give us all inferiority complexes. In the final analysis, analysis of love inevitably proves that our heads are indeed stupid in the face of mystery. There was no alternative than to trust my heart, however analytically stupid it is, and to trust the singularly warm, quickening movement that so often accompanies the experience of love. There are many times, though, when love is required and I feel no warmth at all. Love, after all, is not a feeling. In the absence of warmth, I am forced to search out the central depths of my being, my heart, and to follow its dictates. Our hearts we can all trust; they lead unerringly to love, albeit mysteriously sometimes.

---

recognize the shyness of love. Johann states it beautifully: "One of love's most curious paradoxes is what we may call its reticence. The deeper the love, the less it has to say in its own defense. Its sincerity can almost be measured by its speechlessness. Its very directness imposes silence." (p. 19.)

[7] A.K. Coomaraswamy, *The Dance of Shiva,* rev. ed. (New York: Noonday Press, Inc., 1957), cited by Henry A. Murray, "Dead to the World: The Passions of Herman Melville," in Edwin S. Scheidman, Ed., *Essays in Self-Destruction* (New York: Science House, Inc., 1967), p. 12.

However variously it is experienced, love is One. Understanding love, therefore, is a process of synthesis. Analysis of love, taking it apart in our heads, is beneficial only if the parts can be pulled back together, made whole in our hearts through experience. Indeed, the synthesis that authentic love is, leads to wisdom, and wisdom cautions: "Beware of analyzing love. It can be a defense, an intellectual head-game designed to protect us from the risk of actually loving."

In the operational definition of human love given in Principle Two, love is described in terms of intersubjectivity, communion, interpenetration of beings, subjective giving, receiving and sharing, dynamic mutuality, and mysterious unity. In love therapy terms, this is also a description of the therapist-client relationship. It is important to emphasize that a love relationship is not a "state," but a constant series of acts, an evolving dynamism. Love just doesn't happen. Love is an act of the will, and more, an act of the heart.[8] Indeed, it can certainly be said that love is an art, but not art in the sense of a completed picture; it is, rather, a painting that remains slippery with linseed oil, always being painted.

Now given both the general and the operational definitions of human love, we can progress to Principle Three and a new and fuller understanding of personality structure and its center-most treasure, the psychospiritual heart.

---

[8] The position taken in love therapy is that love cannot be merely an act of the will, for that would necessitate the will being a more fundamental power than love, which would leave the will "powerless," i.e., capable of acting without a more fundamental "energy" or "force" to empower it. Philosophers, particularly Thomists and Aristotelians, may have a fit over the implications of this little statement, for they have always said that love is an act of the will, and stopped there. When love is given primacy as a self-evident principle, it becomes obvious that the will is not the central core of being. Love is. Without love, the will could not exist. Therefore, whether viewed functionally or structurally, it becomes experientially obvious that it is the core of being, the heart, which is given in any act of love, not just the will. (Existentialists, who strive for a more holistic, less abstract, uncleaved, experiential view of the person, will perhaps find this love view more acceptable.)

CHAPTER THREE

The Psychospiritual Heart

Principle Three: The Heart of Personality Structure

The psychospiritual heart is the major structure of human personality, the wellspring and dynamic repository of love, which, in turn, empowers all human functions. The heart includes: conscious and unconscious mind; volition (will); conscience; all the emotions; intuition; character (integrity and all virtues); and the spiritual faculties, including *raison de cœur* and wisdom. At a deeper level, the heart contains the unique mystery of the person which the individual herself or himself will never know. At the deepest level, called *le point vierge*, abides the presence of Supreme Love by whatever name — God, Allah, Great Spirit, Higher Power — Who resides in every person.

Explanations

• Structurally, the psychospiritual heart is the power and control center of the human spirit or soul (psyché) from which love activates and directs all other faculties of thought, will and emotion.

• The existence of supra-rational human powers like wisdom, reason of the heart, out-of-body and neardeath experiences, extrasensory and mystical-spiritual knowledge, refutes the idea that mind and brain are synonymous. Though we cannot know the physical location of the psychospiritual heart, we do know that, experientially, except for highly abstract thought such as mathematics, most higher faculties of the "mind," so-called, are experienced in the chest and abdomen as well as the head. The mind is but one faculty of the heart.

• The unconscious is *not* the major structural component of the mind, much less of the psychospiritual heart. The unconscious is important as a repressed and latent memory file, but the emotions, psychospiritual meaning, and the functions of the will connected with those memories reside far deeper — in the heart, not in the unconscious.

• The psychospiritual wounds that cause mental and emotional problems are not located in the unconscious; the unconscious does not suffer, nor does healing ever occur there.

• Psychological wounds and emotional pain occur and remain only in the heart; human beings can be significantly hurt, emotionally damaged, only where they love, at heart level. Accordingly, that is the only place where healing occurs, at heart level. Thus, we can be hurt only where we love, and only love heals us.

• Analysis of unconscious memories, or even abreaction (remembering and emotionally re-living repressed memories), never has and never will heal an emotional problem. Opening the unconscious memory file does not necessarily open the heart to reveal the source of the wound. Only love opens hearts; only love is permitted access to heart wounds; only love heals.

• Conscience is the faculty of the heart that enables us to know if we are moving toward the good, viz., loving, or toward evil, i.e., toward a privation or negation of love, a pseudo-love. Evil is always presented under the guise of goodness, as a phony love, but a healthy conscience can always discern that ersatz-love. Conscience affirms virtue, any form of authentic loving, and objects to "sin," any violation of love.

• Volition (the will) is the activational power of love that enables us to desire, obtain, or do whatever is perceived as "good," i.e., loving. The "good" perceived, in turn, may be real (authentic love) or misperceived or misrepresented (a pseudo-love).

• Not only is Supreme Love ultimately defined as God, love is equated with reality itself. (This will become clearer in Principle Seven.) It follows that the human personality structure is not self-contained, static, linear and matter-bound as the mental health consensus states; rather, the human personality is permeable, dynamic, immaterial, and thus capable of transcendence. This permeability derives from the fact that all persons are saturated by a singular life force — love — and are "structurally" connected to one another and to the universe by *le point vierge*, Supreme Love, the life principle.

Words have power. A word like personality "structure" automatically starts us thinking in boxy, concrete terms which are antithetical to the kind of thought that is needed to understand the powers and pathways of love. Western, linear, cause-and-effect, materialistic-scientific thinking is quite comfortable with "structures"; boxes and buildings can be measured. But not love, and not the heart. It really does require *raison de cœur*, "reason of the heart" to understand and to "see" the psychospiritual heart, much less "touch" and "read" hearts as is required in psychotherapy. It is with that understanding that the love theory diagrams of personality structure are presented. The first drawing (Figure 1) shows only the primary levels and functions.

Figure 1. Personality Structure in Love Therapy:
the psychospiritual heart, empowered by love, showing
levels/areas of functioning and primary powers.

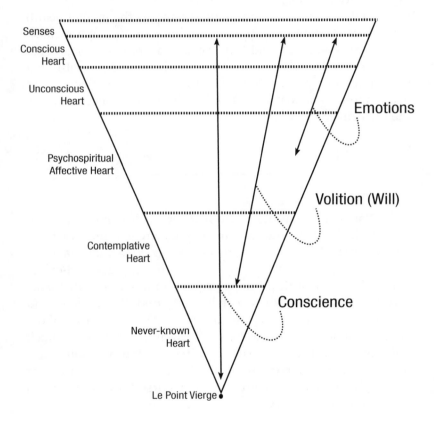

The shape selected to represent the heart could easily have
been the valentine variety, or a square, or the anatomical type.
Who knows? Maybe our hearts look like amoebae, changing shape
with every movement. The upside-down triangular shape of the

heart was selected because it seems to best represent our human experience. Note that the broadest exposure to external reality is experienced in the senses, and that it is the senses that are most easily experienced. Nor is sensing in any way rare; we all do it. So, too, the conscious and unconscious are common powers; they are also closer to external reality than the remainder of the heart's capacities. Above all, note that the heart "narrows" as it goes deeper, and that the accessibility of the heart to the senses becomes more difficult as we go deeper. That, too, corresponds to our experience of both ourselves and others: reaching the greater depths of our own hearts is difficult, and our most treasured, most loving, "heart-moving" experiences are the rarest. Similarly, those human beings whom we most recognize as admirable, grace-filled and rare are those who reach the greatest depths of their own hearts, a rare accomplishment that is rewarded with rare grace. Thus, for example, Mahatma Gandhi, Mother Teresa, T.S. Eliot, and Michelangelo are able to reach our hearts because they first reached the rarest depths of their own hearts and then were able to share them. The greatest poets, artists, saints, and others who have moved the world, are those who have reached the deepest, narrowest, most ethereal and elusive reaches at the bottom of the heart triangle.

There is a beautiful irony, a funny contradiction that we immediately should highlight about this diagram of personality structure. Note that the bottommost area is labeled "never-known heart." That name highlights a fact that we rarely think about: we can go through years of therapy trying to understand ourselves, and we can analyze our unconscious until we have recalled our diaper rashes and re-tasted our neonatal burps, but we will never fully know ourselves. At the center of each heart lies an unfathomable mystery.

Granted that not one of us will ever know the deepest secrets of our own souls is a humbling way to start developing a personality theory: the inorganic atom, the organic cell, a rock, a bird, a flower, the human being, you and I — mysteries all. And granted, it is a weird feeling to think of ourselves as mysteries walking around inside mysteries — mysteries everywhere! But must we feel hopeless? Not at all. As we'll discuss later, the trick to a rich life is to embrace the unknown, love the mystery!

Let us quick-walk through this first diagram with some very brief explanations.

◆ Note again the bottommost area delineating the "Never-known heart." Despite the ancient Greek admonition, "Know Thyself!" and some modern therapists' promises to help you do just that, the "heart of the matter" is that we will never know ourselves, at least not fully.

◆ The boundaries separating the substructures are all permeable, so love pervades the entire structure. Love moves freely from function to function, empowering and coordinating them all. The outer boundary (top) of the personality, too, is permeable; it is thus that we are "open" to give and receive love, permeating others and allowing them to permeate us.

◆ At the bottommost center of the center, at the deepest point of mystery is *le point vierge,* Supreme Love. Note that conscience is heard through every level of being, but begins at *le point.* Conscience, seen in this light, can now be recognized as a faculty which involves far more than morality and the capacity to know right from wrong. Because conscience is so deeply centered in the bottom of our hearts, in proximity to that spark of Supreme Love Whom we all share, it is the faculty that moves us inexorably in pursuit of the good, the true and the beautiful, i.e., conscience moves us to express or to search for love in all that we do every day. Seen in this light, it becomes apparent that conscience has been traditionally defined far too narrowly as a mere good/bad adviser, a benign coach. Conscience is the faculty which empowers the will, providing it with its very substance, the need and inclination toward love and goodness which it needs to operate.

◆ Volition, the will, the capacity to choose, also is grounded in the deepest recesses of the heart, though not as deeply nor as near to *le point* as is the conscience. The will is constantly being informed by the conscience, that is, the conscience incessantly buoys and encourages the will, saying, "Do good. Love always."

◆ Emotions can be seen to emanate from deep within the heart, deeper than the unconscious, but they are not as deeply grounded nor as directly influenced by *le point* as conscience and volition. This is in keeping with our human experience: thus, emotions may be powerful, but the power of the will to choose good over evil, following the dictates of conscience, is greater. So too, in general, all the greater human powers, those which most distinguish human beings as having dignity, beauty, and even heroic virtue, are those that we always perceive as flowing from the deepest recesses of our beings, in greater proximity to *le point vierge*.

◆ Though the relationship is too complex to be shown on the diagram, it may be readily understood that the three functions of volition, emotion and conscience always act in concert. Conscience and emotion both influence volition, always, but we sometime experience a struggle between emotion and conscience to determine which will hold sway over our power of choice, the will, love's final arbiter.

◆ Note that the realm of the unconscious, far from being the vast hidden part of the iceberg, the virtual be-all of the mind that Freud depicted, is in fact a comparatively small structure of the heart. Briefly, functions have been traditionally ascribed to the unconscious that do not reasonably belong to it. The claim that the unconscious runs the mind and heart is like saying that the office files are the C.E.O. of the company.

◆ As the diagram reflects, the psychospiritual-affective heart is the largest structure of personality. Here reside all the emotions, spiritual emotion (a very distinct genre), the aesthetic powers, and many of the finer human capabilities — wisdom, intuition, *raison de cœur* — and others shown in Figure 3, below. Most importantly, it is within this structure of the heart that the greatest repository of love exists, i.e., all the loves experienced in a lifetime, plus all the yet-to-be-activated powers of love. This is also the structure which contains the loves that have been damaged, betrayed, twisted and rejected. Encountering deep heart wounds, people usually say that they just "hurt"; this is where that pain is lodged. This then, is the destination and purpose of psychotherapy, to reach deep into the heart where the bitter lies next to the sweet, where the love that is truth can reach pseudoloves, and healing love can touch suffering love. Reflecting all this "mix" of loves — the pure, the bittersweet, the damaged and the noble — this is the substantial part of the personality that other people "see," the unique blend of love and lovability that we call individuality. Finally, shining through that "mix" is a quality of pure love that is inviolable, the most unique element of individuality that can be discovered even when the remainder of personality has been damaged beyond recognition; this is a transcendental form of love called "beauty," the form of love that is reflected by *le point vierge* from the depths of every heart, thus investing in every person unique qualities of dignity and splendor that are always a joy to behold. It is this transcendent beauty, the brilliance of Supreme Love, which we still see shining through the blank countenance of the chronic catatonic, the glazed eyes of the addict, and the snarling face of the raging criminally insane.

◆ Finally, note that the second level of the diagram, the contemplative heart, is not nearly as large as the psychospiritual-affective heart, and that it adjoins the never-known heart. This depiction again reflects our experience. It is only through contemplative (meditative) silence that we can begin to reach this deeper realm of mystery and the finer, richer, but more elusive qualities of love that lie deep within each of us. Contemplation is not "thought," nor is it "feeling"; it is as close as human beings can come to an act of pure love (for as we noted, love is neither emotion nor thought, per se, but the fundamental source of both). However, as a product of that pure love, contemplation can surface "spiritual thought," insight that is far more profound than ordinary conscious reasoning would ever allow. When I said earlier that all the mystery in life and in us should by no means produce despair, it was because of the hope offered by contemplation. The contemplative person nears Supreme Love, embraces and loves the mystery, and then "knows" mysteries. (Note: people who have practiced silent contemplation, and actually experienced the encounter with mystery, will have no problem relating to this integral part of human personality which I call the contemplative heart. Let me recognize, though, that those who have never practiced meditation or contemplation may be inclined to consider this idea of "knowing mystery" as a contradiction in terms, or as just plain weird. For such doubters, I have two suggestions: talk to a Christian or Buddhist monk or a mystic, people who have spent their lifetimes in contemplation; ask them about their spiritual experiences, and then decide if they are silly enough to be wasting their time. Better still, seriously try contemplation yourself. You'll see.)

This quick journey through the "heart" of love therapy's personality structure necessarily leaves unanswered questions. Figure 1 shows only the primary functions of the heart. There are many more human powers. Figure 2, below, shows powers and functions I will call secondary, but with a huge caveat: these functions are not secondary in importance nor in value, but only in terms of the frequency of human use. They are secondary, too, because they are dependent on the primary powers of thought, volition, conscience and emotion in order to be called into operation. In order to provide a rapid overview of a multitude of human powers, we can quick-step through the secondary functions with brief comments. These remarks focus especially on how viewing personality as a psychospiritual heart-love system provides an understanding of powers that is closer to our experience than traditional models.

Figure 2: The Psychospiritual Heart:

secondary powers and functions all empowered by love, showing relative depth and proximity to Le Point Vierge, Supreme Love. ("Relative depth" means the power varies with individuals.)

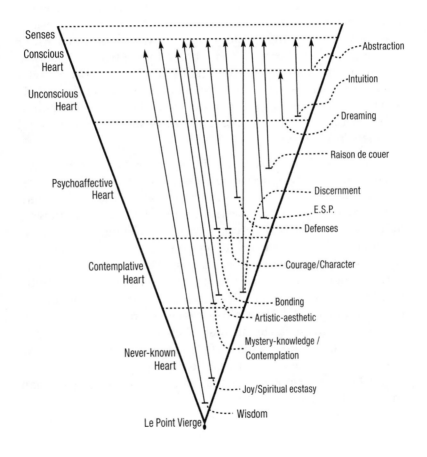

There are sixteen powers or functions shown in Figure 2. Each of the powers is represented by a line that extends from consciousness to varying depths of the heart.

Intuition reaches barely through the consciousness and unconscious and emanates from the shallowest depths of the psychospiritual-affective heart. It is shown as a faculty that is much closer to the conscious level than any of the other powers; only thought and abstract reasoning require less love, i.e., less proximity to the deeper, more mystery-imbued and more powerful love that is available as the center at the heart, *le point vierge.*

Wisdom, at the other extreme, is shown on a line that reaches into the deepest center of the heart — because wisdom is a direct product and gift of Supreme Love. (Briefly, wisdom has little to do with intelligence; wisdom is the gift which allows us to see things the way God sees them. It is precisely because wisdom is a spiritual gift that we are apt to meet an unschooled maid who is full of wisdom, acting as servant to a Nobel scholar who may be intellectually brilliant but utterly devoid of wisdom.) In general, the length of the line representing each faculty is a rough gauge of the depth and intensity of love that is required to exercise that function.

Quick-stepping now, let's race through the remaining functions.

The *artistic-aesthetic* sensibilities and capabilities, if they are authentic, require tremendous love, love in two forms: the capacity to express the transcendental property of beauty, and the power of creativity which reflects Alpha, the creative power of Supreme Love. Who can listen to a Beethoven symphony or read an Elizabeth Barrett Browning poem, or view a Michelangelo *Pièta* or *David,* a Degas dancer, or one of Turner's stormy seas, and not agree that there is a transcendent spiritual quality about them? The capacity to produce such masterpieces came from contemplative hearts. Those artists, in silence, reached deep into their souls and found love that was burning, love that contained beauty that was beyond human capacity to imagine. True art, as compared to craft or skillfulness, always reflects the contemplative heart of the artist, the place where the artisan transcends self by approaching Supreme Love, and there discovers beauty which is, in the most literal sense, "divine." When we recognize that an artist's work is a "masterpiece," when we respond to a symphony or a painting with spine-tingling awe, it is precisely because the artist has enabled us to directly see or hear a mystery, the vision, sound or touch of divine love that the artist discovered in contemplative silence.

Discernment is the faculty of spiritual or heart-level diagnosis. It is a basic tool of spiritual love therapy (discussed in the final chapter), but let's preview it here very briefly so that we can obtain a complete view of personality structure. We need to distinguish: The word "diagnosis" is derived from *dia-* meaning "across" and *-gnosis* meaning "knowledge," so diagnosis should include "across-the-board knowledge," which would include the depths of the heart. But the ordinary tools and training of counselors do not allow such depths to be obtained. In comparison, "discernment" is derived from *-cernere* which means "separate," and *dis-*, meaning "apart." Discernment, in its elementary meaning, "separates apart" psychological signs from spiritual signs. Often, in psychotherapy, all the psychological indicators put together simply do not answer the question, "What is the deepest source of the problem?" The reason is that human beings are psychospiritual creatures. The problem often is both psychological and spiritual, so the psyché, the soul, too, must be diagnosed. Discernment is the spiritual capacity to detect spiritual signs and thus to "know" deeply buried secrets of the heart which have not been revealed. Yes, that seems a little eerie; but it's not. (We'll discuss this a bit more in the final chapters, but this purely spiritual capacity is beyond the scope of this book; it must be shown here as an integral part of personality structure.)

Joy, properly understood, is a purely spiritual experience, as far beyond "intense pleasure" or "great happiness" as the most distant galaxy is from Earth. Joy is always a surprise; it appears only in response to a sudden onrush of unexpected, overwhelming love. The miracle of a new baby, the sudden incarnated evidence of Supreme Love, can bring authentic joy, as can the most intimate, vulnerable, heart-to-heart moments of lovers when love reaches new depths. More often, joy comes in prayer, and always as a sudden gift. The convincing proof that joy is a spiritual gift is that, try as we might, we simply cannot produce the experience by our own efforts. The diagram shows joy emanating from deep within the contemplative heart.

Ecstasy may be viewed as joy multiplied by two, or perhaps ten. Note the line on the diagram: ecstasy is centered at the most extreme depth of the contemplative heart, on the border of the heart of mystery, the never-known heart, so near to direct encounter with *le point vierge* that the purity and intensity of the love becomes too much for the body and consciousness to contain or even withstand. As a result, experiencing ecstasy, people swoon. Consciousness leaves, but the person is not unconscious; rather, consciousness, and all human sensibilities are suspended, just "gone." But where? Even those who have had the experience cannot describe where they "go." Ecstasy is an encounter with Supreme Love which is a blazing fire, a Love which may bring actual fear of being consumed. Much as we yearn for such love, it is too much for us to bear. It hurts! — but in a way too wonderful to describe. This is one of those human experiences of which it is said: For those who believe, or have experienced it (ecstasy), no proof is needed; for those who do not believe and have not experienced it, no proof is enough.

Bonding of infant and mother is a power that needs to be understood in love terms. The sad experience of marasmus babies and the Romanian orphans, discussed in Chapter One, are ample evidence of the disastrous effects of what happens when infant-mother bonding love is totally absent. We die. It is as if this elementary bond of mother's love is the first essential tether that anchors us in this life. Without that lifeline, that anchor, it is as if we just float away from life, ceasing to exist, dying, because love, existence itself, simply did not want us. This elementary mother-infant bonding is essential to the individual's basic psychological formation. In later chapters, "near-total lovelessness" is suggested as the cause of the psychoses, and "gapped," faulty love formation is presented as the cause of sociopathic disorders; both are short steps removed from the total lovelessness that produces death.

Marriage bonding — It must suffice to say here that the bonding of two hearts is a fundamental requisite for the formation of an authentic marriage — viz., no bond equals no marriage. (This bonding is discussed at length in Chapter Six.)

The reality of *ESP, extrasensory perception*, is still debated by many and that is quite understandable. I, too, have great doubts, but the research evidence for some forms of ESP is persuasive. Figure 2 can provide a quick insight for skeptics (and perhaps even a more credible theoretical foundation for ESP researchers, namely, love). When we consider love's intrinsic openness, the porosity and openness of the human personality structure, and of every organic cell, and of every inorganic atom, all four, and then think of ESP in light of the ubiquitousness of love (established in Principle Seven) our basic conception of reality changes. Love flows everywhere and connects everything with everything. Given love as the common medium and energy, and given that love is omnipresent and eternal, i.e., not constrained by the "laws" of matter, time and space as we ordinarily experience them, then telepathy, clairvoyance, precognition and psychokinesis become not just possible, but "almost" understandable. Love is both in time and beyond time. When an ordinarily-porous personality suddenly becomes far more porous, wide open, love allows the walls of time to "collapse" so that future events are known in the present — which is precognition. Far beyond the laws of chance, husbands and wives, linked by love, often know what the other is thinking — telepathy. Scientists have been unable to measure or even find the medium or energy that accounts for such paranormal events. Communication occurs, knowledge is transmitted, objects move, and no physical energy nor medium can be measured by even the most sophisticated scientific instrument. Unable to measure or in any way understand what the energy or medium underlying ESP is, science has named this unknown property *"psi."* Now, given love theory, we can name this mystery and begin to understand it: *psi* is love.

(We should note respectfully that there are religious denominations who hold that all ESP powers are of occult demonic origin. While it is very true that people sucked into heavy occult and satanic practices often began by experimenting with ESP — telepathy, clairvoyance, etc. — I believe it is not true that all such extrasensory powers are intrinsically evil. Like any human capability, a power can be used or misused. "Opening" one's spirit, however, requires spiritual prudence. Chapter Twenty-Five includes the case history of a woman terribly afflicted by evil spirits after she dabbled in the occult.)

Raison de cœur we have already defined. It is that uncanny type of heart-produced knowing that often confounds intellectual understanding, but more often than not results in the wisest choice. It is a power that is closely related to compassion, and both are obviously crucial in the practice of psychotherapy. We'll discuss them in Part II, on love therapy itself.

Character is the power of steadfast love that keeps personality "together" (integrity), and focused on what is authentically good, "virtuous," especially in the face of tribulation and frustration when the temptation is presented to violate authentic love and to compromise the heart with the quick-fix of a pseudo-love. Later, when we discuss psychopathologies, including character disorders, it will be important to see how sociopaths, "heartless" serial killers, for example, become far more understandable in terms of love theory. Love is formational, i.e., love forms us, and we are created out of love. In "normal," viz., loving personality formation, character is formed as the abiding power of the heart in which conscience and volition are fused to become a permanent behavioral "habit" or structure. Psychopathic killers, remorseless, conscienceless, unfeeling criminals, are called "inhuman" and "monsters" because in essential ways, that is precisely what they are: bodies in which the heart and its conscience and volitional powers — character — were never fully formed and fused. Intellectually, sociopaths "know" right from wrong, but they suffer from formational lovelessness. Knowledge without love is meaningless, and thus has no ability to impact behavior; hence the sociopathic criminal's capacity for heartless, meaningless brutality. Love allows character and its disorders to be understood in a deeper and more accurate way.

Courage is the power of the heart to overcome fear. Later, when we discuss emotional problems in depth, we will see that Principle Eleven, on Anxiety, begins "Love casts out fear." It is more than just interesting to note that the word "courage" is derived from the French *cœur* and the Latin *cor*, meaning "heart." Peoples of all ages seem to have known that to "encourage" someone means to "put heart into them." In some severe cases encountered in counseling it is quickly recognized that the suffering person's heart has never been fully formed; therefore, it must be "put in." Love alone can form, create, a heart.

Laughter, when it is authentic, is a sound of pure love, the expression of the heart's sudden realization of the amazing, paradoxical and ridiculous reality of the human condition — frail and foolish, conflicted and absurd, sinful and goofy, but nonetheless lovable, loved and loving. Laughter, like all love, is a gift which can be used or abused, i.e., laughter can be used as an expression of evil, but it can also be a spiritual phenomenon of love's highest order. (Wouldn't Laurel and Hardy laugh if they heard me describe their old slapstick movies as "loving," much less "spiritual"? But they are.)

Dreaming may be difficult to recognize as a power or function of love and the heart. Love, after all, is always an act of volition, a will for what is perceived as good. In addition, dreaming has always been understood as a process of the unconscious mind, so how can the will, much less love, operate while we are asleep? Answering that question requires more explanation of the phrase in Principle Three describing the psychospiritual heart as the "wellspring and dynamic repository" of love. But the brief answer is, "Love never sleeps." Even in sleep, love is always alert, watchful, working and willing — dynamic. Love must never be seen as a static state such as *"being* in love" implies, and if we "have love" for someone, that love must not be thought of as a "thing" that just sits. Deep in the heart, love reposes peacefully, but it is always working hard. If that seems like a contradiction, consider the young mother who lies sleeping with a new baby in the next room. She has had an exhausting day, so when an airplane roars low over her home, and a storm brings thunderclaps that shake the house, she sleeps like a log. But let the new baby whimper barely a peep, and she bolts awake. The mother's love was obviously awake, as was her will. She loved as she slept.

Dreaming, topsy-turvy, bizarre or horrific as it is sometime, is one of the heart's major mechanisms for maintaining sanity, viz., maintaining contact with reality, i.e., love. It has been amply demonstrated that when normal human beings are severely sleep- and dream-deprived, they become irritable, confused, anxiety-laden, and eventually develop depression, paranoid feelings of persecution, and then begin hallucinating. Research also has shown that if we are deprived of dreams one night, we make up for it by dreaming more the next night (R.E.M.-rebound). We need not recount all the dream research to conclude that dreams are vital to sanity.

Love theory suggests a more comprehensive way of understanding the role of dreaming: dreams serve love's general purpose of maintaining personality balance and contact with reality (love) in five major ways: (1) by safely discharging and expressing noxious, dangerous, and otherwise unloving emotions that could not be expressed during waking life; (2) by continuing "sleep-thought" and problem-solving related to conflicts that could not be solved while awake; (3) by using the loving mildness and indirectness of symbolic and disguised meaning to discharge and negate unloving intentions and emotion and/

or to suggest solutions that may be painful; (4) by bringing the deepest creativity of the heart to bear on problems that have defied conscious, waking solution; and (5) by providing, at minimum, a vehicle of expression for frightening, confusing or traumatic events that need to be re-lived until they are resolved; thus, with the re-living being done while asleep, temporary repression, forgetfulness and control are allowed during waking hours so the person can function.

The last-mentioned dream function may be the most difficult to understand in terms of love, so let's address it first. How can "frightening, traumatic" dreaming be called a "loving" function? How can the recurrent, cold-sweat dreams of a war veteran who is re-living a bloody battle, ever be called a loving operation of the heart?

Love at times does nothing but listen. And if the same thing is said over and over and over again, love just listens. And if it doesn't seem to be doing any good, love still listens. Why? Just because the person needs to say it — over, and over, and over again.... Sometimes that is the only thing that the heart can do for a person — just let him vividly tell the same horror story in a dream that ends in a sweat-drenched scream, a dream that occurs over, and over, and over.... Obviously, sometimes the heart of the dreamer does not contain enough love to heal the person and stop the bad dreams; the dreamer sometimes needs more love from outside the heart, from another person, even a therapist. Meanwhile, the heart always does the best it can, letting the person dream.

While that seemingly futile dreaming may not seem loving, consider this clinical experience: by far the overwhelming majority of people I see in counseling who suffer frequent nightmares, night terrors, depression- or anxiety-filled dreams, quickly re-repress the terrifying and depressing emotions upon awakening, and go about their lives, functioning. The bad dreams seem to serve as a meaningful and loving "escape valve." Research has shown that people who are depressed by day often have depressing dreams, dreams of loss and failure. Interesting — but by itself, that study does not tell us the role and purpose of dreams. Sleep disorder is one of the standard, major symptomatic signs used in diagnosing depression, but that symptom can appear in exactly opposite forms, insomnia and hypersomnia. One depressive cannot sleep, the other wants to stay in bed around the clock. Why? Without knowing why, the standard medical treatment has been to immediately drug the insomniac to help them sleep, and to use every means possible to get the hypersomniac out of bed, up and moving. Ultimately, I agree, both goals are necessary. Nor am I a purist who believes that one never treats symptoms. Rather, I would suggest that automatically drugging someone to sleep, or to not sleep, is to treat a symptom of a symptom. Excluding nasal, coronary, and other physical causes of sleep disorders, sleep symptoms are sometimes manifestations of dream disorders. Automatically treating a sleep symptom is to miss the opportunity to explore the dream, which, in turn, may well be the *only* place where the heart is seeing and talking about what the source of the problem is. People who are depressed usually do not know why they are depressed — but their hearts know, and the heart must talk. If the heart cannot talk through its consciousness, it often talks through its dreams. Thus, the heart of the depressed person continues to talk, see, feel, and to remain fully alive — if only in dreams, even when the depressed consciousness is saying, "I just feel dead."

In love therapy, dreams are explored in terms of discovering which one of the five possible loving purposes is being carried out by the dream. Summarizing these dream purposes — discharging dangerous, noxious, fearful, painful, unloving emotions; problem-solving; mild and merciful suggestion of painful solution via symbolism and disguise; creativity; and allowing essential re-living of traumatic events in dreams so as to allow daytime functioning. All five dream functions may be seen as acts of a loving heart that is bearing burdens that the conscious heart cannot bear.

Dream students of other schools will quickly notice that this list of dream purposes does not include two of the most famous theories of dreams: Jung interpreted dreams as archetypes, and Freud saw them as wish-fulfillment. My comments are brief. To Jungians: Love is the archetype of archetypes. And to Freudians: Behind every wish is the wish to love and be loved.

Following is the new love therapy definition of defense mechanisms, followed by four explanations. They may be viewed as corollary principles.

Defenses — mechanisms like repression, denial, projection, displacement and dissociation — have always been seen by the mental health community, forever parroting Freud, as "unconscious intrapsychic processes serving to provide relief from emotional conflict and anxiety."[1] Freud saw much of the energy of defenses being used fighting against the id and its libidinal impulses. The entire Freudian reductionist theory was basically a negative struggle because his first basic premise was — simply stated — dead wrong. As a result, psychotherapy has had a flawed fundamental understanding of why defense mechanisms exist, where they come from, what their purposes are, and how they operate. So with love theory, we must start over, re-thinking what the defense mechanisms are all about.

Defense mechanisms are the positive actions of the heart which serve to protect the personality's existing repository of love, temporarily shelter and hide wounded love until permanent healing can be secured, and by many means expel, isolate or control painful anti-loving forces, principally rejection, fear, hostility and false-guilt.

◆ The strength of and need for defenses is inversely proportionate to the strength of love present in the heart, the repository of authentic love.

◆ Only authentic love can eliminate the use of and the need for defenses. Defenses that are broken down by unloving

---

[1] *The American Psychiatric Association's Psychiatric Glossary* (American Psychiatric Press, 1984), p. 26.

forces will be replaced by alternate stronger defenses. Cognitive and logical persuasion, hypnosis, behavior modification involving punishment, harsh challenges to become responsible, or any other therapeutic technique used to weaken defenses, unless accompanied by love, will have the opposite effect. Love melts defenses; it never breaks them. From an intrapsychic viewpoint, i.e., in the heart's eyes, no defenses are irrational. However, as internal defensiveness increases in proportion to a paucity of authentic love, external authentic love-reality is proportionately blocked. As defenses increase in the face of huge threats to love, therefore, external reality is sacrificed in favor of the internal love that is already possessed. When this happens, it results in an increasing separation from external love-reality and the external appearance of increasingly unrealistic symptoms.

◆ Symptoms are secondary, externalized defenses, i.e., defenses of last resort. More fundamentally, symptoms are external defenses of internal defenses that are working ineffectively in protecting the heart.

Comparing the love theory definition of defenses with the traditional psychotherapeutic view results in very different approaches to diagnosis and treatment. The traditional view, quoted above from the official *Psychiatric Glossary*,[2] still echoing Freud, says that defenses are for the purpose of providing "relief from conflict and anxiety." In contrast, love theory says that the purpose of all defenses is to protect the psychospiritual heart from love-loss and love-damage. Anxiety and conflict are simply symptoms, which themselves are defenses. Anxiety and conflict, in other words, are not the problem, so to define them as the object of psychic defenses is like saying that the object of the body's physical defenses against infection is to prevent screaming. It is simply inadequate, and thus misleading for diagnosis and treatment. On the contrary, when defenses are recognized as having the *positive* objective of protecting and sheltering love, and as being allied against anti-loving forces like rejection, hostility,

---

2 *Ibid.*

false-guilt and fear, an utterly different diagnosis results, one that pinpoints the object of the defense.

In later chapters on specific emotional disorders, this re-definition of defenses will be seen as making a huge difference in the fundamental understandings of diagnosis and treatment.

Mystery-knowledge, as the words audaciously imply, is the capacity of the heart to experience and, to some degree, know and comprehend spiritual realities that are generally under-stood to be absolute mysteries. Though positivist scientists will automatically dismiss such knowledge as not demonstrable or measurable, the overwhelming majority of average people have had spiritual experiences, and from each experience they receive "heart knowledge."

The average person is too humble to claim that she/he has had an experience that could be called mystical. Most equate such experiences with mystics, gurus and saints, and who of us, after all, would claim to belong in that rarified company? But that is a mistake. Most people have had spiritual experiences, at least small ones. Consider: most of us are not geniuses either, but that does not mean we have had no bright ideas, does it?

Perhaps the smallest spiritual event is called the "numinous" experience, and many people can describe the times they have felt it. It is a brief, rather startling, and "tingling" feeling of be-ing touched spiritually. Spiritual writers have written volumes about the numinous, but the best description I've read was an account by poet Ron Seitz of a conversation he had on the subject with the celebrated monk-writer Thomas Merton. A "numinous experience," they agreed, is "when God taps you on the shoulder and says, 'Hi!'"[3]

The numinous experience, though, is just one of many mystical experiences that average people report. Near-death, out-of-body, and ecstatic experiences are not all that uncommon, and from each spiritual experience, people bring back mystical

---

[3] Ron Seitz, "Thomas Merton: A Remembrance," *The Courier Journal Sunday Magazine*, Dec. 4, 1983 (Louisville, Kentucky), pp. 22-28.

"knowledge" that often transforms their lives for the better. Often, words cannot express that knowledge adequately because what was learned was so profound, so entirely beyond ordinary human experience that language is virtually useless. For example, a dentist had a near-death experience in which he was suddenly given a "glimpse" of God and of "the oneness of being." He tried words like "universal fusion," "interconnectedness," and "a collective light" to make me understand "oneness," but following each phrase he'd say, "That's not it." Finally he said, "Look, I know. I saw it. But there are no words to describe it. Let me just tell you that the oneness is a thousand times more 'one' than your wildest dreams of oneness."

A young housewife had been in a major depression for two years, rarely getting out of bed. "I was in absolute despair. I had no hope in anything, and I believed in nothing — not in God, not in life, and certainly not in myself. I just wanted to die." Suddenly one morning, wide awake, she was contemplating suicide when "out of nowhere" she had an out-of-body experience! She found herself hovering near the ceiling, looking down at her physical body on the bed. Then, just as suddenly, "I was totally enveloped in love, God, and I hadn't even believed in God! It was a love so powerful, so glorious, so… no, there are no words." When I asked her to explain, she said, "It's almost like my puny words insult what I know, insult love. I try to say the Light of Love was beautiful, or glorious, and the words never come close to saying what I experienced. People ask if I mean 'unconditional love,' and I say yeah, sure — but the love was so… pure… so saturating! 'Unconditional' is just too weak a word to describe the love. I just quit talking about it. Love is not about words."

That admonition, "Love is not about words," haunted me for months. Centuries ago, Chuang Tzu had said the same thing about mystery-knowledge: "He who says, does not know; he who knows, does not say."[4] Faced with the ultimate truth that love

---

[4] Chuang Tzu is quoted here with the translation given by Thomas Merton, *The Sayings of Chuang Tzu* (New York: New Directions, 1965).

and all its mysteries will inevitably defy words, it would seem that anyone who talks about love and mystery, much less writes about them, is simply displaying how little he knows. And that is true — ultimately speaking.

But love is humbling. It teaches us that there is absolutely nothing "ultimate" about human beings, and that notwithstanding all the ballyhoo in pop psychology and inspirational books about "unconditional love," the hard, humbling truth is that human love is always imperfect, finite, flawed, and conditional. Only God is capable of wholly unrequited love, love that can give and give with no need to receive, love that knows perfectly what it loves, and loves perfectly what it knows, the only Love that even knows what "unconditional love" actually means. By definition, the condition of being human insists that the best that we can do is recognize our imperfections, admit our need, acknowledge our conditions, and keep striving for Perfect Love.

Mystery-knowledge, it is true, is the one capacity that is not, properly speaking, an inherent power of the psychospiritual heart. Mystery-knowledge is not something that by sheer will power we can reach out and grab. Hearts have the capacity to receive it, but not the power to produce it. Mystery-knowledge is a gift — as is all love (the focus of Principle Four, next).

Quickly reviewing the love theory view of personality structure and the heart, it should be emphasized that Principle Three, its nine Explanations, the definition of the three primary and the secondary functions and powers, and its various "levels" of activity do not constitute a "structure" in any sense of being a closed system. The psychospiritual heart, and every level and power of it, is open, both internally and externally. It is precisely that openness that allows heart to reach heart, and heart to reach mystery, the major tasks of psychotherapy.

After a century of universal acceptance of the "unconscious" as the foundation of personality structure, it may seem to some, especially mental health professionals, that the idea of psychospiritual heart as the basic structure of human personality is entirely new and radical. It is not so. Mine is simply the revivification of an ancient truth. In the late fourth century A.D., an anonymous writer known as Pseudo-Macarius wrote, "And when grace pastures the heart, it rules over all the members and the thoughts. For there in the heart the mind abides as well as all the thoughts of the soul and all its hopes."[5] The Psychology of the Heart of Pseudo-Macarius was correct seventeen hundred years ago, and it is none the less true today.

---

[5] Pseudo-Macarius is quoted here by George A. Maloney, S.J., *Prayer of the Heart* (Notre Dame, IN: Ave Maria Press), pp. 26-27.

CHAPTER FOUR

Love Is a Gift

Principle Four: Love Is a Gift

Love is a gift; it cannot be earned by hard work, great achievement, good behavior, or by becoming talented or beautiful. Nor, certainly, can love be begged, demanded, or bought at any price. The giving and receiving of love is governed by the Law of the Reciprocity of Love which states: We always love those whom we allow to authentically love us. As a gift, love must be freely given and freely received. Love is free, freeing, freedom itself.

Explanations

- Love inherently contains a multitude of gifts — hope, trust, courage, confidence, empowerment, peace, truth, beauty and healing.
- Love's first gift is always an act of faith that says, "I believe in you just as you are."
- In counseling as in daily life, love's ultimate gift is freedom, the gift that says, "Because you are loved as you are, you are free to *be* just as you are, not as others, or I, say that you should be; so just be, and be real, free to become who you are."
- The moment of actual internal reception of the gift of love is accompanied by the receiver's free, grateful and humble opening of the heart to the lover, and the automatic reciprocal return of

love; in this sense, loving and being loved is one process. This is the Law of the Reciprocity of Love: we always love those whom we allow to authentically love us.

• The gift of human love must be effective, i.e., it must be received and reciprocated, or it cannot be said to truly exist. Just as a physical gift that is rejected becomes a mere "thing," not a gift, so too love must be received in order to be properly called "love." Authentic love, by definition, implies a reciprocal relationship, a unity of lover and beloved. One-way love, e.g., the so-called love of a rejected lover, may be called "desire," but desire s not love until it is fulfilled, reciprocated.

• Without love, there can be no freedom, for freedom is a product of love. Where love is, there can be neither slavery nor domination. Where love is, there can be none of the interior shackles of the irrational fear, guilt, hatred and pain that we call emotional disorders. Where love is, there can be no exterior chains of familial, social or political repression.

• Freeing people from mental and emotional disorders is synonymous with loving them, no more, and absolutely no less.

In the debate as to whether love must be a gift, or whether it must be earned, love theory's position is best stated in the Song of Songs:

> Set me as a seal on your heart,
>   as a seal on your arm;
> For stern as death is love,
>   relentless as the nether world is devotion;
>   its flames are a blazing fire.
> Deep waters cannot quench love,
>   nor floods sweep it away.
> *Were one to offer all he owns to purchase love*
>   *he would be roundly mocked.*[1]

---

[1] Song of Songs 8:6-7. The italics are mine.

Exactly! What in the world could a person ever do to earn so precious a gift as love? How strong would a man have to be to *demand* the love of a woman? How hard must I work to *earn* the priceless gift of love? How perfect must I become to be *worthy* of the invaluable gift of love? How long must I chip away at my faults before becoming perfect enough to deserve the eternal gift that love is? The very idea is ludicrous.

If the love that is offered to me has a price, it is not love. If I offer to love you and charge you for it, I am not one who loves; I am a prostitute hustling pseudo-love. If you offer to love me only after I have proved myself worthy, or worthwhile enough to deserve love, you will never love me. If I say, "I love you, but...," I am saying I do not quite love you. If you say you will love me *when* I shape up, you have not loved me yet, and chances are you will find more and more requirements when I begin to shape up.

The poet Charles Péguy penned one of the simplest, most profound sentences ever written, so simply profound that we can easily miss its beauty: "When you love someone, you love him as he is."[2] (This quote is presented early-on in every love therapy case.) Love has no exceptions; there are never any ifs, howevers, or buts about it. Love transcends the faults, foibles, blatant sins and sheer ugliness of a person and loves them, if it is ever going to do so, now, just as the person is. Love is always Now, and that Now becomes Forever.

Love that is authentic always — mysteriously somehow — sees deeply into the distant recesses of the heart so as to embrace the is-ness of a person. What I call the heart, philosophers may call the essence. It is who a person is, down deep, at heart level, that psychotherapy must surface and bring into the open. In many respects, I have little regard for the philosopher Nietzsche, but he does capture this idea that the reality of a person, if only potentially, already exists: "What does my conscience tell me? That I shall become who I am."[3]

---

[2] Charles Péguy, *God Speaks*, [on] "Freedom," (New York: Pantheon, 1945), p. 37.

[3] Friedrich Nietzsche, *The Gay Science* [1887], cited in Walter A. Kaufmann, *Nietzsche:*

The is-ness of all persons, says love's gift principle, is that, at heart, way down deep perhaps, far beneath our faults and sin and soul sicknesses, all people are lovable. That is the nature of human beings. It is not something we have to prove. Our lovability is just there. Within the deepest heart of every human being, no matter how evil his actions or the outer levels of his heart, resides a core of pure goodness, lovability that is incorruptible and indestructible. This core of lovability, *le point vierge*, provides dignity and hope for all persons, without exception.

The subtle but pernicious message that one must make oneself lovable, earn love by self-improvement, and become deserving of love by being a "good girl" or "good boy," or nicer, or richer, or more outgoing, or prettier, or brighter, is implicit in many therapy models. Remarkably, even some of the foremost proponents of love theory have failed to see that love is priceless precisely because it is such a pure gift. Dr. Scott Peck, for example, made great contributions toward a psychology of love in *The Road Less Traveled*, but the following paragraph is fundamentally flawed:

> Everyone wants to be loved, but first we must make ourselves lovable. We must prepare ourselves to be loved. We do this by becoming ourselves loving, disciplined human beings. If we seek to be loved — if we expect to be loved — this cannot be accomplished; we will be dependent and grasping, not genuinely loving. But when we nurture ourselves and others without a primary concern of finding reward, then we will become lovable.... So it is with human love and so it is with God's love.[4]

Not So! Not So!

Philosopher, Psychologist, Antichrist, (Princeton, NJ: Princeton University Press, 1950), pp. 133-134. This quote is discussed by Rollo May, "Origins of the Existential Movement in Psychology," in *Existence: A New Dimension in Psychiatry and Psychology* (New York: Simon and Schuster, Basic Books, 1950), p. 31.

[4] Scott Peck, *The Road Less Traveled, op. cit.*, p. 310.

Principle Four of love theory states exactly the opposite of virtually every point in the above paragraph. Thus: if we must first "make ourselves lovable" before being loved, not one of us would ever be loved. If we could only be loved after we "prepare ourselves," we would go on preparing and preparing and never be loved. And if seeking love automatically makes us "dependent and grasping," then all of us are just that. The fundamental "Gift" principle of love theory is that all of us not only seek love, we are pushed and driven to love, and pulled precisely toward that goal, viz., love — both to receive it and to give it. Love is the fundamental motivation and goal of life. How, then, could I not seek it?

The basic argument here relates to the nature of human beings. It is the unalterable stance of love therapy that all persons, by definition, are lovable. Because of that, they are all entitled to love. Yes, even the human skunks, even the so-called dregs of humanity, even the "monsters" who are patently and avowedly evil, we are all entitled to love — just as we are, now, *before* we change. (Note: this is not saying that we have to love or in any way approve of a person's crimes or evil ways; it is saying that we are obligated to seek out the worst criminal's authentic personhood, and to love the person even while we totally condemn his evil actions.)

The most incisive argument I have discovered to support the premise that love is always a gift comes from the New Testament. (Note: in later chapters, I address spiritual dimensions very directly. Here, though, I cite this biblical passage not in a religious vein, but as simple good psychology.) Consider: when Jesus spoke the major commandment, "Love your neighbor as yourself," he did not add, "...when he shapes up and becomes lovable." Nor did he say, "Love your enemies — but only when they make themselves lovable and stop being enemies." Was Jesus a fool? Did he command people to do the impossible, love the unlovable? I think not. I think maybe Jesus understood something about human beings that it is very, very hard for us to grasp sometimes — that there is a core of love that exists down inside all of us, even the most evil person on earth, precisely because God made us, and because something of the Potter always remains indelibly stamped in the clay.

There are no perfect parents, so if we think back to childhood, perhaps most of us can remember being told by a parent (directly or indirectly), "Be good and I'll love you." That's wrong! The only correct message is, "I love you, period," which often translates, "I love you even when you're a brat." A child is good *because* she is loved, not the other way around. Why? Because love forms the child, and the little person's good behavior then flows out of the love as a natural expression of his nature. A child cannot be forced to pay with good behavior as ransom for love. "Earned love" is non-love. Children innately know that, and rebel.

No question, though, some people put the principle of gifted love to severe tests. For example: here is George, who is depressed, lonely and has no friends. George also happens to be rude, crude, obnoxious and nasty. Facing such a character, Peck's belief, that we must "make ourselves lovable," *seems* very logical. It is a sore temptation to say to the guy, "George, if you'd just stop being such a jerk, you'd have friends. You drive people away from you. So shape up! Be lovable!" That simple solution, logical as it seems, is wrong. First, that obnoxious jerk has to be loved, while he is still a jerk, just as he is. Only then, using the love that I give him, will George have a chance of becoming lovable.

But what about truly bad people, not mere jerks, but those who, by any human reckoning, are wholly unlovable — the worst criminals, serial killers, sociopaths who seem to have not an ounce of goodness in them? The hard question is, "If love is a movement toward a perceived good, how do you love people who give the appearance of having no good in them?" Thomas Merton answered: "There is no way under the sun to make a man worthy of love except by loving him."[5] Merton was absolutely correct, but does he not seem to be asking us to do the impossible, love the unlovable?

---

[5] Thomas Merton, *Disputed Questions* (New York: Farrar, Straus and Cudahy, 1953, 1960), p. 125.

No. Merton knew well, and presumed we would know that there is no such thing as an *absolutely* unlovable human being. A loving heart produces loving eyes that allow us to discover love hiding in any person, however buried that love may be beneath venomous rage, cold hatred, stuporous insanity or bloody sin.

Earlier I presented the Law of Reciprocity as a basic fact of love, i.e., that we always love those whom we allow to love us. This simple statement can be easily misinterpreted. Reciprocity in love does *not* mean "giving to get." Loving is not trading. The principle highlights the fact that love can only exist *between* people, and as a measure of their mutuality.

There are, in fact, three aspects of this reciprocity which are involved in very complex ways in every love relationship — reciprocal dependence, reciprocal independence, and interdependence. In authentic love, all three of these dynamics remain balanced, all three remain mutually respected, and all three are mutually and continually given. If I can describe it in a personal way... I love my wife; she loves me. I depend on Joyce in many ways. She depends on me in other ways. I respect her independence, and she mine. Most of all, though, we are interdependent, which means that we operate as one. This oneness, this we-ness, creates mutual give and take which we do without much thought. For example, because we are one, Joyce's independence is as important to me as my own. More precisely, her independence *is* my own, and vice versa. Thus, she will sometimes give her independence to me as a gift, and I will do likewise. At other times, I will refuse dependence on her that I would like to enjoy so that she can go her own merry way independently. She does likewise for me. All this giving and receiving gets very complex. Yet, because all the gifts are freely given, freedom is the result. Love is freeing.

The Explanations describe the innate lovability of people in terms of freedom, and describe psychotherapy as a process of freeing the person by loving them. In emotional disorders, people are caught, enslaved by symptoms, by the masks they wear, by thick defenses and walls, and by lies taught them in childhood.

Love opens the doors of the prison and melts the walls. Emotional problems and counseling are discussed at length in later chapters. Here, the essential point is that love frees people, not to become lovable, because they already are lovable; rather, love frees us to be what we already are, that is, lovable. Psychotherapy, even depth therapy that includes re-parenting, and long-term counseling that is called "reconstructive," cannot re-invent the basic personhood. Rather, love therapy surfaces and frees the authentic personality, and liberates the psychospiritual heart that has been walled in and chained. Using philosophical language, the *being* (person) exists in two forms, in *act* and in *potency* i.e., a person is a being who is actually in existence, plus the being who potentially exists.

An acorn exists in actuality, and in potentiality it exists as an oak tree, but only if it receives the sunlight, water and nutrients it needs to become what it potentially is. But note: no matter what kind of fertilizer or water I use, I will never be able to persuade that acorn to become a birch or a dogwood. It can only become what it already is "potentially." Nor can I say to the acorn, as too many say to those with emotional problems, "Just re-create yourself out of nothing. Don't ask for food and water (love); that's dependency. In fact, acorn, if you want to be an oak tree (a loved and loving person), you have to create that actuality (lovableness) out of thin air." That's baloney!

On the contrary, the lovableness of the person is intrinsic, a fundamental constituent of being, but there is no way on earth to bring out that love, allow it to grow from potentiality to actuality, other than by loving that person.

John Donne said it well: "No man is an island, entire of itself." We need one another. It is not just people needing counseling, but every single one of us who is dependent, or more precisely, interdependent. The idea of the self-made man is the epitome of hubris. We simply cannot fully love ourselves nor anyone else until somebody first loves us.

The principle of reciprocity of love resolves the age-old chicken-and-egg question of which comes first, loving or being loved. The answer is that authentic love is one process, and that giving and receiving are inseparable. Another Explanation explains the chicken-and-egg riddle further by emphasizing that love must be "effective." A gift that is rejected cannot properly be called a gift until it is received. Nor is love *realized* until it is received. That receiving, in turn, is also an act of love.

All this may seem a little philosophical, but in everyday life and in counseling, this loving "versus" being loved question surfaces every day in the form of ripped hearts and marriages torn asunder. Here are two examples:

Luke entered counseling immediately after a failed suicide attempt. His wife had abruptly left him for another man. Luke was both astonished and devastated; he had honestly thought he had the perfect marriage. He had thought that his wife loved him, and he was absolutely sure that he had loved her, and still did. His wife would never give him any explanation for leaving, however, so we could only theorize about what had gone wrong with love. In counseling, Luke agreed, in principle, that we can only love a person to the degree that we know them, so I said, "Luke, you don't know why your wife left you, so we must conclude that there was something very essential about her that you didn't know. Now, if you didn't truly know her, just who was it that you thought you were loving?" That question helped Luke to see that his love could not have been totally authentic, but it took months of discussing "his love" *versus* "her love" before Luke finally began to see that reciprocal love between his wife and him had simply never existed. (This is not to say that there never existed a scintilla of real love; rather, it is saying that there certainly was not enough reciprocity to form an authentic marriage.)

Molly, too, entered therapy after a suicide attempt. She had been jilted a year earlier by a man she truly loved. She could not let go of that "love" and move on to another relationship because she was convinced he loved her, too, and that he would eventually come back to her. She would telephone the man, and he would tell her repeatedly that he wanted nothing to do with her. Even so, she still was convinced he loved her — "He just doesn't know his own mind," she said.

For both Luke and Molly, the problem of loving versus being loved was life-threatening. In both cases, the definition of authentic love as being "effective," and as mutual giving and receiving, obviously was not fulfilled. In these particular cases, both people eventually discovered that they had lost very little *authentic* love, and finally went on to new relationships.

But does the fact that love is not effective, or even that the love may have been based on self-delusion, or even sheer fakery on the part of the person loved, prevent the lover from being truly heartbroken? Certainly not. Molly's love was founded on delusion which, in turn, was rooted in a terrible, lifelong hunger for love. Nevertheless, the pain she felt was totally real. Her heart, she felt, had an enormous hole in it. And Luke, with love gone, felt that he was "empty." For both these unfortunate people, that emptiness caused such intolerable agony that suicide seemed the only recourse. The failure to understand that love is a gift figures prominently into every emotional disorder, as will be shown in later chapters.

The complexity of dependence, independence, and inter-dependence, and of giving and receiving in a relationship, could promote endless analysis. Here, what may seem to be a mysterious summary statement must suffice: I keep myself, gain my life, and realize my independence, only to the extent that I give myself away. Yet, I am able to give myself only because others have first given to me, loved me. Given sufficient love, we mature, and love reveals our openness, and we discover that we need no walls. Then love overflows our own boundaries, for it can never be contained within us, held on to as a "thing." Love is a gift that must be given away. Once we have received it, our yearning to love others burns in us until it is accomplished. But then, to our dismay, we have to do it all over again, because giving love away only increases our supply. It is not just that it is better to give than to receive. Rather, to give love is to receive it, and to receive it is to give it. Either way, love is a life of gratitude for the gift.

CHAPTER FIVE

The Source of Every Emotion: Love

Principle Five: All Emotions Are Love-Derived

All human emotions are derivations, reflections and expressions of love — love-positive or love-negative, love gained or lost, threatened or reassured, rejected or restored, authentic or pseudo, hurt or healed. All emotions are generated by love, and all are ordered to and aimed at bringing about the same end — love given and received.

Explanations

• Love is the light of the heart. Just as all colors are various reflections of light, though light itself is not a color, a glass prism reveals that the "colorless" light actually contains the entire rainbow of colors. In like manner, love is the prism through which all human experience passes, and through which are seen the entire spectrum of emotions, all reflections of love, though love itself is not an "emotion," but something much, much more.

• In the most general, metaphysical terms, love is a movement of the heart toward any perceived good, i.e., it is the total movement of the heart. As love moves out from the heart, it is experienced as the various emotions. The word "emotion" is derived from the Latin *movere*, meaning "move" and *e-*, meaning "out."

• Not just people with emotional disorders, but all human beings at times have difficulty knowing what they are feeling and struggle to express feelings in words. Both powerful emotions and mild, subtle feelings can defy words, so it is not the strength of the emotion that determines the ease of expression. Rather it is the "depth" of love in the psychospiritual heart from which the emotion emanates that determines the ease or difficulty of verbal expression. The "depth" of love (as shown in Figure 2) is the distance between consciousness and the various levels of the heart from which the love-generated emotion springs.

• Severe emotional wounds (love damage) and gross emotional deprivation (love deficits) often lie deep in the contemplative heart, a great distance removed from consciousness, and near to the core of the heart that is "never known"; the greater the distance, the more difficult it is for consciousness to "hear" what the heart needs to express.

• "Emotional disorders" and "mental illness" are misnomers. Except in cases of organic involvement, all functional disorders are love disorders.

Contempt, happiness, rage, guilt, surprise, tranquility, jealousy, sadness, desire, fear, anxiety, hatred, all the emotions and all their hundreds of subtler variations and combinations, including ennui, plaintive remembering, spiritual awe, the spine chilling artistic response, frustrated sexiness, bemusement, and the contagious giggles — they are all demonstrations, reflections, or expressions, positively or negatively, of love.

Most of us do not find it difficult to understand how positive emotions are derivations and expressions of love. Feelings like affection, warmth, peace, mirth, and joy are commonly experienced as accompanying love, so it is not hard to make the connection. But the negative emotions are not so easily seen as love-related. People are accustomed to thinking of love as a simple, single, positive emotion, so how in the world, they ask, can I say that nasty emotions like hatred, disgust, jealousy, and murderous rage are expressions of love?! One man expressed it beautifully: "Look, I was already confused when I came for counseling. Now you're telling me that guilt is love? And hate is love? Lord! Are you going to tell me next that up is down?" Granted, love in negative terms seems contradictory, so following are some brief interpretations of the major negative emotions.

The "opposite" of love is not hate; it is nothingness, an emptiness that might be experienced as an agonizing hole in the psychospiritual heart (typically called "emotional deprivation") or in lesser forms as apathy or ennui.

Anger is the heart's normal response when love is damaged or insulted by injustice in any form — mistreatment, opposition, insult, etc. The love damaged by injustice may be one's own heart, or that of a loved one (which is the same as if the self suffered the love damage directly). The emotional response of anger is automatic and involuntary; it is a response designed to protect and/or restore love. In brief, anger, appropriately understood, is a good and necessary function of love. But there are many misunderstandings of anger. The major mistake is the failure to distinguish authentic love-centered anger from its abuses, i.e., any misuse of anger that results in hurting people physically, sexually, or emotionally. When anger is misused, it is important to understand that it is no longer *authentic* anger; it is simply abuse or hatred. Because anger is such a fundamental dynamic of many emotional disorders, it is the sole subject of Principle Twelve.

Hatred is intense anger compounded by a personal judgment of the other's guilt, culpability, inferiority, and total unlovability. The intent of the judgment felt as hatred is to justify the self as good, better than the one hated, and therefore lovable. Given hatred, authentic self-love is totally impossible because, looking in the mirror, the one who hates inherently recognizes her/himself as unlovable. As a result, ironically, hatred breeds self-hatred in the vain attempt to justify the self as lovable. The one hated is always perceived as stealing goodness or value, viz., something or someone loved, from the one who hates. Finally, in racial hatred, fear of the other race is compounded by feelings of inferiority, but the racist presents opposite feelings — not fear, but power and dominance, and not inferiority but superiority. In all cases, the one who hates is making futile use of judgmentalism in an effort to prove that the self is good, guiltless, powerful and superior, i.e., lovable.

Grief is the normal, immediate response of the heart to love loss. The love lost may be a relative or friend, or it may be part of one's own life. Normal grief following the death of a loved one is temporary; in time, because authentic love never dies, the love that the deceased person gave while alive resurfaces as loving memories, and the remembered love heals the grief. Children of alcoholics, for example, and adults who were emotionally deprived or abused as children, must often grieve through the portions of childhood life and love that were lost. Sadly, but in fact, the love lost through childhood abuse or deprivation remains lost until it is replaced or re-created through a loving re-living of childhood in therapy.

Guilt is the normal response of the heart to one's own violation of love, the automatic reaction to any betrayal, rejection or neglect that compromises the heart's integrity. What is right and wrong is differentiated by the conscience, the faculty of the heart that knows unerringly if love was honored or if it was violated by a particular act. It matters not if the love of another person or the self was involved in the act; if love was violated, the conscience says, "Guilty!" Guilt is the positive voice of the conscience designed to identify, replace and heal love that was violated and thus restore order to life and peace to the heart. (Principle Thirteen is focused entirely on guilt.)

Fear and *anxiety* are emotions that derive from seen or unseen, actual or perceived threats to love that are experienced in the center of being, the heart. Given a threat of love-rejection, love-humiliation, or love-damage in its many forms, the central effects are experienced as alarm in the psychospiritual heart: hearts tremble, quake, shrink, and cower; hearts erect defenses; and hearts prepare for flight or fight. (Two later chapters describe the various forms of anxiety and present new ways of understanding the anxiety that underlies so many emotional disorders.)

Emotions, responses and expressions of the psychospiritual heart, are so varied, so complex and rich that no mere analysis will ever capture them. Poets of all ages have proved that. So, too, the chart shown at the end of this chapter, "All Emotions as Expressions or Responses of Love," must be understood as simply a bare-bones sketch that shows how each and every emotion eventually can be understood in love terms. "Thinking in love terms," with a mind and heart "set" on love will be described in later chapters as a basic "method" of love therapy. The "Emotions" chart can provide no more than a sip, a tiny sample of how we can better understand the heart-level meaning of what any of us are feeling.

This principle makes no exceptions in its assertion that all emotions are derivations and expressions of love, but as an Explanation suggests, all of us have difficulty at times finding mere words that can express some of those feelings. Over the years, psychology, as a science, has produced countless analyses and taxonomies of emotion on lots of pie charts and grids, all in an effort to simplify our understanding. During those same years, poets continued searching for the exactly right gossamer, ethereal, wingèd, silv'ry, or vaporous word to describe feelings that simply will not come "trippingly on the tongue" as Shakespeare or any of us would prefer.

Clearly, both science and art, charts and poems, conceptual analyses and novels, taxonomies and symphonies can help us in our struggle to capture and express the ever-elusive emotions. But is it reasonable to ask, "Which does a better job expressing emotion, science or art?" Love theory answers without hesitation: Art! Figure Two in Chapter Three, showing personality structure, quickly shows us that there is almost an inverse relationship: science relates to consciousness as art relates to the "heart of the matter" of emotions and the deeper recesses of the human spirit. Thus, in addition to citing Jung, Karl Stern, Frankl or Walsh, a love therapist struggling to find ways to express elusive emotions is just as likely to point to the work of "counselors" with names like Goethe, Van Gogh, Mozart or Yeats.

Chart 1: All Emotions as Expressions or Responses of Love		
When my love is...	**Love's response is...**	**Because love's goal and need is always...**
Hurt, treated unjustly by someone	Anger	Restoration of justice, the measure of love's inalienable rights/needs
Violated by my own sin (my abuse of my own love standards and integrity)	Guilt	Honoring the command of Conscience for a clean heart– openness, honesty
Overtly threatened, physically or emotionally, by a visible danger to love	Fear	Life – the enduring wholeness of love of self and others
Covertly threatened by an undefined danger to the heart (injury to love of self or others)	Anxiety	Same as above
Threatened with annihilation, destruction at the deepest core of the heart	Angst, panic	Same as above, compounded by the mistaken belief that love can ever be totally destroyed
Vested and projected into the future as a promise of love's continuing existence	Hope	Eternal life. (Hope is an integral component of all authentic love)
Misused (by myself) as an expression of pseudo-power	Unjustified anger, abusiveness	Realization of authentic power which, in abuse, derives from pseudo-love

CHAPTER SIX

The Five Acts in Every Authentic Love

Principle Six:
Love Is One, With Five Basic Acts in Every Type

All authentic love of whatever type involves the same five essential actions of the psychospiritual heart: (1) movement of the heart toward a known and actual good that is perceived; (2) giving of the heart and receiving of the heart of the other; (3) affirmation of faith, trust, and hope in the other (and self); (4) permanent commitment to the other, i.e., a heart-held promise that the gift of self to the other will continue, for better or worse, until death and beyond; and (5) bonding to effect psychospiritual heart-to-heart unity. Though there are many types, love is one. "Love" that omits any of these five essential heart actions is a pseudo-love.

Explanations

- All types of love — self-love, marriage and sexual love, the symbiotic love of mother and infant, love of relatives and friends, purely spiritual love of God or people who have died, or love of animals, nature, groups, country and humanity — all require the same five actions of the heart if the love is authentic.
- Love of things, inanimate objects, per se, is impossible because things cannot reciprocate love, therefore bonding is impossible. Rather, things — money, art, houses, etc. — can be loved only

in so far as the thing contains, reflects, and thus indirectly and vicariously gives the love of the creator of the thing (as in art, or any beautiful thing), or in so far as the thing provides an authentic good that contributes to valid self-love.

• Pseudo-loves, notwithstanding the intensity of warm and pleasant emotions that accompany them, are not love. Love is not a mere emotion. Pseudo-loves can be compared to hallucinations: both seem real to the one experiencing them, but both obscure reality. (The word "love" is insulted, and millions of people are misled daily by the linguistic fallacies implicit in such common news headlines and movie themes as "love-pact suicides," "love triangles," "love murders," lust portrayed as "love-making," and greed defined as "love of money." These are all contradictions in terms; all are pseudo-loves. Authentic love may be hurt, but it is never voluntarily sick, nor does it ever affirm evil.)

• The third of five actions implicit in love is described in Principle Six as "the affirmation of faith, trust, and hope in the other"; this is one act with four parts as described in the Introduction. Love is a quadruplex integer. Love is "one" in that it is a single existential experience that is complete in and of itself. Thus, love is one unified act of the heart, not four.

• Though not usually, the type of romantic love called "being in love" may be an early stage of authentic love. It may also be a flitting flight of fancy that signifies little more than a momentary soaring into sentimentality. Yet, many of those who have been graced with mature, authentic love can testify that being in love can be more than mere sentiment, that it is sometimes an experience of enduring truth that seemed to be "infused."

• Inevitably, human love is imperfect, so there may be a tendency to confuse flawed or damaged loves with pseudo-loves. The two can be distinguished by asking whether the five essential actions described in the principle are present. Love can be buried beneath a mountain of damage and pain, but if the love is authentic, the five criteria still will be present. Pseudo-loves, however, may be painless, even blissful, but one or more of the action-criteria will always be found missing. The commitment may be missing, or the trust, or faith, or what is subjectively perceived as good may be objectively evil.

• Notably absent from Principle Six's five criteria for determining authentic love is any mention of emotion. The equation of love with feelings of warmth, bliss, and other sentiments is a persistent media- and culturally-induced myth that positively contributes to the epidemic rise of divorce rates, violent crime and suicide. People dissolve marriages, hurt "loved ones," and even kill themselves because they have been mis-taught that they must always "feel" love. As shown in love theory's diagrams of personality structure (in Chapter Three), love pervades the heart, but its source lies far deeper than the emotions, grounded in the deepest recesses of the soul. There, the movement of love may be powerful, even while at the shallower, emotional level, nothing is felt.

• The five criteria of Principle Six provide a foundation for teaching the basics of authentic love in the schools. Children's early understanding that love can be tough, that it requires character, and that it is far more than a feeling, could not just save them from unhappiness later on, it could save their lives. At present, prayer, God and religion are legally banned in the United States' public schools; teaching "love" is not a religious concept, but it would provide invaluable benefits to children that parents of any religious persuasion, or none, could readily agree upon.

Principle Six may be another of the love principles that some may view as iconoclastic. There is no question that its intent is to shatter the popular images of profane, glitzy, muddle-headed, lusty, romantic, and other false "loves" that have adorned the altars of the movies and soaps, and so thoroughly mangled public understanding of what real love is all about. There are thousands of idols masquerading as real love, and love theory's fervent desire is to topple them all. Our focus here, though, must be limited to the areas of greatest professional controversy and public misunderstanding. In the process, several new therapeutic concepts will be introduced that have evolved from the development of love therapy.

Self-Love and the Self-Definition

The "Love is One" principle makes it clear that self-love, if it is authentic, requires the same five action-criteria as loving other people. Firstly, if I love myself validly, I have moved my heart to affirm what is truly good about myself. Secondly, I can both give to myself and receive from myself, and this presumes I can allow myself to have access to my full heart and to just be me, without masks or defenses. Thirdly, I believe in myself, trust myself, and invest hope in myself. Fourthly, I have made a commitment to myself, that is, I have promised to stick with me and not reject or disown my own being even when I am very imperfect, as I inevitably will be. And fifth, I have gained access to my own heart and bonded with myself, i.e., I have affirmed the deep integrity and mystery of my heart and fused with the goodness residing in me. While providing psychotherapy to many people, like any counselor, I have encountered my share of tough cases of individuals who apparently would not or could not get better, people who persistently viewed themselves as something less than worms, and could not change the idea that they were somehow rotten to the core. Often, these people hang on to symptoms like glue, so that therapists too often give up on them, labeling them "intractable" or "not amenable to treatment."

Self-love in such "intractable" cases often stays near zero despite the fact that the therapists did everything possible to improve the person's "self-image" and "self-concept." In love therapy, when the focus is kept on what authentic self-love means to the person, one discovers that there is something much deeper and more important than the traditional concepts of self-image and self-concept. It is the person's "self-definition."

Self-Definition

Definitions, by definition, do not change; they must reflect truth, which is unchangeable. Deeper than a person's self-image, a "view" of self which might be quite superficial, and deeper than self-concept, a person's "ideas" of self, which can be heartlessly intellectualized, love theory focuses on "self-definition," the unique *is-ness* of personhood. A "chair" is a seat, usually having a back to lean against. On Monday, Wednesday or October, the dictionary definition of "chair" does not change. Similarly, children are taught, and then fully accept, self-definitions which may be entirely false, but which then become integrated as permanent labels and descriptions of self. Self-images and self-concepts then merge into definitions that folks are just stuck with. Far too often the definition is inaccurate, and when a person has a mental or emotional disorder, it can be accepted as axiomatic that that person is living with a self-definition that contains pernicious, insidious, or sometimes blatant lies.

Parents, teachers, relatives, the "big people," are all viewed by the child as authorities in relation to him- or herself. The child looks into parents' eyes, like looking in a mirror, and sees the self reflected back. Whatever is reflected, be it true or false, the child absorbs like a sponge — innocently, trustingly, indiscriminately, never questioning nor even suspecting that what the mirror's depiction of him or her will be anything but the pure truth. If the mirror says, "You're a good girl," the child says, "I'm good; that's what I am," and that quality enters the definition. If the mirror says, "You're a smart little girl, and pretty, strong, kind and clever," that is precisely what the child accepts as self, by definition. Most importantly, if the mirror says, "I love you, just as you are," the little girl says, "I'm lovable; yep, that's who I am."

If, though, the mirror says, "I love you, but…, but this or that is wrong with you," that is no love at all. All that the child then absorbs, as an integral part of his self-definition is, "There's something wrong with me." Love has no "buts" about it. If the mirror says, "I'll love you only when you learn to pick up your toys," the child's definition becomes "not yet lovable," which might as well be "never." Love is always now. Love with ifs, howevers, buts, or exceptions is not love; these negative amendments to love add up to one inescapable message of the mirror: "You are unlovable." When that terrible, destructive, oh-so-wrong message is given, that becomes the self-definition, and the foundation of a tragedy, a life of suffering.

Notice what happens. Given a definition of self as "unlovable," when authentic love is offered to that girl or to the grown woman, she must reject it; it simply does not fit her definition. That woman has been forced into a lifetime cycle of "playing duck" with love; love falls off of her like water on a duck's back, never sinking in. If someone says to her, "I love you," her self-definition automatically kicks in to reply, "But if you only knew the real me, you wouldn't love me," or, "Surrrre, you love me... but what's the catch?" or "Okay, you love me; now what do you really want?"

So long as a self-definition as "unlovable" remains, emotional problems can never be healed. Nor can a false self-definition merely be amended; "less" unlovable is still unlovable. Rather, the whole damnable unlovable definition has to be discarded, junked. This will not happen until the person is totally convinced that the mirror — parents in ninety percent of cases — lied. They may not have meant to lie; they may have been reflecting their own disorders. Nevertheless, the parents' lies must be aggressively and angrily repudiated before a false self-definition can be replaced by one that accurately reflects the intrinsic goodness and lovability of the person.

Falling in Love

Romantic love, the "falling in love" experience, has neither the permanence, nor the volitional (act of will) quality, nor the commitment required of full, authentic love. Falling in love is a preliminary, temporary state in which the heart opens wide, and reaches out to all the most beautiful qualities perceived in the other. The other is seen as Wonderful! Extraordinary! and as having rare and exquisite qualities that no other person on earth possesses. To the newly-in-love, she is an Angel! and he is a Prince! and each of them is convinced that the other is the embodiment of quintessential perfection. These incomparable, gorgeous, heavenly qualities are of such inestimable value that great vulnerability is worth the risk, any risk. Long-held defenses are suddenly dropped, and each of the lovers suddenly stands totally open to the other, naked to the soul, ready to offer all that she and he has to the beloved. Relieved, then, of the weight of defensive armor, lovers suddenly find themselves soaring above the earth, walking on air! Hearts trip and flutter and rockets flare! Bells ring! Flags are raised! For the lovers, all of life becomes the celebration of an obsession. She is the *only* girl and he is the *only* boy, and whether their ages are seventeen or seventy, the lovers become younger and younger as life becomes excitingly new, perfect and glorious.

Many therapists believe that falling in love is not love at all. Thus, Scott Peck says that it is a "misconception" that falling in love is love or even "one of the manifestations of love,"[1] and he goes on to offer one of the best analyses of the falling in love experience in print. The essence of the phenomenon of falling in love, Peck says, "is a sudden collapse of a section of an individual's ego boundaries, permitting one to merge his or her identity with that of another person."[2] With one vital exception, I agree with Peck's analysis, viz.: we agree that falling in love is highly sexually motivated; that it is full of illusions; that the will's action is missing; that it is not permanent; and that it is a far cry from the fullness of love. Still, I believe that falling in love *may* be real love, albeit just the beginning. Falling in love is the seed of a flower that may grow and in maturity bloom in lovely profusion — but

---

[1] Peck, *The Road Less Traveled, op. cit.*, p. 84.
[2] Peck, *ibid.*, p. 87.

only if the seed has good earth in which to germinate, only if it has the water and nutrients it needs, and only if weeds do not strangle it.

Falling in love, I believe, must be viewed as minimally realistic, maximally unrealistic, but most importantly, supra-realistic. The unreality is easy to see: while falling in love, the loved one is perceived as having few or no faults — and that is unreal. The good qualities are highly exaggerated, and that is unreal. Beneath that exaggeration, though, is some reality.

The heart of the falling in love experience is seen in its supra-real aspects. We fall in love primarily because we see the "super" qualities of the loved one, those unique, hidden attributes of the person that have been called the *individuum ineffabile*, ineffable individuality, the one-of-a-kind combination of rare and beautiful qualities that lay deeply buried in the heart of every person, those singular and even sacred qualities that are given to everyone who has ever lived, the qualities that mark them as very, very special. Our hearts open, and we "fall for" the utterly unique, "unknowable" qualities that we are mysteriously permitted to see in the heart of the other, those aspects of the person which are, in reality, super!

Consider, for example, these three married couples. First couple: he is ugly as homemade sin, and she has a face that would stop a clock. Couple two: she is widely regarded as a loudmouth busybody, and he is known as an obnoxious jerk. Third couple: he is a guy whose best friend can't stand him, and she was voted Miss Unpopularity. And yet, boggling the minds of all who know them, all three of these couples are madly in love. These are the ones of whom the catty so unkindly ask, "What in the world does she see in him?" But she surely sees something, and that something that she sees is obviously not obvious to the rest of humanity. A moment's reflection will show that this is not an exception, but the rule. To one degree or another, those three imperfect couples are all of us who fall in love and marry. Is that hard to admit? Aren't we all "Odd Couples"?

Look around. The married couples we see come in all sizes and shapes, both in personality and physically. One hard look produces the most telling questions: What in the world do all these people see in all these people? How could so many people manage to find someone who fell in love with them? More bluntly: how could it happen that so many people who seem so downright unattractive, or so weird, or so standoffish and unknowable, or just plain mean and nasty, stumble across the one person who could fall in love with them?

The cynic's answer is, "Love is blind." On the contrary, I answer that people fall in love because all of us, at special times, have extraordinarily acute vision, the capacity to see through the facade of another person and into the heart. There we see the interior reality of the other, the oft-hidden beauty, unique goodness and rare qualities that make that person what they are in reality. We see the deepest truth about the person, the supra-real. "There's just something special about her," he says. And then he falls. And if she reciprocates, the seed of authentic love is planted.

What I have just described is *mature* falling in love. What distinguishes the mature from immature is the realistic perception of the other's heart at a very deep level. Of course, there is the immature kind also.

I remember counseling a fifteen-year-old, Jenny, who told me she was going to get married. She had met Henry just the previous week and he was "just gorgeous." I asked what had happened to Tom, the guy she had been "in love with" and raving about for the two previous weeks. "Oh, he was a baby," she exclaimed, "Tom was just fifteen; Henry is a real man." How old is he? "Seventeen!" When I asked if she might not be rushing things a bit, she answered with great certitude, "Oh, no! The first time I laid eyes on him I fell in love with him." After basking in Jenny's glowing descriptions of Henry for long enough, I said, "Jenny, it seems like I've heard you talk like this before, but my memory fails me. Let's do this: you think back over the past year, and tell me the names of any guys you've been in love with, and I'll write their names down." As expected, Jenny's memory was amazing, "Well, there was Larry, then Danny, then Doug, then John...." When the list was complete, it showed that Jenny had fallen in love thirty-two times during the previous year. No kidding!

Looking at the list I had recorded for her, Jenny laughed. After contemplating the history of her love life for a while, she said, "The funny thing is, I thought they were all the real thing.... Hmmm.... Well... maybe I should wait on getting married, eh?" When that decision was firmed up, Jenny added an afterthought that might well sum up what puppy love and immature falling in love experiences are all about: "Gosh, all those guys... Know what? Maybe I was just practicing. You know what they say: practice makes perfect!"

After the early teenage days, with maturity, falling in love becomes less fickle, more discerning, deeper, less a matter of body, sexuality, pretty and handsome, and more a matter of the finer sensibilities of the heart that take more time to "practice" and develop. As we mature, we do indeed seem to learn that beauty is more than skin deep — although the epidermis has its rightful place. As we gain some wisdom, our hearts grow and our eyes open wider. Then, when we finally fall in love in a mature way, if it is truly mature, our love is not very blind at all. With practice, as our hearts grow in age and grace and wisdom, as we learn to listen to our hearts and not just our bodies, it is as if our hearts teach us to how to see more and more deeply into the hearts of others. Then, one day, after having peered into scores of hearts, we suddenly discover the heart that is right, "perfect" for us, and we fall head over heels. The seed falls on fertile ground and we fall in love. This is the bare beginning, but it is an essential aspect of love because all the potentialities for goodness, beauty, truth, openness and unity that growing love will make possible are discernible in the seed. The "magic" of the experience is that in mature falling in love, we do see the reality of the very best that lies in the interior of the heart of another person, the *individuum ineffabile*, the unique mystery.

Of course, a seed has to be cultivated, and that is hard work.

If love is to take root and grow to maturity, the decision to work cannot be avoided. Bad weather, periods of hunger and thirst and the threat of marauder weeds inevitably afflict every plant. Given the work of cultivation, the seed will never fail to grow and then flower. The flower of love is never seen in the seed of falling in love, though. That requires an authentic marriage (discussed below). People who have been happily married for many years, though, can look back and testify that the truth of their marriage, all the essential and best ingredients, were all contained in the seed.

One man's testimony, if it is indeed the truth, is truth for all, so allow me to share my own "falling in love" experience. It was a doozy. (Please note: while the following experience is remarkable by anyone's standard, and even though it is a love story that has thus far withstood the test of time [forty-three years], I caution everyone to *not* follow this example.)

I met Joyce, my wife, at a party at about nine o'clock at night. Within five minutes, we had isolated ourselves in a corner, away from the noise of the party, and began sharing life stories, laughing, and talking more and more intensely. An hour later, we left the party, found some privacy, and began talking even more earnestly. By the third hour, we were talking heart-to-heart, sharing soul-deep secrets and yearnings. Within four hours, I had fallen in love with her, and by 1 A.M., I proposed, she accepted and we were engaged. Exercising as much prudence as we could, we waited six months to get married, but the "seed" that would flower into full, mature, authentic love was undeniably present within hours. After lots of rough times, struggling times, rocky times, I can say without any doubt that I knew Joyce very accurately, and loved her in a very real way, that first crazy night. Since then I've fallen in love with her a thousand times all over. She is my flower, the heart of my heart. Even now, though, after all these years, when I look closely, I can still see the seed. It is there, as alive as ever, the power that gives life to the blossoms. It is the heart of Joyce, and now of me. I knew over forty years ago, and I know now, that that seed will never die.

Falling in love is romantic, yes, and full of pretty words, yes, but the essence of it is a moment of rarest silence. Words fail and fall away as we come face to face with a spellbinding beauty in the other that is the unutterable truth. It is exactly as the noble Cyrano de Bergerac tells his love, Roxanne:

> Love hates that game of words!
> It is a crime to fence with life — I tell you
> There comes one moment, once — and God help those
> Who pass that moment by! — when Beauty stands
> Looking into the soul with grave sweet eyes
> that sicken at pretty words![3]

"Love is truth." There is a moment that is, and will always be, the dominant, most treasured and pervasive truth of the lives of those of us who marry, the moment of falling in love, the Moment of Truth. That is the ethereal split second during which we are allowed to see the rarest sacred splendor, the quintessential beauty and truth that is hidden deep in the heart of the beloved. That moment is a mystical experience; it is as if the knowing of the beloved is supernaturally infused. Some may say that mystics experience love that is greater, but I say that those who fall in love, maturely, truly, are mystics — and once a mystic, always a mystic. Who knows but that mystics are simply those who remain open and vulnerable enough to keep falling in love over and over again.

The Test For Authentic Marriage

Is it not remarkable that everyone bemoans the national fifty percent divorce rate, but that the level of failed marriages remains depressingly high year after year? Given that single fact,

---

[3] Edmond Rostand, *Cyrano de Bergerac* [1897]. Translated by Brian Hooker (New York: Bantam, 1959), p. 109.

is it condescending to ask whether the average person knows what authentic married love is all about? It also seems reasonable to ask whether many of these divorces might not be occurring unnecessarily. Over the past three decades, the questions as to whether to get married, or not, and whether to stay married, or not, seem to have left half the marriage-aged nation adrift, confused, with no way to answer the questions.

When couples come for counseling, often angry, hurt, confused, and questioning if it's time for divorce, the five action-criteria which define authentic love form the foundation of a "test," or what might be called a "heart guide," for helping people evaluate their marriages. First, though, we need some consensus about what marriage and married love actually are. Principle Six describes all authentic love, which would include married love, in terms of five criteria, five interior events: (1) movement of the heart toward a known and actual good; (2) heart-level giving and receiving of selves; (3) faith, trust, and hope invested in one another; (4) permanent commitment; and (5) bonding, heart-to-heart unity. Moving step by step toward the question of bonding, the final test, following is the interpretation of married love which I offer to every couple entering marriage (and/or divorce) counseling:

"The first big question, no matter how long it's been since your wedding, is, 'Were you authentically married?' Now, we know that a marriage license and a ceremony do not make a marriage. Love makes a marriage, and that love has to be mature. Children cannot marry. Why? Because they are not yet capable of knowing others deeply enough. We can only love what we know. So the first question is, 'Did you have accurate, mature knowledge of your spouse? Did you know him/her at heart level?' If not, you were never married. If you did, we can go to the next test.

"The second mark of authentic love is the giving and receiving of yourselves, your hearts, to one another. This is a totally interior event. Love is a gift. Only you know if you became vulnerable, opened yourself up, and *gave* yourself without reservation to your spouse. By the same token, you also know in your heart if you were *given* the heart of your spouse. If hearts were not mutually given and received, there could not have been a real marriage; if they were, there are still three more tests.

"The third test has several parts: married love means that when you opened your hearts, you had faith, trust and hope in one another. Those are indispensable parts of love. So, if you said, 'I love you, but I don't believe in you at all, or I don't trust you at all, or I don't have enough hope to believe you'll love me next year and forever,' then the absence of any one of the three — faith, trust, or hope would mean you were never authentically married. But if all those were present, there are still two more tests....

"Test four: Were you totally committed? Commitment means a permanent promise of love, including love's faithfulness, and of love's trust, and of love's hope. If you had an affair, it means — note the word — you adulterated your love. By itself, an affair does *not* automatically mean there was no commitment ever; it may mean only that you violated your own heart, and that you need to heal it by renewing your promise of fidelity. On the other hand, if you carried on a constant string of affairs, it may well mean that you were never really committed, and thus never married. Still, in even one affair, if you discovered that you actually could give your heart to someone besides your partner, it means that you had never committed your heart to your spouse. But given commitment, there's one big question left....

"The fifth, final and biggest question about your marriage is this: Is there a bond between you, a heart-to-heart unity? A bond is like a vaccination; if it 'takes,' it's an integral part of you and you can *never* take it back; it's a done-deal even if you decide someday that you don't like your vaccination scar. Here's another example: a marriage bond is like mixing two glasses of colored water together, one blue and one yellow. Once they are mixed to produce green, you have green, and you can never separate the molecules and the colors and go back to blue and yellow again. It's the same with bonding: if two hearts are joined to become one, it's like conjoined twins sharing one heart. You'll share that same psychospiritual heart till death parts you.

"Now, those five interior events create the special kind of love we call marriage, so before we talk about your marriage or divorce, the question is: Were you authentically married in the first place? Was there, and is there an inseparable bond?"

After presenting this five-step "heart guide," it is amazing to watch couples' reactions. Their responses are totally unpredictable. No matter how troubled, unhappy, symptom- and storm-filled the marriage is reported to be, a counselor cannot predict how a couple will evaluate their marriage after they have been given just a moment to reflect. Just as amazing, once the heart test is presented, almost invariably people can answer immediately and with total certitude, "Yes, we are truly bonded, married," or, "No, I was never authentically married."

Some couples come to counseling seriously talking divorce, and describe their marriage as a living hell. I have heard people describe daily shouting matches, screaming and fighting in which the house is nearly destroyed. They both yell that they "can't stand" the other. She "hates his guts" and he "despises her," and their angry glares seem hot enough to start a fire. But when I say, "Okay, okay, I believe you! — you're both angry as hell, and there's an ocean of hurt, and you're not getting along at *all*, but please try to answer my question: Is there a bond between you? Are you authentically married?" Often as not, her response might be, "Yes, dammit, the bond is there, and yes, it's a real marriage, and yes, I love the big dummy, but I tell you I hate him and I'm not going to live with him!" And his response might well be the same. Authentic love can be buried beneath a ton of confusion and hurt that may take months to unravel and heal, but midst the reality of that buried and hurting love, in the third fundamental component of it, next to faith and trust, there lies hope. Beyond all external appearances, beyond all the voluble, heated and painful emotions, love's hope sometimes still whispers loudly enough to save a marriage that presents every external appearance of being doomed. The counselor's first job is to help the couple listen to their hearts, to the tiny whispers of hope instead of the shouts of emotions. It bears repeating again and again: love is not a mere emotion. If it were, no marriage would ever survive.

At the opposite extreme, another couple may come for marriage counseling who have never had an argument. They are simply unhappy in vague ways they do not understand. Both partners agree they "should" be happy. They get along okay. Each likes and respects the other. Each thinks the other is a nice person. Both have been faithful. Sex is fine. Neither has ever seriously emotionally hurt the other. Their unhappiness seems totally inexplicable. Yet, when the five-step heart guide is presented to this couple, a marriage that seems basically very sound is discovered to have been built on quicksand. By the second step of the test, a wife might say, "Faith in him? Believe in him? I don't know.... He keeps to himself — like he's in a shell. A month after our wedding, it dawned on me that I didn't *really* know him at all... so how can I believe in him?" Or, in response to the commitment question, he might confess, "Well, I've honestly tried to love her, and I thought I did, but when you described commitment, I have to admit that I married on the rebound. I guess I *kind of* love my wife... but I have to admit that if my old girlfriend would give me a chance, I'd be gone in a minute." Conclusion: even though the couple asks for "marriage" counseling, no faith equals no marriage, and no commitment means no marriage. Thus, there is no authentic marriage to counsel — just two unhappy people who are living together and clearly should not be.

By no means, though, should this "test" be considered only a framework to determine if the marriage is bona fide. It is also a quick and accurate diagnostic tool. Solidly committed, bonded, but troubled couples, after hearing the five "heart actions" involved in love, can often zero in on their basic problem area. Whether that is shaken trust, hurts caused by arguments over money, growing emotionally apart, sexual difficulty, or poor communication, the two immediate advantages of the test are, first, the couple has reaffirmed their original and continuing mutual bonded love, and second, their attention is immediately focused on the "heart of the matter" of any marriage problem

— hurt, shaken, and disrupted love. Given this solid foundation and focus at the outset of marriage counseling, the test spares the couple endless hours of roaming all over the ballpark, talking about extraneous petty issues. A third, and perhaps the greatest value of the test, is that when a solid foundation of committed, bonded love is reestablished, the couple instantly remembers the *positive* reasons they got married in the first place, the love they share. In turn, that remembered love inherently brings with it two other qualities that are sorely needed in a shaky marriage: hope and healing.

Pseudo-Loves

Metaphysically, love is defined as "a movement toward the good," or more precisely, "to will the existence of that which the intellect apprehends as good."[4] In the broadest sense, anytime we do anything at all, we are moving toward something we perceive as "good." Obviously, that perception may or may not be objectively accurate, but if we perceive a good, and move toward it in thought, feeling, or deed, we nevertheless are loving in an accurate metaphysical sense. Many emotional problems derive precisely from the capacity of human beings to be deceived or to misperceive goodness and then love something or someone who is not good at all, and in fact may even be quite evil.

Authentic love is always good, true and beautiful, but there are also pseudo-loves, loves which are ersatz, twisted, deceptive, destructive, phony, and yes, even malignant or murderous. Some pseudo-loves are quickly perceived by an onlooker. An addict "loves" heroin. A jealous husband kills his wife because he "loves" her. A pedophile tells a child, "I love you," and then sexually abuses her. A masochist "loves" punishment. Those who are prey to their own pseudo-loves rarely see the pseudo

---

[4] Dulles, et. al., *op. cit.*, p. 263.

elements, even though they are blatant and bizarre to everyone else. Yet, some pseudo-loves are not so easily detected. There are the insidious, pernicious kinds of pseudo-love which sometimes require months of intense psychotherapy to unravel.

A young man suffering panic attacks began counseling by saying, "I had a Super-Mom. She loved me to pieces. She did *everything* for me." In counseling, he began to trace his anxiety to fear of failure, failure at even the simplest tasks — because only Super-Mom could do things "right." Sadly, he eventually discovered that his mother was overprotective, controlling, hostile, and that he had received little mother love but much "smother love" — pseudo-love, little authentic love at all.

A woman with a severely emotionally disturbed mother had been sexually abused throughout childhood by her stepfather. He had also sexually abused her three sisters. She "loved" her stepfather, though, and initially felt no anger toward him at all — though she vaguely knew what he did was wrong. It took months of therapy for her to understand that this stepfather's "love" was entirely venomous, pseudo. He would inflame the disturbed mother against one of her daughters, and then come to the girl's "rescue," interceding to "protect" her from the mother's wrath, and all he asked in return from the then-grateful girl was a sexual favor, which he always called, "a little love." In truth, this pedophile manipulated the entire family, using and abusing "love" to control them all. In cases like this, complex systems of pseudo-loves compounding pseudo-loves must be unraveled and exposed. The only effective detector of the most insidious and evil pseudo-loves is authentic love.

In one sense, every symptom can be best understood as a pseudo-love. Though painful and destructive, every symptom has what therapists call a "secondary gain." The symptom serves some purpose. A symptom of depression, though painful, may prevent having to deal with a package of loss, guilt, and hatred that seems more painful than the depression. Panic attacks, though excruciating, may have a secondary gain of allowing avoidance of a repressed traumatic memory. The secondary gain always seems to serve some "good" purpose. Thus, in the broadest understanding of love as a "movement toward the good," we arrive at an undeniable but paradoxical conclusion: all symptoms are pseudo-loves, but emotionally suffering people "love" their symptoms.

It is the basic contention of love therapy that, except for organic problems, all mental and emotional problems involve pseudo-loves (compounded by love deficits, rejection, and love deprivation). When our most elementary needs for love are unfulfilled, or when love is provided in twisted, manipulative, perverse, punishing or even evil forms, all called pseudo-loves, emotional problems result, inevitably and inexorably. Now, once it is recognized that all emotional disorders are damaged love problems, the cure for all disorders becomes obvious: authentic love precisely targeted to heal the damage. And that answer, that hope, is as oh-so-simple and as oh-so-complex as love itself.

Types of Pseudo-Love

Every age and every society has its own unique pseudo-loves — false, deceptive and destructive forms of "love" that receive tacit if not actual legal approval and institutionalization within society which makes them seem "normal." Likewise, every human being, even the saint, has had pseudo-loves, a "love" for something that seems "good" at the time, but is actually destructive. Every bad habit, sin, or human failing — and we all have them — has a pseudo-love motivating it. In counseling, it can often be seen that the pseudo-loves that underlie emotional disorders have their origins in society-at-large. Culturally or individually, pseudo-loves can be exposed by applying Principle Six's five criteria for determining authentic love.

As shown earlier, faith and love are one (together with trust and hope). Thus, if I believe that I can steal your soul, or you mine, that faith could prompt me to "love" your soul, and then to kill and eat you before you can eat me. Yes, that's cannibalism, a false-faith and pseudo-love, and in our enlightened era we call that primitive. Similarly, the old Chinese practice of foot-binding, based on the pseudo-love of small feet on women, we would call brutality. Yet, there are modern forms of socially- and media-promoted pseudo-love that are every bit as deadly or crippling as cannibalism and foot-binding. The following brief examples highlight some of the more common ways that media-hyped and culturally-promoted pseudo-loves directly produce or exacerbate emotional disorders.

The Pseudo-Love of Body Beautiful

In the seventeenth century, the artist Rubens painted nude female forms which universally are considered masterpieces. His models were decidedly fleshy, hippy and plump — the ideal in his era. Later, in the nineteenth century, big buttocks were admired, so women wore bustles. By the quarter of the twentieth century, the hour-glass figure was in vogue. That's when the "sexy" voluptuous comedienne Mae West was a big hit. A few years later, though, the "flapper" years began and women's figures were totally de-emphasized. For a couple of decades then, the body fashion was generally thinner. Then the big-breast craze began. That's when Jane Russell, Marilyn Monroe, Gina Lollobrigida and a few years later, Dolly Parton became big hits. The breast focus increased then, so that in order to be loved, a stampede of women raced to undergo silicone breast enlargement surgery.

Simultaneously, the ideal image of women became skinnier and skinnier, so coincidentally, thousands of teenage girls and young women developed anorexia nervosa and bulimia — starving, vomiting, taking laxatives, and in effect cannibalizing themselves in order to become "lovable," that is, skinny.

It seems reasonable now to ask, which practice is more primitive? — Cannibalism? The deformation to produce the old Chinese ideal of small feet? Anorexic and bulimic "self-cannibalism"? Or the modern practice of cutting breasts open to make them bigger?

Quickly, some caveats are necessary. Granted, the major causes of anorexia and bulimia involve deep emotional pain, and the irrationality of the society-produced pseudo-love of skinniness is usually a secondary cause. Yet, that secondary cause is directly responsible for the huge increase in emotional disorders expressed in this particular form over the past twenty years. Too, there certainly are cases in which extremely small-breasted women, together with those who have undergone mastectomies for cancer, may need breast reconstruction or augmentation in order to feel "whole" or "feminine." A purist position that breasts are totally unimportant would be as extreme as saying that having a nose is of no consequence. However, when women with slightly small or average-sized breasts (whatever that is) run by the millions for augmentation, they must be viewed as victims of societal- and media-created pseudo-loves and diagnosed accordingly.

In counseling, the fickle pseudo-loves of society sometimes require more exposure and treatment than clients' individual damaged loves. Clearly, prevention would be far more effective. Through aggressive education regarding societal pseudo-loves, groups like the National Institute of Mental Health could undoubtedly reduce the numbers of eating disorders and unnecessary breast surgeries dramatically. That would mean, of course, that N.I.M.H. would have to do battle with the diet, exercise, and fashion industries, as well as some plastic surgeons who are exploiting the pseudo-loves of skinniness and big breasts for the sake of a fast buck. (Note, by the way, that the industries' and surgeons' ill-gotten fast bucks are also pseudo-loves.) Meanwhile, women beware: in a few years, fickle fashion will surely change — it always does — and the Rubens fleshy body and small breasts may be fashionably "in" again.

Religion-Induced Pseudo-Loves

As a member of the Association of Christian Therapists, I receive more than my professional share of referrals of religious people by priests and ministers of many denominations. Sadly, but all too frequently, the emotional problems are directly traceable to church teachings which are distortions of truth — pseudo-faith and pseudo-loves. Following are just a few of the more common pseudo-loves taught in some churches.

If religious Christians are asked, "Do you subscribe to Jesus' prime commandment, 'Love your neighbor as yourself'?" every single one answers, "Of course." But if they are then told, "Now reverse the clauses in that commandment. It's the same thing, isn't it? — 'Love yourself as your neighbor' — do you do that?" Amazingly, not only do a huge percentage of people answer, "No," many of them will say they thought that they *shouldn't* love themselves, at least not very much. Why? Their church taught them to be "humble."

The virtue of humility is widely mis-taught as a pseudo-love that values and promotes self-abnegation, putting one's self down, refusal to admit that one is in any way good, bright, beautiful, talented, or, in short, lovable. Properly understood, humility demands the simple truth: I am indeed good and truly lovable because I have received many loving gifts from many people and from God. Truth and humility demand that I celebrate my goodness, my gifts, and my lovability. Denigrating oneself, self-demotion and rejection of self-love are in fact ingratitude, false humility, and ironically, pride.

The most destructive pseudo-love taught by some denominations is one that could not sound better: the love of *perfection*. That sounds like an oxymoron, doesn't it? What, after all, could be wrong with perfection? The problem rises when the biblical admonition, "Be ye perfect..." is taken literally, and then strictly enforced by church authorities who roundly condemn the teeniest sin in the name of God. The result is a purulent mix of perfectionism enforced by judgmentalism which produces a profound fear- and guilt-laden depression stemming from the false belief that one is hopelessly condemned by God. Suffice to say, the pseudo-love of perfection, i.e., perfectionism, is a sin, and judgmentalism is a killer.

Though it may seem entirely abstract, it is true nonetheless that, excepting organically-induced disorders, there can be no serious emotional problems in people who thoroughly believe that God loves them. Love protects the heart, so in the presence of Perfect Love, destructive fear, false-guilt, hatred, jealousy and the like would be warded off, and emotional wounds would be quickly healed. Of course, the problem is that imperfect human beings cannot receive Perfect Love — no, not even saints are perfect. The secret of the saints, I believe, must be that they have discovered that, imperfect as they are, God loves them anyway, and not in the hereafter, but now, as they are, warts and all. On the contrary, the pseudo-love called perfectionism, and its deadly hit man, judgmentalism, are clear diagnostic signs of a faith problem: the inability to believe that God's love is bigger than a wart.

Religious pseudo-loves may well be as numerous as those existing anyplace else, including brothels. The history of "holy" wars, terrorism, and murder perpetrated "in the name of God" is ample testimony that the pseudo-love of "God" may be the most deadly of all. During the Inquisition, "heretics" were burned at the stake "in the name of God." The Ku Klux Klan killed African American people "in the name of God." Many Black Muslims teach that white people are "devils" "in the name of Allah." Jews and Arabs have warred for centuries in the name of Yahweh on one side and Allah on the other. Islamic fundamentalists, "in the name of Allah," and led by their religious leaders, blew up the World Trade Center in New York. And Catholics and Protestants who fought for decades in Northern Ireland both claimed to have God on their side. Poor God. Throughout the ages and throughout the world, the atrocities perpetrated "on God's behalf" would require volumes to simply list. How can we explain such tragic and barbaric ironies? The hard truth is that we probably cannot. When religious-speaking people twist the meaning of "love" and

"God" in order to justify mayhem, war and terrorism and murder, that is called, not just pseudo-love, but evil. And when we face evil, our effort to explicate pseudo-loves is stopped in its tracks. Real evil can never make sense because it is the antithesis of truth and thus totally inane and insane. Suffice to say here, when we encounter the most extreme religious perversions of love, we are probably looking at the ultimate in pseudo-loves, naked hypocrisy. Authentic love exposes it.

Power as a Pseudo-Love

Ultimately and essentially, the only authentic power is love. All power is derived from love, and though the motivation ordinarily is not blatantly obvious, the goal of every use of power is to be loved or to love. Needless to say, there are a thousand ways that power can be misused as a pseudo-love. Power can be exerted violently, economically, or sexually — to name just three of the more common ways.

A husband batters his wife, a mother abuses her children, a teenager explodes and hits a teacher — and in the course of counseling, when the violent person finally is able to identify the feeling that just preceded the experience of rage, the answer almost invariably is "powerlessness." All too often, identifying that deep sense of impotence, counselors say, "Aha! That's it!" and treat the powerlessness directly. Assertiveness Training may be used to help the person express anger appropriately, and interviews may be focused on exploring when and how the feeling of powerlessness overcomes the person. Those are good and necessary therapies — but they miss the heart of the matter of violence.

Violence, at any age, is a child's way of capturing love by storm. Anger (as Principle Twelve will discuss in detail) is a natural and normal human response to injustice, any love violation (whether accurately or inaccurately perceived). For the very young child, deprivation of *anything* might be perceived as an injustice because the toddler loves everything and wants *everything*, with no limits, and with no distinction between objective good and bad. Deprived of love (anything), a very young child might have a tantrum, or get violent and hit his mother — "Bad Mommy!" This same childish rage underlies adult abuse and violence in any of its forms.

The heart of understanding violence lies in hearing the desperate cry for love that lies behind it. The violent person is a child screaming, "If I can't have love (any perceived good, be it a cookie or a country), I'll take it with power!" The violent child (of any age) does not understand that love is a gift that can never be taken by force, so he/she pursues loveless power, which then becomes a pseudo-love. Effective therapy in relation to violence must be focused not only on the obvious issues of power and powerlessness, but on the sources of both, love and its absence.

Granted, it is not quite that simple. The ways that power can derive from love or pseudo-love may require wending our way through a maze of psychic twists and turns. Yet, in the counseling office, in industry boardrooms, or at the State Department, what is suggested in this discussion of pseudo-loves is that power is largely misunderstood. For example, when the notorious Saddam Hussein was jockeying to overpower Kuwait, it is doubtful that anyone in the State Department or among the Joint Chiefs of Staff of the Armed Forces ever used the word "love" in their analyses of the man. Yet, unless Saddam was understood fundamentally as a disturbed child desperate for love, if only his saber rattling and his (pseudo-love-produced) power maneuvers were analyzed, there could be no basic understanding of his motivations. Without such love-centered insight, the tyrant would remain unpredictable. And indeed, both before and after his defeat in the Gulf War, he was just that. Though it may seem impossibly farfetched, what is suggested here is that if a nation's foreign policy were love-centered instead of power- and pseudo-love centered, instead of sacrificing military lives and billions of dollars fighting hostile nations, a way could be found to deliver the basic goods that even, and especially, tyrants need — love, authentic power.

The massive misuse of power by the world's politicians may be exceeded only by criminals, but in relation to criminals, too, fundamental understanding has been missing. For prison wardens, police or judges to ever use the word "love" in efforts to understand a criminal is virtually unheard of. On the contrary, the word "love" has been anathema in the criminal justice system. Criminals blatantly misuse power so the perception has been that to speak of "love deficits" as the cause of criminal behavior is the language of weak, bleeding-heart liberals. Instead, the only acceptable policy has been to answer criminals' misuse of power with State power by cracking down and punishing, using "legitimate" power to out-power illegal power. Again, the fundamental truth has been missing: love is the only legitimate power, so any use of power without love is illegitimate, pseudo, and inevitably counterproductive and destructive, even if that power is wielded legally by the State. The result has been that the very concept of rehabilitating criminals has become a pitiful joke. Granted, the very idea of actually loving a murderer, a rapist, a robber, or any violent person may seem positively silly if not revolting. Still, until the truth dawns on society that criminals must be *healed*, that only love heals, and that rehabilitation logically demands love, the prisons will continue to expand and the cities will increasingly become war zones.

Victim and victimizer, though they seem to reside at opposite ends of the spectrum of power, both suffer from the same deficiency, a gap in the psychospiritual heart that is felt as powerlessness — a gap that only authentic love, real power, can fill. Given love, the lion lies down with the lamb, the warrior becomes a pacifist, the coward finds courage and the victim and criminal both become healed. One interpretation of the most well-known biblical passage on love says, "Love never fails."[5] We must conclude this short section on love and power by affirming that love will never fail the criminal justice system or political policy either. It just hasn't been tried.

---

[5]   1 Corinthians 13:8.

CHAPTER SEVEN

Reality Is Love

Principle Seven: The Love Principle of Reality

Ontologically, reality is love. Reality, the totality of being, all that authentically exists — materially, psychologically and spiritually — is love.

Explanations

• Theologically, God is Love; Love is God. Supreme Love, God (by whatever name) created all things, not out of "nothing," (the word used by many theologians) which obviously does not exist, but out of the only thing that did exist, God's own substance, Love.

• Reality is sustained in existence by love.

• Ontologically, reality, considered as being, was preceded by love; love is the essence, the being-ness, of being.

• Materially, physically, love is the "spiritual substance" from which the atom, the building block of material reality, was created. The mysterious "space," "flux," or "ether," which exists between and binds together the electrons, protons, quarks, and all the micro-particles that collectively form the atom, the fundamental "stuff" or "energy" of the atom which quantum physicists have long sought but never identified, is love.

• Biologically, organically, love is the singular, omnipresent life force, the ubiquitous constant, the elemental dynamic energy which creates, directs and sustains the existence of the cell, the basic building block of all life, human, animal and vegetable.

• Love is the first and most fundamental natural law, i.e., love is life, and vice versa, biologically, psychologically and spiritually.

• Evil — imperfection, defects, sin — is not being, but a privation of being, an absence of love; thus, *by itself*, it does not exist. Evil "exists" only relatively, as a privation of the being. All being, insofar as it actually exists, is good — because being is love. The "relative existence" and "privational reality" of evil does not negate the truth of the principle that reality is love. (This difficult concept of evil as a "privation" of reality is explained by philosophers such as Dulles, *et al.*[1] It is discussed here, albeit too sketchily, only because we are trying to define the broadest concept of "all reality.")

• That all of reality is love is self-evident — just as self-evident as it is that love is the fundamental drive, goal, and *raison d'être* of human life (Principle One). The proof that love is the Alpha and Omega of reality lies in palpable human experience, *raison de cœur*, reason of the heart.

• Epistemologically, (in the study of the philosophy of how human beings "know,") love precedes knowledge. Love creates the power to know. Precisely because of this, with great love, human beings sometimes can know and understand mysteries that seem impossible to know. Under certain circumstances, human beings have the mysterious capacity to "know the unknowable," to plumb mysteries about other human beings, God, and spiritual reality that seem impossible.

---

[1]   Dulles, *et al, op. cit.*, pp. 294-297.

Following such heady philosophical stuff, it bears repeating that the purpose of the Love-Reality Principle and its Explanations is to provide psychotherapy with an essential and long-needed definition of reality upon which a personality theory can be grounded. Philosophy itself is not our purpose, however. A basic philosophical statement is essential, but we can't do much with love that is floating around the ethereal clouds of abstract thought. Love has to be brought down to earth, incarnated, enacted. Therefore, I will not provide even the minimum defense and discussion this principle and its reflections may well need and surely deserve. Rather, I must bank on the only proof that love can ever provide for itself, that it is self-evident. Given acceptance of the self-evidence, the principle and its corollaries are fairly obvious — with one exception.

The exception is the fourth Explanation, the definition of love as the essence of physical, material reality. That idea could be a brain-blocker for some. Frankly, I have imagined it causing physicists to either throw up or to get the giggles, so the concept needs some explanation.

The proposition that love is the fundamental force, energy, flux or ether that governs the atom is clearly deducible once it is accepted as self-evident that no other reality could be more rock-bottom fundamental — but it still may seem somehow farfetched. The reason for the difficulty is that we can easily experience love as a psychological reality, but we have difficulty grasping any real connection, much less commonality, between ourselves and inorganic, material *things.* It is difficult, but much less so, to feel or intuit something in common between a walrus and me, or even an artichoke and me. After all, when we read of Francis of Assisi talking to "Brother Bird" and "Sister Flower," we are warmed by his love and feel some of the same affinity as he did with all creation. Modern-day environmentalists and animal rights activists are clearly expressing their conviction of the organic connection of all living things. But at least animals and vegetables are alive! They are organic, as I am, and they are composed of cells, as I am. It is a lot tougher to feel some kinship between myself and a rock, a carbon atom, or the toilet brush. The definition of love as the elemental energy that not just governs the atom, but as the "substance" of which it is created, clearly warrants some explanation. The argument begins with creation.

Whether the universe began with one big bang, or a series of snaps, crackles and pops, or with one big breath of God that was bigger than a circus tent,[2] or in six days of really fast work as the Bible literalists believe,[3] is not the most salient question. Rather, the question is what was the pre-existing power that activated the bang, whisper, ping, sigh or zapp that started the universe rolling?[4] That power, we know, had to form and energize billions upon billions of atoms, which in turn formed all matter, the material galaxies. That power was love. Let me prove that.

The proof that love is the power that creates and controls the atom lies with two unlikely bedfellows, the Bible and Physics. If we prove that love powers the atom, the building block of material reality, we obviously prove that love, *en fin*, is reality. (Note: for atheists and agnostics who doubt anything biblical, I nevertheless would proffer the challenge of the second half of the love-reality argument which focuses on Physics.)

With some creative but straightforward deduction, plus a tiny, irrefutable, logical step in Physics, science proves that the biblical rendition of reality is quite correct. First, we need to apply

---

[2]   Archibald MacLeish uses this image of creation in his play, *J.B.*

[3]   The "six days of fast work" are described in Genesis 1:1-27. Note: there are some who very seriously argue that God's creation occurred in six *days,* meaning six 24 hour periods. Others say a Genesis "day" could mean several billion years. Still others argue that evolution disproves creation altogether. For the record, I affirm God's creation and evolution, both. Debating precisely how that creation came about, however, seems like an endless wrestling with mystery. Therefore, rather than pretend to resolve the debate, perhaps I can enrich it by recalling the funny old (evolutionary) question: Did Adam and Eve have navels?

[4]   How did creation begin? Maybe the astronomers' theory of the "Big Bang" is correct; maybe not. In any case, evolution does not negate the idea that God began creation. Therefore, I propound another equally scientific concept, Mullaney's "Little Ping" theory, which is this: One timeless day, God was just hanging around the void and got bored, so He said, "I think I'll create something." So He pointed His finger, and "PING!" there was the first atom, or maybe all the galaxies. That ping was the first materialization of love. So, if there was a Big Bang, the Little Ping came first.

the newer understanding of God offered in the New Testament to the story of creation recorded in the Old Testament.

The most incisive *definition* of "God" ever given is biblical: "God is love."[5] Logically, the obverse must also be true: Love is God. It follows that we can interchange the words "God" and "Love" with logical consistency. Now, applying that understanding to the creation story presented in the first pages of Genesis, look what happens when we substitute the word "Love" for "God."

> In the beginning, when Love created the heavens and the earth, the earth was a formless wasteland, and darkness covered the abyss while a mighty wind (literally, a wind of Love) swept over the waters.
>
> Then Love said, 'Let there be light,' and there was light. Love saw how good the light was. Love then separated the light from the darkness... the first day.
>
> Love made two great lights, the greater one to govern the day, and the lesser one to govern the night; and Love made the stars... Love saw how good it was... the fourth day.
>
> Then Love said: 'Let us create man in our image...'
>
> Love created man in Love's image; in the divine image Love created him; male and female Love created them... the sixth day....
>
> Such is the story of the heavens and the earth and their creation.[6]

Creation, all of reality, the Genesis account says, began with Love, Love alone, and then Love began creating matter. Creating out of what? Obviously out of the only thing that existed, love. So Love went to work, atom by atom.... Biblically, it is clear that reality is love.

---

5 John 4:16.

6 Selected verses from Genesis 1:1-27.

Would physicists agree? They obviously have not reached that conclusion yet, but all the findings of modern physics point to love as the ultimate answer to the atom that has been right under their electron microscopes all along.

Modern discoveries in atomic or particle physics and quantum mechanics have penetrated the reality of our physical universe — matter, and its relationship to energy, space and time — to a degree never conceived of eighty short years ago. The physical world, matter, has been found to be comprised of smaller and smaller bits and microbits — atom, nucleus, neutron, proton, electron, piton, positron, neutrino, quark — which behave in such paradoxical, surrealistic, "impossible" ways that the "laws of nature" we once thought so certain and immutable have been replaced by a "law of uncertainty"[7] that is universally held by physicists. The microparticles of matter thoroughly defy such common-sense notions as whether a thing is there or not there, stationary or moving, whether a particle can be two places simultaneously, or indeed, even there at all until it is measured.

Perhaps the most quoted paragraph summing up this weird physical world we live in is the remark of J.R. Oppenheimer, head of the Los Alamos (atomic bomb) project:

> If we ask... whether the position of the electron remains the same, we must say "No"; if we ask whether the electron's position changes with time, we must say "No"; if we ask whether the electron is at rest, we must say "No"; if we ask whether it is in motion, we must say 'No."[8]

Thus, it seemed, the more that physicists discovered about the atom, the less likely they were to reach conclusions. The atom, and thus material reality, continued to be an endless string of question

---

[7] In 1931, Werner Heisenberg received the Nobel Prize for this theory, which is alternately called the Principle of Indeterminancy.

[8] J.F. Oppenheimer, *Science and the Human Understanding* (New York, 1966), p. 40.

marks. Werner Heisenberg, spelling out that uncertainty, says:

> Atoms are not things. The electrons which form an atom's shell are no longer things in the sense of classical physics, things which could be described by concepts like location, velocity, energy, size. When we get down to the atomic level, the objective world in space and time no longer exists, and the mathematical symbols of theoretical physics refer merely to possibilities, not to facts.[9]

At the atomic level, so much that appears to be material is found to be not material that physicists are hard pressed to find a suitable term for the "space" or "flux" or the "medium" that holds matter together. Two centuries ago, scientists universally agreed it should be called "ether." Much later, the astronomer V.A. Firsuff postulated that matter is held together by "mind-stuff" he called "mindons." This was updated to "psychons" by Sir Cyril Burt in the late 1960's.[10]

As this enigmatic atomic "ether" or "mind-stuff" was plunged into deeper and deeper mysteries of the material world, an equally inexplicable mind-stuff was being named as Psychology delved deeper and deeper into mysteries of the mind. Parapsychology, seeking explanations for telepathy, clairvoyance, telekinesis, precognition, synchronicity, Kirlian photography and the like, could never find any measurable "energy" to account for the phenomena. Yet, researchers reasoned, there must be a "substance," something that is beyond matter, space and time that accounts for paranormal events. This immeasurable "immaterial substance" was given the name Psi.

---

[9] Werner Heisenberg, *Der Teil and das Ganze*, Munchen, 1969, pp. 63-64. Quoted in Arthur Koestler, *The Roots of Coincidence* (New York: Random House, 1972), p. 51.

[10] Firsuff's "mindons" and Burt's "psychons" are discussed in Koestler, *ibid.* Koestler presents a masterful, concise history of the development of Physics, relating it to the parallel development of Psychology and Parapsychology.

Under strict laboratory conditions, without touching a test object in any way, a gifted person moves the object using only a mysterious power of the mind; this is psychokinesis. No energy of any kind can be measured, so what is the power? Psi.

In "distant viewing," an experimenter is sent at random to designated sites that have distinctive features, and spends a designated time just looking at the target site. Miles away, in a locked room, a subject, the "percipient," using telepathy or clairvoyance, describes or sketches on paper what flashes through his mind. Result: the percipient's descriptions match the target sites the experimenter was viewing with a success rate exceeding chance of one in a million million.[11] Again, no energy, no power of any kind can be measured. The unknown energy is Psi.

Using Kirlian photography, a lilac bud is photographed. The "aura" of the plant becomes visible. (This may be the same halo or glow that some psychics claim to see surrounding all living things. The aura may also be the halo shown around the heads of saints.) Shooting out of the lilac bud, one sees rays of energy, plumes, whirling fireballs, and small spikes of light. Then the bud is cut in half, and again photographed. The "gone" half of the bud still shows up on the photograph.[12] How can "something" be photographed when there is nothing there? Psi.

When we view these two extremely different studies of reality simultaneously, both physics and parapsychology culminate in what must be called, by whatever name — ether, unknown energy,

---

[11] Arthur Ellison, *The Paranormal: A Scientific Study of the Supernatural* (New York: Dodd, Mead), p. 31. N.B.: Both prudence and wisdom demand that paranormal events be evaluated with a sharp discriminating eye. The entire field of parapsychology must be viewed with extreme caution. Suffice to say here, there are some seemingly supernatural events, Kirlian photography, for example, which surely are not spiritual at all, and perhaps someday will be understood. Similarly, some rare human powers of perception may have natural as opposed to supernatural explanation which eventually will be understood. However, some so-called "psychic" powers are indeed supernatural, and demonic, while some spiritual healing powers are God-given. Chapter Twenty-Five provides case examples of both. It bears repeating: discriminate! Discern the sources of supernatural powers. Failure to do so, as will be shown later, can be deadly.

[12] Sheila Ostrander and Lynn Schroeder, *Psychic Discoveries Behind the Iron Curtain* (New York: Bantam), p. 233.

psychon, mindon, or Psi — nothing other than mystery.

And this mystery I call "love."

Love is the power or energy that underlies and explains the composition and behavior of all matter? Yes. Love is the final answer of quantum mechanics? Yes. And of parapsychology? Yes. Love is the central force and energy of the atom? Yes. Love is the flux, or medium, or ether, the psychon or mindon that exists *between* the microparticles inside the atom and governs their actions? Yes. But that is a totally unheard-of, radical idea! Yes.

We can surely expect that physicists will argue that I have answered their mystery of the atom with a solution that is another mystery: Love. Serving as my own devil's advocate, I might even argue that I use an illogical circular argument back to a non-answer. My response is that all mysteries are not created equal. I can in no way directly know nor experience ether, mindons, the energy inside the atom, nor Psi. Love is a mystery of a *different order*. Love is mystery I can know, *experience*, and sometimes even feel.

However this argument is received by physicists, eventually they must admit that no matter how small a particle they find within the atom, be it a micro-mini-neutrino, or a super-teeny-weenie-quark, the "final" answer to the atom will forever remain a mystery. Therefore, when I assert that the power that creates and governs the atom is love, it must be recognized that that conclusion can *never* be refuted. Debated, yes, but refuted, never. Reality is love.

Now, once we affirm the equation of love and reality, it becomes necessary to affirm that the universe and everything in it is open, permeable. Just as the interior of the atom shows us that what appears to be physical is largely non-physical, it logically follows that the universe is also comprised of two, open, intermingling dimensions, the one we call "physical" (which is itself atomically porous and immaterial), the other purely immaterial, spiritual — and both dimensions are united by love. This openness, this permeability that love brings to the human being is a foundation stone for understanding human personality structure (cf. Principle Three). Given the Reality Principle, it is important now to see how "open" persons relate to one another and to the "open" universe. Figure 3 shows the relationship.

The diagram that follows shows all that exists, the universe, with its openness and permeability, and it shows how the atom, persons, and the entire material dimension are also spiritual, and thus open to a purely spiritual universe. Only evil is utterly closed to love.

Figure 3: The Love-filled Universe

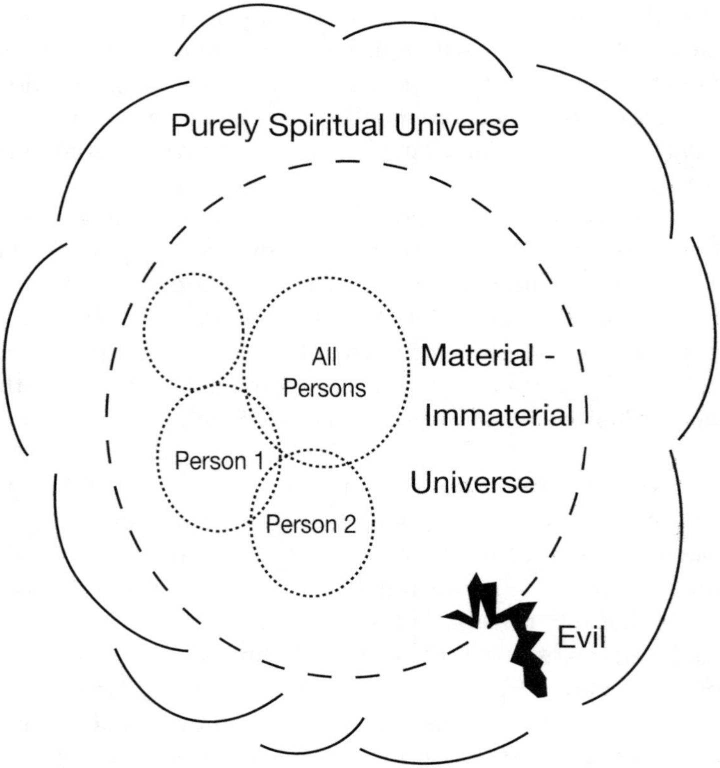

Purely Spiritual Universe

All Persons

Material - Immaterial Universe

Person 1

Person 2

Evil

Love demands openness. More accurately, love is openness. That permeability which is imbued by love is shown by the dotted lines, which are all intersecting. This view of reality can be summed up this way: Love (God) is omnipresent, everywhere and in everything; yet, love must be free, which requires that human beings be afforded the possibility of choice, willingness to be open or shut, porous and receptive to God and to other people, or closed, defensive, not open to anyone. The porosity of all persons allows spiritual connectedness among all, from which we can theorize that the increased love of one person accrues to the benefit of all humanity. In the linkage of the smaller porous circles, Person A and Person B, we see how it is possible for two people to love one another, i.e., move beyond the confines of separate beings to "become one" with one another. The larger circles show the porosity of the universe with its commingling of physical and immaterial dimensions. This openness of the universe allows us to understand how human beings, living as we do in physical reality, can also experience spiritual reality: Love (capital L) God, is not separate from us at all; He is as close as our love and openness allow Him to be. In other words, the universe is *not* distant and incomprehensible in its vastness; it is as near as an act of love.

This "open universe" theory is not entirely new, but it may seem so to many who have been indoctrinated by the materialist-scientific theory which says that reality can be boxed and measured. Though he did not center his theory in love, and did not view the person, God, and the universe in the utterly commingled unity as I present above, it was Carl Jung who broke away from Freudian materialism and forged the way in Psychology to show that the universe is open, and that openness to spiritual reality is essential to healing and emotional wholeness. Jung's writings were vast, entirely too huge to be succinctly summarized here, but Morton Kelsey incorporates Jung's views in his own effort to show that Psychology's view of reality must honor an open universe. In Kelsey's words, "Jesus... undoubtedly believed that there were two interacting dimensions of reality, physical and non-physical, both created by God, and both good."[13] That good-ness, I might add, is love.

There is an old joke about an "intellectual" being a person who has both feet firmly planted in mid-air, astraddle of the question. That has been the not-so-funny position of mental health professionals on the question of reality. We counselors make authoritative statements about whether a patient is "in touch with reality," and how schizophrenics "distort reality." We use Reality Therapy and Realness Therapy, speak often of "reality testing," diagnose "unrealistic expectations" and "feelings of unreality," and we even dare say that delusions and hallucinations aren't "real." Until now, though, therapists would have been totally embarrassed if we were challenged in Court to prove our pro-nouncements by defining "reality." Love theory's principle of real-ity is intended to end that embarrassment. Granted, the principle reaches "far out" intellectual heights, but the entire effort of love therapy is to bring love down-to-earth, down from the pulpits, into the streets and into the earth of suffering souls.

Given Love's Reality Principle, we can now develop therapy that is grounded in every way — grounded in every organic cell, grounded in every atom, electron and neutrino of the material universe, grounded in self-evident experience, and grounded in the human heart. And of course, as we search for grounding, let us not forget *le point vierge*, which some have called the Ground of Being.

Next, all this grounding allows us to figure out what a hu-man being adds up to be: a sum of loves.

---

[13] Morton T. Kelsey, *Christianity as Psychology* (Minneapolis, MN: Augsburg, 1986), p.56. In a chapter titled "A Place for God in Psychology," Kelsey summarizes Jung's extremely complex view of spirituality, and shows a diagram (p. 37) of how Jung would picture physical and non-physical dimensions of reality inter-acting. In a chapter titled "Living in an Open Universe," Kelsey makes the case for the "open" view of reality very convincingly.

CHAPTER EIGHT

The Person: A Sum of Loves

Principle Eight: Love Defines the Essence of Personhood

Positively speaking, after discounting all human deficiencies, failures, and privations of being, all that any human being essentially is, and existentially is becoming, is the totality of her or his loves, the sum of loving and being loved that creates and forms the psychospiritual heart. Given that love creates the human being, it follows that love is the most elementary of inalienable rights, and that love is the standard and measure of normalcy, viz., only love is normal.

Explanations

• As Principle Seven defined reality as love, and evil as a privation of love, so too, when the relative unreality of evils and privations like emotional pain, personality faults, hatreds, and destructive habits are subtracted, the remaining authentic, positive and real elements that comprise the human person are all derivations and expressions of love.

• The inalienable human rights of "life, liberty and the pursuit of happiness," affirmed as self-evident by the Preamble to the Constitution of the United States, derive from the higher and more fundamental inalienable right to love and be loved — for without love, there is no life, no liberty, no happiness, no equity, no justice, no law. It is self-evident that the U.S. Constitution should be amended to include the most fundamental right to love and be loved. Love is the supreme law from which all other civil and criminal laws derive, and without which they become impossible to enforce or interpret.

• If love is the fundamental reality of the human person, it follows that only love is normal, and that loving and being loved must be the standard of normality and of sanity. Evil is a privation of reality, so even if psychological tests reveal that a huge majority of people harbor fears, hatreds and mild emotional disorders, to say that such "mild evils" are within "normal limits" is to say that some degree of unreality is "normal," which is irrational. Defining "normal" by any "average" is to compromise, dilute and thus demean human dignity and capacity. Only love is normal.

Admittedly, at first blush, this principle sounds like an embarrassing oversimplification. All that a human being essentially is, is the sum total of his or her loves? That sounds too simple, deceptively simple. So let me face the devil's advocate's obvious questions....

All that I essentially am is my loves? What about my senses — my sight, touch, hearing — are they not part of me? Answer: yes, but not *essential* parts. Helen Keller, with neither sight nor hearing, proved how non-essential the senses are. The essence of the person is love.

Question: But what of my knowledge — isn't that different from love?

Answer: There are two levels of knowledge we must consider; we'll call them essential and non-essential knowledge. Non-essential knowledge includes all types of knowledge that have no direct love-connection. Algebra, the migration patterns of the aardvark, and how to speak Gaelic (even though I'm Irish), are examples of non-essential knowledge; they have no vital love-connection, nor would my essence change a whit without such knowledge. Similarly, I "know" some people as nodding acquaintances, but they are not essential parts of my being because I haven't loved them. On the other hand, my knowledge of God, wife, children, parents, relatives, close friends and counseling clients, those I love and who love me, are essential to my very being. Essential knowledge is that which is loved. More precisely, *knowledge does not fully exist until it is loved*; it is the act of loving that produces essential knowledge. So the answer to the question as to whether knowledge is separate from love is "No." All that a human being essentially is, is the total of her or his loves. (Principle Nine, next, addresses the truth-love connection in more detail.)

The self-love equation seems like an oversimplification because love itself is so rich, so profound and life-saturating that, like the forest, we miss it midst the trees. Love has a right to complain about being taken for granted. How often do we think about the blood coursing through our veins that is keeping us alive? Perhaps never — until we experience our first heart attack. When the chips are down, though, we stop taking essential things for granted. It is possible that most of us never realize just how thoroughly and totally our loves comprise our essential beings until we reach our death beds. Then, if we are sane, we reach the most acutely "normal" point in our lives: we love — our lives flash before us; our hearts unfold and we recount all that ever really mattered in our lives. In those dying flashes of memory, like looking in a mirror, we watch as the complexities of our lives crystallize. Vanities, trivia and phoniness are stripped away till all that can be seen in the mirror is the image of who we essentially are. Denuded of superficialities and all but what really counts, what then do we see? We see all the people who have loved us, and all whom we have loved, mixed with some loved places, a loved toy from childhood perhaps, and a little loved music. On our death beds, as we count the moments that really counted, it is doubtful that any of us will regret not having spent more time at the office, or wish we could have made more money, or seen more football games, or played more bridge. No, dying, we will recount and treasure our loves — for love, after life is all said and done, is the only treasure we can take with us. Love never dies.

Defining personhood in love terms answers a question that is so simple that mental health practitioners rarely ask it: "What is the elementary substance, the essence, of the being we call human?" Or, in the existential sense of becoming, "What precisely is it in a human being that becomes?" Though the questions sound abstruse, the answers make all the difference in how people with emotional problems are treated. Some theorists answer the question in terms of sexual energy. Others say that humans are simply highly evolved animals, or that the essence of the human is electrochemical energy. Still others answer in terms of words like "mind" or "psyche," without ever saying what a mind or psyche really is. Still other theorists, though, just never bother to ask the questions. Without a conviction that even the most psychotic patient is a person who fundamentally *is* love, there is an inevitable tendency to depersonalize people, treat them as objects. Granted, every professional ethical code verbalizes the necessity of treating every individual with "respect," and defines that respect as a basic human right. However, when those codes do not explain precisely *why* the person is due respect, the code becomes ungrounded, hollow.

In some mental hospitals, that depersonalizing tendency is evident every day. "Charley" becomes "the schizophrenic in room 212," and "Annie" becomes "the depressive sitting over there next to the catatonic." In fact, Charley is a man who loves his wife, his kids, the Yankees, and the Three Irish Tenors, and Annie is a lady who loves her sisters, Shakespeare and Pavarotti. But both Charley and Annie have lost their identities, lost their loves, and nobody on the ward has even asked about those loves. Why? Only love can find a lost love, and love is always a risk; it can get you hurt. Maybe nobody has asked about the lost loves simply because love is a hell-of-a-lot of work. More than likely, though, the loves of Charley and Annie have not been found because the professional staff has been trained with some scientific theory that has not focused upon what a human being fundamentally is. Love isn't very scientific.

This "self equals love" definition also zeroes in on a problem that is central to virtually every emotional disorder: identity. Be it depression, anxiety, psychosis or obsessions, virtually every problem presented in the counseling office brings with it the big question, "Who am I?" The identities of many people with disorders are hidden, distorted, fractured, or lost behind masks, confusion, pretenses, symptoms, and walls of defenses. The problem of identity has seemed so terribly complex that, in one sense, the entire fields of psychology and psychotherapy have been devoted to solving the riddles it presents. Each of some three hundred major diagnostic labels listed for emotional disorders speaks to various identity problems, and each symptom, each defense, mask, and mannerism of the person expresses something about his identity. Yet, the people with the disorders, the lost, frightened, or bewildered ones suffering the symptoms of the identity problems, aren't much interested in the theoretical complexities. They want a simple answer to a simple question, "Who Am I?" Sadly, despite the hundreds of schools of therapy developed, therapists virtually never answer that question. In fact, most professionals would probably consider it therapeutically taboo to respond with anything more substantive than the traditional, "Well, who do you think you are?"

Breaking with tradition, love therapy answers directly, "Who are you? You are the total of your loves, the sum, the reflection and expression of everyone and everything you have ever loved, and you are the sum of everyone who has ever loved you, including God who loves you, and I who love you. You are all the loves in your heart, both the love you can know and the love that will always be a mystery. Who are you? You are love, an utterly unique and special love. That's who you are — just love. You are the one who is struggling to discover and rediscover the unique loves that comprise the center of your being, your heart. You are the one whose loves have somehow been hurt, and you are the one whose love has given you the courage to seek healing, which is the wholeness that only love can bring."

Needless to say, that answer, "You are love," often takes months, even years, to absorb and understand. Once heard, though, people in love therapy never forget it. At the deep heart level where self-evident truth rings clear, everyone understands, even while not understanding fully. The heart invariably knows more that the head, and knows first.

In some ways, the process in love therapy is the opposite of most therapies. Virtually all therapies help their clients assemble facts, feelings and experiences, gradually building a picture of identity. Love therapy starts with the *a priori*[1] answer to the "Who Am I?" question: "You are love" — and then works backward, assembling facts, feelings, and experiences to help the person reaffirm and realize the answer.

Sadly, without a conviction regarding what a human being fundamentally is, many therapies wander aimlessly, collecting mountains of facts and feelings which remain ungrounded, and thus leave the identity-damaged person as lost as ever.

This does not mean that the love-as-identity answer is a quick fix, however. Hardly. A computer programming teacher once told me that he had not felt anything at all for thirty years. "I am a machine who works on machines," he said. At age eight, that man had been locked in a coffin for hours by some other kids "as a joke." Emotionally, his life stopped in that coffin. After

---

[1] An *a priori* argument is one which starts with a cause and moves to the effect, or from general law to a particular instance. The opposite, an *a posteriori* argument, moves from effect to cause, from actual observation of experimental data to a conclusion about the cause of that observation. In so far as Psychology is a science, it is based on observation, data, and *a posteriori* conclusions. That is a necessary scientific approach to understanding human behavior. However, love therapy starts with the recognition that even if science were able to assemble the totality of data about human behavior, that totality of data would still not tell us what a human being fundamentally is. Hence, we are forced to use an *a priori* approach to defining the person. Thus, love therapy starts with love as the self-evident truth, and then assembles observations and data to support its argument.

months of therapy, after abreacting (re-experiencing) the horror of the possibility of being buried alive, and after finally recognizing that he had a heart that did indeed feel, he said, "My heart died in that coffin." My response, "Love never dies," became the theme of his life and the subject of every therapy session for many months. Gradually, the "machine" became a fully feeling human being. Love is a panacea, yes, but it is not a quick magic elixir. It's a hell-of-a-lot of work.

The "Person as a Sum of Loves" principle ends with the bold statement that love is the central and primary standard and measure of normalcy. Thus, it is love, not the statistical average range of behavior that is the only rational gauge of sanity. Clearly, love is held up as an "absolute," and that may not be very popular in an age of relativism in which unfettered "freedom" is commonly held up as the highest value. But if some still argue that love is not primary, consider: for the sake of love, people sacrifice their lives, freedom and happiness every day. People die for love! But if we ask people what they would sacrifice for a loveless life or loveless freedom, the universal answer would be "not a nickel."

When we assert that "only love is normal," the consequences may shock the system of thought of what the world-in-general considers "acceptable," "standard" and "average." At the risk of seeming preachy, it is necessary to recite the following litany of new versions of "normal" that love produces.

The love standard insists that it is abnormal, sick, to hate, even a little bit.

It is abnormal to be selfish — even in a "me-generation" in which altruism is viewed as passé.

Love insists that promiscuous sex is unloving and therefore pathological, even if it seems normal because "everybody's doing it."

Dog-eat-dog business in which competition is unfairly crushed is sick, even in a dollar-dominated society driven by market forces that insist that ruthlessness is just "good business."

Children being love-deprived by both parents working only in order to fulfill materialistic values — house beautiful, fashionable dress and big cars — is abnormal, even if all the Joneses with whom we are competing are doing the same thing.

For both the individual and government, it is abnormal not to be generous, loving, in relation to the poor.

Harboring *any* amount of bitterness, grudges, and unforgiveness is abnormal, even though it is the practice of the overwhelming majority of people.

Acts of revenge, inherently unloving, are sick, no matter how grievous the offense that is being avenged.

The inability to love one's self fully, though very few people do, is abnormal.

The refusal or inability to love *anyone*, even the most despicable bum — and yes, even enemies — is abnormal.

Any use of power that is not love-derived and love-motivated, whether in the family, business, or politics, is abnormal, sick.

In brief, love is the norm of human behavior, and there is nothing average about it.

The natural consequence of promoting love as the standard of normalcy is to raise the standard of expectations in virtually every aspect of life. When love becomes "standard," it radically changes, elevates and upgrades consciousness in every respect. Self, others, work, education, business, government — everyone and everything become cast in a new light, and radical change inevitably follows. But is love radical? Of course not. Love is normal. Only not loving is radical.

CHAPTER NINE

Love and Truth are One

Principle Nine: Love Is Truth, a Knowable Mystery

Love is truth; truth is love; they are one. Thus, the test of authentic love is whether it corresponds to the truth of the person, a truth that resides in the heart of mystery. Mysteriously, human beings possess powers of love which enable us to love the mystery of a person and, in the loving, know the unknowable. This is the *"individuum ineffabile,* the unspeakably unique,"[1] the truth known only in loving, the truth that is a singular reflection of *le point vierge,* the Ground of Being, God, or Supreme Love (by whatever name) which is the source of love and ultimate truth residing in the unknowable center of the heart of every person.

Explanations

• The paradox presented by the inseparable unity of love and truth is this: only that which is known can be loved, and only that which is authentically loved can be authentically known.

• The measure of any human relationship, and the special test of psychotherapeutic diagnosis and treatment, is (again and again) best expressed by Péguy: "When you love someone, you love him

---

[1] This concept, the *individuum ineffabile,* is surely not my creation, but unfortunately I have been unable to recall where I learned it and thus cannot provide an attribution. I can only express great gratitude to the anonymous author.

as he is."[2] That "is-ness" is knowledge that can be obtained only through love, intersubjectively. The existence of *le point vierge* at the center of the human heart means that, at the deepest level, notwithstanding external appearances and behavior, and even despite themselves, all persons are lovable.

• The connection between *le point* and everyday experience is this: every time we love, every time we experience being loved by others, we have been touched by the power emanating from *le point vierge*. This is transcendent Love that is immanent, a down-to-earth reality. Indeed, that is a spiritual paradox, but one that we concretely experience: when we love most intensely, our hearts warm, move and even soar; that "soaring" is often a spiritual experience. A person is a psychospiritual being; in reality, the psychological and the spiritual cannot be separated. By intellectual abstraction it is possible and sometimes necessary to separate psychological from spiritual, and objective, scientific knowledge from the subjective heart-known. Indeed, love demands balance. In love therapy, both angelism and scientism, hyperspiritualism and hypermaterialism, are deemed short-sighted, inherently untruthful, unloving and ineffective. In the unity of love-truth, there can be no contradiction between science and spirituality, for the psychospirituality of the person is not divisible. Truth is one.

Principle Nine refers to the centermost mystery of the person as God "by whatever name." I have no wish to, nor could I impose beliefs on anyone, but this principle does presume unanimous agreement that even endless probing of the depths of self, or any human being, will invariably reach a level that can only be called "mystery." That mystery has gone by many names (below), so if atheists or skeptics are more comfortable calling the mystery by another name, be it "infinity," "the ultimate X factor," or "the

---

2   Charles Péguy, *God Speaks, op. cit.*

amorphous fuzz of existence," then so be it. The first intent of Principle Nine is to logically demonstrate that if psychotherapy is in any way considered a science and if science is concerned with truth, then we must grapple directly with the inescapable mystery that positivist science can never touch. I call that mystery *le point vierge*, or Love (capital "L"), or God.

No one captures the heart of *le point vierge* with more succinct insight than Sr. M. Madeline Abdelnour.[3] Here is a summary of her description...

There is a rich tradition behind *le point vierge* that stretches well beyond denominational, racial and cultural lines, links Western thought with Eastern, unites Christian and Jew, oriental and occidental, black, white, yellow and red. Augustine, Meister Eckhardt, Plotinus, Alexander of Hales, Bonaventure, Albertus Magnus, Thomas Aquinas, John of the Cross, Teresa of Avila, Massignon, Suzuki and Dionysius — back through the ages, East to West, *le point* has been given many names: synteresis, *Wesen* of the soul, *scintilla animae* (sovereign point of the spirit), *Apex ventis*, Divine spark, *Nada* (nothingness), *leb* or *lebab* (Hebrew, deepest heart), Omega point — but all point to the same nameless, unknowable point that only a few extraordinarily loving souls are ever permitted to see.

As we examine *le point vierge*, we must be ever mindful of the third Explanation which emphasizes that love must be balanced, never hyperspiritualized. Yet, *le point vierge* is purely spiritual, so it must be expressed in those terms. In later chapters, we will see how the spiritual has very practical application.

To my knowledge, the phrase *le point vierge* is not used in either Old or New Testaments, but in the latter, it is clearly implied in this assertion: "God is love, and he who abides in love, abides in God, and God in him."[4]

Now, either it is possible that God can abide, live in a hu-

---

[3] Sr. M. Madeline Abdelnour, S.C.N., "Le Point Vierge in Thomas Merton," *Cistercian Studies* (Kalamazoo, MI: Cistercian Publications), pp. 153-171.

[4] 1 John 4:16.

man being, or it is not. With those who believe He does not, I simply will not argue. For the vast majority who do believe in one God, the question becomes: if God lives in you, whether you call Him Yahweh, Jesus, Buddha, Adonai, or Allah, where is it exactly that He lives? It is in the center of the center of the heart called *le point vierge*. No one describes it more beautifully than Thomas Merton:

> Again, that expression, *le point vierge*, (I cannot translate it) comes in here. At the center of our being is a point of nothingness which is untouched by sin and by illusion, a point of pure truth, a point or spark which belongs entirely to God, which is never at our disposal, from which God disposes of our lives, which is inaccessible to the fantasies of our own mind or the brutalities of our own will. This little point of nothingness and of absolute poverty is the pure glory of God in us. It is so to speak His name written in us, as our poverty, as our indigence, as our dependence, as our sonship. It is like a pure diamond, blazing with the invisible light of heaven. It is in everybody, and if we could see it we would see these billions of points of light coming to-gether in the face and blaze of the sun that would make all the darkness and cruelty of life vanish completely — I have no program for this seeing. It is only given. But the gate of heaven is everywhere.[5]

Those who would seek to understand *le point* at the mysti-cal level I can only refer to the spiritual writers named above by Abdelnour. Becoming a mystic, of course, is the only way to even begin to know the diamond, the blaze, the heaven, the poverty, the nothingness, the mystery of Absolute Love that dwells within

---

[5] Thomas Merton, *Conjectures of a Guilty Bystander* (Garden City, NY: Doubleday, 1966), p. 142.

each of us at *le point*. Throughout this book, however, the challenge has been to discover how love is brought down to earth, incarnated, activated, enacted, realized, experienced, and especially, experienced as healing. The question therefore is, what is the down-to-earth connection between *le point vierge* and everyday, not-so-mystical, garden-variety experience?

At the minimum level, the experience of powerfully loving someone may be proof enough for many that love is far bigger than we are, that we could never manufacture the capacity to love with our own puny human powers, and that the source of love is somehow "beyond" us in a way that can only be called "transcendent" or even "divine." If proof is needed that love has suprahuman origins, it is readily provided by personal experience. Most of us have had the experience of saturating warmth, soaring and heart-tripping joy and even ecstasy that accompany a powerful love event. The birth of a baby, a loving sexual encounter, or maybe the warm embrace of a relative or friend might have produced those feelings. Note this: try as we might, we cannot, at will, just sit down and reproduce those powerful love experiences on our own. The power, the source of such love transcends the human. So where did the power come from? *Le point.*

But there is even stronger evidence that the power source of love is transcendent. At its best, love surges, springs and leaps into a passion that becomes an all-consuming fire, a roaring blaze that enables human beings to transcend themselves entirely. People die for love! Mothers die saving their children. Husbands give up their lives in the stead of their wives. Captive servicemen die of torture while protecting the lives of their comrades. And every day, everywhere, people are sacrificing great chunks of their lives — their time, energy, money, work, blood — because they love with a power that is beyond life. Love of this noble order makes a mockery of any attempt to explain human love in ordinary psychological terms, much less behavioristic, animalistic terms. The unsung martyrs, the millions who have died for love, are living testimony that love is beyond self and beyond life. But "beyond" is where? It is at the center of the center of the heart, *le point vierge,* the abode of eternal Supreme Love Who is both in us, and far, far beyond us.

Of what practical consequences is all this focus on the spiritual dimension of people? The love-truth principle highlights the fact that the person who walks into the office for counseling is not just a scientific puzzle, not an assemblage of readily reachable pieces, but an *individuum ineffabile,* a truly ineffable mystery whose individuality is so unspeakably unique that he/she will baffle and elude scientific understanding every time. Her essence, his "is-ness," her uniqueness, inevitably will defy diagnosis if the counselor can obtain no more than scientific knowledge of her.

As the second Explanation emphasizes, the deepest, most important levels of knowledge of a person are obtainable only by loving them. "Diagnosis" (*dia-* meaning "across" and -*gnosis* meaning "knowledge") demands thorough, across-the-board knowledge. If a professional is going to be thorough, the mystery of the person cannot be omitted as if it were somehow irrelevant. On the contrary, the very roots of many emotional disorders may well lie deeply buried in the substance of that mystery. This is so often true that, indeed, diagnosis without love should be considered malpractice.

It is both a mystery and an undeniable fact, as this principle highlights, that we have the power "to love the mystery of a person, and in loving, know the unknowable." The resulting "known mystery" produced by love defines a level, type, or field of knowledge which is clearly distinguishable from the kinds of knowledge gained through the ordinary scientific (non-loving) observation, interviewing and assessment used in psychotherapeutic diagnosis, no matter how careful and thorough that examination might be.

Good professional diagnosis includes many areas of information: presenting problems and symptoms; developmental, family, work and social histories; history of the symptoms; medical history; and assessments of various areas of functioning. In the process, facial expressions, body language, appropriateness of emotions, reality contact, verbal tone and many other observations are made, all in an effort to identify and understand the person and problem. Collectively, all this information would be called empirical knowledge. It is all good, and essential for diagnosis, but it has not even touched upon the mysteries of the heart wherein the actual source of the problem might well lie.

Loving the person, intersubjectively joining the person heart to heart, will produce another, very distinct form of knowledge, the "known mystery." Having said that, I must stop here to make a frank admission: I have never known what to call this level or form of mysterious knowledge which only love can bring. Perhaps philosophers have a better name for "known mystery" or "love's knowledge," but let me simply call it the field of "love-known mystery." It is a basic affirmation of love therapy that diagnosis can never be complete without loving the person enough to reach and penetrate this deeper, hidden region of the heart.

In discussing the love-known mystery of persons, some have asked, "But how do you reach that deep love of people?" Because we rarely talk about such mysteries, there is a tendency to think there is some magic to it, some kind of refined, esoteric professional technique. Nothing could be further from the truth. Reaching the love-known mystery is as easy as loving.

Love is easy? Earlier I said (and sometimes complain) that love is a "hell-of-a-lot of work." There is no contradiction. As Gibran's *Prophet* says, "Work is love made visible."[6] Without love, work can be sheer hell. With love, work is not just easy, it's fun. The only real work, hell always, is in refusing to love.

---

[6] Kahlil Gibran, *The Prophet* (New York: Alfred A. Knopf, 1964), p. 28. N.B.: Though Gibran is widely esteemed as a wise man, there is strong evidence that both he and his "prophet" are false prophets. See John Ankerberg and John Weldon, *The Facts on Spirit Guides* (Harvest House: Eugene, OR, 1988), p. 24. Gibran mixes beautiful truths, such as this one connecting love and work, with dangerous lies that would destroy Christianity if they were believed. Gibran was a medium whose writings were dictated by so-called "spirits" who claimed to know Jesus when he walked on earth. Thus, these spirits, or Gibran, say: "Jesus was a man and not a god.... It's a pity his followers seek to make a god out of such a sage." Kahlil Gibran, *Jesus, the Son of Man* (New York: A.A. Knopf, 1959), p. 113; also see pp. 43 and 109. This is evidence enough: the only "spirits" who would say such things are dangerous ones. Compare those in Chapter Twenty-Five.

To say that loving is easy, though, does not mean that it is simple, at least not exactly. Rather, love is like a fire. The flames of the fire, like the truths residing in the mystery of the heart, are both one and many. Sometimes, if I watch a particular tongue of flame, it will stay steady enough for me to understand it — its size, its colors of orange, red, blue or yellow, and the directions that it leaps and bounces. Other flames I see and *poof*, they're gone. Still other flames appear, then hide, smolder, then jump back up in the same spot as before. Love-known mystery is like that, as simple and as complex as fire. Separate tendrils of flame can be seen within the fire, but they can never be separated from the whole.

Describing diagnosis with a fire analogy may seem more akin to poetry than science, and so be it. The mysteries that human beings contain so completely transcend empirical science that the love-known truth can never be expressed in respectable professionalese. Yet, as the first Explanation insists, "Only that which is authentically loved can be authentically known." A professional diagnosis demands thorough knowledge, that is, authentic loving knowledge.

Diagnosis in love therapy includes both empirical knowledge and love-known mystery, and the latter may well be expressed in the ethereal terms of poetry, painting, music, or even unintelligible sounds and images that the heart expresses. If this sounds totally unorthodox, or even weird, let me emphasize again that we are talking about a level of knowledge that is indeed utterly different than the manageable, measurable, more linear and boxable kind of knowledge that is obtained by empirical methods.

Love-known mysteries of the heart may well appear as surrealistic landscapes, or as strange mixtures of melody and cacophony, or as odd blends of Greek tragedy and theater of the absurd. Often, a therapist loving someone who has been traumatized, can "see" the portions of the heart that have been slashed and torn, and "hear" a terrified scream of the heart that remains long after both conscious and unconscious emotions have been fully expressed. Secrets of the heart are heard only by loving hearts. It is just such secrets that are the essence of successful diagnosis and treatment.

Following is a brief example of how a heart is expressed. This note was sent to me by a woman with chronic depression:

> I had to tell you. You kept asking me where my heart was. Well, I finally found it after I left you last night and I've been crying ever since. My heart has a big hole in it. The whole bottom of it is just empty, hollow. God, it hurts! I know now that neither of my parents ever really loved me, at least not much. It's weird. I haven't cried in years, and now I can't stop. What's weirder is that the depression is almost gone. I'm sad, but mad! I keep *hearing* my heart. It's an empty kettle drum. It's been empty — silent for years. Now it's Booming! I'm sad, and I'm mad as hell — but I'm alive again!

This hurting woman had correctly identified the underlying cause of her depression as love deprivation. But that did not fill the terrible void she felt. That required a "heart transplant" (which we'll discuss in a later chapter). The good news that her note signified was that she had allowed me to reach her at heart level. Love had melted her defenses. Progress would come trippingly along after that breakthrough.

Collectively, the nine principles of love theory are an attempt to provide a new view of the human personality, to wit, we are beings who are made to love; love is our reason for being, our fundamental drive and goal and the rock-bottom motivation for every thing we do. Thus, barring some physical insult that damages our brains, if we receive authentic love, and love others and ourselves in an authentic way, we will remain sane and healthy psychologically and spiritually.

But what happens when our loves are damaged or deficient, or when we ourselves deliberately reject love in the pursuit of toxic and damaging pseudo-loves? Then we suffer, and/or we inflict our suffering onto others, and that can lead to mental or emotional disorders. Explaining those disorders and how love can heal them is the purpose of Part II and the nine additional principles of love therapy.

Part Two

LOVE THERAPY
Principles Redefining Emotional Disorders

As one is, so is his love. For
this reason, we can find in love
the most decisive symptoms of
what a person is.

Ortega y Gasset[1]

---

[1] Ortega y Gasset, *On Love* (Cleveland: World Publishing Co., 1957), p. 178.

CHAPTER TEN

The Heart of Emotional Disorders

Principle Ten: Emotional Disorders Are Wounds of the Heart

All emotional and mental disorders, (except the organic), are wounds of the psychospiritual heart, symptomatic expressions of love damaged, love rejected, betrayed, perverted, twisted, lost, or never received. The heart is created by love, so the most severe mental illnesses must be understood as consequences of hearts that are partially unformed.

Explanations

• Psychic wounds and the suffering they cause are located not in the unconscious or conscious mind, but far deeper, in the center of the soul, in the psychospiritual heart. Just as the senses are not damaged by witnessing a traumatic event, neither are the conscious nor unconscious memories damaged by recording that event, nor do they feel direct pain. The proof of the principle is experiential: traumatic suffering is felt and experienced not in the brain, but in the deepest center of our beings, in our hearts.

• It is not by accident that peoples of all languages and of all ages have said that their hearts freeze or shrink with fear, break with rejection, become heavy and empty with grief, are crushed by defeat, and sink with disappointment; and in the face of tragedy, when people say they are heartsick, they mean exactly that. People have always known that their hearts are the deepest parts of their beings. Less than a century ago, a pseudo-science, psychoanalysis, named the unconscious as the deepest element of being, and that is not true, and people knew it. Universal experience still affirms that people love with their whole hearts, and that those hearts sometime get sick.

• The heart is a reservoir of all loves, and an emotional or mental disorder is a manifestation of damage or deficiency in one or more of the loves residing there. It is only hurt loves that experience suffering.

• All symptoms are defenses, efforts of the heart to express the hurt love. Albeit painful, no symptom is as painful as the damaged love, which is precisely the reason for the symptom, to protect damaged love.

• The purpose of defense mechanisms — denial, projection, displacement, etc. — is not to protect the person from anxiety and conflict as has been traditionally taught. Rather, defenses defend love. Anxiety and conflict are *wanted* as protections (secondary gains) against the direct suffering that is being experienced in the heart by the damaged or threatened love.

• The straightforward suffering of an emotional or mental disorder is in itself a sign of courage, and evidence of the suffering person's love for other people. Contrariwise, sociopaths and the most evil people rarely experience overt emotional suffering. Thus we see that emotional pain that is refused, and projected onto others, is the cause of most of the world's evils.

• In general, the severity and chronicity of mental and emotional disorders is a direct measure of the extent of love deprivation sustained in childhood, and/or of love damage, love threat, or love loss sustained in later life. Though love deprivation can never be scientifically measured, a therapist can intersubjectively and psychospiritually "know" the degree of emptiness in a person's heart, and then roughly gauge not just the amount of love that healing will require, but the exact form and age-level of the love that must be replaced.

• Love is creational. Paralleling the ontological equation of love and reality, the distortions and loss of contact with reality seen in psychoses, and the problems of finding identity and the real self that are typical in all emotional disorders, can be generally understood as an equation: the greater the love lost or distorted, the greater the loss or distortion of reality; by the same measure, restoring love restores reality in direct proportion.

• Only love protects the heart from injury and the threat of injury. Pychospiritually, the protection of love may be visualized as an aura (like a halo or shield of light) that surrounds the healthy heart. (See Figure 4, below). Normally, that aura is created by the parents' gifts of love in childhood, so that in emotionally healthy people the aura is "thick" and strong enough to shield the person from threats to love. In psychosis, the aura may be nearly absent. In mild emotional disorders, the aura can be visualized as "thin" or "gapped" in certain areas, resulting in involuntary vulnerability and corresponding severity of symptoms.

• The proof that the heart's love damage, and not the unconscious, is the seat of mental and emotional disorders is provided every day by average, loving, non-professional people. Foster mothers of seriously disturbed teenagers, uneducated women who would not know an Oedipus complex from an apartment complex, often bring exquisite healing to kids when every professional has failed, and they heal without surfacing even a shred of unconscious material.

Indeed, this principle presents a radically different view than the traditional picture of emotional disorders. Though I am not saying that the unconscious is unimportant, I am clearly saying that if the unconscious is viewed as the end-all-be-all of emotional disorders, as it has been for the past century by virtually the entire mental health world, that chances of healing are enormously diminished because we are not even seeing where the painful wounds are located. Emotional wounds lie deep in the soul, at its center, in the psychospiritual heart.

Principle Ten and its first Explanation topple the unconscious from the throne upon which it was placed by the Freudian belief system about a century ago. In fact, the "unconscious,"
that old sacred calf, is about as "scientific" a concept as ether,[1] the
four humors,[2] phrenology,[3] or orgone.[4] Having said that, let me
race to admit that the concept of the "psychospiritual heart" is in
no way a scientific concept, either. The great difference is that it
does not pretend to be. I cannot prove the existence of the heart
any more than Freud could prove the existence of unconscious.
Starting with a *tabula rasa*[5] — no mindsets nor preconceptions
— we would all admit that none of us has ever seen a mind, an
unconscious, a heart, soul, psyche, or spirit, nor, in reality, do we
know where any of them are. Nor can we absolutely disprove

---

[1] "Ether" is defined as "an imaginary substance regarded by the ancients as filling
    all space beyond the sphere of the moon, and making up the stars and planets"
    (Webster's New World Dictionary). Reading pre-late-nineteenth century manu-
    scripts, one sees "ether" treated very "scientifically," viz., "ether" was such a
    commonly used word that it came to be regarded as "fact." Eventually, ether
    was the word used to describe the mysterious "substance" that comprised the
    interior of the atom (See Love Principle Seven). One also sees "ether" used to
    describe paranormal phenomena. I use the word here as an apt comparison to
    the word "unconscious." Neither is a "scientific" concept, but modern Mental
    Health has treated the unconscious as such for so long that it has taken on the
    aura of "fact." In comparison, we cannot pretend that the "psychospiritual heart"
    is a scientific concept either. I do assert, however, that the "heart" corresponds
    to a larger truth which is confirmed by human experience. The self-evidence
    of love as the "substance" of the heart is the sole "proof" of its primacy. That is
    a proof which the unconscious does not offer. There is, of course, the argument
    that the unconscious could not affirm itself because it is unconscious; that is,
    of course, an oxymoronic argument.

[2] The four humors — blood, phlegm or yellow bile, choler, and melancholy or black
    bile — were considered in old psychology and physiology to be the cardinal
    fluids which determined one's physical and psychological condition.

[3] Phrenology was the theory that mental powers and character could be deter-
    mined by analyzing the shape and protuberances of the skull.

[4] Orgone was an energy postulated by Wilhelm Reich (1897-1957) as permeating
    the universe, the personal supply of which an individual suffering an emotional
    disorder could replenish by sitting in a small cabinet, the orgone box.

[5] *Tabula rasa*, in Latin, literally means a scraped tablet, a blank slate. René Des-
    cartes said that beginning with a "blank" slate, the mind assuming nothing,
    was the sure way to begin developing a philosophy. From his *tabula rasa*, his
    first principle then emerged as "I think, therefore I am." In contrast, my *tabula
    rasa* first says, "I am loved and therefore I love."

other "quasi-material substances" that scientists have proffered, like psi, mindons, and chi. Nor, by the way, is there agreement about angels, demons, ghosts, spirit guides, poltergeists, Santa Claus nor even (Saints preserve us!) leprechauns. Clearly, both the heart and the unconscious have some eerie companions, and just as clearly, we are talking about matters of, not scientific fact, but faith, belief systems. Modern psychotherapy was founded on a belief system that crowns the unconscious as "god," the ultimate tenet of faith regarding human beings. Now, backed by the proof of universal human experience, and reason itself, Love's Heart Principle affirms the existence of unconscious, but deposes it to a secondary function, and re-crowns the heart as the rightful occupant of the throne, the monarch of the soul.

The third Explanation, describing mental and emotional disorders as damage to one or more loves, and the protective aura of love that surrounds the heart, described in the second-last Explanation, are shown in Figure 4. Letters A-K refer to the legend beneath the diagram.

The immaterial forces us to use metaphors. The advantage of Figure 4's "picture" of the heart is that it corresponds to the metaphor that all nations of all ages have used to describe the deepest movements and events of the soul; this is the universal wisdom depicted in folk language cited in the second Explanation. The immediate advantage in counseling is that the heart allows patient and counselor to speak the same language. Therapists rarely notice, and clients are reluctant to admit it, but ordinary people are often frightened, intimidated by the very idea of their "unconsciousness" being probed or exposed. Why? Because they do not know what the unconscious is; they simply can't relate to it; it does not seem real to them. On the other hand, in love therapy, when clients are asked, "Can we just talk heart-to-heart? What is your heart saying?" people quickly begin revealing feelings and experiences that actually include unconscious material, but much more — the deeper and more sensitive, secret yearnings, soul-deep aches and hidden wounds of the heart. The reason for this easier, more straightforward, honest and open communication

Figure 4: The Psychospiritual Heart — showing love's protective aura, authentic loves, and common heart wounds. See legend below.

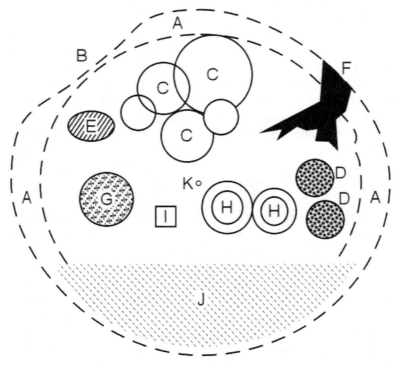

LEGEND:
A. Love's protective aura (or shield, halo) against threat. In a healthy heart, the aura is "thick," intact, and under voluntary control.
B. "Thin," or gapped love aura which permits threats to love to invade the heart too easily — as seen in anxiety and phobic disorders.
C. Assemblage of authentic, healthy loves, including self-love. In a hypothetically perfect person, these loves would fill the entire heart.
D. Unhealed heart wounds.
E. Guilt, from self-induced heart-violation (sin).
F. Trauma, causing rupture of aura and severe heart wound.
G. Love loss from rejection or death — as seen in depression or grief.
H. Healed love wounds, with newly created, "stronger" love auras.
I. Secret spot, a place of survival in which abuse and neglect victims often hide.
J. Love deficit sustained through love deprivation, shown here at a level often seen in moderate depression (but which, when it engulfs the majority of the heart, can produce psychosis or suicide).
K. *Le point vierge* — the area of pure and total love in which God resides, a place that is inviolable, unreachable and unknowable within every person.

corresponds to reality, specifically, the reality that the psychospiritual heart contains far more of what is essentially real and human than the unconscious does. The unconscious, stripped of its pseudoscientifically manufactured functions, is simply a latent memory file. The heart, though, is the repository of loves, and people instantly know that, affirm the truth, relate to it, and pour their hearts out.

In practice, I show Figure 4, the diagram of the heart, to every client, first asking them to identify the healthy loves in their lives ("C" on the diagram), and then asking how the love-wounds, deficits or traumas apply to them. I ask people to bring their own drawings of their hearts into counseling sessions, and change the drawings as therapy progresses. They will draw concentric circles around heart wounds as they are healed ("H"), draw in other dark circles ("D") to represent old wounds that they have remembered, add new light circles as new loves ("C") are developed, erase a dark circle as a love-loss ("G") is healed, and add to or subtract from the aura as they find specific areas in which love seems better protected ("A") or more threatened ("B").

Only love protects us from the threats of the world, so the love aura is a frequent topic of discussion. Without love's protection, fear enters the heart unimpeded. For example, a woman came for counseling because of a terrible fear of storms, a severe phobia that caused terrible palpitations and hyperventilation. When she looked at the heart diagram, she immediately could dismiss most of the types of heart wounds depicted. She knew her parents had loved her dearly, so there was no basic love deprivation (J). There had been no big traumas (F), no severe rejections nor love-losses (G), nor even any significant heart wounds (D) that she could identify as unhealed. Emotionally, she seemed to be an exceptionally healthy person. However, when she looked at the "thin" love aura (B) and related it to her phobia, she immediately recounted that her mother, too, had had a terrible fear of storms. She had always been aware of the similarity between her mother's fear and her own, but it was only now that she began to see why she was so affected. "I thought I had just learned the fear, but it wasn't that simple, was it? Learning just affected my head, but the problem was in my heart." When thunder and lightning occurred, her mother would huddle the children in the middle of the living room away from windows, away from the telephone, television or anything electric. She would then light votive candles, pray for God's protection, and visibly tremble all through the storm. Viewing the "thin" love aura, the insight quickly came: "So I was basically right when I said Mom really loved me. She did all the time — except when a storm came up outside. There was no love in a storm... so I was afraid, just like Mom. She couldn't give me love that she didn't have herself, right?" Right.

Obviously, each heart's depiction is unique and must be customized. Sometimes, rare experiences and subtle nuances of emotion that accompany some heart wounds are difficult to "picture." For example, a fifty-year-old woman from an alcoholic home grew up with terrible love deprivation (J). As she sketched her heart, that deprivation encompassed a full three-quarters of her heart. But then, at age thirty-five, she had had a spontane-ous spiritual experience in which she had experienced an over-whelming unconditional love that saturated her entire being, and changed her whole emotional life. For seven years, she had remained on an emotional "high," feeling loved by God. (No, she was not manic.) When she sketched that healthy love (C), it, too, encompassed more than three-quarters of her heart. When I noted that three-quarters (deprivation), plus three-quarters (healthy love) equaled one-and-a-half hearts, she said, "Darn it, that's what I've been trying to tell you; that's exactly how it feels: there's this terrible sick part of my heart that came from the sick childhood, but the love I experienced from God was just as real. My heart is both. And you're right, I just don't add up." Beyond her confusion, though, she was quite sure of one thing: "All I know is that one day, God came out of hiding, here (pointing to *le point vierge*, K on the diagram) and saved my life."

Sometimes, too, people have to struggle to "find" their hearts. The heart of the person with schizophrenia is obviously "lost," not just because of a fractured and splintered "mind," the traditional professional understanding, and not only because the schizophrenic's heart has been splintered. Most schizophrenias, I believe, are caused by the heart never becoming completely formed in the first place. Principle Eight defines the person as the sum total of her/his authentic loves, and describes love as creational. Some persons with schizophrenia have suffered near-total lovelessness, resulting in hearts which were left substantially *uncreated*. Surely the psychotic heart is lost and wandering in un-reality, but this is a heart that cannot be "found" until love makes it, creates it from bottom up, and provides it with a protective aura of love. Until that is done, the schizophrenic's partially-made, aura-less heart is too vulnerable to threat and fear to make any sense of external reality. (Chapter Nineteen, on psychoses, offers a more detailed explanation.)

There are, though, people who are not psychotic at all, and may function quite well in their work, who have no idea where their hearts are. In general, these are people who grew up in families dominated by the defense mechanism of denial. Alcoholic or abusive parents, for example, disallow children expressing what is in their hearts, but worse, they discourage them from experiencing any feeling or thought that even approaches heart-level. The reality of the heart is denied; it does not exist. In the alcoholic or abusive home, children are exposed to every form of bizarre and painful hell, but are forbidden to react in any realistic emotional way. For example, a drunken parent may savagely beat every child and tear the house apart at night — but the next morning, the entire family, led by the alcoholic's rules, carries on with their lives as if the previous night's terrifying debacle had never happened. Reality, both physical and emotional, is simply erased, denied.

As adults, people who have lived in deep denial typically experience a group of related symptoms: psychic numbing or emotional anesthesia, depersonalization, feelings of unreality, emotional constriction, selective amnesia, and various levels of dissociation, i.e., the isolation and splitting off of emotion from ideas and situations. When victims of denial are asked what their hearts are saying, or even where their hearts *are*, they haven't the foggiest idea. It is as if the entirety of their inner beings do not even exist — almost as if their hearts were never created. Yet, the personas, the faces, these denied beings present to the world vary enormously.

For example, two women and a man I have seen in counseling presented totally different external demeanors:

One woman had only one emotional response in her repertoire: she cried. When she was angry, she cried. When she was sad, she cried. When she was confused, jealous, in conflict, afraid, or guilty — whatever her emotional state — she cried. In her alcoholic home, tears were the only permissible expression of emotion.

The second woman's singular response was to smile. As she described being beaten savagely by her father, she smiled. As she voiced fears of abandonment and desolation, she smiled. Speaking of resentment, obviously angry but apparently not feeling it, she smiled.

The third client, a man, simply did not talk. All effort to engage him in discussion was like the proverbial pulling of teeth. Trying to say anything at all to his abusive father always got him in trouble.

In therapy, after each of these three people described horribly painful events, when I asked what they were feeling, their standard response was, "Nothing," or "I don't know." When I asked if they knew who they were, i.e., as an identity, the answer was the same. When I asked where their hearts were, the first woman started crying, the second just smiled blankly and broadly, and the man silently brooded. And yet, before long, given just a little love, the freedom to just *be*, it was as if one could sense each of their hearts "peeking" to see if it was really safe to come out of hiding.

Despite their utterly different exterior emotional appearances and symptoms, in love therapy, each of these three persons was diagnosed as having "hidden heart syndrome." Unlike the psychotic person whose heart is partially unformed, people who have been victimized by years of denial, notwithstanding very different symptoms and diagnoses, share a common heart malady, a heart that has been buried, hidden away, denied.

The destructiveness of the defense called "denial" is often underestimated, I believe, because the traditional interpretation is that it is only emotions that are denied. There is far more. What is fundamentally denied is reality, and that reality includes the reality of self, not just emotions, but huge parts of the person's entire being — emotions, thought, heart and soul.

As therapy progresses with the hidden heart syndrome, as the victims begin to rediscover their hearts, a common "picture" of the heart emerges. These people very typically have a "secret spot" in their hearts which they have always kept separate from the main body of their inner beings, a place which they often describe as "tiny." The secret spot is in a corner of their hearts that they guard fiercely because this is the safe place to which they withdrew and silently and secretly allowed themselves to do what was strictly forbidden by the abusive or alcoholic or otherwise denial-enforcing parent: *be real*, feel, and even, in daring moments, express to themselves the anger or fear or even the love that was totally unacceptable in the home. In counseling, when love finally begins to free people to be able to draw the diagram of their hearts, people with "secret spots" will typically draw a large circle, as in Figure 4, drawing more dark areas representing heart wounds and traumatic experiences, but then they will draw a tiny circle or square in the deep center of the larger circle and then say, "The big circle is my heart, I guess, but I don't know what's in there because I feel like nobody. But here's where I am, in this little place here (the secret spot). I never let anybody into that spot. That's mine! That's the part of me that nobody can take away from me. When Dad (or Mom) would go on a rampage, when all hell was breaking loose, I'd go inside me, into this little corner, and I'd be safe."

The importance of discovering the secret spot of the heart cannot be overemphasized. When people dissociate, they are often "found" in the secret spot. When they appear "unreachable" in therapy, often they can be found to be protecting the secret spot. In brief, if the person is going to be helped in therapy, the secret spot of the heart has to be discovered.

The greatest importance of the secret spot is that for these victims of abuse and denial, it is as if most of the strongest and healthiest functions of the heart are "condensed," squeezed, as it were, into this tiny room in the heart.

Obviously, only love of the purest kind is permitted entry into the secret spot of the heart. This means that the quadruplex of faith, hope, trust and love, as described earlier, must be wholly present in the client-therapist relationship. Once the therapist is allowed entry to the secret spot, it is then fairly easy for client and therapist to "spread" the strengths of the secret spot to the whole heart.

The third Explanation highlights the Heart Principle's assertion that all emotional and mental disorders are in fact love wounds, and the fourth Explanation emphasizes that, notwithstanding the huge variety of symptomatic expressions of pain, the seat of both woundedness and suffering is hurt love. Symptoms, whatever they are — anxiety, depression, hallucinations, delusions, phobias, mania, flight of ideas, or any of a hundred others — all are the various voices of love expressing suffering. Moreover, all symptoms are in fact defenses, painful lesser-of-evils, so to speak, designed to prevent the greatest suffering, love-loss and love-damage.

This needs to be stated explicitly: whereas traditional teaching has always distinguished symptoms and defense mechanisms as two separate functions, love therapy insists that symptoms *are* defenses, and that both serve to express love's suffering and to defend against its further damage or total loss.

Depression, for example, is typically seen as a major symptom, and efforts are made to relieve it. When it is recognized that the depression is a defense of love as well as a symptom, we are forced to recognize that some essential part of the person, the heart, wants the symptom precisely because it defends love, expresses the cries for love that has been lost, and protects the heart from even more and worse love-loss that it fears.

Immediately we must register a caveat, and this caveat expresses precisely the conflict inherent in depression: of course, at one level, the person does not want to be depressed even though, at the same time, at a deeper level, the person does want depression as a safeguard against further love-loss. The lesson is this: any effort to relieve depression without first helping the person to safeguard his existing loves and find a replacement for the love that has already been lost, is wrestling with the impossible. Even if the symptom of depression is quickly relieved, by medication, for example, if the love-loss is not restored, the depression is bound to return. This is precisely the reason why so many depressions prove recurrent or chronic. Quick-fixes do not work with depression or any other disorder. Only love heals. Only love truly fixes. It may not be so quick, but by definition, love is patient.

Anxiety, too, the other most common symptom, is also a defense, both a "desired" protection of the heart's loves, and the heart's chosen method of expressing the hidden fear caused by the threat to love. It may help to note that anxiety is a less severe symptom/defense than depression. Depression is caused by love that is already lost or considered lost by the depressed person, whereas anxiety is caused by the "mere threat" of love-loss. Of course, anxiety is terribly painful, but it is inherently more hopeful than depression — as is evidenced by the far higher incidence of suicide with depression. But anxiety and depression do not differ in terms of their purposes. Both are the heart's ways of protecting love.

Anxiety disorders are discussed at some length as love problems in three later chapters. Here, the major point to be made is that the heart's positive, desired reason for expressing itself through anxiety has barely been recognized. Therapists have long recognized the mechanism called "secondary gain," the fact that even though a disorder causes pain, there is always a hidden benefit in having it. Here is an example....

A sixty-year-old widow had lived in almost total isolation on a farm for two years following the death of her husband. Then, for six months, she had a series of monthly panic attacks — terrible anxiety, hyperventilation and palpitations — that had caused her daughter to rush the woman to the hospital for a "heart attack." Panic attacks are horribly painful, horrifying experiences, so what possible "secondary gain" could there be? After talking with her five minutes, the gain was obvious. She talked about feeling so guilty about causing her daughter so much trouble, having to rush her to the hospital all of the time. She had told her daughter, "Honey, I just wish you didn't have to see me like this all the time." In fact, the *only* time this mother ever saw her daughter was on these trips to the hospital. The daughter was a selfish adult brat, and the only way that the mother had unwittingly discovered to gain her daughter's attention, a "semblance of love," was to "die," have a "heart attack."

Ordinarily, what therapists have always called "secondary" gain is absolutely primary. As with the lonely widow above, anxiety is always about the threat of love loss. The exact form of anxiety is always designed to both protect the heart and to express what is happening in the heart. In this case, this lonely mother's psychospiritual heart was indeed breaking from both grief and the neglect of her daughter, but that pain could only be expressed through physical heart symptoms.

An analogy may help. Physically, when the body becomes very cold, it develops "goose bumps" and shivers. The goose bumps increase the surface of the skin and hold heat in, while the shivering muscle increases blood movement to the body. In anxiety, the psychospiritual heart is threatened and becomes fearful; that heart then "quakes," trembles with the exertion of guarding love against the danger of loss, the strain of the "fight-or-flight" for love, and the body follows suit, doing as it is commanded by the heart: it trembles.

Clearly, the connection between the many physical expressions of anxiety, and what is happening at heart level, is difficult to understand sometime. The language of the heart is psychospiritual, and that tongue often can be expressed only through metaphor, symbolism and art. That is the difficult task of psychotherapy, to find ways to understand, translate and express the psychospiritual language of suffering love.

The headaches and neck pain that are symptoms of many anxieties might be found to be expressions of one heart's "stiff-necked," stubborn rebellion and repressed anger, while another heart may be saying that a spouse is literally a "pain in the neck." There are about forty common symptoms that can accompany anxiety. While there are metaphors and symbols, heart language, that are commonly found to be expressed by particular symptoms, there is no pat formula for understanding every heart and every anxiety. Suffice to say this: even in the worst anxiety, hidden fear of death, it is never physical death that is the actual threat, but rather the death of love. Love is life. When people describe anxiety attacks as being "scared of death," or say "I thought I was going to die," they are expressing a metaphor of the heart, which, translated, is saying, "The core of my very being, the most treasured loves of my deepest heart, were threatened with annihilation."

Principle Ten's goal is to fundamentally reinterpret what mental and emotional disorders *are* in terms of their purpose, operation, and basic nature. Treatment with love therapy begins, says the Heart Principle, by recognizing that mental and emotional disorders are signs of suffering love — love twisted, mangled, missing or infected — and that the source of the wound lies, not in the unconscious, but far deeper, in the center of the soul. The remaining principles and chapters are attempts to express what hearts are saying, or whispering, or screaming. Diagnosis in love therapy requires understanding the language of the heart, and that is a language which only another listening heart can hear and interpret. It is a language that is heard only from inside the heart, a sacred place that permits entrance only to another loving heart.

Now oversimplifying just a little, we can summarize: excluding physiologically-centered problems, there is only one mental or emotional disorder, wounded love, and there is only one thing that heals those wounds — love. How love does that is the subject of the next principle.

CHAPTER ELEVEN

Anxiety: Threats Against Love

Principle Eleven: Love Casts Out Fear

Only love protects us in this world. Apart from love, there is only aloneness, separateness, and that is intolerable. Apart from love, everything — the world, other people, God — causes fear. Because the self is comprised of the sum of loves which make up the psychospiritual heart, all anxiety can be understood as deriving from the threat of love being rejected, diminished, damaged, or lost. The most severe anxiety, traumatic threat, produces a sense of aloneness, lovelessness, which is tantamount to the annihilation of self, non-being; hence, the heart, the whole being, quakes.

Explanations

• Anxiety is far more than an emotional response to threat: it is the shudder and shriveling of the heart, the core of being, in expectation of the partial or total destruction of love.

• The "fight or flight" response is an action of the heart designed to protect a loved one (including one's self) who is threatened. More precisely, love protects itself by fight or flight.

• The severity of anxiety symptoms produced by a given threat is inversely proportionate to the amount of unthreatened, protecting love that remains within the individual heart. (Hence, for example, an identical threat may have little impact on a very stable person, while pitching an emotionally fragile person into an anxiety attack.)

• Only love empowers us; threatened loss of love, therefore, produces feelings of powerlessness, which is experienced as weakness, shaking, and even the loss of all power, fainting.

• The forty or more symptoms associated with anxiety are the best evidence that anxiety is heart-deep, a response of the total being. A severe threat of total love-loss is a threat of iminent non-being, so blood vessels, eyes, sweat glands, brain, skin, endocrine glands, every part of both body and spirit are directed by the heart to respond.

• In love, there is no room for fear. When a mother's arms totally enfold a baby, the child has no fear, regardless of the horrors raging outside. Thus does love heal adult anxieties. Love casts out fear.

• The essence of love's healing of anxiety is expressed in the words "encouragement" and "courage." "Courage" is derived from the French *cœur* meaning "heart." With encouragement, as new love is given, it "expands" the heart so that fear is crowded out. As the heart grows larger, being supplants non-being, and the person develops the "courage to be."[1]

Depending on how one counts, there are some two hundred official names given to mental and emotional disorders,[2] and anxiety lurks very near the core of virtually every one of them (i.e., of functional disorders — excluding the organic). As noted earlier, one major benefit of understanding disorders from a love

---

[1] *The Courage to Be* is the title used by existentialist Paul Tillich (New Haven, CT: Yale University Press, 1952). The phrase is used here as a precursor to later principles which will show that both anger and courage must be understood existentially, as heart-deep movements of being.

[2] D.S.M. IV, *op. cit.*

perspective is that it brings a more incisive and simpler under-standing. If we can grasp the relationship of love to anxiety, we can make huge strides toward reaching the "heart of the matter" of all disorders.

Psychoses, phobias, paranoia, panic, psychosomatic and sexual — everything from anorexia to zoophilia — every disor-der involves anxiety, and that anxiety is an expression of a threat to love. That is the fundamental, simple truth that guides love therapy. It is also true, of course, that anxiety causes quaking of the psychospiritual heart, and that shuddering sends disturbing ripples throughout the whole central nervous system, the entire being. When that happens, the complexity of physical, emotional and spiritual symptoms and defenses can be thoroughly baffling. Any thought process, any feeling, any decision or body part — or all of them — may be afflicted as the anxiety emerges. The fundamental understanding offered in Principle Eleven is that each disorder, each symptom and each defense has a common, albeit disguised purpose — to express a specific way that love has been threatened and/or a precise way that the self (the balance of existing love comprising the undamaged portion of the heart) is being defended and preserved. Granted, disorders and their symptoms are complex, but this principle highlights the simplicity underlying that complexity: the simple common thread running through all anxiety disorders and their multiplicity of symptoms is a threat to love, a threat which can be so severe as to (falsely) signal the extinction of one's existence. Examples may help.

Three people — one suffering paranoia, another with panic disorder, and the third with a mild superiority complex — would appear to have little in common. The paranoid person thinks strangers are always talking about him (called "ideas of reference"); the person in panic suffers heart palpitations, hy-perventilation and trembling; and the one with the superiority complex alienates everyone by popping off about how great he is. Symptom-wise, disorder-wise, the three appear to have little in common. And indeed, given the dozens of modern personal-ity theories in use in the marketplace, one could easily find fifty "fundamental" explanations that have nothing in common. Love therapy provides the common ground. Note that the first sentence in each of the following three "heart statements" is identical:

The paranoid person is saying, "*I am afraid nobody loves me. So I am alone. That's terrifying. I feel like nobody.* No, no that can't be true. Everybody loves me (reaction formation),[3] so I'm *not* afraid. See? Those strangers are talking about me (ideas of reference),[4] so I'm not nobody; I'm important enough to be talked about. That's proof that I'm lovable."

The person with the panic attacks is saying, "*I'm afraid nobody loves me.* So I'm alone! That's terrifying! Without love, I'm defenseless, powerless, just like I was when I was a child and Mom wasn't there. I'm going to be annihilated! Then I'll be unloved, totally unlovable. Oh, run! I'll take the love I have left, and run. Run! (flight)."

The person with the superiority complex is saying, "*I'm afraid nobody loves me.* So I am alone! Oh, that's terrifying! No, no, that can't be true. I'm not vulnerable; I'm super. I'm not inferior; I'm superior (reaction formation). I'll convince everybody (and myself) how super-lovable I am."

These three "heart-statements" are prototypical of every functional disorder. Be it a phobia, a psychosis, a mood or behavioral or delusional disorder, the fundamental anxiety is always the same: love, the core of being, is threatened. Given that threat, the resulting disorders, defenses and symptoms are variations on

---

[3] "Reaction formation" is a defense mechanism which allows us to literally flip our emotions and impulses inside-out. Love, for example, can become hate, and vice versa, or moral righteousness may disguise repressed desires to be a big sinner. The defense is usually signaled by the feeling in the counselor, "This person doth protest too much...."

[4] "Ideas of reference" are incorrect interpretations of casual events and external happenings as directly relating to oneself. In the extreme, these ideas can form the basis of a delusion, a chronic false belief. In love theory, these delusions are seen as pitiful attempts to ward off the intolerable feelings of A-loneness engendered by lovelessness. For example, the interpretation might be, "Those strangers are talking about me. Well, at least I'm important enough to be talked about, which proves I'm lovable." Ideas of reference are defensive solutions in that they provide at least a modicum of human contact, albeit sadly, from a safe distance.

the single theme — to express, preserve, or protect love, or to take existing love and run away with it, or to fearfully enter a fight for love, or, if extremes demand it, to create facsimiles of love, delusions or hallucinations, or even a whole new persona (depersonalization disorder, multiple personality) who pretends to be loved. Indeed there are endless variations on the love-anxiety struggle, but every disorder begins with the same heart-statement, "I am afraid I am losing love...."

Quickly, lest these "heart-statements" give a misleading impression that we need only find a simple verbal formula that underlies a disorder, it must be recognized that anxiety has little to do with words. Nor will any "thought" adequately express it, as the cognitive therapists hold. Nor is anxiety a mere emotion. Rather, as the Threatened Love Principle of Anxiety indicates, anxiety is centered in the heart of being, so it is the whole being that quakes when love is perceived to be in danger.

The distinct sense of utter "aloneness" that accompanies the worst anxiety has no English term that accurately describes it. The German word *angst* generally describes anxiety as soul-deep trembling unto death. The word has no exact English translation, but Hendrik Ruitenbeek captures the sense of its absolute terror: "*Angst* embodies that fear, total and indefinite, which encompasses alienation, isolation, despair, and death."[5] That still does not adequately express the element of stark aloneness that accompanies severe anxiety. Erich Fromm[6] speaks of the "separateness" that is intolerable, but neither does that word adequately express the unique state of solitary being that accompanies anxiety in severe disorders.

After struggling for years to help people describe that horrific state of aloneness, I began interpreting it this way: "That sense of separateness is not just 'lonesome.' And neither does

---

[5] Hendrik M. Ruitenbeek, "Some Aspects of the Encounter of Psychoanalysis and Existential Philosophy," in Ruitenbeek, Ed., *Psychoanalysis and Existential Philosophy* (New York: E.P. Dutton Co., 1962), p. xv.

[6] Erich Fromm, *op. cit.*, p. 9.

'aloneness' nor 'solitude' adequately describe it. This is a state of alone-beyond-alone-beyond-alone, an interior feeling that 'nobody's home and nobody's ever been home.' It is an empty agony, a hollowness that is utterly desperate. But there has been no English word for this separateness, this horrific desolation. It is not merely 'alone,' so I began hyphenating the word, using the long pronunciation of 'a-,' calling it the state of being absolutely 'A-lone' — alone beyond alone beyond alone — 'A-lone!' Given that description, an amazing number of people respond, "Yes! That's the feeling; oh, God, it's horrible."

"A-loneness" is the wordless terror that accompanies the sense of infinite distance between self, others, God, and self itself. I have come to believe that this state of A-loneness is a central factor in understanding not just anxiety, but all serious emotional disorders.

The Threatened Love Principle relates anxiety to the threat of love being diminished or lost, and earlier, Principle Eight defined the human being in terms of the sum total of loves residing in the psychospiritual heart. These two principles, together, tell us why that state of A-loneness, emptiness and separateness is experienced in every disorder.

The extreme opposite of love is not hatred, as popular understanding has it; it is nothingness, and that non-love is experienced within the human heart as A-loneness. In turn, the A-loneness is invariably accompanied by fear that ranges from mild anxiety to stark terror — because the impending threat of love-loss is the equivalent of personal annihilation, ontological non-being.

The human heart cannot tolerate a vacuum. One way or another, using scores of symptoms and defenses, the heart will rise to fight the emptiness — take flight to escape it, isolate it, dodge it, disguise it, or fill it with a hundred various pseudo-loves: money, power, sex, food, an irrational obsession or compulsion, fantasies, or even (as in hebephrenic schizophrenia and multiple personality disorder), a whole new persona.

But when all efforts to defend or escape the emptiness fail, the A-loneness, nothingness, begins to break out of a heart that can be pictured as broken. Therapists call that crumbling of defenses "decompensation." In lay terms, it is a "breakdown." But if the actual object of fear is the "nothingness" that is becoming "exposed," then perhaps we can more accurately say that failed defenses leads to an "A-loneness break-out."

In severe mental illness, psychosis, the A-loneness overruns defenses, breaks out, and virtually consumes the entire being. Anxiety becomes terror. Instead of experiencing love, the touchstone of reality, the heart of the person blatantly suffers the emergence of a vacuum, non-love, non-reality. But that nothingness is intolerable, so the heart uses the pitiful remnants of love remaining, shards and splinters of love, in a frenzied effort to assemble, jig-saw-puzzle style, some semblance of reality. Yet, many pieces are missing, so bits of remembered love (reality) float willy-nilly, unattached to other pieces. What emerges is the splintered personality of the psychotic, a phantasmagoria of jumbled images and word salad, a fabricated, make-do, hallucinatory and delusional mix of the unreal — non-love — and the table scraps of love that remain in touch with reality.

Later chapters focus the psychoses and various anxiety-related disorders. Love simplifies our understanding of anxiety, but by no means does that make it simple.

The Principle's third Explanation, however, provides a "gauge," a proportion, that enables us to more easily evaluate the severity of disorders. That Explanation says: the severity of anxiety produced by a given threat is inversely proportionate to the amount of unthreatened, protective (healthy) love that is present within the individual heart. The ratio can be stated obversely: lack of anxiety (peace) is directly proportionate to the amount of unthreatened, protective love present in the heart.

A quick, first glimpse at the implications of the love-anxiety ratio can be gained by observing two men, co-workers, faced with the financial threat of sudden unemployment. Their skills, work experience, intelligence, number of dependent children, bank savings, debts, and actual prospects for finding a new job and regaining security, are all identical. The first man gripes, worries a little, but sets out in relative peace to find a new job. The other man, faced with an equal amount of actual threat, falls apart; he is rushed to the emergency room with palpitations, sweating, unable to breathe, convinced he is having a coronary. He is diagnosed "Panic Disorder," given medication, and sent for counseling. Two men; identical threat; the threat rolls off the back of one man while it crushes the other — what made the difference? The "amount" of love present in each man's heart, the sum accrued over a lifetime.

Only love empowers us (the fourth Explanation). For the fortunate man who was relatively unfazed by the threat of unemployment, years of love from parents, family, friends and God had constructed a strong heart that enabled him to love himself, have faith and trust in himself, and to confidently hope that he would land a new job. That same love had given him self-confidence and courage (heart) in the face of adversity.

Given a paucity of love, the heart of the co-worker was too fragile; threat entered too easily. That threat, unemployment, triggered the abrupt surfacing, the "break-out" of non-love, the heart-vacuum that he had been defending against for years. His love deficit produced what might be visualized as the mirror-opposite of his stronger co-worker's responses. Faith in himself quickly became total loss of confidence. Self-trust became uncertainty and inability to make decisions. Hope became hopelessness, and instead of loving himself when he needed it most, he began self-abasement, blaming and kicking himself for being unemployed (blaming the victim).

How many anxiety symptoms the panicking man experienced is directly connected with the love deficit of his heart. Of course, we cannot "quantify" love nor its deficits in any objective way. Love can never even be known except through intersubjectivity. Yet, in a diagnostic interview, if it is loving, truly intersubjective, heart-to-heart, an experienced therapist can reach and assess that heart and obtain an accurate assessment of the "amount" of love that the person has been given, and/or been able to receive, throughout his life. That "subjective measuring" of love is one of the essential arts of psychotherapy.

Finally, two of this Principle's Explanations speak to how love heals anxiety: "In love, there is no room for fear." How that works is discussed at length in later chapters. Suffice to say here, as love fills the psychospiritual heart, it "crowds out" fear and calms the anxious, palpitating physical heart. As it pushes out anxiety, love courses through the central nervous system, stops the rapid flow of adrenaline, cools the pumping sweat glands, reverses the dilation of the pupils, forces blood out of the tensing muscles of arms and legs and returns it to the internal organs, and slows the respiration. How can love have all those effects on anxiety? Because love issues in the opposite of anxiety — peace. More accurately, just as love is truth, so too, love is peace, and peace dispels all need for fight and flight. Peace basks safely, warmly and lazily in the arms of love, its mother.

CHAPTER TWELVE

Authentic Anger Is Loving

Principle Twelve:
Anger Is the Normal Human Response to a Violation of Love

Anger is the normal human reaction to injustice, any violation of love. In its authentic form, anger is the voice of a heart that has been hurt, a voice which is controlled and proportionate to the injustice, a voice purposefully expressed so as to restore and heal love that has been damaged. Thus, authentic anger, as contrasted with its abuses, can be identified in light of the same ontological definition as love itself — as a movement toward an authentic good, viz., restored justice.

Explanations

• Authentic anger can be distorted in two extreme ways, both of which can produce pathology. At one extreme is abuse — physical, emotional, or sexual — and at the other extreme is passivity, cowardice, the refusal or inability to express anger even when justice and love, of others or self, are clearly being violated.

• The biblical admonition, "Be angry, but sin not"[1] captures well the balance required of love's anger. There are two clauses in the

---

[1] Ephesians 4:26. Two other translations of this quote are, "If you are angry, let it be without sin" (New American Bible) and "If you become angry, do not let your anger lead you into sin" (Good News Bible).

sentence: "Be angry," which is to say, "Of course you'll be angry sometime; when your love is hurt, that's perfectly normal; so *be* angry" — "but sin not," which implies, "But don't hurt anybody with your anger; don't violate love by becoming abusive, or judgmental, or by allowing your anger to turn to hatred."

• Psychological well-being demands that anger be acted upon, released and resolved, ended — by appropriate verbal expression or benign physical ventilation, and finally by forgiveness. Anger, and the injustice that created it, are stored in the psychospiritual heart as dynamic, living realities; therefore, an injustice must be righted in order for wholeness, love, to be restored. It is the denial or unwarranted repression of anger, the refusal to recognize and respect it, which directly causes abusive anger and explosions of violence at one extreme, and cowardice, or living as a victim with illness-producing repressed rage, at the other.

• No matter the chronological age, rage is the infantile explosion of uncontrolled power in response to the threat of powerlessness, which, in turn, is produced by the perceived threat of severe lovelessness, destruction of the heart.

• Destructive, abusive, murderous rage in adults is a response to early childhood injustice, love's betrayal, deprivation or destruction. The love damage originally experienced by the rage-filled adult was truy unjust, but it has never been forgiven. The original injustice (of parents, typically) may be projected on to all people. Victimization may breed a victimizer. Or, the rage may be expressed through self-punishment, or denied with the aid of alcoholism or addictions.

• At the other extreme, the inability or refusal to ever express appropriate anger, even in justified and necessary self-defense, is also a result of early childhood (usually parental) injustice. This is victimization in the form of spirit-breaking punishment of the child's justifiable anger, or a more subtle form of victimization — teaching a child that anger is immoral, always wrong, or something to be feared.

• Co-dependent adults, children of alcoholics, chronically battered wives, masochists, and anxiety-laden people of many types, lead their lives as proverbial "doormats," perennial victims, totally unable to feel, much less express anger, no matter how mistreated they may be. Appropriate self-love mandates anger when love suffers injustice.

• Loving anger is never judgmental, never condemning, never abusive. Authentic anger is directed at the act of injustice, at the sin, never at the heart of the one who perpetrated the injustice, never at the sinner. The goal of appropriate anger, therefore, is never to punish nor to reap revenge; rather, its goal is to simply stop, prevent, or correct a wrong, to right an injustice, and to restore love.

• The expression of anger is indeed a fundamental human "right," as teachers of Assertiveness Training correctly proclaim, but it is much more. Anger is an inherent component of love which is essential to the preservation of life, viz., love. Anger is a simple fact, a truth that must be lived, expressed, if love is to be maintained. " Right" may be exercised, or not, without diminishing personhood. If, though, necessary and appropriate anger is not expressed, then the unjust maltreatment of love goes unchecked, and personhood is diminished. Eating is a right, but it is also essential to life. Similarly, anger is a right, but it is more: it is essential to the integrity of the person.

• Love is the most fundamental human power, the power of powers, and all abuses of power derive from love deficit or love damage. A love deficit inherently induces a sense of powerlessness, but the reactive use of abusive power, "superpower," is pseudo-power.

• Love is to authentic power as rage, abuse, and all hostile acts are to powerlessness and pseudo-power; this ratio implies a proportion that can be used to evaluate the severity of love deficits underlying abuse- and rage-related disorders (e.g., cold-blooded serial murderers lie at the extreme end of the spectrum of lovelessness/powerlessness).

• The greatest anger is always preceded by a deeper feeling, a unique response of the heart that goes by the simple name "hurt." Strangers can annoy us, frustrate us, step on our toes, but only people we love can truly "hurt" us. Anger may be a defense that allows us to temporarily avoid feeling heart-deep hurt.

• Much of the abusive anger seen in the schools, streets and families is endemic to unjust social systems. Simply pursuing "more justice" has not and will never be the answer to systemic societal anger. Love principles provide the mandate and guidelines for effective revolutionary change in education, corrections, human services, governmental, and other systems.

———————————

Opening the newspaper in the morning, or watching the news on TV, we are deluged with horror stories — assaults, riots, children brutalized, rapes, drive-by murders, drug murders, and murders for no apparent reason. Surely everyone would agree that we live in an angry world and that it seems to be getting angrier every day. Yet, here, the Loving Anger Principle says, "Not so. Authentic anger is good! It is an expression of love. The problem is *not* anger, but its abuses; and the simple answer to all that modern rage and mayhem is love, including *more* authentic (loving) anger."

Simple? Yes. Truth always is. It is also a simple truth that our societies need wholesale reorientation, a revolutionary answer to the problem of violence and hostility that is ripping individuals, families and nations apart. Some of those revolutionary answers are implicit in the Anger Principle. Following are just two examples of the revolutionary changes suggested in the Explanations.

"Corrections," so-called, the prisons and jails of the criminal justice system, correct precious little criminal behavior, serve as a "crime school" for some inmates, embitter and harden the hearts of others, and are widely acknowledged to be a huge societal joke, a wrong idea awaiting correction. The Loving Anger Principle suggests some hard questions and provides answers....

Question: If the most violent criminals are said to possess an "anger disorder," and if part of that disorder stems from having a lifetime of rage stuffed in their hearts, and if the second Explanation, above, is correct in saying that anger *must* be expressed and resolved, ended, then question: how does imprisonment resolve and end repressed rage?

Answer: It doesn't.

Question: Then what happens to that rage?

Answer: It remains within the prisoner till he is released; then his violence and crime resume, energized by repressed rage that has had time to fester during the tenure in prison.

Q: But doesn't punishment, imprisonment itself, correct the rage?

A: Absolutely not.

Q: Then what could actually correct, remove the prisoner's rage?

A: Love — love that respects the simple truth that rage is a living force, a dynamic reality of a wounded heart, a kind of psychic pus that must be drained off so that love can reach and heal the open wounds that are causing the rage.

Q: Love prisoners? *Love* murderers and thieves and rapists? What kind of bleeding-heart-liberal answer is that?

A: The truth, the only answer that can possibly work. (And by the way, love just might be the only concept that is both conservative and liberal; take your choice.)

Q: Alright, how do you drain off rage?

A: It's done in mental hospitals and therapists' offices every day — in brief, by using punching bags, safe plastic bats and pillows to physically punch and pound, safely and benignly expressing the anger, effectively ventilating and dissipating the raging energy, while simultaneously talking about the wounds, the injustices suffered, and how to forgive, how to let go of the anger once and for all. A huge milestone that prisoners *must* be helped to reach is forgiveness.

Q: Outrageous! It sounds like you want to turn prisons into giant therapy rooms using love therapy?

A: Hey! What a great idea!

Q: But where could you possibly get all the therapists, and the sheer quantity of all the love that would be required? It sounds impossibly expensive.

A: Love is free. So are volunteers. Therapists are expensive, but a totally new Corrections system can be designed that could be cost-effective. Besides, nothing could be more expensive than the abysmal failure of the present correctional system.

Q: The whole notion is radical. You must realize that you'll be either laughed to scorn or pilloried if you dare suggest the idea. Do you dare? Isn't it obvious that your love idea is bound to fail?

A: First, I dare. Secondly, love never fails. Love just hasn't been tried.

In support of the audacious suggestion above, compare the following: this is a lesson from history.

Many trace the beginning of modern humane treatment of the mentally ill to 1793 when Philippe Pinel, as the new administrator of Bicêtre Hospital in France, released the mental patients from their chains, and began treating them with kindness.[2] Prior to that time, not only were the mentally ill chained, they were subjected to bloodletting, purgatives, emetics, filth, torture and burning at the stake. In 1793, it was "obvious" to the world that mental patients had to be chained and that Pinel's kindness toward them was utter folly. Pinel was considered mad by his contemporaries. Two hundred years later, as I suggest not just kindness but love for the inmates of prisons, will I be considered mad? Love is mad? Or is it not true that the present "correctional" system, so-called, and anyone who would dare defend it, has a pre-Pinel mentality?

---

[2] A brief history of Pinel's courageous movement to unchain the mentally ill is given in Franz G. Alexander, M.D. and Sheldon T. Selesnick, M.D., *The History of Psychiatry: An Evaluation of Psychiatric Practice From Prehistoric Times to the Present* (New York: Harper & Row, 1966), pp. 112-113.

A second revolution implicit in Principle Twelve concerns Education.

One of the most pitiful ironies of our day is this: many schools now keep statistics on how many guns children bring to school, how often teachers are physically assaulted by children, the number of drug busts of children, how many children are suspended for violence, and the cost of armed guards patrolling the school halls to keep children from killing one another — and all these statistics generally have risen year after year.

Question: If it is a fair conclusion that modern educational theory and methods fail to train children to deal appropriately with anger and fail to address the blatant rage of some of them, what is fundamentally wrong?

Answer: Principle Twelve shows the inherent linkage between anger and love, and Principle Nine defined the inseparable ontological and psychological unity of truth and love; together, these two principles highlight what is missing in educational theory. They illustrate not only why teachers are unable to cope with the children's increasing violence, but why too few children learn so little truth — even the three Rs.

Q: So the answer to the educational system is love? But don't teachers already love the children?

A: Many do — when they are allowed to do so by the system. The educational system, though, is mortally flawed because it has not understood that love must be given absolute first priority. Love and truth are one; asking a child to learn without love is like asking a fish to swim without water. Give a fish water and it will swim; give love and the child will learn. But in the present system, no one has taught the teachers the essential relationship of love to learning, much less spelled it out as their first responsibility.

Q: But how do you make love the top priority?

A: The hard way — with a revolution of the educational system. Re-think it from bottom-up; that is, start with new, fundamental philosophical premises — that love and truth are one, and that learning occurs only when motivated by love — and then re-build the system. In a nutshell, the goal is to build an educational system in which love is blatant and ubiquitous. Given top priority, love will pour out of the teachers, saturate the kids, and then love will start showing up in the school subjects: kids will love math, love history and spelling.

Q: Learning is motivated only by love? What about motivating kids by giving gold stars for good work? Or what about behavior modification — rewards and punishments? Isn't your only-love-motivates-learning principle an over-generalization?

A: No, love motivates all human behavior (Principle One). Specifically, a gold star is simply a symbol, a re-presentation of the teacher's love. Behavior modification can work if the rewards offered the child are loving. Remember the broad metaphysical definition of love? Love is a movement toward a perceived good. If a reward is good, it is loving. As for punishment, by itself it will not work; if, however, the punishment (e.g., "Time-out") is offered with the promise that it is loving, then it can work. Children innately know they need discipline, limits, and that if they are not disciplined when they need it, they are not being loved. Kids also know when a punishment is for them, a gift, and when it is merely the selfish, hateful spleen of the punisher.

Q: So your answer to violence in the schools, and education in general, is to overhaul the whole system with love at the center. But again, how? Even if we accept that love and learning, and love and nonviolence are inseparable, how do you apply these principles to teachers and schoolchildren?

A: And don't forget school superintendents, administrators, the N.E.A. and education's political leaders. A revolution has to be top-down as well as bottom-up. So then — how? First, you teach love. This entire book is saying this: many people don't understand love, don't understand that their own motivations are all love-grounded, and don't understand the love-and-learning, the love-and-anger, or the basic love-and-life relationships. Those relationships can be and need to be taught. It must be understood that learning about love does not automatically produce more actual loving; love always requires a free choice. Rather, teaching love will remove impediments to loving, and thus free people to make choices to love. For example, if children learn that their defenses, their angry acting-out behaviors, are all love-related, then they have a chance to be more forthright by just asking for love directly. Now, when I say teach love, I mean *classes* in it — from the elementary to high school to college levels. We speak of the three Rs as basic — reading, writing, 'rithmetic. It should be "three Rs and L."

The two examples above can only hint at the wholesale reorientation of social systems that love theory can bring about. The same principles can be applied to business-labor relations, the judicial system, and community-neighborhood relations (especially with regard gang wars, homelessness, and the justifiably angry effects of poverty). Until now, in the United States and throughout the world, the highest value and concept that has been applied in guiding these systems has been "justice." Surely, justice is a good and necessary virtue, but often it is just not enough. Justice is simply not achievable without love. More importantly, justice is inherently less than love. Consider, for example, the effectiveness of justice and love in relation to street gang violence or homelessness.

The highest goal of justice is to provide to each person according to his "due," i.e., his rights. In contrast, love's goal is far higher: it is to provide to each person according to his "need," whether or not he has a legal right to that in which he is in need. As the chronic problems of gang wars and homelessness prove, justice fails. Why? Because the homeless have earned nothing, so by law they are "due" nothing. Similarly, gangs are "due" nothing, and they have forsaken all rights by violating the rights of others. Gang members have been "brought to justice" repeatedly, but the street wars continue and increase. Given the standards of justice, society can turn its back on these people and be legally "right" and smugly righteous in doing so because, after all, the unrighteous are "due" nothing. There's only one problem with justice and with being legally right: it just doesn't work.

In comparison, if governmental and voluntary social agencies were to ask, "What do gang members and the homeless *need*?" (notwithstanding the fact that they are due nothing and have no rights), then massive programs of intervention would emerge that could tremendously diminish the problems within a few years. The demands of justice are always minimum, and hence ineffective. In contrast, if city governments and social agencies were to focus on a social problem and ask, "What does love demand that we do?" then success would be virtually assured. Why? Because the demands of love are maximum, generous, dictated by need — reality. In brief, that is the incentive and rationale behind the revolutions implicitly promoted by the love principles: they are realistic, practical. Love works; and without love, nothing works.

Thus far, discussion of the Loving Anger Principle has focused on whole social systems. Most of the Explanations, though, speak to how anger and the abuse of anger operate within the individual.

It is perhaps the Explanation that speaks of anger as the response used by the heart when love is "hurt" that best describes the methods and goals of love therapy. "Hurt" is another of those oh-so-simple, uncomplicated, unprofessional-sounding words that love therapy embraces as uniquely descriptive of suffering souls. In counseling, after anger has been endlessly discussed and cussed, stormed and spit, pounded into pillows, vented and splattered, the time comes when I again ask, heart-to-heart, perhaps whispering, "Now, what is your heart saying? What's beneath all that anger?" This is the question that reaches the "heart of the problem." The answer that comes is almost universal, a plaintive, soul-deep answer that is often accompanied by wrenching tears — "Oh, it hurts. It just hurts." When the anger has been terrible, and we reach the agony that caused it, people will often fold over in pain with their hands clenched tightly over their chests, holding, protecting and soothing their hearts.

Beginning therapy, people who are able to express anger may rave and rant, but they will oft times not have the foggiest idea what their anger is all about. Moreover, when the therapist tries to steer them to look deeper, to look for the root of the anger, they resist — angrily. As a rule of thumb, the greater the anger, the greater the defense, the greater the hurt. As therapy progresses, that "stored" anger is gradually spent and the session eventually comes when heart-level is reached. Only then, heart to heart, vulnerable, defenseless, open, can the person allow the source of the anger to be exposed — a gaping wound in the heart. Painful as that moment is, it is a blessing, for only when the open wound is exposed can it be healed. Only then can healing love reach wounded love.

How love heals is the subject of other principles. Here, we should highlight two salient points: first, anger itself is not healed, for the wound lies not in the anger but in its source, a heart that can be pictured as gashed. This realization is vital in that it demonstrates again that *only love heals*. Therapies like assertiveness training and behavior modification, and therapy exercises aimed at expression and ventilation of anger, are often good and necessary steps on the path toward healing — but they actually heal nothing. Only love heals, and then only when the wounded heart is exposed. Similarly, analysis alone, gaining knowledge of the cause, by itself heals nothing. Only love heals.

The second vital point is that the universal expression of "hurt" that is found to underlie anger demonstrates that anger is always a defense — even when it appears as an attack. There is no contradiction here: it is not just in sports that "the best defense is a good offense." Rather, the question is what is anger defending? It is, of course, the psychospiritual heart, the core of being.

The purpose of a principle is to simplify, and to facilitate understanding. The Loving Anger Principle distinguishes between authentic anger (we might even call it "righteous anger") and distorted or pathological anger of two kinds — at one extreme, abuse, and at the other, passivity, cowardice, the inability or refusal to express necessary anger. The Principle's simplicity is aimed at cutting through the endlessly complex ways that anger figures into virtually every emotional disorder. Thus, when therapy is successful, the "answer" as to the source of anger is always simple — love that was "hurt." Reaching that goal, however, may require tracking anger through dozens of mazes, the defense mechanisms. Two brief examples might help.

Displacement — When this defense begins operating, anger is transferred, shunted away from the person who caused the unjust heart wound, onto a safer object. For example, a man was deeply hurt by his father. For years he transferred that anger toward father figures, bosses. He dared not express anger to either bosses or father, though, so when he arrived home from work, he kicked the cat almost every day, and sometimes abused his wife and children. Note: kicking the cat was a defense of a defense of the heart wound — all very complex until the man was able to unravel it all and say of his father, tearfully, "He really hurt me."

In cool, detached tones, the same man described how his father abused him, beat him bloody. When I asked if he was angry about the way his father treated him, he answered in the same flat tone, "No, there's no sense in being angry; it was a long time ago." This is the defense called dissociation — the emotion, anger, is separated, split off from the causal events, and not felt. With therapy, the anger is finally acknowledged, and then it emerges as an explosion. Only then, beneath the anger, which lay hidden behind a flat, dissociated demeanor, can the wounded heart be exposed. Healing then begins when the anger is spent and the man can say, "It just hurts."

Often, defenses cover other defenses in a tangled web. Understanding Principle Twelve, though, can often allow the counselor to take an important, timesaving shortcut. Rather than analyzing all the circuitous routes that anger can take through dozens of defenses, a powerful love can sometimes melt all or many of them at once. As the Principle states, only love protects us against the many threats in this world, so we know at the deepest heart level that in the presence of love we are safe, safe even from the harm experienced in the past. In that loving atmosphere, a therapist often can penetrate beyond the defense level to reach and speak directly to the heart. Once the heart is reached with love, a simple question then produces remarkable results — the question, "I know you're angry, and you have a perfect right to be angry. But can you just tell me now, what hurts? What hurts?" Remarkably, when asked in the context of loving, that simple little question short-circuits defenses, disarms and melts anger, and produces tears, tears accompanied by the soul-deep, honest admission of a wounded heart, "Oh, it does hurt. It just hurts."

In describing this "loving shortcut," we are again handicapped by the limitations of the printed word. Words alone will never convey love. Suffice to say, if I ask you, without love, to tell me your heart-level hurt, you'd never tell me. Given a powerful love, though, any of us will rush to bare our souls.

Thus far, the focus has been on overt anger, and the pain that lies beneath it. At the other extreme, as two Explanations describe, are forms of anger that are not just covert, but so thoroughly hidden that the anger seems nonexistent.

By far the majority of people entering counseling have repressed, avoided and stuffed anger all their lives. These are the scapegoats, the doormats — victims. But there are degrees of victimization, too. At the far extreme are people who have been brutalized, kicked around all their lives, the pitiable whipped pups of humanity whose spirits have been broken. They have suffered abuse for a lifetime, so they expect nothing else. When abused, they whimper, but go right back for more abuse, never expressing the slightest anger.

Authentic anger, as this principle emphasizes, is a function of love. From that perspective, we see that anger is good and necessary, and that it requires strength, power. In contrast, the extremely and chronically abused simply do not have the power to be angry. Since Freud, mainstream theories of personality have held that if people are abused, their anger must be present unconsciously, but in repressed form. That is simply not true. In the traumatically abused, anger is not repressed; it is simply *not present* because substantial portions of their psychospiritual hearts have been demolished. Beyond having "broken spirits," those who have been terribly abused have had their hearts virtually ruined, nearly razed; there is so little undamaged, healthy love remaining in their hearts that there is simply not enough power to be angry. In love therapy, it is recognized that these devastated hearts have to be not just healed but reconstructed, and more — re-created. The heart that is missing must be replaced, and only massive infusions of love can accomplish that. Love is not just healing; it is creational. In a later chapter, this type of intensive love therapy is described as "heart transplant."

The practical consequences of this "destroyed heart" view of the traumatically abused, and the utter absence of their anger, cannot be overstated. Every day, battered wives, abused children, rape victims, and alcoholic co-dependents — victims of many kinds — are being unwittingly subjected to further maltreatment by people who are actually trying to help them, their counselors. Following the spurious theory that the anger of the abused is just repressed, therapists push, probe and analyze, insisting to the abused people that their anger is present "unconsciously." Ever passive, compliant and obedient, the abused people accept the burden placed on them by their counselors, and feel guilty because they cannot voice the anger the counselor wants. This is not just a waste of time; it is abuse, albeit unintentional. We have all seen pictures of emaciated, starving children who are too weak to cry. That is the picture of the hearts of many of the traumatically abused — too weak to cry, and certainly too weak to muster the power that is required to be angry.

Other common and mistaken themes of present-day treatment of the abused are the premature use of anger exercises and confrontation. In the first-mentioned, rape victims are told by therapists, "That rapist took your power away! Get it back, get angry! Punch that pillow and pretend it's him." In confrontations, victims are led to face their victimizers and to "Let 'em have it; tell 'em how angry you are! Get your power back!" All too typically, these kinds of treatments are initiated long before the abused person is ready, viz., long before they have the "heart" for it, before enough love has been restored to create the power to be angry. The result: the abused one "fakes" anger, or simply fails. Anger exercises and confrontations are good and necessary forms of treatment, but a ravaged heart must first be empowered, loved, before expecting it to have the power to express anger, or even tears.

At the far opposite extreme of the traumatically abused are the chronic abusers. Given the understanding above — that appropriate anger is a function of love, and that anger is one of the powers of love — abuse can be understood as a violation of love, of power, and of authentic anger itself. Though the psychology of abusers is no less complex, and is surrounded by a hodgepodge of defenses, love therapy enables us to cut through the maze, find the heart of the matter, and treat abusers more quickly and effectively.

Effective treatment with abusers has a first priority objective: stopping the abuse in its tracks. The typical chronic abuser maintains his cruel behavior by voicing two consistent themes (defenses): first, "I couldn't help it; I just blew up before I knew it; I just lost control" (denial of responsibility). The second frequent theme is projection of responsibility on to the victim: "I didn't want to hurt her; she just made me do it. If she hadn't made me so mad, I'd never have hit her." The first love therapy response to these typical abuser defenses is this: "Let me offer you a very professional interpretation of all those excuses for beating your wife — Bullshit!"

Just as the severely abused have no power to be angry, we can deduce that the abuser, who obviously can show power and anger, just as obviously possesses enough love (albeit misused) to exert power. Given love and power, we can also be certain, therefore, that the abuser possesses another faculty that the abused often do not have, the power to choose — volition, the will to be angrily abusive, or the power to choose not to be abusive. Given this amount of love, this much power to make choices, love therapy's second forceful interpretation to the abuser is this: "There is no damn excuse for your abuse, ever. You have the capability to choose *not* to be abusive. The power behind your anger is living proof that you also have freedom of choice."

Typically, abusers will resist freedom of choice, insisting time and again that, "I can't help it! She makes me so mad I just see red, and then before I know what I'm doing, I've hit her — like in blind rage." Abusers try to be very convincing with their "I couldn't help it" routine, so it is vital that the therapist be more convinced, and more convincing, that the abuser's anger is *prima facie* evidence of the existence of love, and thence of the power to choose. Given that conviction, following is the love therapy response to the abuser's claim of "uncontrollable" abuse:

"Look, you're telling me you're helpless, that you have no choice about your rage and violence. It's not true. I want you to think back to the last time you hit your wife — to just *before* you hit her. Think back, and slow down the events. Just before you swung at her, there was a split second, just a brief interval, but maybe two or three seconds, when you *did* have a choice. In that split second, if you're honest, you'll remember that *you thought about it*, to hit her or not to hit her. You freely chose.

"Now what we'll do, what *you'll* do, is train yourself to pay attention to that split second. Then the first decision you'll make is to *stretch out* that thinking-time by slowly counting from one to ten, or to twenty, or however many numbers it takes for you to calm down, think and decide not to be abusive. Look, I'm tying this string around your wrist to remind you: When you're angry, pull hard on that string; it's a strong string so it will hurt you and remind you to *think*. *Decide* if your wife can possibly be responsible for your abuse. She can't be. Abuse is a decision, an action, not a reaction. So don't con yourself with that 'poor-baby-can't-help himself' baloney. Remember, there's *no* excuse for abuse, *ever*."

Treating abusers begins with what many would call "tough love." Indeed the love must stay "hard," directive, and if necessary, chastising until the abuse has stopped. Yet, if the abuser is to be healed, he too must be understood and loved.

Very typically, abusers have been abuse victims, so they must understand the cycle of abuse, the way it is handed down from parent to child, sometimes over many generations. The abuser's own victimization must be recognized, but he must also understand that someone must stop the cycle. The abuser, too, was unjustly treated; therefore, he has an absolute right to be angry about that injustice, but absolutely no right to inflict his anger and pain onto others, as his parent(s) did. In love therapy, "tough love" with an abuser is a delicate mix of both compassion and authoritative direction, warm acceptance of the person mixed with forthright condemnation of his abusive behavior. Ultimately, the goal of treatment of the abused/abuser is exactly the same as with his victims, to reach the open wound in the heart, and to heal it with love.

One Explanation describes a ratio: love is to authentic power as rage, abuse and hostility are to powerlessness and pseudo-power. This inverse relationship is helpful in evaluating the progress of people given to rages, as well as in interpreting why and when the rages occur. People will punch holes in doors, smash a bowl of food against a wall, fly into a screaming fit, or hit someone, and invariably not understand what they were feeling. Here are three typical explanations that raging people offer: (1) "I was just so frustrated! *Nothing* was working. Then I lost it." (2) "She kept backing me in a corner; *nothing* I said was right; then I just blew, hit her, and tore up the room." (3) "Nothing was going right. I couldn't win. Then a dish slipped and broke. That's when I tore up the kitchen and started beating the kid." Frustration; being backed in a corner; nothing working; nothing right — all are code words for *powerlessness*. For the therapist, that power vacuum is easy to see, but it is often very difficult for the power-less people themselves to see or accept. Often, in fact, the more rages and abuses, the more unwilling the person is to accept the idea that they are in fact feeling powerless. Why? The love/power ratio explains it: the greater the distance into rage and abusiveness (pseudo-power), the further away the person is from authentic power and love, and thence the more pain of lost love, and thence the greater defensiveness.

For the "toughest" macho man who beats up everybody, the admission that he in fact feels powerless and unloved will initially be met with sneering scorn. He may counter with, "Powerless? I ain't afraid of nobody, man." So he would like to pretend — but he is mortally afraid of the lovelessness that he senses to be lurking inside himself. The macho man is a coward acting like a hero. Beneath the lip-curling snarl and heroic swagger is a bully who runs from himself, a crying baby. But macho abusers are stubborn cases. They hang on tenaciously to their defense, abusive pseudo-power, precisely because they have so little authentic loving power going for them. Helping them gives "tough love" a new meaning: to love these macho-jerks is tough for the therapist. It requires courage, authentic power — and huge patience.

Because of the limits of language perhaps, many are inclined to say that evil is simply the nth degree of anger. We think of the raging evil of serial killers, for example, and place evil in the same category as abuse — just a whole lot worse. That is not true. Real evil is in a category all its own and has little relationship whatever to ordinary human anger. Actual evil is inhuman.

Earlier, I described above how "ordinary" abusers commonly operate out of a love deficit. There are, though, some people who have been given ample love by parents, family and friends who, exercising free choice, misuse the loving power they have been given in order to destroy love. That is evil.

Serial killers like Dahmer, Gacy, and Bundy, and political killers like Hitler, Idi Amin, and Saddam Hussein are not wild-eyed maniacs, nor are they emotionally disturbed like ordinary abusers; these are sane people, in total control of their emotions, who freely chose to become monsters, and freely chose to kill, destroy and befoul humanity. These are not mere "angry" people. They are evil. They freely chose to defile the love they possessed. In contrast, authentic anger is the normal, healthy human response to an unjust treatment of love. That is the extreme opposite of evil.

There seems to be no better or more concise way of summarizing love therapy's psychology of anger than to repeat the biblical prescription, "Be angry, but sin not."

CHAPTER THIRTEEN

Guilt – The Voice of My Own Violated Love

Principle Thirteen: Guilt is the Normal Response to the Violation of One's Own Love

Guilt is the cry of a self-inflicted heart wound. The one self-evident and absolute law of the human heart is to love everyone, including one's self, and to love always. Guilt is the natural human reaction to our violation of that law. Guilt is the normal psychospiritual response of the heart to sin, which is defined psychologically as well as spiritually, as any deliberate violation of love. Authentic guilt is far more than an emotion; it is the whisper of love uttered by the Conscience, which is the innate power of the healthy heart to keep itself inviolate, innocent, and loving always. In contrast, false guilt, which is involved in many emotional disorders, is a mere emotion. At deeper levels of the heart, Conscience unerringly confronts both real and false guilt with truth, and its voice will not be stilled until the heart has been healed of sin's wounds, and false guilt's lies, by the restoration of love. This natural human affinity for loving truth, Conscience, is present in seminal form at birth.

Explanations

• Conscience, as a major component of personality structure, is a heart-deep repository of love that performs an entirely positive function, the preservation of the innocent goodness that is

fundamental to the integrity of the heart. Thus, from the beginning of life, conscience presents the meaning and dictates of love
to consciousness in order to encourage the pursuit of goodness
(love) and the avoidance of evil (anti-love). Conscience whispers:
"There is no excuse for not loving."

• The deepest seat of the power of conscience is the purest love
which abides at the center of the heart of every person, *le point
vierge* (God or Pure Love, by whatever name). Thus, a child growing up on an island alone, without parents or social standards
to guide him, would still possess the core power of conscience
that would encourage him to pursue love, avoid evil. Conscience,
therefore, is as fundamental to the makeup of the infant as the
startle reflex.

• The values, prohibitions and standards taught by parents
and society (church, school, television, etc.) are, at most, second
and third-level tiers of conscience. These teachings and dictates
become integrated into conscience only insofar as they are presented in a loving context, and only then to the degree that they
conform to and reinforce the original body of love that created
the conscience. Thus, parental and social values and dictates
that do not conform to the individual's seminal conscience are
rejected. Similarly, when societal values change, the individual
conscience remains relatively constant, homeostatic, seeking always to maintain the balance advocated by the love that created,
not just conscience, but being itself.

• The creational, seminal love that forms and informs conscience continues growth throughout a lifetime, but is substantially formed by mid-teen years (14-16). The existence of this
seminal conscience is the reason that it is reasonable for society to
hold each person responsible for his/her own behavior. Though
parental figures and society are secondary and tertiary formational influences, at the deepest heart level, the seminal conscience
always knows right (love) from wrong (non-love), even when it is
incorrectly taught by parents and society.

• The effect of guilt is to activate conscience so as to block and stop the flow of life-giving love in that area of the psychospiritual heart responsible for the particular decision to violate love. In a relatively healthy heart, that blockage of love causes pain, a "pang" of guilt. When the pain of guilt reaches consciousness, its purpose is to signal the need for repentance and atonement — reconciliation of the heart with itself, and a return to the natural state of an innocent, loving heart, called peace. Any deliberate anti-loving act (sin) creates a blockage and stoppage of love, which, in turn, splits the heart, separating the loving, alive body of the heart from the part which is threatened with a love-starved death. This painful split, and the temporarily "moribund" area of the heart that stopped loving, explains the gloomy, "dead," grief- and depression-like feelings that accompany severe guilt. But atonement is the saving grace that heals the split. To "atone" means to make amends or reparation. The origin of the word "atone" is the middle English *atonen,* or "at one." The heart that was split by a love violation is made whole, at one, reconciled with itself by atonement. Only when the heart is without guilt, *at one* with itself, alive with integrity, can it find peace. (Note: Though professional therapists may be uncomfortable with the religious sound of a word like "atonement," I use it here because it seems like fundamental good psychology. In comparison, the last three Explanations are straightforward spiritual principles.)

• True guilt and false guilt must be distinguished. A huge preponderance of guilt suffered by people with emotional problems is utterly false. False guilt, at the emotional level, feels exactly like real guilt, even though in reality the person did nothing that was actually wrong. Rather, the person was *forced* to feel guilt. Sexual abuse victims, especially, but victims of any abuse will invariably suffer false guilt. The guilt that victims feel appropriately belongs to the abuser, for guilt was inherent in the abuser's acts. (Thus, if someone throws a bucket of mud on you, you will *feel* dirty even though you in no way caused yourself to be dirty.)

• The array of defenses utilized to cope with both real and false guilt run the gamut: denial, projection onto others, intellectualization, isolation of affect, dissociation, self-punishment, rationalization, etc. Powerful love, and a counselor's absolute non-judgmentalism, can melt and cut through defenses. Analysis alone can never relieve a whit of guilt, and may in fact serve to strengthen defenses. Love alone heals the guilty heart.

• For adults seeking relief from guilt, it is imperative that they know precisely what they have done wrong, and why it is wrong, viz., precisely how they deliberately violated love. Too often, adults operate on consciences that were falsely or incompletely formed as children. When guilt is found to be real, it is also imperative that the degrees of culpability (responsibility) versus inculpability be determined. Many immoral acts that are objectively called "sin" or "crime," when mercifully viewed in the context of an emotional disorder, must be called "symptoms."

• Just as love is inherently free and freeing (Principle Four), in order for an objectively immoral act, a love violation, to be called a sin or a crime, the act of violating love must meet two requirements: (1) Free, full consent of the will, and (2) full knowledge that the act is wrong, anti-loving. To the degree that either of these requirements is missing, culpability is missing, and to that same degree there is no real guilt.

• Because the law of love is absolute, severe guilt following a great love violation inherently proves the human need for absolution, the restoration of innocence, the return of the heart to the normal state of loving. Absolution, authentic resolution of severe guilt, without God, is a therapeutic impossibility. The person suffering from catastrophic guilt caused by unspeakably evil acts may incur damage at a depth of the psychospiritual heart that can only be called "mystery." For a therapist to presume that he/she has the skill to penetrate and know that mystery, reach the guilt, provide forgiveness and absolution, and restore that heart to love and peace is the epitome of hubris, the presumption that the therapist is God. A therapist who does not believe in God, or one who feels unable to lead a guilty patient to God by spiritual counseling, is ethically bound to acknowledge that limitation and to refer the person for qualified spiritual guidance.

• Unresolved catastrophic guilt may totally block the flow of love (life) in the heart, producing intolerable feelings of anguished, unrelenting death. If the person can find no hope for resolving the guilt, the state of *anomie* (normlessness; no way to turn; disoriented emptiness) may ensue, which is one short step from suicide. At that point, the only therapist who can prevent suicide is one who her/himself believes, at heart level, that God can and will forgive *anything*.

• The conscience of the atheist, agnostic, or nihilist suffering severe guilt obviously must be respected. Yet, the conundrum presented by these nonbelievers is this: "Forgiving one's self" for terrible love violations inevitably proves impossible, but meanwhile, neither can the person affirm any "Higher Power" or "Supreme Being" who could forgive him. Even boxed in by such an apparently hopeless dilemma, love offers hope. The self-evident "heart-reaching" nature of love transcends theologies, philosophies and reason itself. Often, an avowed nonreligious person can affirm "love as the highest power," while remaining unable to believe in a personal God. The return of a nonbeliever to a belief in "love," however she/he defines it, transcends religious argument, and may result in the relief of guilt at the deepest spiritual mystery level of the heart (even while, paradoxically, the person continues to intellectually disclaim belief in anything spiritual).

• Over the past several decades, as never before in history, values and the concept of guilt have been politicized and diluted by controversy. Name any high moral value and one can find a strong social lobby attacking that value. All this social turmoil about what is right and wrong directly causes emotional problems. Increasingly, people come into therapy with hearts torn by guilt, but thoroughly confused by the politics of it. Yet, no matter how debated or watered down guilt issues might become, the individual heart *knows* when it has violated love. The voice of conscience, love's protector, does not allow dilution, equivocation, political compromise or escape. Its indictments and verdicts are absolute because love is absolute. When we have transgressed the law of love, we know it — absolutely. For this reason, both psychologically and spiritually, guilt can be resolved, erased, only by *absolution*. Interestingly, that word derives from the Latin, *absolutio*, which means "acquittal." Even in ancient languages, guilty hearts knew they needed forgiveness that is as definitive as a trial and acquittal by judge and jury, an absolute declaration of "not guilty" or "forgiven and no longer guilty." Obviously, the easiest way to resolve guilt, for those who believe, is to go straight to God for absolution. For nonbelievers, as the prior Explanation describes, love can still bring absolution. Only love absolves guilt.

If there are any emotional problems in which guilt is not a major issue, it's not many. In therapy, I seem to be hearing someone's confession just about every day. No, I am not a priest, but as a therapist discussing guilt, I sometimes speak very directly of God. Is that a scientific sin?

Whatever Became of Sin?[1] Nearly forty years ago, the eminent psychiatrist Karl Menninger asked that question. Menninger beautifully explicated the relationship of sin and guilt to emotional disorders. But did the professional community listen? Doubtful. "Sin" is still considered an "unprofessional" word. We also know that there is no professionally designated category of mental/emotional disturbance called "Guilty Conscience," though, beyond doubt, some emotional problems are purely attributable to that malady. The professional psychological and spiritual (clerical) worlds still do not see that their realms must be reconciled. Toward the end of his book on sin, obviously feeling the pinch from both sides, Menninger asked, "Will the clergy tell me, a psychiatric cobbler, to stick to my last? And will not my own

---

[1] Karl Menninger, *Whatever Became of Sin?* (New York: Bantam 1978 edition/ Hawthorn Books, Inc., 1973).

colleagues perhaps endorse that prescription, with some raised eyebrows about my fall from scientific grace?"[2]

Menninger was not refuted; he was simply ignored — and that, I believe, was a professional sin. But sin is still not recognized by many professionals; for many, God is still a defense mechanism ("projection," as Freudians would call it); and guilt is merely an id-superego conflict that can be scientifically manipulated and analytically reduced to nothingness. But the graceful Dr. Menninger wryly predicted that he would receive no more than a "raised eyebrow." Why? Because "Science" remains god. Surely Menninger must have laughed at his mild jibe at his colleagues as he wrote of his fall from "scientific grace." Science is a god dispensing grace? That's funny!

But it is not at all funny when a patient has committed some unspeakable act, is devastated by guilt, on the verge of suicide, and has a Science-adoring therapist who relies solely on his own great skills and will not even consider a spiritual approach to the suicidal guilt.

Who is the counselor, speaking only on his own authority, who can say to the father who set fire to and immolated his child, "You are forgiven"? Who is the analyst who can say to the mass murderer, "I forgive you," and not be laughed at? A mother has sold her eleven-year-old daughter to a pimp; where is the behaviorist who can devise a behavior modification program to dissolve her guilt? The purpose of such hard rhetorical questions is certainly not to criticize any particular school of therapy. Rather, it is to demonstrate that when human beings commit inhuman acts that are so barbaric, so vile, so evil that the guilt they incur is correspondingly scarlet, gut-ripping and deadly, there is no personality theory and no therapy that is merely "psychological" which can, by itself, ever effectively ameliorate such guilt, much less provide soul-cleansing absolution. Guilt of such huge proportions can be absolved only by authentic spiritual experience (as described in the last three Explanations).

---

[2]   *Ibid.*, p. 265.

When positions like the above are presented, there is the inevitable risk that some will respond by categorizing love therapy as pastoral counseling or as *solely* a spiritual approach. Let me hasten to reaffirm that that is not the case. For too long, love has been left languishing in churches, saving the saved. In fact, the intent of love therapy is to bring love down-to-earth, *out* of the pulpits, and yes, out of the confessional box, and down to the ordinary human street level where it is most needed. Love is a psychospiritual reality. It just happens that when we treat colossal guilt, reality demands that we focus more on the spiritual than the psychological levels of love.

When some professional therapists view love therapy's guilt principle and its focus on Conscience, they may ask immediately, "What happened to the Superego, the Freudian theory almost all of us have followed for years?" Answer: It's gone, discarded, placed in the good-riddance file along with other sophistic and silly theories like phrenology, the orgone box, the four humors, blood-letting, and chaining the mentally ill. The superego theory is simply not true. Love's Guilt Principle revivifies the Conscience, and grounds its creation and development from earliest infancy in the concept of seminal love.

The radical difference between the origins of the superego and the origin of seminal love define utterly distinct views of the nature of human beings. In several previous principles, I have shown that the psychospiritual heart, not the unconscious, is the fundamental structure of the person. The superego, together with the id and ego which comprised the Freudian unconscious, must be deemed invalid concepts accordingly. It may be helpful to specifically compare Freud's superego with the love therapy conscience and its seminal love.

In Freud's view, the superego evolved out of the id, the sexual and aggressive instincts that formed the initial nucleus of personhood. The superego grows as one outcome of the resolution of the Oedipus complex; the child incorporates the image of the same-sex parent, and this internal representation of the parent becomes the prohibitor of unacceptable impulses, the ego-alien impulses of the id. Granted, my summary of superego theory is extremely abbreviated, but it does contain Freud's fundamental ideas on the superego.[3] It is only those elementary concepts that are crucial in our comparison of love therapy's conscience and seminal love with Freud's superego.

First, the conscience in no way evolves out of physical instincts, sexual or otherwise. Rather, the infant is born with a psychospiritual heart which is intrinsic to personhood, i.e., the child is born with a central core of love which is as much a part of personhood as breathing. That love, by definition (viz., love as a movement toward goodness) provides the infant with a lifelong drive toward what is *good*. In other words, the baby is born *good*, and therefore intrinsically knows the difference between good and evil before taking its first breath. It is that original seminal love, *infused* by virtue of creation (Divine Love), which is the primary foundation of conscience.

Quickly, parenthetically, it might be noted that the paragraph above not only refutes Freudian atheistic ideas, but it may be interpreted as a criticism of a lot of Christian theological teaching. Many churches place so much emphasis on "Original Sin" that they seem to totally overlook the fact that human beings are created by and thus born with "original love." Some churches, in fact, seem to teach people that they were born evil. That is an idea that is not just as silly as Freud's sexual instinct (id) theory, it is a repugnant, pernicious idea that causes pathological guilt, false guilt.

Back to the superego again.... Note that the superego's abiding substance, the only guidelines for right and wrong, and the *final* determinants for whether the person will experience guilt, are solely the incorporated parental and societal representations of what is prohibited. In comparison, per the third Explanation, love therapy views parental and social influences within the

---

[3] *The Basic Writings of Sigmund Freud*, Dr. A.A. Brill, Ed. (New York: Random House, Modern Library, 1938, 1966), pp. 12-13, 859-861.

conscience as, certainly not unimportant, but second- and third-level forces. The primary substance of the conscience is the body of original love that *forms* the person, the conscience being one of several important and *integral* functions of that love.

How the conscience develops, the interplay of the original seminal love and parental influences, how and why that seminal love in some people becomes so buried beneath mountains of pain that it seems nonexistent (as in sociopaths, for example), the role that conscience plays in each emotional disorder — these and a hundred questions need exploration. In the following, we can focus on only the more common problems involving guilt and conscience that surface in counseling. Of these, none is more common than three forms of false guilt.

Forms of False Guilt

False guilt, as an emotion, feels exactly the same as real guilt; yet, its origin is diametrically opposite. Authentic guilt is a freely chosen, internally generated response of the heart to a love-violation by the person him- or herself; thus, real guilt is a free act of love by the person's own conscience which is intended to restore and heal love. Contrariwise, false guilt is not freely chosen, and the person feeling it has not violated nor damaged love in any way. False guilt is guilt that a person is *made* to feel, *forced* to feel by another person, even though the one feeling it is absolutely innocent. The conscience of a person who has been forced to feel false guilt has been short-circuited, either bypassed entirely or manipulated into sending the heart a lie, a "guilty" message when there has been no personal wrongdoing.

There are three distinctly different origins of false guilt, each of which plays an enormous role in many emotional disorders:

Learned False Guilt — Needless and baseless guilt is too often taught to children by parents. Guilt-producing beliefs that are simply untrue, and attitudes based on cognitive errors, are often passed from generation to generation. How many non-orgasmic women have counselors seen whose mothers taught them that "sex is dirty" and that only "loose" women (guilty ones) enjoyed sex? Too many. Perfectionist parents, making impossible demands, produce anxiety-laden, workaholic children who are filled with false guilt because they are not perfect. The moral theological errors that "self-love is a sin of pride" and "the virtue of humility means that you shouldn't like yourself very much" doom children to false guilt and low self-esteem.

Abuse-Inherent False Guilt — The guilt and shame that are invariable and inherent concomitants of rape, incest and all sexual, physical and verbal abuse may be the most difficult forms of false guilt to understand, both for the victims themselves, and for society at large. A woman is abducted off the street, raped and battered. She screams and fights, but there is absolutely nothing she can do. Afterward, what is the strongest, most painful emotion she feels? Shame. Guilt. But guilt is an emotion that tells us we have done something wrong; what did she do wrong? Absolutely nothing. Nevertheless, her shame is overwhelming. The rape victim then meets in a group of women, all of whom were sexually abused. She hears a sixty-year-old who was molested at age five describe guilt she has hidden all her life, and she hears incest, date-rape, marriage-rape and childhood molestation victims all describe the same feelings of guilt. Finally, the group unanimously agrees that not one of them did *anything* wrong, and that there is no objective reason any of them should feel guilty. But what do they feel? Guilt! Shame! Do they realize it is false guilt? Yes — but they still feel it. So where does the guilt come from? The guilt was inherent in the acts of abuse they sustained.

If I push you face-first into a stack of cow manure, you're going to feel dirty and smelly no matter how clean you were before. Any abusive act inherently contains and imparts guilt just like that manure. A victim of verbal, physical or sexual abuse feels guilt because they were *forced, made to feel* emotions they were never intended to feel. The false guilt that victims feel actually belongs to the victimizer as real guilt that was inherent in violent acts.

Deprivation-Induced False Guilt — Early childhood love deprivation, euphemistically called emotional deprivation, induces a subtle, insidious form of guilt that causes the person to feel guilty for *everything* — for "living," for "breathing," for "being." In counseling, this is the most difficult form of guilt to heal because it is so totally elusive; the guilt can be linked to no particular event, person, age or place. It is like struggling to grab a fistful of wind, or more precisely, a vacuum. Earlier, we noted that the opposite of love is not hatred, it is nothingness — and that is exactly the source of the problem, the terrible emptiness caused by love-starvation.

Talking to love-deprived little children, there is a word that almost every one of them uses to describe their most basic feeling: "bad." If you ask them why they feel "bad," many of them will immediately answer, "Cause I'm bad." These sad little kids intuitively know their ontology very well, if not their logic. They know that love is a movement toward the *good*, and that the opposite of good is bad, so if they are not being loved, it "logically" follows that it must be because they are "bad." In very young children, the nebulousness of this unnamed guilt is still fresh, so if you ask, "What did you do bad?" they will very typically say, "Somethin'!" They can never quite name what that "somethin'" is that they've done that was so bad.

In later life, love-deprived adults, saturated as they are with guilt feelings that stemmed from "nothing" will sometimes actually *do* something bad in order to find some temporary solace, some "something" that is bad that enables them to say, "Aha! *That's* why I feel guilty!" Yet, because the false guilt was born of non-love, nothingness, love-deprived adults scour their souls and flagellate themselves looking for real guilt, but end up back at square one feeling guilty for nothing and "everything." If *any* thing goes wrong for *any* body, the love-deprived adult will automatically say, "I'm sorry."

Obviously, there are multifarious dimensions of all three forms of false-guilt — symptoms, cognitive errors and compensatory defenses and actions — a thousand blind alleys that can lead both victim and therapist on that many wild goose chases. Dealing with false guilt must begin by recognizing that the *feeling* is quite real — "Yes, you feel guilty" — and that guilt always derives from a love violation. But the real question is, who did the violating? Certainly it was not the victim. Yet, and sadly, it is the victim who has the task of "letting go" of that false guilt, and that "letting go" is called "forgiveness." Granted, the very idea of forgiving a rapist, forgiving a parent who battered me, forgiving a child molester who created shame that very nearly ruined my life, or forgiving a parent who refused to give me the elementary love that I had an absolute right to expect, seems outrageously unfair, virtually impossible. And the fact is, it *is* unfair. It is, nevertheless, the *only* way to heal false guilt. Indeed, often, the forgiveness that is required to heal false guilt is beyond human capacity and can only be called supra-human, or spiritual. Forgiving the most terrible levels of false guilt is as outrageous as the most "impossible" and humanly "absurd" Christian admonitions: "Return good for evil," "Pray for those who persecute you," and the craziest of all, "Love your enemies." God knows I hate preaching, but I must say what I believe: without God forgiving for us, in us, we are often stuck with the false guilt and other unfair effects of the most heinous abuses. Forgiveness is always possible and available to us (and in Principle Fourteen, "Unforgiveness blocks healing," we'll see that it is absolutely essential to emotional health).

The final Explanation describes the politicization of guilt and resulting moral relativism, confusion, and worldwide controversy about right and wrong, as social problems that directly cause emotional disorders. Notwithstanding the relativism, the principle defines the psychospiritual heart as invariably *knowing*, in an absolute way, when it is guilty, and when it is in need of absolution, not relative but absolute forgiveness, acquittal. Thus, says the principle, so long as the human heart remains, hope remains that nations will not implode under the weight of their own corruption. That microcosmic view of the Explanation is true enough, but it does not provide answers to the two crises mentioned: what do you *do* about the moral relativism and the mushrooming crime and social problems that result from it? And at the individual level, what do you *do* to help people who have committed unspeakably vile, inhuman acts, resolve very real guilt that is killing their souls?

Love alone absolves guilt, but when that guilt is horrendous, people seem to know that there is no nifty psychological formula that can provide a quick fix. Intuitively, by listening to the whispers of conscience, every heart seems to know that, proportionate to any horrible crime or sin, a correspondingly proportionate amount of suffering must be undergone as atonement. That suffering may be in the form of x-amount of time, or x-degree of intensity of acutely feeling the scourge of the guilt. In some countries, atonement may require an actual scourge — as with the flagellants who whip themselves bloody on Good Friday in reparation for their sins. Whatever the method, atonement, self-forgiveness, and letting go of guilt seems to demand suffering. Why? If love alone absolves guilt, what is the connection between love and suffering?

The fifth Explanation, which describes the "blockage," and "stoppage" of the flow of love in the heart that is caused by guilt, inherently describes suffering. That Explanation depicts the psychospiritual heart as "split" by virtue of guilt cutting off the love-supply. One cannot fail to find an analogy in a physical "heart-attack" when the blood supply is cut off in a blocked artery. In both the physical and psychospiritual heart, when the life-giving nutrient is cut off — physical blood or psychospiritual love — the heart responds with pain, and suffering continues till the blockage is removed. Suffering, of itself, does not remove guilt; it is, however, an inevitable and necessary symptom, something that we must be willing to endure in the process of facing and admitting guilt, renouncing evil (my anti-loving act), and returning to love. It is love, not suffering, that absolves guilt.

But the process of absolution begins with facing guilt forthrightly, saying, *"Mea maxima culpa"* ("Through my great fault"), that is, admitting culpability, dropping all the excuses (defenses), admitting what I have done wrong, expressing sorrow, and setting a new course to rectify my heart. That dropping of defenses, the willingness to finally be honest and to open my heart, inevitably involves suffering. Harkening back to the analogy of the physical heart, open heart surgery automatically brings pain. Undergoing "open heart" to remove a guilt blockage can be excruciating. It takes tremendous courage.

Compassion and Aggressive Compassion

"Courage," let us recall, is derived from the French, *cœur*, meaning "heart." That realization points to the agonizing dilemma and the huge need of the person struggling with catastrophic guilt. With a heart that is split, blocked, the person has access to only a fraction of a normal heart at the very time when he/she most needs courage, a great heart, in order to face the guilt. The answer to the dilemma is obvious: alone, the guilt-plagued person may be truly helpless. The trap in which the person has ensnared the self, which can happen to any of us, is poignant proof that no man is an island. The love that can heal the greatest guilt always must come from someone other than the guilty person themselves. This love — from counselor, clergy, or friend — is the power of mercy that can "enhearten," "encourage," put new heart in to someone who may have well-nigh ruined his own heart. This is one of the most powerful acts of love. It is called "compassion."

> The word compassion is derived from Latin words *pati* and *cum*, which together mean 'to suffer with.' Compassion asks us to go where it hurts, to enter into places of pain, to share in brokenness, fear, confusion, and anguish. Compassion challenges us to cry out with those in misery, to mourn with those who are lonely, to

weep with those in tears. Compassion requires us to be weak with the weak, vulnerable with the vulnerable, and powerless with the powerless.[4]

And, I must add, compassion requires us to be guilty with the guilty. The compassionate spirit which must be a constant pursuit in love therapy is beautifully captured in the mere title of Henri Nouwen's *The Wounded Healer*.[5] Automatically, that title calls forth images of humility, mildness, mercy, non-judgmentalism and acceptance — all attributes of love that are essential to good therapy. The wounded healer "must look after his own wounds but at the same time be prepared to heal the wounds of others."[6] When a person has faced and accepted responsibility for personal guilt, a wounded healer intersubjectively shares the burden, suffering with the guilty person, but bringing courage by merging her or his (mostly, let's hope) healed heart with the damaged and split heart of the one who is guilty. There is virtually nothing that is objective or scientific about the actual healing of guilt. Love is a "communion," "an experience of intersubjectivity," "an interpenetration of beings." A wounded healer's compassion further defines love as a heart-to-heart with-ness in suffering.

There is, though, another form of compassion that sometimes is required in order to reach and help people who are blatantly guilty, but in denial, rationalizing, using a thousand silly excuses to justify even vile and vicious behavior that could never be rationally justified. In people who are guilty of abuse — physical, sexual, verbal or substance abuse — denial of guilt is very common, and denied guilt is not amenable to ordinary, mild compassion. With those who are denying or otherwise defending

---

[4]   Donald P. McNeill, Douglas A. Morrison, and Henri J.M. Nouwen, *Compassion: A Reflection on the Christian Life* (Garden City, NY: Doubleday, 1982), p. 4.

[5]   Henri J.M. Nouwen, *The Wounded Healer* (Garden City, NY: Image Books, Doubleday, 1979).

[6]   *Ibid.*, p. 82.

against the acknowledgment of real guilt, love therapy utilizes "aggressive compassion."

Aggressive compassion is confrontational love. For those who still hold on to the mistaken popular notions that love is always sweet, or in any way weak, aggressive compassion and confrontational love may be difficult to grasp — for the first goal of this love is to enable the person to experience pain. The love does *not* cause the pain. Rather, it simply recognizes the truth, that a severe love violation has blocked and split the heart of the guilty person, that that split is *already* causing pain, and that the person is using defenses, excuses and rationalizations in order to avoid experiencing that pain. Compassion recognizes that so long as both guilt and pain are hidden, they cannot be healed. The abusive one has erected walls around conscience. Aggressive compassion offers love through tough confrontation, saying in effect, or directly, "Look, you're guilty as hell and I still love you. But you've buried your conscience, friend, so here, use mine for a while." Only a wounded healer can say, "You're guilty as hell!" while allowing the guilty person to recognize that he/she is not being judged, that it is one's guilt, not one's personhood that is being confronted. The wounded healer, too, has suffered guilt, survived, and can say with aggressive compassion that melts defenses, "It takes one to know one."

Politicized Guilt

The last Explanation addresses guilt in the social context, specifically the way it can be politicized and diluted. The holocaust of Nazi Germany is perhaps the classic example of how an entire people can be charmed and bamboozled into believing that barbarous evil is somehow good, guiltless. Through the 1960's in the United States and till the early '90's in South Africa, racism, even including lynching, and the firebomb murder of children in churches, was deemed "guiltless" on the basis of abstruse, misinterpreted biblical verses. Skinheads and white supremacists still use such "righteous" politics. Today, too, the blood of innocent gun victims floods the streets, but gun sales increase — guiltlessly — politicized by the National Rifle Association's propaganda. Most churches still teach that premarital sex is wrong, but the explosion of illegitimate teenage births, and the huge majority of sexually active young people, testify to the more persuasive and explicit sexual rhetoric of TV videos and soaps, rap songs and movies. Within the past thirty years, the increase of moral relativism seems to have generated a new social law, comparable to a perverse law of physics: for every traditional moral value taught, there is an equal and opposite societal promotion of an immoral value — except the latter is a better financed lobby. There are, in fact, some who advocate the abolition of guilt altogether, preaching that if you ever feel guilty about anything at all, there's something wrong with you.

Yet, despite all efforts to escape, dilute, or deny it, the enormity of the world's guilt hangs like a huge pall over each of us, darkening our vision. Millstones of guilt, miraculously borne on the winds of the media, are hung on our necks with each newscast. It becomes part of daily life, like taking out the garbage, to rid ourselves of the world's guilt, try to not see it, try to not feel its weight. Daily, we mention the latest serial murders, or the latest genocide, drug war or any of a thousand atrocities, agree that "Oh, that's terrible!" — and then promptly forget it. And indeed, who can blame us? Who, in fact, can even *express* what this amalgamation of societal guilt feels like?

Amorphous World Guilt

It is not psychotherapists nor sociologists who can express the effect of the world's guilt on each of us, nor is it they who can express the heart of excruciating guilt suffered by one who has committed a terrible crime or sin. It is always the task of art to express the inexpressible.

The poet T.S. Eliot, in *Murder in the Cathedral*, voices the horror of the world's guilt when the King's knights murder Thomas Becket, the Archbishop of Canterbury. The King demands obedience. Thomas responds, "I give my life to the Law of God above the Law of Man." Thomas dies a martyr. Eliot's Chorus, speaking for the world, then cries out, enunciating guilt as never before nor since:

CHORUS: Clear the air! Clean the sky! Wash the wind!
Take stone from stone and wash them.
The land is foul, the water is foul, our beasts and ourselves defiled with blood.
In life there is not time to grieve long.
But this, this is out of life, this is out of time,
An instant eternity of evil and wrong.
We are soiled by a filth we cannot clean,
united to supernatural vermin,
It is not we alone, it is not the house,
it is not the city that is defiled,
But the world that is wholly foul.
Clear the air! clean the sky! wash the wind! take the stone from the stone, take the skin from the arm, take the muscle from the bone, and wash them. Wash the stone, wash the bone, wash the brain, wash the soul, wash them, wash them![7]

This chorus was intoned, I believe, not just when Thomas Becket was slain, but after the deaths of Lincoln, John and Bobby Kennedy, Martin Luther King, Jr., Egypt's Anwar Sadat, Italy's Aldo Moro, and Israel's Itzhak Rabin, after the near-total genocide of the Native American race, during the slaughters in Nazi Germany, Cambodia and Rwanda and after the deaths of millions of other good people who were assassinated, but more immediately:

---

[7] T.S. Eliot, *Murder in the Cathedral* (Harcourt, Brace, 1935) in Maynard Mack, Ed., *World Masterpieces*, Vol. 2 (New York: W.W. Norton, 1956), pp. 2206-2244.

that chorus of pain, sorrow and guilt is sung every day by mental patients longing to express soul-grinding guilt in tearful words instead of symptoms — and still more, it is spoken by every one of us every day as we struggle to survive in a "world that is wholly foul." Guilt's Chorus is us.

The "open universe" described in Principle Seven means that we are all connected so that each person's acts of love accrue to the benefit of all humanity. By virtue of that same openness, the weight of each person's guilt is borne by all. We cannot pick up a newspaper without guilt rubbing off on us. We fight the feeling, but the world's guilt, an amorphous slime, seeps into our bones. The guilty world is a hard, hard way of life. We say we do not deserve the world's guilt, and that is both true and not true. Yet, we all violate love, so we are part of it.

But where is hope? How can we cope? What is it that can wash the bone, wash the brain, wash the soul? It is, of course, the daily absolution that only love can provide. Love alone can cleanse us and thus allow sanity for any of us. The hope of which we can be very certain is this: despite our foulest deeds, love will continue to wash the world and to keep it beautiful — and us, too, if we can allow it.

CHAPTER FOURTEEN

Unforgiveness Blocks Healing

Principle Fourteen: Unforgiveness Blocks Healing

Forgiveness is an essential prerequisite for healing every emotional wound or disorder. Unforgiveness blocks healing. Healing of each heart wound underlying a disorder can be accomplished only if that wound is exposed, open, vulnerable, and love-accessible. Culpable unforgiveness requires judgment of another person or self; it is a deliberate choice of hatred, bitterness, the venomous desire for revenge — all of which are antithetical to love. Inculpable unforgiveness, though never chosen, must be replaced by the choice of forgiveness if healing is to become possible. Once unforgiveness is chosen or incurred, it fills the wound of the heart and saturates the memory of the experience, thus excluding the possibility of love reaching and healing the wound.

Explanations

• Culpable differs from inculpable unforgiveness in that the former always includes hatred, and is always the act of a responsible adult who makes a free choice with sufficient knowledge to have chosen to forgive. Inculpable unforgiveness was never a matter of choice, so the person is not responsible for its presence — although responsibility and forgiveness must be achieved if healing is to become possible.

• Culpable unforgiveness derives primarily from judgmental-ism. Such unforgiveness always includes a moral judgment of the one perceived as inflicting injury. That judgment is actually a fivefold act: (1) a conclusion is drawn regarding the interior motives of the injuring party (which typically requires "mind-reading"); (2) a conclusion is made that the injuring party is morally "bad" and deserves punishment; (3) a conclusion is induced that the injuring party judged the one injured; (4) an erroneous conclusion is reached that a "counter-judgment" is needed to maintain the integrity of the heart; and (5) a conclusion is reached that the injured one has the right to act as a judge who has the godlike right and capacity to both unerringly understand and to thereby render judgment on the heart of another human being.

• The purpose of unforgiveness is always self-righteous justification, pseudo-love of self, the artificial propping up and inflation of self by using an inflexible negative judgment: hatred. The purpose of this rush to judgment is to fabricate "adjudicated definitive proof" that the real or imagined negative judgment by the injuring party is untrue, and that, on the contrary, the unforgiving one is good and lovable. Ironically, therefore, the purpose of unforgiving hatred is love, albeit pseudo.

• There are two forms of inculpable unforgiveness: (1) unforgiveness that is inherent to repressed heart wounds, i.e., forgiveness that I am not even aware I need to accomplish, and (2) conscious, hate-filled unforgiveness which was induced by parents or authority figures, usually by teaching, which occurred without the person's volition and/or without knowing the reason for the hatred. In the latter, the person may be consciously aware of hating, but feels impelled to do so by false "righteousness" incorrectly taught by parents, or, the hatred may be totally automatic, "just there," for reasons that have been totally repressed. This might be called "false hatred," analogous to false guilt. (Often, racial and ethnic hatreds are examples of inculpable unforgiveness; taught by parental example, children grow up hating another race, religion or nationality, never having had the opportunity to think out "why." The children are wounded by their hatred.

Though they did not choose the hatred, they must nevertheless assume responsibility for it, and let go of that hatred if they are to be healed. That letting-go is called forgiveness.)

• It is important to distinguish normal anger, both conscious and repressed, from hatred and culpable unforgiveness. The differentiating determinant is not intensity of emotion, but intention, choice. Anger and rage are *reactions*, normal human responses to love violations (even though rage is infantile). Hatred and unforgiveness are *actions*, initiatives, free choices of judgmentalism.

• Authentic forgiveness is not possible prior to the expression and ventilation of nonjudgmental anger (cf., Principle Twelve on anger).

• Anger, the appropriate and natural human response to injustice, can be pictured as flowing from a wound in the heart. Once the anger is expressed, without judgment, it leaves an open heart wound which, though painful, is accessible to healing love.

• When wounds are sustained in childhood and then repressed, mere recall of the wound will not produce healing. Rather, once a childhood wound is identified, the normal human responses to heart injury — pain and anger — must be allowed to surface and be experienced. Then forgiveness must be accomplished if healing is to occur. Thus, unforgiveness blocks healing even when we are not aware we need to forgive.

• Unforgiveness plays a major role in virtually every emotional disorder. The more chronic, resistant to treatment, and intractable the disorder is, the more likely it is that unforgiveness is a major factor blocking healing.

• The one who is the object of unforgiveness is always perceived as more powerful than the unforgiving person in some significant way. Hence, any person or group who is perceived as a threat — to security, life, self-esteem, or any facet of love — may become an object of entrenched, unforgiving hatred. The felt "need" for hatred is directly proportionate to one or more of the love deficits of the one who hates. In general (though not always), those who hate most have been loved least.

- Pseudo-forgiveness, e.g., "forgiveness" propelled by even the most well-intentioned religious motive, is often detectable by the presence of seething anger remaining just below the surface of consciousness. Repressing or suppressing anger is no substitute for forgiveness, authentic pardoning, the conscious, deliberate repudiation of the judgment once made.

- The conscious choice of judgmentalism, hatred and unforgiveness is the simultaneous choice to inflict an emotional wound or even a disorder upon oneself. The biblical admonition, "Judge not, lest you be judged,"[1] is not just a spiritual caution; it is a basic human intrapsychic law. Judgments, hatreds and unforgiveness are dynamic, virulent forces that invariably boomerang, poison the soul and thus inflict suffering upon the perpetrator. To judge another is to judge and sentence oneself to a living death, for the violence of hatred ravages the heart. Some emotional disorders are solely attributable to self-induced judgment.

- To forgive means to refuse to judge. To forgive means that we pardon, grant clemency, have mercy, let go of anger and of any claim of a right to revenge or punishment. To forgive is to repudiate and forsake any prior judgment. However, to forgive does not mean to deny that I have been hurt; it is not to deny that I have suffered injustice; it is not to deny that my love was violated, not to deny that I have been sinned against, not to say that the one who hurt me was not wrong, and not to say that I have no right to be angry. Rather, to forgive is to "be angry, and to sin not."[2] To forgive is to *be* angry, and *then* to let go of that anger.

- Forgiveness and unforgiveness both emanate from the deeper reaches of the heart wherein our psychology stretches thin and we find ourselves dealing with the spiritual dimensions of our beings. Thus, for most people, forgiveness of self or others often brings God into the discussion. Atheists, materialists, and other nonbelievers, if they can affirm Love as a Prime Mover in their

---

[1]   Matthew 7:11.

[2]   Ephesians 4:26.

lives, can achieve forgiveness when all else has failed. Whatever the belief system, however, it must be acknowledged that forgiveness is one of the highest forms of love, and that unforgiveness is the most deadly violation of love.

Most people would identify themselves as being to some degree "religious," and most would identify big-time forgiveness, both receiving and giving it, as involving God. In order to demonstrate the relationship of unforgiveness to emotional disorders, we might picture a man in prayer. This man has been badly hurt, heart-wounded; he is full of hatred for the people who hurt him, and he is adamantly unforgiving. Racked by pain, though, he reaches out to God, pleading, using both hands to gesture. With his right arm extended and hand open, he says, "Oh, God, I am in agony; heal me, love me, fill my wounded heart with your love and take this pain away; heal me!" But with his left hand clenched in an angry fist, blocking his heart, he adds, "But don't take away my hatred!" Thus, God Himself, respecting the person's freedom, cannot heal the man.

The form of love that heals guilt is called *receiving* forgiveness. Forgiveness is love that cleanses. The form of love that heals anger is called *giving* forgiveness. Forgiveness is love that pardons, refuses to judge, lets go. It becomes clearer, doesn't it? Guilt and anger are closely-related emotions, two expressions of the same wounded heart whose love was hurt, both healed in the same way, through forgiveness received or forgiveness given.

Forgiveness

What is forgiveness? For reference, a dictionary definition of "forgive" is: "to excuse for a fault or offense; to renounce anger or resentment against; to absolve from payment of (e.g., a debt)."[3] Of course, that definition cannot answer the many tough questions about forgiveness, like: why is it so difficult to forgive? Why do we sometimes say we just cannot forgive ourselves or someone else? Why do we hold on to bitterness and venom that eat us up inside and poison our whole view of ourselves, others and life itself? A trickier question, one that we rarely consider is, what do we get out of unforgiveness? Why do we think, beyond all reason sometimes, that we desperately need our bitterness? Indeed, why do some people kill and commit every kind of barbarous act rather than give up their unforgiveness? Finally, there are those whom depression leads to suicide! Am I correct in saying that their unforgiveness, of self or others, is often the single driving force that proves more powerful than life itself?

In order to answer these questions, let us take as an example a depressed client who has recognized his long-repressed anger and guilt, and is ventilating it all over the counseling office, splattering rage and tears in all directions, but does not know what to do with it. Following are a series of explanations, all based on love theory, which I frequently offer. (Please note that these lengthy interpretations are never given this way in actual practice. What is shown here may be several interpretations given over several weeks, compressed into one.) Each is preceded by a typical argument that clients proffer while resisting forgiveness.

Client: Forgive them?! Oh, I just can't!

Counselor: Can't? Well, let's review.... You're saying your mother and Henry and those other jerks really hurt you. They rejected you, cut your heart out and betrayed you. They've

---

[3] *Webster's II New College Dictionary* (Boston, New York: Houghton Mifflin, 1995), p. 439.

ruined your life, you say. I suggested forgiving them, and you looked at me like I was crazy, and said, "No way! I can't!" But let me ask you, don't you mean *won't*? Well, just so you understand what you're deciding, let's look at the choices. First, it's true: you don't *have* to forgive. You've got lots of other options. One — you can put the anger right back inside you, repress it like you've been doing for years, and stay depressed. That's an option. Two — you can use the anger and go bust them all in the nose. Three — if hitting them is not enough, you could kill them. Four — you can choose not to hurt them, and not to resolve the anger, and just stay in the active rage you're in now for the rest of your life. Five — you can take the anger out on somebody else; take it out on your kids; or spend your life hitting walls. Six — you can blame God; spend your life cussing Him for creating those jerks in the first place. Or Seven — you can forgive them.

Client: Okay, okay... but I just don't know how; I don't even know what forgiveness is!

Counselor: What is forgiveness? It means to pardon, to grant free pardon for remission of an offense. Do you see the word "give" in "forgiveness"? Well, what you give is clemency, which means to give mildness, to give mercy. You read of governors giving pardons to convicted criminals. Or you read of a judge granting clemency. The judge recognizes the criminal is guilty, but eliminates the punishment anyway. That's forgiveness. When you forgive, you are a judge who refuses to judge. Right now, you're a judge who's judging, and you want to be jury and executioner, too, right? But you have the power to simply grant mercy, refuse to judge. Did you ever hear the biblical admonition, "Judge not, lest you be judged"? Why do you think it says that? Because no human being is fit to be the judge of another. Why aren't we fit? Because we aren't capable of looking deeply enough into the hearts of other people to enable us to understand their motives and to really know why they did what they did. We can't read hearts perfectly, so we don't know other people's consciences and just how culpably guilty they are, if at all. It takes perfect love to be a moral judge, and God knows none of us have that. All we can do, then, if we don't judge, is let one another go. Just let them go. Free them. Let go; that's forgiveness.

Client: If you only knew how bad they hurt me, you wouldn't ask me to forgive them!

Counselor: I'm not asking you to say they didn't hurt you. You've told me how they hurt you and I believe you completely. They did. They were jerks, skunks! What they did to you makes me angry, too. They were dead wrong! In a word, they're sinners. In this case, those sinners sinned against you. They sinned; they hurt you. You called them dirty bastards. You don't have to say they're *not* bastards. They're still sinners. Now if we agree that they are sinners, let me ask you, have you ever sinned? Well, so did I — just once. Believe that? Of course not. We all sin; we all hurt one another. I have. So have you. You've hurt people. So what do you do when you hurt somebody, sin against them? You ask for forgiveness for yourself, right? You ask the person you hurt or you ask God to forgive you, right? And if you're real sorry, you pray. You might even say the *Our Father*, the *Lord's Prayer*. Remember what it says? "Forgive us our trespasses, as (which means 'just like,' 'in the same manner,' 'to the same degree') we forgive those who trespass against us." "Forgive us our debts (our sins) as we forgive our debtors (those who sin against us)."

Stubborn Client: Can't forgive? Won't forgive? I don't know. I've tried, but I'm not forgiving.

Counselor: You know, sometimes we think we *need* our bitterness. It's like we think the unforgiveness is a friend even though it is eating our guts out, eating us alive. It's like we'd lose something if we gave it up. It's almost like we would be *wrong* to let the bad guys go unpunished. Sometimes we think that if we forgave them, it would mean they were right in what they did, hurting us. Do you know what we think unforgiveness does for us? We think it justifies us. We think we need bitterness to prove that we were right and they were wrong. They rejected me, put me *down*. So my bitterness, in my mind, keeps them down, and justifies my saying I'm better than they are, so I'm *up*, not put down. Let me say it again: you don't need your bitterness to justify being who you are. If you forgive them, it would never make them right; it just means that you show mercy to the jerks and let them go. Let them be them; let God be the judge of who they are and who you are. You just be you. That venom you're hanging on to is not your friend, and it's not doing a damn thing but hurting you.

Guilty Client: I've forgiven the others. It's *me* I hate! Me I can't forgive! I'm rotten! God could never forgive me!

Counselor: Oh? So what am I? Am I the last rotten one that God will ever forgive? Did it ever occur to you that God might just scratch His head wondering if you know more than He does, that you know the limits of His powers of forgiveness? Think now: don't you think God is loving enough to forgive anything — *any*thing?

Client: I wish I could believe that. (tears) I just can't.

On that sad and desperate note, we must pause in this explication of the dynamics of forgiveness, recognizing that we are facing a person who is in the midst of a spiritual crisis. There are times in the course of counseling when Psychology becomes an empty gas tank and simply sputters to a halt. The client quoted above was ravaged by such horrendous guilt that the only way to escape seemed to lie with God. When that happens, many therapists will stop the therapy process and refer the person to the clergy. That's fine. That surely is the best course for counselors who themselves do not believe in a spiritual dimension, or who do not feel comfortable leading a spiritually conflicted person to God and peace. As a Christian counselor, I will quickly recognize that there are some wounds that are sustained by human beings which are just too deep for human hands to touch, so to speak, and levels of agony that God alone can reach and heal. Encountering that point, if the client is comfortable with the idea, I will not hesitate to pray with the person, asking God to do the forgiveness for them and in them.

Here, though, concluding the discussion of the principle, it is necessary to reassert the principle's absoluteness: unforgiveness blocks healing absolutely — stops healing right in its tracks. In later chapters, as love therapy cases are described, the subject of unforgiveness will not always be specifically mentioned. It can be accepted as an absolute given, however, that if love's healing is ever claimed, it was only after unforgiveness and bitterness, the true villains of every emotional disorder, had been vanquished... just loved away.

CHAPTER FIFTEEN

Love Heals

Principle Fifteen: Only Love Heals Emotional Wounds

Love heals. All emotional disorders are symptomatic expressions of love damaged, love rejected, betrayed, twisted, perverted, neglected or missing. The result is a love deficit, a soul-deep wound sustained in the very center of being, the psychospiritual heart. To heal is to make whole. Love is creational: it is wholing. Love therapy seeks to find and expose the wounds, melt defenses, drain off toxic hatred that is infecting wounds, encourage forgiveness, correct love that has been distorted, and infuse healing love so as to make empty hearts whole. Therapeutic love must be authentic, skillful, accurate, timely, wise, and as transparently open, powerful and unconditional as human limits allow. Healing takes place only heart-to-heart, midst the openness of intersubjective communion, during fleeting "healing moments."

Explanations

- In counseling, objectivity is of value only insofar as it serves and guides subjectivity, heart-level action. Objectivity and science must be allowed to become defenses of neither the counselee nor the therapist.
- Every method used in the love therapy treatment process

— many models and methods of psychotherapy, psychological testing, group and milieu therapies, etc. — must be balanced and orchestrated so as to bring about those synthesized, singularly powerful, subject-to-subject, experiential events during which healing love reaches, infuses and supplants wounded love. These "healing moments" may be fleeting, so concentrated openness must be maintained in order to keep the therapeutic atmosphere heart-to-heart. (Existential "healing moments," a complex study in themselves, are described in Principle Eighteen.)

• Love does not "break" defenses (for example, by coercing a person to confront a traumatic memory that the person is too fearful to face). Rather, love melts them. All defenses — repression, dissociation, denial, projection, etc. — may be pictured as various shields, like bandages, that cover and "stick to" a wound in the heart in order to protect it from pain. Love provides the courage (new "heart") that the person needs to withstand the unavoidable pain that accompanies removing entrenched, "stuck" defenses, thus allowing a long-hidden wound to be opened wide. Love's warmth penetrates the shield and melts the adhering grasp of the defense. Because love casts out fear (Principle Eleven), the essence of defensiveness, love simply makes the defense unneeded.

• Love is creational; it adds to and enlarges the healthy heart, expanding personhood, the interior of being itself. When the heart has been wounded, slashed, part of it sometimes has been destroyed, cut away. Love is wholing, healing; it is the only "substance" capable of repairing, replenishing, and filling the missing areas of the heart. As food nourishes the body, only love can feed a hungry heart.

• When psychosis is diagnosed and no physiological cause proved, it can be presumed that a substantial part of the psychospiritual heart has sustained a near-total love deficit, viz., that a large area of the heart has been so love-starved that vital areas of personhood have been left uncreated. Only love creates the interior reality of the person, and only love allows the person to face external reality without fear. With gross love deprivation, reality becomes splintered, "schizophrenic," or subject to capacious moods, "bipolar" (manic-depressive), or unable to trust and suspicious, "paranoid." Given near-total lovelessness, the massive therapeutic infusion of love that is needed may be called "heart transplant." In psychosis, interior reality cannot be merely corrected, it must be created. Only love creates.

• Love has the power to reach *straight through* the unconscious so as to bring about heart-level healing, sometimes without a shred of unconscious memory ever being surfaced. In contrast to virtually all traditional models of therapy in which the unconscious is deemed primary, love therapy insists that healing ordinarily occurs bottom-up, not top-down; that is, wounds at the deeper heart level are healed first, and as a result, unconscious memories and repressed emotions pour out, not vice versa. Moreover, it can be accepted as axiomatic that, without love, no repressed unconscious material can ever be produced in therapy.

• Love is a light that shines into the darkness of the wounded regions of the heart. It is only when wounds are exposed to full light, gaping wide open, vulnerable and undefended, that love can infuse, fill and heal them.

• Love finds its own way, forges its own path to reach the wound in the heart. Defenses, guilt, hatred and unforgiveness cause darkness, but that darkness cannot withstand light. Love unclutters the heart, sweeping aside both conscious and unconscious distractions and trivia as surely as light chases darkness. Love then treats and heals the wound directly, often before any significant conscious understanding or unconscious memories are produced.

• Therapy, this principle says, must be infused by wisdom. Precisely how love heals will remain forever a mystery. Plumbing that mystery is the province of spirituality, beyond natural science. Thus, while pursuing and integrating the truth found through psychological research, love therapy places great weight on the discoveries of literature, art, philosophy and religion. Science produces truth at a level of empirical knowledge — fact; poets and mystics discover truth at a higher level — wisdom. Wisdom, very briefly, is a spiritual gift, the capacity to see and understand life and mysteries of the human heart, the very way that God sees them. Need we argue that a seriously disturbed, suffering soul has never been healed by facts? Wisdom knows that "at the deepest level... all things fade into mystery: *Omnia Exeuent in Mysterium*."[1] And at the heart of mystery, wisdom finds love, and discovers that it is only love that produces wisdom.

Principle Fifteen synthesizes all the previous principles into one bold, fundamental tenet, one law: "Love heals." Those two little words reflect a mountain of complexities, and perhaps a few dozen controversies. Properly understood, they could even revolutionize the mental health system, and that is the intent. That, of course, would first require changing some very old, very entrenched, and very sacrosanct ideas that form a "mindset" of the collective professional mental health community.

The first Explanation highlights several major changes in perspective that love provides. In love's healing, the principle says, objectivity must serve subjectivity. That is nearly the diametric opposite of the way the mental health system operates, and the opposite of the way many professionals think. Since the days of Freud, the mental health profession has attempted to consider itself a science, that is, primarily objective. As such, mental health schools, in psychiatry, psychiatric nursing, social work, psychology, art therapy and occupational therapy steep their students in the sciences, and as fitting final preparation for professional healing, demand that the students write a thesis or dissertation — scientific research, or a very objective treatment of a suitably scientific topic. In contrast, love, the essence of healing, is never communicated objectively, and in the actual conveyance of love, science is in the distant background, if indeed its presence is felt

---

[1] *Omnia exeunt in mysterium*: "At the deepest level, all things fade into mystery." The quote is of Thomas Aquinas, in Dulles, et. al., *op. cit.*, p. 7.

at all. Healing moments are entirely heart-to-heart, subject-to-subject. In fact, it can be fairly said that the more rigidly objective a healer is, the less likely that person is to heal anybody. First, then, "Love heals" implies the need for a revolution in mental health education, a wholesale change in priorities with weight being placed on the subjective being of the healer, and on the subjectivity of the healing process. This means, as an Explanation affirms, that the priority in mental health education needs to be placed on the humanities, on literature, philosophy, theology and the arts, the goal being to place the student on the road to wisdom, the high road, a difficult road that is built not with facts, statistics and empirical knowledge, but with love-derived and love-infused transcendent psychospiritual insight and sagacity.

No matter how mildly or lovingly it is worded, the mental health profession must be confronted with this: the mental health system got off on the wrong foot about a century ago, and it has been on the wrong foot ever since, stuck with a way of thinking about human beings that was and is born of defensiveness, a mindset that is shortsighted and counterproductive to healing.

Shortly after the turn of the last century, Freud called the unconscious a scientific concept and began promoting psychoanalysis. But if "Love heals" is true, then it logically follows that "analysis," per se, never healed a living soul. If healing occurs, that change occurs at the very center of being, in the psychospiritual heart, not in the unconscious. Nor is there anything "scientific" about the unconscious, nor, in fact, about the id, ego, superego, libido, Oedipus complex, pleasure principle nor any other of Freud's theological, philosophical and mythological ideas. Did he have some valid insights? Absolutely. But his fundamental ideas were fatally flawed fabrications born of defensiveness. When Freud's writings are interpreted in light of love theory, it is very clear that he used "science" as a defense against threats that he perceived in love. The majority of mental health practitioners, following Freud's basic path of the "scientific unconscious," have been on the same wrong foot ever since.

The first Explanation says it plainly: "Objectivity and sci-

ence must not be allowed to become defenses of the therapist."
Those were Freud's defenses, hidden behind the altar of science,
the sacred cow.

Early on in his career, Freud recognized what a vital role
love played in his patients' lives. Sometimes he used the word
"love" openly as he began to subjectively explain his own internal
experience, especially his thoughts, feelings and dreams about
his parents. But quickly, then, his defenses rose. He back-pedaled
from the word "love" and began substituting intellectualized, less
heart-touching, "scientific" substitutes for love like "cathexis" and
"transference." Yet, Freud still felt the powerful force of love, as we
all do, so his defense was to "reduce" the threat he felt from love
by whittling human nature down to a "fundamental" instinct,
the id, a sort of rudimentary sexual energy.

What was Freud's problem? Why was he so hung up on sex?
A good case has been made by E.M. Thornton that Freud never
overcame his early and well-documented cocaine addiction, and
that his heavy focus on sex is a well-known effect of that narcotic.
We also know that he did not resolve the conflicts involving the
love of his father and mother. His notion of the "universal" Oedipus complex, a truly cockamamie idea, was born of that love
conflict. It is manifest in his writing that Freud was afraid of his
father and, given love theory, it is also evident that he never received the love needed to resolve that fear. Instead, he displaced
and projected father onto God, and rejected both by projecting
them onto the sky, far away. Freud's atheism, his fixation on sex,
his fear of his father, and all of his "scientific," intellectualized,
"objective" defenses were the result of love deficits and the love
conflicts that he never resolved. The sad summary statement about
Freud is that he came face to face with love in his patients, and
then, tragically, rejected love, and defended that painful act with
elaborate, hyper-intellectualized defenses he called "science."
Even more tragic is the fact that a huge percentage of psychotherapists still adhere to the Freudian belief that the unconscious is the
primary construct of the human being, and with cool detachment,

continue analyzing and objectizing patients in the name of science — and it is all a giant defense.

But why? Why has it been so easy for thousands of psychotherapists, some of the brightest, kindest, warmest and best-educated people, to fall into the mindset that holds the unconscious and scientific objectivity as sacrosanct ideas? The answer may be deceptively simple: because it is easier. It is far easier to think than it is to love. It is easier to be objective than to be subjective. It is easier to analyze than to synthesize. It is easier to read data and charts than to read souls and hearts. It is easier to be abstract than to be real. It is easier to discount the mysteries of spirituality as immeasurable than to embrace and experience them. It is easier to gain a mountain of empirical knowledge than the first scintilla of wisdom. And it is certainly easier to be a brilliant scientist than it is to be a totally authentic, open, vulnerable, and warm human being called a "counselor" who is called upon to give and give and give from the marrow of his or her heart all day long. In a nutshell, repeating a phrase, love is a hell-of-a-lot of work, a hell-of-a-lot harder than science.

Tracing the basic historical conceptual and oh-so-human flaws in the evolution of mental health is the easy part. Words come easier when we are talking about science and objective facts. Similarly, we can blithely say that "Love heals" captures the conceptual heart of what it will take to get mental health off the wrong foot and on to the right one. Finding words to describe "love" and "healing," however, both of which are wholly subjective experiences for both therapist and client, is excruciatingly difficult. Words to describe its ineffable ecstasies and agonies, beauties and conflicts, comedies and tragedies, have been rhymed, sung, painted, narrated, and dramatized. But if Plato, Browning, Teresa of Avila, Blake, Cummings, Frost, all the writers of the Bible, and thousands of other authors have not captured the elusive subjectivities of love, we never need think we will succeed in doing so. Does that mean that finding the many meanings of the two little words, "Love heals," is a fruitless endeavor? Not at all. It just means that we finally are forced to face our humanity with all its limitations, acknowledge our pain and quandaries, but this time remain open and vulnerable, willing to struggle with mysteries rather than to take the easy way out by irrationally reducing life to manageable, scientific ids, chi squares and computer bytes.

Given acceptance of the need to vulnerably pursue the experience of love in psychotherapy, and to struggle to express those experiences in words, we immediately come face to face with two problems that the greatest poets and mystics have barely touched — finding words to describe the experiences of being *inside* a therapist-client love relationship, and the terrible challenge of expressing the thoughts, feelings, and the existential state of hearts in which love has been slashed, twisted, paralyzed, rejected or betrayed. The Love Heals principle begins by describing emotional disorders in just such terms, but few have even come close to adequately describing those excruciating experiences.

Of the mental health professionals, it is the existential therapists who have come closest to finding words to express here-and-now experience. For that reason, love therapy banks heavily on their experience. Chapters Seventeen and Eighteen are devoted solely to Existential Love Therapy. The existentialists, however, have not zeroed in on love as the fundamental force and goal of human life to a much greater extent than other schools of therapy. Love therapy gladly assumes that task. Yet, to their credit, the existentialists have clearly broken with the Freudian "scientific" defense that has kept most schools boxed in by objectivity, measurement and "heartless" empirical data. The existentialists search out experience, phenomena, life as it is in reality, here and now, with all its immeasurable loose ends and fuzzy imponderables.

Using the existential approach, then, can we find words to describe the inside of the therapeutic love experience, and the experiences of hearts that have been battered, shredded, deserted, starved and mutilated? Many volumes, and many case transcripts, will be needed. Here, with just one brief case example, we can provide a beautiful glimpse of the experience of love's healing.

The Case of Mary Lou

A fourteen-year-old girl had grown-up in an isolated shack in a southeastern Kentucky "holler." Mary Lou was a victim of brutal physical abuse and incest. She ran away from home, hitch-hiking, and made it to the outskirts of a city, to a field. There she had lived for four months like a little animal in the shell of a wrecked car. Junk food and blankets had been provided to her by the boys who lined up to have sex with her. When brought to a youth shelter by police, she was filthy, lice-laden, syphilitic, and combative, a feral child[2] who literally snarled. After finally obtaining a social and medical history and psychologicals, a multi-disciplinary team had diagnosed the girl as both Borderline and Anti-social Personality, and established her prognosis for ever leading a normal life as "near zero." After eighteen months, two experienced therapists had failed to faze her and the prognosis, if possible, was even poorer. Then she was sent to a second group home. There, the "group home mother," a barely literate woman in her fifties, Mamie, somehow reached and began to utterly transform the girl within three months. After another year, to everyone's amazement, Mary Lou began to emerge as a happy, bright, well-mannered young lady. Six months later, both previous diagnoses of emotional disorders were removed, and her prognosis changed to "Excellent" — but not before some debate among the professionals who had tried to treat her. They simply could not believe that the change in the girl was real. They suspected Mary Lou's good behavior was a "con." Nor could Mamie explain her "treatment methods"; she just knew the girl was "better." I was asked to evaluate Mary Lou.

The following "interview" is actually a reconstruction, a synthesis of four interviews. This is the heart of Mary Lou's ac-

---

[2] The adjective "feral" describing Mary Lou means "wild, untamed," which is accurate. The word "feral" is often associated with those extremely rare cases of young children being found who had grown up alone in the wilderness, even with wolves. Mary Lou was not *that* unsocialized. Here, "feral" describes a scratching, biting, kicking, wild-eyed little girl who bared her teeth, raged and cursed, but barely spoke otherwise.

count of her amazing turnaround. She spoke very slowly, with a
heavy Appalachian mountain twang, using words like, not "his"
but "his'n" and not "ain't" but "hain't"....

B. (Brennan Mullaney): Wow! Are you the same young lady I met
    after the police brought her in? You're like a different girl.
    What happened?

Mary Lou (laughing): I guess ol' Mamie happened.... But I'm not
    a differ'nt girl. Mamie says I'm jes becomin' the real me, the
    me God made.

B.: That's great.... But how did you do it — change so fast?

Mary Lou: I didn't! Mamie kind of done it fer me. She's so funny....
    How did *she* do it? Oh, I was terrible to her. I'd scream and
    yell at her, and call her names, and hit her and kick her...
    and she'd grab me and hug me (laughing). She'd squarsh
    me into her big ol' boobs and she'd start... kinda rockin' me,
    and whisperin'... and if I kept fightin' her, sometimes she'd
    start a-hummin', just a-hummin' and a-rockin', or singin' her
    church songs... (getting teary). I don't know how she did it,
    but that ol' lady's plum pow'rful.

B.: Can you tell me what the tears are saying?

Mary Lou (more tears): No... 'cept'n... Mamie taught me to cry. I
    never cried in my whole life! That's the first thing she kept a-
    whisperin'. She'd say — you know how she talks — "Honey
    chile, you hain't really mad at me. You're jes hurt, baby. Who
    hurt my baby so bad?" I kept fightin' her for a long time.
    I'd cuss her, and she'd hug me harder, ever' day! And she'd
    hum and whisper, hum and whisper....

B.: What did she whisper that stopped you fighting her?

Mary Lou: Oh, I'll never ferget that! One day I had a real hissy fit
    — tore up my room, and I was a-screamin' and a-cussin', and
    she got me in that ol' bear hug again, and she said it again,
    "Chile, you hain't really mad. You're jes kinda hurt" — and
    then she said (tearing)... she said, "Baby, when you gonna
    let me in? Jes let me in. Let me take that hurt. Jes give that
    hurt to ol' Mamie.".... And I looked up and there was tears

a-comin' down her cheeks, and a-fallin' in my face... and somethin' jes... broke up inside me. I started cryin' for the first time in my life, and it was like a dam broke. I thought I was gonna die, jes break plum in two. H'it was awful. I cried so hard my throat was a-achin' and my jaws hurt, and there was this terrible pain in here (putting her hand in the middle of her chest). I cried and cried and cried and cried and cried. I didn't think I was *ever* gonna stop....

B.: But you got through it...

Mary Lou: I reckon. I cried for four or five hours that first time, and off and on all the next week.... And Mamie would always jes hold me. She'd say, "Baby, did you know that tears is the only water that runs uphill? Tears are prayers, 'cause they come straight from the heart, and God sees ever' one." She'd say God was a-cryin' with me 'cause he hurt when I hurt... Do you believe that? Do you think God cries with us?

B.: Well, if Mamie said that, I'd say there's a good chance it must be true — it sounds like she knows God pretty well.

Mary Lou: Oh, she does! She's jes beautiful.

B.: She sure is.... But tell me, is that what caused your big change, that Mamie cried with you, and hugged you?

Mary Lou: I don't know. That was part of it. H'it's kinda weird. She jes *wouldn't* give up on me, and lak, she got *inside* me (laughing)... I'd be a real snot, and she'd hug me and whisper, "Hush, chile, that hain't the real you." She'd say, "You can't fool ol' Mamie by pretendin' to be mean, 'cause you hain't!" Then she'd say, "I know the real Mary Lou and in her heart she's full o' goodness." Know what? At first I thought she was plum crazy! Nobody in my entire life ever told me I was good.

B.: You said she got inside you?

Mary Lou: In here (pointing to her chest). H'it don't make no sense a'tall, but she made me believe it... (tears again). She loves me.... H'it don't make no sense... but she does. There I go a-cryin' again. (Smiles, wipes her eyes.) Mamie always said my heart was a-runnin' down my face.

The case of Mary Lou is an example of love therapy at its best, and it was administered by a woman with a sixth grade education. Mamie had never read a psychology book, nor did she know that "Prognosis — near zero" meant that several very qualified professionals had concluded that she didn't have a prayer of taming the wildcat Mary Lou. Mamie had little knowledge, but more wisdom than the entire professional multi-disciplinary team put together. And she had just one simple technique, a love that Mary Lou aptly described, "pow'rful."

The case of Mary Lou illustrates many of the Explanations of Principle Fifteen: the first — the method was wholly subjective. The third Explanation — Mamie's love "melted" Mary Lou's defenses; her irresistible warmth penetrated the angry defensive wall surrounding the girl's heart, erased her fear and provided her with the courage, the "added" heart, needed to withstand the inevitable pain involved in opening a wounded heart. The fourth Explanation — Mamie's love was creational. Abuse, incest, gross neglect, abysmal poverty, social deprivation, and a horror-filled childhood in an isolated rural hollow, had left Mary Lou with a heart that was not just slashed and gapped, but one that had been largely "uncreated." Mamie's love healed Mary Lou by filling the wounds with love, yes, but also by discovering and realizing great pieces of Mary Lou's heart which had been buried in darkness. The fifth Explanation: Mamie's love was a true "heart transplant." Mary Lou's diagnosis as borderline personality, though not quite as severe as a full-blown psychosis, was a severe mental illness. That diagnosis was compounded by the "feral," wholly unsocialized, wild components of her personality that a diagnostic label cannot express. This little girl was primitive, uncreated. Mamie "gave her own heart" in full measure. The sixth Explanation — Perhaps the most remarkable fact of this case is that the majority of healing occurred with hardly any unconscious memories being surfaced. This illustrates many of the fundamental tenets of love therapy — that "analysis," knowledge alone, heals no one; that the unconscious is not the end-all-be-all of personality structure, but only the "latent memory file" which may or may not figure prominently into the far deeper heart-level essence of healing; that healing, per se, is a totally subjective process; and that recall of unconscious memories often comes after, not before, healing occurs. (This important and perhaps controversial view is discussed at greater length below.) The seventh Explanation — Love heals like a light shining into darkness, but only when that darkness, the painful wound, is opened wide, vulnerable, no longer defended. It is important to note that "opening a wound" means far more than mere recall of a memory. An unconscious memory can be surfaced *without* the wound being opened. Contrariwise, a wound can be opened *without* conscious recall of what the wound was all about, i.e., with only the deeper, heartfelt pain exposed. This is what happened with Mary Lou as Mamie loved her and melted her defenses. Tears rushed out like a dam breaking, and Mary Lou thought she would "break in two." We can picture a butchered, largely empty heart — darkness — being "wholed" by the light of Mamie's love.

The eighth Explanation — that "love finds its own way" to reach wounds is evident in Mary Lou's healing. For weeks, while the essential change in the girl was taking place, she and Mamie discussed few specifics of her trauma-filled history. Love "swept aside" both conscious and unconscious distractions to reach the "heart of the matter," painful wounds and malformations that lay at the very center of Mary Lou's being.

The final Explanation speaks of how love "fades into mystery." That mystery is easy to see in the healing of Mary Lou. It was certainly, as the Explanation claims, more a matter of wisdom, the stuff of prayer, poetry and mysticism, than of positivist science. The mystery of love's healing was perhaps more astonishing in this dramatic case, but the Love Heals Principle presents a reminder and a challenge to every professional: if the most science-minded therapists will reexamine their most successful cases, those in which a very disturbed person made a remarkable improvement, they will discover that, beyond the many reasons for the improvement, the bottom-line explanation is always a loving mystery. All good therapists, I submit, have a lot of Mamie in them. They love, they heal, and then look back in awe, humbled by the mystery of their own love.

Quickly, though, lest I leave the false impression that healing is always or even typically so devoid of thought, searching dialogue, treatment strategies and methodologies as in Mary Lou's case, I should emphasize the obvious, that this was a very rare case. It was selected, not to demonstrate methodologies, but to illustrate the heart of the meaning of the words, "Love heals." Methods are ways to transmit love, but love transcends methodology. Methods are ways to reach wounds needing healing, but methods themselves do not heal.

The second Explanation emphasizes that every method used in the treatment process must be "balanced and orchestrated" so as to bring about those "synthesized, singularly powerful, subject-to-subject experiential events in which healing love... supplants wounded love" — called "healing moments." That Explanation expands upon the sentence in the main body of Principle Fifteen which describes healing love as "authentic, skillful, accurate, timely, and wise." Thus, although Mary Lou's healing and Mamie's "methods" describe the bottom-line results that treatment is designed to produce — "healing moments" — those bottom-lines are rarely reached by such direct, nonverbal, non-cognitive, tactile and tearful "methods" as Mamie's. On the contrary, it is far more typical for a therapist to follow labyrinthine ways and utilize a wide variety of treatment methods, most of which involve hours of talking around dozens of key concepts, before each healing moment is reached. Principle Sixteen, next, continues with the description of love therapy's methods of healing. Though it is difficult to separate love's healing from the methods through which that love is transmitted, Principle Fifteen's focus is on what healing *is*, what mental and emotional wounds *are*, where wounds are located, and what happens when healing love infuses a wound.

The sixth Explanation brings into stark relief the distinction between the unconscious, the central psychic structure of most traditional therapies, and the psychospiritual heart, the basic personality structure of love therapy. In the case of Mary Lou, no unconscious material about her lifetime of terrible physical abuse and incest were surfaced until long after she had been substantially healed by Mamie's "pow'rful" love. Though it is extremely rare for so very little "talking out" and "figuring out" to accompany healing, it is not unusual for deeper heart-level healing to come *first*, and for unconscious memories to come later — not always, but typically. Almost all traditional therapies hold the opposite, i.e., that the wound lies in the unconscious, so an unconscious memory must be produced first, before it can be healed. That is simply not true. There are strong arguments that favor the view that the psychospiritual heart is the primary location of healing, and that heart-level healing typically precedes the surfacing of unconscious memories.

First, if we ask *where* emotional wounds are located, and where healing takes place, and then trust our own individual experience, and/or watch and listen to people talking about where they feel both emotional pain and healing, it will readily be confirmed that human beings *experience* both emotional suffering and healing in their torsos, viz., in their chest, belly and physical heart areas, far more often than in their heads and brains. Freud's diagram of the unconscious shows it in the brain. In contrast, where the psychospiritual heart is physically located, I would never dare guess; the center of our being is obviously indefinable, spiritual as well as psychological.

Secondly, the overwhelming number of emotional problems and full-blown disorders are healed by parents, relatives, good neighbors and friends, not by professionals. Thus, many of our most effective "healers" might not know an unconscious id from a mathematical pi. Yet, they heal. How? Did they use analytical, gestalt, transactional, or free association methods to surface repressed emotions and unconscious memories? No. Did they use cognitive, psychodrama, or behavioral therapies? No. Ask them, and they'll tell you they "just talked." How did they talk? "Heart-to-heart." Then ask those healers if they gave the hurting person some great insight, a profound dream interpretation perhaps, or maybe an explanation of their unconscious defenses or cognitive errors, and the answer will again be, "No." What, then, did they give the person? "Just love."

The third, most convincing argument that love's healing *precedes* the surfacing of unconscious material — the opposite of the traditional view — is provided by a closer, more existential look at the typical therapy interview. The sixth Explanation is based on that view when it states an axiom: "Without love, no repressed unconscious material will ever be produced in therapy." A moment's reflection will affirm that none of us would reveal our innermost thoughts and feelings to a cold, detached person whom we knew cared not a whit about us. It takes warmth, acceptance, at least a modicum of love to allow a person to be the least bit open, much less open enough to reveal a well-defended feeling or memory. But the instant a defense is loosened and a repressed thought, memory or feeling begins to emerge, healing has already started to happen — which proves that healing often does occur bottom-up, at heart-level, before any unconscious material ever surfaces. The many ramifications of this "bottom-up," heart-centered view of healing will be clarified in the next principle, on methods of therapy.

Principle Fifteen describes love therapy as the process of finding and exposing soul-deep heart wounds, and the third Explanation explicitly states that those wounds must be "opened wide," which makes pain an invariable and unavoidable prelude to healing. Healing love can then be precisely targeted to fill the open wounds, but the pain that accompanies healing must be expected and faced with courage. Typically, our terribly human task in counseling is to search out the pain and follow it to the heart wound.

Though a therapist may have encyclopedic diagnostic knowledge, it takes courageous love to move beyond symptoms to discern and decipher heart-deep pain. One Explanation recognizes that, *en fin*, healing will always remain a mystery. We must note that even the very beginning of the healing process, accurately discerning heart pain, is itself mysterious.

Looking back at Principle Two, as I tried to find words for human love, I described it as standing in another's shoes, looking out at the world through their eyes, seeing as they see, feeling as they feel, yearning as they yearn.... This intersubjective merger of being with being, soul with soul, heart with heart, has precious little to do with thought, but it can produce a level of knowledge that completely transcends deductive reasoning, interpreting observations, or analyses. This "heart-knowledge," as I'll call it, often produces a sudden, sure, synthesizing awareness of pain that is present in someone's heart, pain which they are not even consciously aware they have, pain that is far deeper than any manifest symptoms would indicate, pain that is deeper than the person's "psychology." This is knowledge which can only be called psychospiritual. Love allows the counselor an intersubjective, intra-heart *experience* of the person's pain, an "inside" view that no amount of objective analysis would ever produce. That experience of a person's pain and the "heart knowledge" it produces is the invaluable and essential prelude to healing — but it comes at a price. The price is the therapist's willingness to suffer with and for people, to love them enough to assume and bear their pain even before they do, even while they are still unwilling or unable to accept that pain.

Intersubjectively, from the inside of another's heart, a counselor experiences pain that is sometimes nearly impossible to describe in words. Indeed, we are not trained to do that. We are trained only to observe symptoms, the view from outside, i.e., the objective view. Surely, observing and naming defenses and symptoms is necessary and helpful, but it is not helpful enough — because the core problem is not the symptom, but the heart wound.

Words inevitably are found wanting when it comes to describing both the subtleties and roaring horrors of heart-level suffering. The language of hearts is rarely easy to understand, and the utterances of some hearts may indeed seem incomprehensible. As love allows us to fuse heart with heart so as to experience the other's pain, we can sometimes use analogies and literary allusions to help a person accept and go though the pain that is an inescapable accompaniment of exposing wounds and getting healed. Here is a case example...

An anxiety-torn woman constantly smiled. Even as she described horrible events from her childhood, she smiled. I could feel acutely a huge pool of what seemed to be sheer agony that she had sealed away and never allowed herself to experience. I said to her, "You mentioned going to the opera sometime. Know my favorite? — It's *Pagliacci*. That was one of the great tenor Caruso's famous roles. Pagliacci is a clown. His face is painted white with a big red nose, and a big wide smile. But his beloved has been unfaithful, and his heart is breaking, so he sings the great aria, *Vesti la giubba*. He sings! His voice soars! And then the clown laughs! And then he cries. But the show must go on, so he laughs! But his heart is breaking, so he cries.... I think I'll call you Pagliacci. Why do I think there are tears behind your smile? You smile. I smile. You smile again. I smile with you. But when will you *cry*, Pagliacci? Let me cry with you, too. I will, you know."

The languages of the human heart simply cannot be translated into sterile professional terms. Were that not so, humanity would never have evolved poetry, drama, opera or the novel. The assertion of the Explanation that psychotherapy must place greater weight on the arts than on science is simply a recognition of the way our hearts live and operate — not like boxes, charts, gears and linear equations, but like kaleidoscopes, cornucopias, phantasmagoria and collages of feelings, thoughts, decisions, perceptions, memories, and a thousand agonies and ecstasies, all richly mixed, blended and sometimes jumbled, but always centered and held together by a beautiful mystery. Applying science to the human heart is extremely helpful, yes, but a chemical analysis of the pigments that were used in the *Mona Lisa* tells us precious little about her mysterious beauty. Similarly, even the most rigid scientist understands why the Tin Man in *The Wizard of Oz* asked for a heart instead of an unconscious. One of the last Reflections simply reasserts some truths that cannot be lost — that psychotherapy requires more than science and skills; it requires wisdom and art and the courage to embrace the mysteries that every heart presents. Indeed, love always seems to begin with awe.

Yet, this heavy emphasis on the heart and mystery does not mean that science is not essential, or that all prior theories and methods of therapy are passé. On the contrary, love therapy utilizes, blends and orchestrates scores of concepts and techniques. The methods of love therapy are discussed in the next principle.

Chapter Sixteen

Love Therapy: One Way, Many Methods

Principle Sixteen: All Effective Therapies Are Love-Centered

Love therapy is love-centered eclecticism, a singular way of healing mental and emotional disorders which subsumes and unifies many models, concepts and methods of therapy, and orchestrates their application so as to bring about those intersubjective, experiential events during which love infuses and heals wounds in the psychospiritual heart.

Explanations

- Therapeutic love must be authentic, skillful, accurate, timely, warm, accepting, patient, mild, trusting, hopeful, and as powerful, generously giving, transparently open-hearted, and as unconditional as human limits allow. Both in its giving and receiving, love is always humble because it is recognized as a gift (cf., Principle Four). Love is never judgmental because love's inherent justice honors the ultimate right of every person to forgiveness, absolution of guilt, and the return to the wholeness of love (Principle Fourteen). Though never condemning, neither does therapeutic love shrink from telling the necessary truth even when it is painful, nor from confronting evil. (Chapter Twenty-Five addresses dealing with authentic evil in a spiritual way.)
- Virtually any theory, method or concept of psychotherapy can

be to some degree effective in healing so long as it is predominantly love-centered and administered with love.

• If any therapist, using any method, effectively heals, it is primarily because the therapist, whether aware of it or not, effectively loved the client.

• As a singular "way" of healing that brings together diverse methods and concepts from many models of therapy, love therapy provides the basic philosophical premises, encompassing spirit, general conceptual direction, and guiding principles for diagnosis and treatment. As a "way," not a method, love therapy may be viewed as the flagship in a huge armada of therapy models, techniques and concepts, or as one constant fire, a whole within which many tongues, tendrils and sparks are essential parts. Authentic love, of its very nature, prevents "methodolatry."[1]

• When love is allowed to serve as the goal, direction, and guiding principle of any therapy method, that method instantly becomes more effective. Similarly, when a recognized concept or mechanism of human behavior is reinterpreted in light of love as the fundamental goal and drive of life, the meaning and purpose of the concept is dramatically changed and expanded. (For example, Freud was very correct in his observation of the existence of various defense mechanisms, but wholly incorrect in his interpretation of those defenses; love utterly transforms our understanding of their nature and operation.)

---

[1] "Methodolatry" is a word coined by Rollo May, which he seems to define as the "uncritical acceptance of limited assumptions" which so often marks modern science. Every "scientific method," May reminds us, "rests upon philosophical presuppositions." "It is a gross, albeit common error, to assume naively that one can observe facts best if he avoids all... philosophical assumptions.... The result in our day is that science gets identified with methods of *isolating* factors and observing them from an allegedly *detached* base." Rollo May, "The Origins and Significance of the Existential Movement in Psychology," in Rollo May, Ernest Angel and Henri Ellenberger, Eds., *Existence: A New Dimension in Psychiatry and Psychology* (New York: Basic Books, Simon and Schuster, 1958), p. 11. This is precisely the reason that love therapy's philosophical foundations are presented first, in the Introduction and Principles, especially Principles One and Seven. Yet, for love therapy, too, the caution against methodolatry is well-taken: thus, should a love therapist find her- or himself "in love with love," the reminder should be given that an "in-love" feeling is not a guiding principle; "in love" is not yet love.

• In the love therapy way of healing, several different therapy models, methods and concepts may be utilized with a single client, but each approach is orchestrated and fused to culminate in an existential, subject-to-subject, here-and-now healing moment, an experience by the client of therapeutic love reaching, infusing, and filling an undefended, open wound in the psychospiritual heart. Thus, for example, gestalt, art, cognitive and behavioral therapies may be utilized in preparation for accepting love and healing, but the actual healing moment is always an existential, intersubjective experience of love that transcends any method or concept that was utilized as a medium for love's delivery. Objectivity serves subjectivity.

• Love-centered diagnosis is based on the principle that love and truth are one (Principle Eight), and that thorough knowledge as to the source and operation of an emotional disorder is found at heart level wherein the wounds of damaged love are located. Diagnosis requires objective evaluation of observable symptoms, coupled with subjective, psychospiritual discernment of the heart-level pain and wounds.

• Love-centered treatment of disorders is a planned process of assembling and coordinating the use of various therapy methods and concepts so as to systematically heal wounds in the heart. Selection of treatment approaches always is based on the question, "What does love specifically demand?" Healing each heart wound requires selection, from among scores of therapy models, the one(s) which will most effectively allow melting defenses, or exposure of the heart wound, or catharsis, or correcting cognitive errors, any or all of which may precede or accompany the actual healing moment, the subject-to-subject event during which healing love infuses and supplants the wound in the heart.

• The skillful, creative process of customizing an intersubjective encounter in which love is precisely tailored to heal a specific heart wound is a highly intuitive art. There is art in communicating love, art in timing love, art in enabling a person to receive love, art in accurately targeting a specific wound, and art in selecting the intensity and forms of love that a specific individual is ready to receive. An art can be learned, but it is primarily a matter of talent. Unlike other arts, though, loving is a talent that every human being possesses and can exercise at will.

• Even a little love goes a long way in healing. In general, the more emotionally damaged and love-deprived an individual has been the more imperative it is that the therapist search out and clearly identify the little love that has enabled the person to survive. By extending and expanding that little love, emphasizing the positive, strength is gained to tackle the negative. In severe cases, diagnosis, identifying problems, inherently a negative process, must be deferred until the person has found a little love to cling to.

• Love's "healing moments" are intersubjective, here-and-now, experiential, existential events. While many models and methods are orchestrated and utilized in love therapy, all of them are administered with love. Thus, the overriding atmosphere and mode of thought and feeling of love therapy is heavily weighted with existential concepts and methods, both of which are reinterpreted and revised in love terms. (Principles Seventeen and Eighteen focus on existential love therapy.)

• Love and truth are ontologically and psychologically one. (Principle Eight). Thus, "love" that does not conform to truth is not authentic love even though warm, pleasant and other so-called "love" emotions are very strong. Love is not a mere emotion (Principles One and Two). Similarly, truth that is not loved (integrated into one's being, "taken to heart") is not the psychological truth even if it is ontologically true. This principle of love-truth unity both requires and allows love therapy to consolidate many disparate therapy models into a cohesive whole. (Thus, love therapy may conjoin objective, "heady," heavily truth-centered approaches like psychological testing and cognitive therapy, with the more existential, emotive, heavily subjective models like gestalt, expressive, art or existential therapies, while correcting or altering any model to bring about love-truth wholeness, i.e., healing.) In individual treatment, the concept of love-truth conflicts becomes an all-purpose tool for reinterpreting every defense mechanism, every relationship problem, and every mental and emotional disorder.

• The first goal of therapeutic love is simply "reaching" the client at heart level. "Reaching" means melting defenses with love and bridging the gap between two individuals, client and therapist, so as to allow the earliest stage of intersubjective unity wherein healing becomes possible.

———————

As "love" is described in the first Explanation, in ideal and absolute terms that include every virtue, anyone who contemplates loving a friend, a relative or even themselves may well object, "Mercy! Who can be that perfect? You'd have to be a saint to love!" Even more upsetting, when mental health providers read that love therapy includes any and every model, method and concept of therapy ever developed, they may protest, "Ouch! Love therapy not only demands that I be a loving saint, but that I know everything!" Quickly, therefore, we need to highlight the phrase in that first Explanation which is intended to keep love down-to-earth and human, i.e., "Love must be... as open-hearted and as unconditional *as human limits allow.*"

There has been a great fad raging in religious and pop psychology circles for the past decade that extols and promotes the idea of "unconditional" love. Invariably, discussing love therapy, someone in the audience will say, "You're talking about 'unconditional' love, aren't you?" My response is, "Absolutely not! Only God can love unconditionally." Human love, by definition, is finite, always imperfect, flawed, incomplete, so it is vital that we understand and accept those limits. The idea that love ever can be truly unconditional has damaged people. Consider this: doesn't "unconditional love" imply perfection? — love that contains not one scintilla of self-interest, love by a lover whose own complex, subtle and varied needs can be *totally* set aside, love that is so perfectly open, purely giving, and utterly selfless that it out-saints the saints? If I try to love unconditionally and fail, as I inevitably will, I feel guilty, inadequate, unloving. If I claim that I am loving unconditionally, I am living a sham, posing, not acknowledging human limits which truth demands that I admit. That untruth is unloving. The unconditional love craze, like romantic movies and novels, surely meets some human needs, but it also inflicts misconceptions on people who are struggling to discover what real love is all about. Does it not seem wiser to pursue love that is a little more forgiving, a little less demanding, a little more human?

Love therapy advocates love that is "authentic." That is the first adjective used to describe therapeutic love in the first Explanation. "Authentic" means "real," and the reality of being human means being imperfect, always just a little tarnished and unsaintly. By this reasoning, a good counselor's love, if it is authentic, must at times invariably include such open admissions, "I screwed up; I'm sorry," and, "You're right, I was unfair." Earlier, we quoted Charles Péguy's profoundly simple formula: "The only way to love a person is as he is."[2] Surely Péguy would not mind if I add a necessary assertion of the obvious to his verity, that "as he is" universally means "finite, imperfect, limited, human."

By the same token, it is obvious that the average counselor has no more than a smattering of knowledge of the total body of concepts and models of therapy available. A therapist could read round the clock and still barely dent the huge body of professional literature. There are many thousands of studies of anxiety, thousands on depression, scores of models and hundreds of methods available. That information overload was one of the major motivations for the development of love therapy. Many in the mental health field have dealt with that glut of knowledge by calling themselves "eclectic," but as noted in the Introduction, that can be tantamount to irrational dabbling. "Eclectic" which means only "selecting from various systems" (the dictionary definition) with no singular, underlying, guiding fundamental principle to

---

[2] Péguy, *op. cit.*

unite those various systems into a cohesive whole, surely cannot heal. Pure eclecticism is like building a house, using a steamroller, a spatula and a dentist's drill for tools, starting with the roof first, using a biologist's nomenclature and a racing form as a house plan. If that makes no sense, one need ask how an eclectic use of dozens of therapy models and hundreds of concepts of personality dynamics, each of which have different underlying philosophies, makes much more sense.

Love Therapy is love-centered eclecticism. Though a wide variety of models, methods and concepts are used, love therapy has one basic premise, one underlying philosophy, one overriding "way," and one ever-present goal. Similarly, love therapy's personality theory views all human beings as having one fundamental drive, one ultimate goal, and one unifying, dynamic spirit. Love therapy is eclectic, yes, but its centering in love allows unity in diversity.

But if the many methods and concepts that love therapy incorporates have very different, even contradictory philosophies, how can love therapy unify them? Answer: *change* the philosophies so that they are not contradictory, viz., keep the basic idea of a method, but change the rationale surrounding it, and then alter and/or extend the method so that it is more directly focused on producing an intersubjective healing love moment. Likewise, keep what is valid and true in a therapy model or concept; change the rest so that it is love-compatible.

The fifth Explanation gives the example of Freud's ideas on the defense mechanisms. I gratefully acknowledge Freud's observation of the fact that various defense mechanisms exist, while wholly rejecting the philosophy and theology of psychoanalysis, including the id-libido theory, the Oedipus complex, and the entire animal-like personality structure into which Freud placed the defenses. Love theory accepts the raw observation of defenses, but virtually starts over in explaining what a human being is (Principle Eight), and how the human personality is structured (Principle Three). This example demonstrates that love-centered eclecticism does not mean merely "selecting from various 'whole' systems." On the contrary, love therapy's eclecticism is more like customized tailoring. Often, only a kernel of truth is selected, and that truth is then recast, re-explained in light of love principles.

Clearly, the task of showing how love therapy adopts, adapts, molds and melds a huge body of methods into one love-oriented system will not be accomplished in one book, nor indeed in one lifetime. The love principles provide some guidelines, but constant creativity is a hallmark of any love. There is, though, another subtle but important guideline that is essential in the ongoing task of selecting and merging so many concepts and models. Implicit in the body of love principles is a mindset, a "way" of thinking about people and disorders that can guide the intuitive process of selecting methods and concepts. That mindset can be stated as a simple rule: "Love, and think constantly 'in love terms.'" Following that rule, love "almost automatically" surfaces the right therapy at the right time and helps the therapist adapt the method or concept to the individual patient in the most effective way to bring healing. Granted, that sounds a little "magical," and the idea of a "mindset" on love may sound a little dogmatic, so let me explain....

Every counselor has a dominant mindset, a consistent way of thinking which reflects his or her basic theoretical beliefs, or, in other words, "terms" that generally dictate the direction of thought processes. Thus, for example, Viktor Frankl thinks predominantly "in terms of meaning"; Aaron Beck's mindset is "in cognitive terms"; Jung thought "in terms of archetypes"; Freud's mindset was "in terms of the unconscious and sex"; behaviorists think primarily "in stimulus-response-conditioning terms"; Virginia Satir thinks "in conjoint family system terms"; the existentialists' prime focus is "in terms of being or here-and-now existence" — and there are dozens more major mindsets which correspond to the many major schools of therapy. There are three immediate points:

First, the only unusual aspect of love therapy's "rule," to

"think in love terms," is that I am pointedly recognizing the inevitability of mindsets, and forthrightly saying that a "love set" must be paramount if healing is to occur.

Secondly, as established in the Introduction, logic says that all of the scores of mindsets floating around, each corresponding to a different "basic" premise about human behavior, cannot possibly all be correct. There may be *some* elements of truth all in them, but logic insists that there is only one rock-bottom fundamental truth about what makes us tick.

Thirdly, one person cannot have two or five or ten mindsets at the same time without becoming at least a little fragmented, a wee bit nutty. Only a unidirectional mindset can allow eclecticism to be used sanely.

Loving and thinking "in love terms" almost automatically surfaces in the therapist's consciousness the right therapy to use at the right time. How that occurs is not "magical," but it is indeed a complex process. This "automatic selection" from among eclectic possibilities is a product of the love-truth equation described in last Explanation, above, and in Principle Nine. Love is truth. This means that in any experience of authentic love, the corresponding truth which is inherent in that love can be simultaneously experienced — and vice versa: any truth fully experienced implicitly denotes a corresponding love of that truth. Moreover, a truth about a person cannot be fully known until that truth is fully loved. This reciprocal love-truth relationship is an infinitely complex subject that requires bringing two levels of thought, ontology and psychology, together, as one, in the form of an existential experience. Yes, that seems to be heady stuff — until it is brought down to earth. The next two Principles, on existential love therapy, explore the subject in more detail. Here, I introduce the idea of the love-truth equation in order to show how a mindset on "loving, and thinking in love terms" brings with it a rather "automatic selection" of the correct therapy method from among the hodgepodge of eclectic possibilities. A case example should provide a more down-to-earth grasp of how love-centered eclecticism works. In the following case excerpt, I will interrupt the dialogue to describe how I was "thinking in love terms," while simultaneously considering several eclectic therapy approaches.

Love-Centered Eclecticism with Kathy

Case Summary: Kathy, age thirty-four, an attractive mother of two, second marriage, has just started her third therapy session. She is tentatively diagnosed with both Major Depression and Post-Traumatic Stress Disorder. She has seen a psychiatrist every three months for three years and is taking antidepressant medication. She grew up in an alcoholic family, emotionally deprived, viz., love-starved. She was sexually abused by her father's drunken friends on two occasions, but refuses to discuss it. A sex life "near zero" is just one result. She withdraws usually, but suffers acute anxiety when she has flashbacks. In the following interview, she sat down and immediately started crying...

Kathy (severe tremors; crying): I'm just falling apart. Oh, God, I just want to die. Jerry (her husband) tries to help, but he just doesn't understand — and neither do I! I just can't deal with anything. Everything's wrong! I just feel so guilty. Everything's going wrong, and I'm just no good for anything. The kids are miserable, the whole family's unhappy, and I know it's all my fault. Jerry wants to make love, and I just can't. Then I feel guilty again. Everything's wrong! All I do is sit and think about how rotten my life has been. It's hell. It's shit, all of it.... I just feel so... alone. I'm just empty. Nothing means anything — I'm just lost.... And when I start feeling that — empty, hollow — it's like I just don't feel anything, like I'm numb, dead.... I'm sorry. I don't cry like this at home. Then I see you and I just fall apart. (More tears.)

Possible Eclectic Therapy Approaches Considered: A dozen or more therapy techniques will eventually be required to help Kathy, but the first question is which one to call upon in immediate response to her anguish. Therapies immediately called to mind by her opening statements include the following: typical of people in depression, she overgeneralizes negativity, as seen in her words that she's "no good for *anything*," and "*everything's wrong*." Cognitive therapy could be employed to deal with the exaggeration and illogicality of those thoughts, and probably surface some "hidden, automatic thoughts"[3] lying behind them. However, Carl Rogers' nondirective, client-centered therapy would assume that, given "unconditional positive regard," and the genuineness, accurate empathy, and warmth of a therapeutic relationship, Kathy "will discover within herself"[4] the solution to her problems, including the cognitive ones. But focusing on Kathy's "emptiness," the very real misery she has endured, and the invariable feelings of hopelessness that accompany depression, Frankl's Logotherapy[5] could well help her find the meaning in her life that seems so absent now. From another perspective, Kathy's problems are inseparable from the whole "miserable, unhappy family," so a Virginia Satir[6] approach with conjoint family therapy could certainly help. Long-standing sexual dysfunction is a constant problem, so eventually some sexual therapies may be needed, but not yet. Kathy's guilt, anger, fear, hopelessness, and psychic numbing (dissociation), broken only by flashbacks on past traumas and the "shit" of her life are bubbling emotionally and require some immediate relief. A Perls' Gestalt[7] approach,

---

[3] Beck, *op. cit.*

[4] Carl R. Rogers, *On Becoming a Person* (Boston: Houghton Mifflin, 1961), p. 33. This one statement about discovering "within one's self"... "the capacity... for growth, and change and personal development" seems to be as close as Rogers ever came to stating his first, basic principle regarding what a person is. He calls it his "overall hypothesis." Rogers' full attention was always focused on how to develop a helping relationship, and indeed, he helped people. He did not call his helping relationships "loving." He seems to equate love with just one "emotion" among many. In fact, in the index to this basic Rogerian book, the word "love" is not even listed. Yet, a rose by any other name is still a rose. Rogers demonstrates that his "unconditional positive regard" is indeed love, and that he is one of the most loving counselors God ever made. He describes "unconditional positive regard" in pp. 62-63 and 283-284; by any name, I read "love."

[5] Frankl, *op. cit.*

[6] Virginia Satir, *Conjoint Family Therapy* (Palo Alto, CA: Science and Behavior Books, Inc., 1983).

[7] Fritz Perls, *Gestalt Is* (Moab, Utah: Real People Press, 1975).

emotionally confronting her neglectful parents and sexual abusers by "imaging" them in a chair in front of her, helping her drain off some of the pain, could surely help. So could Reality Therapy[8] by assuring her that she could assume responsibility for her life. A transactional analysis[9] approach could help her by casting all the problems in "parent-child-adult" roles and helping her discover how those roles were in conflict. Karen Horney's "Tyranny of Should"[10] is clearly operating to increase Kathy's guilt. And the list goes on and on. The possible approaches to therapy are so numerous at any point in psychotherapy that, clearly, unguided eclecticism — simply picking the therapy that "seems best" — with no standard or guide to determine which approach is best, is at best a crap shoot, capricious if not damaging.

The Love Therapist's Heart Process: The effort to love and to think "in love terms" is an act of the therapist's whole being, a very deliberate effort to be with Kathy subjectively so as to feel what she feels and understand what she is saying from inside-out. The therapist is thinking, yes, and feeling acutely, yes, but deeper than both of those active functions is the action of the therapist's heart. Who can describe this heart action? We must fumble for words because the heart is psychospiritual, largely beyond words — but let me try.

I could feel Kathy's pain pour over me. Not waxing poetic, let's just say that I felt a terrible weight heaped upon me, smothering me, as if the whole world had suddenly turned rotten and had smacked me in the face. More succinctly, it hurt like hell — which is exactly the word she had used. Listening to her, identifying with her pain and allowing myself to feel it, gave me a sick feeling. It was like entering her heart and finding myself chest deep in pus. Clearly, she had poured out a lot of horrors in the first two inter-

---

[8] Glasser, *op. cit.*

[9] Eric Berne, *Games People Play* (New York: Grove Press, 1964), and Berne, *Transactional Analysis is in Psychotherapy* (New York: Grove Press, 1961).

[10] Karen Horney, *Neurosis and Human Growth: The Struggle Toward Self-Realization* (New York: Norton, 1950).

views. Problems and pain were surfaced, but none were resolved, healed, so she was getting overwhelmed, sinking, "decompensating."[11] There were so *many* problems. Question, therefore: what was love demanding first? She seemed to be pouring her heart out, so why wasn't I hearing what it was saying? There was something missing. What? She had poured out problems and pain, but I felt talked at, not with. Why? Had she told me? Yes! Indirectly, she had told me the bottom line, the one thing that was causing the most pain: she was "empty" and "alone." Yet, she cried only with me, she had said, so her tears were talking. What approach, then, did love demand first? What was her heart saying? None of the several models, methods and concepts considered earlier was applicable yet. What was required was love therapy in its most direct form, called "reaching" (the final Explanation above), just loving, trying to reach intersubjective communion with a woman whose aloneness *was* her emptiness, and surely a large part of her depression. First, then, I had to *reach* her, be with her.

B. (Brennan Mullaney): Kathy, can you tell me what all those tears are saying?

Kathy: No.... (Cries harder, head buried in her knees.)

B: (After waiting for her tears to slow.) Kathy, can you listen to me? (Tears eventually stop and she looks up.) Let me ask you a kind of strange question. I'll ask it twice so you can hear the *way* I'm asking it. The words are, "Kathy, have you ever talked to anybody?" — but listen to my heart; listen to the

---

[11] "Decompensation" is a rapid deterioration of defenses which then allows a quick escalation of painful symptoms and pathological behavior. More graphically, defenses fall and the person "falls apart." Typically, this is what happens just prior to a person landing in a mental hospital. In order to prevent decompensation, the love therapy view is that love must "melt" defenses; they should never be aggressively "broken." From a broader perspective, love is our only effective defense. The appearance of decompensation, therefore, is a signal that a quick and massive infusion of love is needed. That fast, huge dose of love can often prevent hospitalization and the necessity for big increases in medication. Yet, when a risk assessment shows that a person is in imminent danger to themselves or others, and love is not "reaching" the person, then love demands prudence: the person should be hospitalized immediately.

way I'm asking it — Kathy, have you ever, ever in your life
really talked, really opened up, let somebody in, and *really*
talked, heart-to-heart?

Kathy: (looking stunned at the question) Ohhhhhh.... Nooo.
(Crying hard — heaving sobs.)

B: (Now moves to sit next to her, hugging her. She clings, hard, like
a scared child.) Kathy, it's time. Will you let me in? In! There's
a big spot in you that has been alone all your life, and that's
the emptiness you feel. Just let me in. Let me love you.

Kathy: Ohhhh, nobody's ever loved me.... I'm afraid.... Everybody
I love, I lose. (Clings harder, buries her head in therapist's
chest.)

B: I know, I know.... Maybe it has seemed like that, so we'll talk
about that later, but right now, try to believe this: I'm not
going away. I'll be right here. Do you know what I mean
when I say, "Let me in?" In!

Kathy: Into my heart?

B: Right. I want you to let me be part of you, just like you're part
of me. Hon, you've been badly hurt, I know. I really know.
And when people get hurt that badly, they get afraid, and
afraid to trust anybody. So they pull back inside themselves
trying to stay safe. But then you're all alone, and that's even
worse. See? — I know you, Kathy. Don't you think maybe
it's time to let somebody *in* — to be really with you? Are
you letting me in?

Kathy: Ohhh.... (Tears again, followed by full minute of silence)....
Know what? Something just happened inside me. (Smiling
through the tears.) It's true — I've never really talked to *anybody*, let anybody *'in'* as you call it — but I think I must have
just let you in. It's weird. You've always asked me if I knew
where my heart was, and I wasn't sure. Then, a minute ago,
you said something — what was it? — about being alone all
my life. All of a sudden I realized how true that was, and I
thought my heart would just... just split open or something.
God! It hurt! Right here (pointing to her chest). That was the

worst pain I ever felt in my life!.... But you kept saying, "Let me in," and I finally knew I had to... so I did... and that was the absolutely best feeling of my entire life — even though that horrible pain was there, too. Weird.... Bittersweet! That's the word. Sweet and bittersweet.

B: Bittersweet — Hurting, but somehow feeling good?

Kathy: Oh, more than good! It's sort of incredible, wonderful! It hasn't quite sunk in yet, but I know that you... you love me, and that's just.... Do you really?

B: (laughs) Really love you? Sure I do! Kathy; you're easy to love. But test me if you need to; test me a hundred times. The real test, though, is what does your heart say?

Kathy: I know you do.

B: Good — Listen to your heart, Kathy; it's a good one... But you said bittersweet. I know the sweet, but what's bitter?

Kathy: Well, bitter's not the right word. I'm not bitter. I'm just.... It's just a lot of hurt, I guess. I never knew how much pain I had in me. It all came out at once when you saw how alone I always felt. Lord, all the pain hit me at once. It was like my heart... exploded! But the very next minute you said, "Let me in," and all of a sudden my heart was back together, better than ever.... Know what? Now I know why I couldn't find my heart — it was hiding.... Hey, you better not leave me, buddy.

Kathy had diagnosed herself beautifully — a "heart in hiding." Typical of so many people who grow up in alcoholic homes, she had a terrific fear of abandonment: "Everybody I love, I lose." So she guarded her heart, letting no one in. Unable to believe that anyone could love her, she would need repeated reassurance that the therapist's love was real. Eventually, she would let her husband "in," and then others, but many interviews, many months, and an assemblage of many other models and methods of therapy would be required in the process. Virtually all of the dozen or so "eclectic possibilities" mentioned above would be needed.

The interview with Kathy is a rather typical love therapy interchange. What distinguishes it from other therapy approaches? That question again surfaces the terrible difficulty in capturing the meaning of love. In one sense, this entire book will have to serve as an answer. Yet, there is a quality or "spirit" of therapeutic love that perhaps we can distinguish. Therapeutic love is proactive, almost aggressive, and it is blatantly open, transparent, determined, insistent, and very deliberately and intensely warm. For example, it is far more intense, more subjectively personal, and far more intimate than Carl Rogers' "unconditional positive regard." Mere "regard," of any kind, seems entirely too passive, too cool, too distant to reach an extremely defensive person. Therapeutic love is far more than "regard," and more than acceptance, non-judgmentalism, accurate empathy, or kindness, though it certainly includes all of those. This is love that openly, shamelessly, guilelessly, even brazenly begs that it be accepted by the hurting person. Therapeutic love so yearns to heal that it strips off all professional aplomb and reaches out with a naked, transparently open heart, reaching and stretching beyond itself to touch a wounded heart. Yet, this "reaching love" is as confident as a beautiful, innocent child who knows it is irresistible, but as wily, strategic, farsighted and sure as an old Grandmaster at the chessboard. "Reaching love" includes a unique fusion of compassion, wisdom and the passion to heal. There's the word: more than anything else, love that reaches to heal must be passionate.

Staying with Kathy's case, we can show how other therapy models are changed and subsumed into a unified love therapy treatment approach.

Earlier, I listed a dozen therapy models and methods that could be used eclectically to address one or another of the many needs and wounds that were implicit in Kathy's initial big gush of pain and confusion. The first approach was love therapy's "reaching." That love effectively melted a thick shell of defenses that had kept her so painfully alone. Her heart was now, if not wide open, at least thoroughly ajar and reachable. Now what? Which of her other numerous needs, using which therapy approach, should be used next?

I also noted earlier that staying love-centered allows a rather "automatic selection" from among eclectic possibilities. There are actually two levels in this process: diagnosis and discernment. With diagnosis, we can identify problems, and rank them according to both priority and amenability, i.e., according to how severely each problem is affecting her functioning, and how ready she is to let go of her defenses. Discernment, though, is a "heart-level assessment," a psychospiritual capacity that love makes possible. Discernment is "spiritual diagnosis." Thus, the conscious reasoning of diagnosis may indicate that problem "A" is the priority, whereas discernment, the therapist's *raison de cœur*, that mysterious, deeper reasoning of the heart, may either confirm the diagnosis, or it sometimes may surprise the therapist and point to another problem altogether. Following is an example — continuing with Kathy's third interview.

At the beginning of this interview, I was seriously concerned that Kathy might need hospitalization. She was decompensating, overwhelmed with problems, losing defenses, and in her words, "falling apart." In the last ten minutes of this interview, there was an obvious need to help her break down "all" her problems to individual, smaller, manageable problems. She had repeatedly "overgeneralized negativity." Her initial burst of pain was just full of irrational generalizations: *"Everything's* wrong!"; "I'm no good for *anything"* and "can't deal with *anything";* "It's all hell, all shit," and the grand summary, "Life is rotten." These generalizations can often be changed fairly quickly with cognitive therapy, so I used the remaining few minutes to quickly interpret her cognitive errors, and to give her some homework designed to help her regain some focus and control. I repeated five of her negative over-generalizations, and asked her to go home and write down the *specific* problems behind those generalizations.

The fourth interview began with Kathy recalling the profound impact of the last session — the first time in her life she had felt somebody truly *with* her so that she wasn't so devastatingly alone. That terrible, desolate A-lone feeling had swept over her time and again during the week, but each time she had remembered me saying, "Let me in," and she knew she had, so she immediately felt better. As expected, though, she kept wondering whether I really "loved" her. How was that possible after such a short time? Did I just say it and not mean it? It was hard to believe.

Her alcoholic father and co-dependent, neglectful mother had not loved her nearly enough, she felt. She knew she had not let her husband love her, nor even her children, so how could a counselor? We agreed she would have to test me, even though she "sort of" knew I loved her.

She had done her homework well. She had brought a list of specific problems three pages long. It was during the discussion of these many specific problems versus untrue generalizations — a continuation of cognitive therapy — that discernment, *raison de cœur*, surprisingly surfaced in me to abruptly change the therapy approach.

It should be noted that in the first interview Kathy had said that she had been twice sexually abused, but she had adamantly refused to say any more. It wasn't important, she said, and even if it was, she was not going to talk about sexual abuse, period. She had been in therapy twice previously with other therapists and had never discussed it. Given that much defensiveness, I had placed sexual abuse on the back burner altogether, thinking it would be months before she was ready to discuss it.

It should also be noted that even while using a cognitive therapy approach, a rather objective and "heady" process, it is important to continue to maintain a mindset on love and thinking in love terms. That mindset allowed a surprising breakthrough.

B: (Commenting on her new cognitive interpretations of her many generalizations last week.) Good. You did good. You thought in terms of specifics. What do you say now about your big conclusion that all of life is rotten?

Kathy: Well, I still can't say it's a picnic, but it's not all rotten. (Looking at her list.) See? I've got "rotten" broken down. I still say my father was rotten, rotten to the core, and my old neighborhood was pretty rotten, but not all of life.

B: Is life still all "hell," all "shit"?

Kathy: (laughs) No, see? (Pointing to her list) The "hell" is mostly the anxiety feelings and the depression. The "shit" is a glob of god-awful feelings in the pit of my stomach that I just don't understand.

B: But eventually you will, Kathy; give us time. Now what about not being able to deal with "anything"?

Kathy: Oh, I see it now. I can still do my job, and I'm still a halfway decent mother. We've got some real problems with the kids, but you said we'd work on them, too. So I guess I got that one, too. Be specific, right?

B: Right. Now, you said it two or three times, *"Everything's wrong."* Is it now?

Kathy: ... I don't know. I don't want to talk about this.

B: Pardon?.... I'm not understanding.... Don't want to talk about what?

Kathy: (Eyes welling with tears)... (whispering) I don't know.

B: (Totally puzzled) Can you tell what you're feeling?... Thinking?

Kathy: (Bends forward, hiding face in her knees, arms folded over her head).... No, no... no.

B: We were talking about over-generalizations and you were doing just fine. Then I asked if you still felt, "Everything's wrong." Do you?

Kathy: ...Yes! (Cries hard.)

B: Can you tell me why you feel that way?

Kathy: ...I don't know, I don't know.

B: Well, it's not just the generalization. It's the words, isn't it? "Everything's wrong." Who said that, Kathy?

Kathy: (Screaming the words) I did!

B: When? "Everything's wrong" — when did you say that?

Kathy: (Still crying, head on knees)

B: (Suddenly knowing) It was when you were a little girl, wasn't it — when you were sexually abused.

Kathy: Ohhh. No, no, no, no, no, no.

B: (I move to her side, not touching her.) Kathy, I'm here. Can you let me in there, too? I think you need somebody with you, hon.

Kathy: (Flinging herself at therapist, wrapping arms around him.) Oh, its wrong! It's terrible. It's wrong — wrong, wrong, wrong.

Kathy: (Choking on her tears) Ohhh. No, no, no, no, no.... (whispers) Yes....

Slowly, bit by bit, the story came out. At age nine, Kathy was home alone at night. Her father and mother were both out at a bar. One of her father's drunken friends came to the house and raped her. He could not penetrate her, but kept trying, hurting her. When she tried to scream, he put his hand over her mouth and kept trying to quiet her, saying over and over, "Everything's alright. Shhhh. Everything's alright." Then, when he finally released her, he sat and talked to her for a long time, still saying, "Everything's alright" — but everything would stay alright only so long as she didn't tell anybody what had happened. Nobody would believe her, he said, but he threatened her anyway: everything would be alright so long as she just never told.

Each time the rapist said, "Everything's alright," Kathy would think, "No, it's wrong." Afterward, as the nine-year-old replayed his words, "Everything's alright," she would repeatedly counter with the thought, "No! Everything's wrong!"

How I knew, with no doubt whatsoever, that "everything's wrong" related to sexual abuse cannot be explained by the context of the interview, nor by nonverbal communication. Was it intuition? Intuition is based on tiny clues, verbal or nonverbal, but clear hints that hindsight can usually discover. No such clues could be found. In the initial interview, she had said that she had been sexually abused, but she had adamantly refused to discuss it further. Nor was there anything that she said before or after saying, "Everything's wrong" that spoke to anything resembling sexual abuse. Was it blind luck? Of course that could never be objectively ruled out. There is only my subjective experience that can be checked. In this case, I suddenly knew with great certainty that Kathy's severe reaction to the words, "Everything's wrong" related to sexual abuse. That knowledge came from discernment. Later, Kathy would confirm that she "didn't have a clue" as to why she was reacting so painfully to the words, "Everything's wrong." This, I believe, was also an example of *raison de cœur,* heart-level knowledge, reasoning that transcends conscious reasoning, a knowledge that love alone can produce.

These little vignettes from two interviews with Kathy illustrate many of the points of Principle Sixteen. To summarize: a mindset and heart-set on loving, and thinking in love terms, means that diagnosis expands to include discernment, so that objective knowledge of a problem is fleshed out with psychospiritual knowledge obtained intersubjectively. Intense love quickly melts defenses, thus "reaching" the client far more quickly so as to produce surprising, timesaving breakthroughs in a case. Love is truth, and vice versa, but the fruits of that fusion of ontology and psychology are discovered only heart-to-heart, in the vulnerably open context of subject-to-subject communion. Notwithstanding the variety of models and methods of therapy utilized to reach the point, actual healing, a "healing moment," always occurs in an utterly non-objective context, during a nakedly subjective, mutually openhearted, existential encounter. Just as all the scientific and objective knowledge of canvass, pigments, and oils will never produce the talent for a masterpiece painting, neither is objective scientific knowledge the essence of mental and emotional healing; love heals. The brevity of the actual healing moment is related to the principle that a little love goes a long way. The latter, in turn, highlights the fact that all modes, methods and concepts of therapy and personality theory must be orchestrated toward reaching one end, zeroing in on a specific heart wound with love that reaches a crescendo of intensity in a healing moment.

If the dialogue with Kathy has provided a glimmer of the

"spirit" of love therapy, that is the priority. In the final analysis, love is always very simple. That simplicity is usually hidden, though, midst a maze of complexity. Like fire, many constantly changing individual tongues, embers and sparks burn as one. By analogy, the oneness of love therapy is the spirit of love, the whole fire that governs and unites it. That oneness is composed of truths derived from every method and theory ever written.

Continuing to follow Kathy's progress, following are the highlights of how other models and techniques were adapted to fit the love therapy model.

Relaxation techniques for easing anxiety, derived from behavioral therapy[12] were taught to Kathy early on. These were coupled with the use of loving imagery. Specifically, Christmas morning with her children was the time during which she could most readily re-experience love in her imagination. By recalling Christmas while breathing slowly and deeply, she could ease the anxiety symptoms. Though this exercise began as a band-aid, she eventually learned that love did indeed cast out fear (Principle Eleven).

I noted that logotherapy ("meaning therapy") — was helpful in treating the hopelessness inherent in Kathy's depression. Love therapy significantly expands or changes logotherapy by aggressively stating, "Love is the meaning of life. Love means everything." In Chapter Twenty-Three, on depression, I identify "loss" as a main ingredient in the beginning of all depression. That loss, however disguised, is always a love. Given loss of love, meaning is lost with it. As a result, without love, searching for meaning, and logotherapy itself, become meaningless. In the beginning, Kathy could find authentic meaning only in the love of her children. There was "some kind of real meaning" in the love of the therapist, but it was still "too surprising" to understand.

---

[12] A detailed description of a relaxation approach called PSR, Progressive Self-Relaxation, is offered in Spencer A. Rathus, Ph.D. and Jeffrey S. Nevid, Ph.D., *BT Behavior Therapy: Strategies for Solving Problems in Living* (New York: New American Library, Signet, 1977), pp. 14-29.

Much later, she would discover that the therapist being a "man" had a very distinct meaning for her. Her husband's love had a similar skewed meaning.

Fritz Perls' Gestalt approaches, especially the "Saying Good-bye" technique described by Tobin,[13] were utilized in helping Kathy reach and express long-repressed feeling toward her deceased parents, an alcoholic father and an equally disturbed mother. Visualizing her parents in a chair in front of her, she would speak her mind, pouring out anger, fear, rage and pain in its many forms, exposing her heart for the first time. As modified by love therapy, these Gestalt approaches were never concluded until a step toward forgiveness (Principle Fourteen) had been achieved. Guiding the process, I would steadily nudge Kathy's imagery and dialogue with each parent toward the heart of the matter — love abused, love tricked, love abandoned, love faked, and worst of all, the love that was just never there for her. Gestalt, which translates as the "whole," *is* love.

Kathy was given assertiveness training.[14] As modified by love therapy, she began to understand that she not only had a basic human right to assert her thoughts and emotions, but indeed love demanded it. As she grew stronger in her ability to empower herself, even expressing appropriate anger, her overwhelming feelings of powerlessness started to wane. Loving herself, she began to understand that love is authentic power.

Given love's empowerment, Kathy could discuss the sexual abuses more openly. Her sex life with her husband had been virtually destroyed by the two childhood rapes, but she began to see that rape is an abuse of power that has no relationship whatever

---

[13] Stephan A. Tobin, "Saying Goodbye in Gestalt Therapy," in Anthony G. Banet, Jr., Ed., *Creative Psychotherapy: A Source Book* (University Associates, Inc., 1976), pp. 212-221.

[14] Robert E. Alberti and M. L. Emmons, *Your Perfect Right. A Guide to Assertive Behavior* (San Luis Obispo, CA: Impact Publishers, 1970, 1974, 1978). This is a basic book on assertiveness, but many books on the subject have appeared. Universities offer courses in assertiveness, and people entering mental hospitals often receive assertiveness training as a routine treatment. It is an extraordinarily valuable tool.

to authentic sexual love. As she then discussed the two rapists' brutal control and misuse of power, she began to see that rapists are, "at heart, weak, empty, powerless men." Soon thereafter, as she contrasted the attributes of Jerry, her husband with those of the rapists, she changed her definition of rapists: "They're not men at all." Jerry, a mild, loving guy who loved her, would never dream of forcing himself upon her. When she understood how, as a defense, she had displaced and generalized her fear and loathing of the rapists onto all men, indicting them all, including Jerry, she began to experience a happier sex life.

No sexual therapies were ever needed, but it was only after we used more imagery techniques to "confront" the rapists that the authentic power of her love and sexuality began to emerge. Even then, residues of deep shame, the false guilt that is an almost-invariable result of sexual abuse, were hard to shake.

Group therapy with other women, all of whom had been sexually abused, was the most effective approach to Kathy's false guilt. Every woman in the group shared that same all-pervasive, bone-deep sense of shame. The affinity and closeness which their similar terrible experiences provided, bonds born of suffering, allowed them to say to one another, "You're not guilty!" more convincingly than any individual counselor ever could. When the group collectively declared "all-out war on false guilt," Kathy's sex life improved dramatically.

As a child in an alcoholic home, Kathy had learned two extremely distorted views of responsibility: gross irresponsibility, viz., denial of reality, on the one hand, and perfectionistic super-responsibility, on the other. Glasser's Reality Therapy,[15] reinterpreted in light of love principles, was consistently used with Kathy during those times when she resorted to denial, quitting and giving up in the face of anguish and flagging hope. Reality therapy's major theme is a compassionate but tough, here-and now approach that says, no matter how "sick" or problem-laden

---

[15] Glasser, *op. cit.*

you are, you are still responsible for your life; you can and you must be responsible, and there are no excuses. As modified by love therapy, a tight analogy is drawn between "responsibility" and a "commandment." Thus, the Christian commandment is singular: "Love God, and love others as you love yourself." When reality therapy and love therapy are presented together, the principle is stated, "Your first responsibility is to love, and there are no excuses. You can love; you can be responsible enough to love yourself and others. Now, the guideline for prioritizing your responsibilities is this: which responsibility does love demand that I exercise first?"

Many other models and techniques were altered and subsumed into the unified loving treatment of Kathy. Hundreds of other concepts must be incorporated in the treatment of the full range of disorders. The wealth of knowledge that we cannot touch upon here must be left to the devices of other theorists and therapists. Clearly, that will require one of the highest forms of love: creativity.

Because love is pychospiritual, therapy is never complete until the person has grappled with and discovered the spiritual dimension of his or her being, and has found a path toward continued spiritual growth. (Love's spiritual healing is addressed in Chapter Twenty-Five.) Kathy said she was reared a "pagan" with no belief system whatsoever. After practicing silent contemplation, she discovered a "spark" of God inside her, which she called "Love, big L." She then began an intense spiritual search, bouncing from church to church, studying all, and learning to pray. At that point, we terminated therapy. She returns for a session now and then. The bond is permanent.

Love-Centered Art Therapy and Play Therapy

An eight-year-old, Mimi, presented symptoms of anxiety and depression. Her divorced parents had joint custody of Mimi, so she and her little brother were shuttled back and forth weekly between parents, both of whom had remarried. That constant disruption of her life was an obvious source of some of her anxiety, but the larger problem did not surface until during play therapy, our hand puppets started talking about what their hearts were saying. Mimi said her puppet's heart was "hurting," and sometimes, when nobody could hear, the puppet cried — but she could not say why. It was only when we started drawing that the problems became obvious. Kids almost always know where their hearts are, so using art, when the focus is kept on love and the heart, the source of the love disorder quickly became graphic.

Mimi immediately knew the meaning of the adage, "Home is where the heart is," so I asked her to draw a picture with that title. Using colored markers, she drew all the members of both households — parents, stepparents, and children. She drew herself in both places with her valentine-style heart exposed. In her mother's house, Mimi's heart was multicolored, large and pretty. The heart she pictured in herself at her father's house was solid black except for slices of red in it, obvious gashes. Drops of red fell from the gashes. In both hands of Mimi's stepmother were swords, dripping red, and the stepmother's heart was solid black. Her father's heart was outlined in blue, but empty inside.

This little girl's problems leapt off the drawing. Talking about the drawing, Mimi said her stepmother was like Cinderella's stepmother and the Wicked Witch in *Snow White*, "but meaner." And she drew her father's heart as empty because Mimi wasn't sure if he loved her. After all, how could he if he allowed the stepmother to be so mean to Mimi? Though art is used in love therapy as it is in most other therapy approaches, Mimi's drawing illustrates how a pointed focus on love and the heart can reach the heart of the problem much more quickly and graphically. This is not to suggest that a therapist "dive into the heart" in the first interview. Defenses must be respected. More importantly, love alone opens hearts, and love alone heals. As for art, it heals nothing except as a medium for love, but as all the great masters testify, it is a great medium.

Just as love is an ultimate concept, love therapy is, by definition, comprehensive, i.e., it subsumes the truth inherent in all other theories and methods, and it changes, adapts, and orchestrates approaches so that healing occurs in the most effective, efficient way possible. Indeed, love is a panacea — theoretically. Were there a therapist who could love perfectly, and knew all theories and methods, and how to orchestrate them all lovingly, love therapy would indeed be the cure-all for all psychogenic disorders. In practice, though, given human limits, a love therapist, like everyone else, has to learn what I call "the fine art of muddling through" — but maybe not quite as much. Loving muddling is easier than the plain kind.

CHAPTER SEVENTEEN

Existential Love Therapy

Principle Seventeen — Healing Moments Are Brief, Intersubjective, Transcendent, Existential Love Experiences

Beyond all models and methods utilized in the counseling process, the actual healing moment always arrives in the context of a brief, intersubjective, existential event, a "healing moment." That brief instant transcends time, space, materiality and causality, and fuses many emotions, concepts, images and volition into a singular experience of love that effects change in the core of being, the psychospiritual heart. No matter the method, it is the existential, here-and-now way that love is experienced that provides cohesion and unity to the counseling process. In practice, therapeutic loving, and thinking in love terms, often requires the setting-aside of the Western World's linear, cause-and-effect, objective and abstract thinking in favor of a more experiential, subjective, intimate mode of thought which in love therapy is called "love-thought."

Explanations

• Being is love; becoming is loving. Love is the essence of existence (Cf. Principle Seven).
• In the positive sense of what is, authentic human existence, as both being and becoming, is loving — no more, and absolutely no less (Cf. Principle One).

• Love is truth, and vice-versa; they are one (per Principle Eight). In order for a person to integrate a particular truth into his or her being, that truth must be "taken to heart," i.e., truth must be loved in order to become fully real.

• When a truth is perceived by an individual, but to some degree not loved, and therefore not integrated, that truth is unrealized and thus psychologically unreal to that same degree. Perceived but unloved truth may cause confusion, anxiety, and even a fracturing or splintering of being.

• All defense mechanisms — projection, displacement, denial, etc. may be understood in one of three ways: (1) as various maneuvers the heart employs to protect itself against lies, untruths which assault the heart but cannot be loved and integrated precisely because lies are intrinsically unlovable; (2) as efforts to disclaim a truth because it is painful, or (3) as the deceptive protection of a pseudo-truth which has been accepted as a pseudo-love.

• Repressed unloved truth causes enduring confusion and anxiety as it clutters the unconscious pathways to the heart. Unloved truth can exist only as a continuing contradiction of the integrated loved-truth that forms the central core of the heart. In conflict, I inaccurately "know" truth "A," but the heart knows better, truth "B"; or, I "deny" truth "A," but the heart knows better, that truth "A" must be accepted and loved. In either case, the conscious and/or unconscious are at war with the heart. Defenses and symptoms are the many ways this conscious- unconscious- versus-heart war is expressed in the form of mental and emotional disorders.

• The fulfillment, actualization and realization of individual human existence is measured not in terms of achievement, possessions or status, but by being loved and loving. This is best expressed in existential terms: the actualization of human potential is a process of becoming-love, or of bringing-love-into-being. Authentic human existence, i.e., being-truly-alive, means living-as-loving, or living-in-love (not to be confused with mere romance).

- Psychotherapy is the loving, existential process of entering an intersubjective I-Thou relationship in order to understand at heart level how the person's lifelong love-goal — fulfilled living-in-love has been damaged, followed by the loving-healing of that heart-level damage.

- The unitary reality of love-truth, i.e., love as the essence of existence, allows a cohesive view of the human being, and thus reconciles the age-old object-subject schism that has separated essentialist from existentialist schools of philosophy, and Eastern from Western modes of thought. These splits have heavily influenced all theories of personality.

- The phenomenological experiences of time, space, causality and materiality, always subjects of special interest for existential therapists, receive very new understanding when studied in love terms. For example: only love-time is real time. Anxiety, which causes a race to fight or flight to protect love, produces existential fast time. Depression, which deadens existence following love loss, induces slow-time. Psychosis, a response to fractured love, may distort, fracture or destroy time altogether. Similarly, the perception of real-space corresponds to love-space; space becomes distorted as love is distorted. So, too, because love is freedom itself (per Principle Four), the capacity to transcend determinism and the capricious influences of chance are directly correlated with the power of love; existential experiences of cause-and-effect become distorted as direct reflections of the damage done to love's freedom and the capacity to freely choose. Materiality, the existential, subjective way that the substance of the "real" world is interpreted, e.g., as black, cold and colorless in depression, all rosy in mania, hot with anxiety, and topsy-turvy or disappearing in psychosis, is a direct reflection of the equation between love and reality.

Though it certainly has not been so mangled as "love," the word "existentialism" surely has been befogged, abused and bastardized. Federico Fellini and Ingmar Bergman movies, often called "existential," are wonderfully entertaining, enthralling, but leave most of us utterly puzzled. They may be good fun, but some may ask, "Is that existentialism — the study of bewilderment?" In literature, the writings of Franz Kafka and Albert Camus are just as baffling, but trenchantly black, brutal, weary, dreary, and despairing. Yet, Kafka and Camus are often presented as classic representatives of existentialism. If such depressed writers are models, then one would have to ask, "Is it possible to be an existentialist if one is happy?" In painting, the multi-planed, jigsaw faces of Picasso, and the melted watches and bizarre figures of Dali often are seen as existential, as are the jumbled blotches and squiggles of lesser modern artists. Must one see life in weird glimpses in order to be an existentialist? In drama, the "theater of the absurd" presented plays that made no sense whatsoever, but the nonsense in itself was supposed to somehow make "existential" sense. And that provokes the oddest question of all: is it possible to be an existentialist and still make sense? Listening to the arts, one would be tempted to conclude that confusion, despair, fragmentation, terror and nonsense are the hallmarks of existentialism. It is not so!

Perhaps because of such confusing artistic interpretations of the existential, many therapists have clung all the more tightly to "scientific" facts, such truths about human beings as can be measured, categorized, labeled and boxed. Science has a problem, though: love does not fit into boxes, nor do human beings. Surely, there are "objective" things we can say about love, i.e., about its "essence," but if we are going to live it, love is utterly "subjective," a matter of "existence." Thus, notwithstanding the fact that both "love" and "existentialism" have been bloodied, befuzzied and blasphemed, let us trust that by putting those words together, "existential love therapy" can help us transcend some of the confusion that has been evident in both the arts and the sciences.

To spare the reader a long philosophical discourse, let's just note that "Existentialism," à la Rollo May and Ludwig Binswagner, "is the endeavor to understand man by cutting below the cleavage between subject and object that has bedeviled Western thought since shortly after the Renaissance," a cleavage that has been "the cancer of all psychology up to now."[1]

That object-subject "cleavage" that Binswagner described has permeated American thought more deeply than European, and far more than Oriental. And it is not just a split between subject and object. Throughout this book, we have struggled with parallel cleavages between art and science, heart and head, spirituality and materiality, reason and *raison de cœur*, the immanent and the transcendent. Though we have highlighted these splits, there is nothing new about them; Western thought has a long history of cancerous cleavages.

Aristotle and St. Thomas Aquinas cleaved reality in several ways. For example, they said that "being" has "essence" and "existence"; that being is composed of "prime matter" and "substantial form"; that being can be viewed in terms of "substance" or "accident," and that "being" exists both in "act" and in "potency." Those were some of the "classical" cleavages. Many schools of philosophy then lined up on "sides" of the splits.

Rationalists like Spinoza and Hegel lauded reason (devoid of experience). Empiricists like Locke, Hume, and Mill, and Positivists, like many modern day scientists, argue with the Rationalists and deny that reason can arrive at any universal conclusions, so they laud "objectively demonstrable experience." Subjectivists, like Kant, insist that what is "true" for the human mind can never be verified. So much for the history of philosophy, a history of taking sides after splitting reality.

The fundamental problem of the subject-object cleavage is that both modern science and ancient philosophies have searched for "truth," but the truths discovered were abstract, depersonal-

---

[1] Rollo May, "The Origins and Significance of the Existential Movement in Psychology," in Rollo May, Ernest Angel and Henri F. Ellenberger, Eds., *Existence, op. cit.*, p. 11.

ized, and therefore, unreal and inhuman. Rollo May uses the example of adding three apples to three to make six. The mathematical truth would not change if we substituted unicorns for apples, nor would the mathematical truth change whether apples or unicorns actually exist or not. Here the truth is only abstract. "A proposition can be true without being real." It would be both true and real, May notes, only for the person who has the apples.[2]

After providing this support for the existential argument, I must make an audacious assertion: neither the essentialist nor the existentialist philosophers are correct. Unwittingly, as the existentialists attempt to correct the harm done to reality by the essentialists' focus on abstract truth, the existentialists are simply, again, jumping to the other side of the cleavage. As existentialists attempt to redress the balance in favor of individual, experiential reality, they forsake the ideas of essence and objective truth as necessary. Thus, for example, while May makes a point of saying that existentialists do not *deny* objective reality, the fact is that the existentialists, like the essentialists, have never truly reconciled the split of the human being into subject versus object.

Be it ever so bold, what is suggested here is that Principle Seventeen and its Explanations, particularly the first four, which we might collectively call the "love-truth-being-realities," provide the nucleus for a system of thought that finally reconciles the subject-object cleavage. More pointedly, when love is factored into the historical body of philosophical thought, and given the primacy that both abstract reason and total human experience demand, that is, when love is recognized as the first premise of all thought and experience, then the unity of subject-object love impels re-thinking of ontology, epistemology, theology and psychology from bottom-up. The subject-object whole, whether viewed as an abstract, microcosmic, universal truth, or as a microcosmic slice of individual here-and-now human experience, is both essentially and existentially unified by love.

---

[2] May, *ibid.*, p. 13.

Such bold, sweeping statements deserve mountains of explanation, but our purpose here is to provide the necessary philosophical grounding for Psychology. As a philosophy, we can only summarize: all the cleavages that have bedeviled all philosophies — subject versus object, matter versus form, essence versus existence, material versus spiritual, abstract versus "real" truth, head versus heart, etc. — are all reconciled, united by the recognition that authentic living is loving, that truth and love are inseparably one, and that love is the essence of all that exists and the actualization of any potential reality.

It is against the yardstick of the realized human existence as love-filled life that mental/emotional disorders are best understood. Psychotherapy, therefore, is the loving-existential process of entering an I-Thou relationship trying to understand at heart-level how the life-historical universal love-goal of each individual has been damaged, and then healing that damage with love. This understanding often comes in existential love-language.

When rejection has been experienced — rejection by a parent, spouse, anyone loved — the terrible hurt is experienced as "being-destroyed-by-love-withdrawn." In the extreme, rejection is an experience of "being-no-more," an experience that life has stopped because the person was "not-allowed-by-love-to-be." In this painful state, missing love is the same as missing being, missing life altogether. The rejected person moans, "Part of me (of my being) is just gone, empty." In love therapy, this missing, empty part of the "I" is clearly identified as the "unloved I," a part of the self that has sustained loss and emptiness which surely must be grieved and eventually accepted (by many means). But the saving grace is always what remains of being after the unloved-I is subtracted. This is the "loved-I," the "loving-I," the indestructible life of love that can always be discovered to have survived even when the pain of rejection makes it *seem* that the totality of being has been destroyed. (People who commit suicide following a love loss, and those who withdraw permanently into psychotic depression following rejection, would seem to refute this idea that a "loved-I" *always* remains following rejection and love-loss.

It is not so. The fact that no one was able, or allowed, to help these devastated people rediscover the loved-I that survived within them, does not mean that a surviving love did not exist.)

As clients disclose all varieties of negative, unloving emotions, destructive actions, and pernicious life-deep decisions, it is often helpful to identify the sum of all this negativity as comprising a "non-love-life," and to clearly differentiate it from the positive, loving aspects of the person's being, the authentic "love-life." Asking a person to do an inventory of their lives in "love-life" and "non-love-life" terms is helpful in identifying problems and conflicts. It sometimes brings surprising results. While a person is looking at a written list of his/her non-love-life, the simple question, "Do you really need or even want this non-love-life?" can issue in a sudden "change of heart," a simple but firm decision to stop self-destructive patterns, to stop living on resentment, regret and hatred, to forgive, and to start loving again.

Looking at the "love-life" and "non-love-life" inventory also can show a person, often to their surprise, that what they listed in the love category is actually non-love. For example, a forty-year-old man suffering panic disorder, a workaholic corporate executive, had listed in his love-life inventory the whole series of business projects and money-making schemes that had kept his life in an anxiety-soaked tizzy. When I said, "So this is what living and loving means to you? — these projects and deals?" he first cursed, and then started crying. The love-truth, he soon admitted, was that all the busyness projects were a race to be a "big deal" so that somebody might think him worthy of love — because he surely did not. When he returned the following week, he had listed all the corporate projects in the non-love-life category. Soon after, he left the corporate world "to begin life."

The love-life inventory is a rather holistic way of enabling individuals to bring the love and truth of their lives together, as an experienced unit, by using the "love-thought" mentioned in the Principle. That non-abstract, experiential mode of loving-and-thinking-together, by itself sometimes resolves love-truth conflicts. The anxiety-driven executive suddenly saw that a huge part of his life was a lie. As the country song says, he saw that he had been "lookin' for love in all the wrong places." His own love melted his own lies, and suddenly all his defenses melted. Money, status and achievement were not bringing him love, so he set out on a whole new course to become "real" by bringing-love-into-being and being-truly-alive.

This panic-suffering executive had been on the "fast-track," not just racing through life, but anxiously racing life. Time was his enemy. The Explanations allude to the new understanding that love brings to the phenomenology of time.

When people realize that they are being internally driven through life in a race against time, in fast flight, it is helpful to talk in terms of "love-time" versus "clock time," or "fear-time." The subjective experience of time as the "flowing of life," as described by Ellenberger, *et al,*[3] takes on a whole new meaning when life is experienced in a love context.

Consider: in moments of peak love experiences, people are heard to say, "Time stood still." Experientially speaking, who knows, maybe it did. In the midst of an intense love experience, we say, "I wish this moment could go on forever" — and in a certain sense, it does: the exquisite time-of-loving lives on in our hearts and memories till the day we die. Time was "captured" by love, made to stand still.

Anxiety causes a flight in time that parallels the intensity of the flight from threat, whereas love, because it casts out fear (Principle Eleven), causes anxiety to wane and thence causes time to slow down. Love-time is real time. Anxiety-time is fast-time.

Viewed in terms of time, depression is hopeless and thus futureless. With no future to look forward to, time crawls. Depression is past-oriented. The depressing past, though, is like a stagnant pond, covered over with scum, full of rot (bad memories, resentment). It stinks, and it does not move. It is still, timeless.

---

[3] Henri F. Ellenberger, "A Clinical Introduction to Psychiatric Phenomenology and Existential Analysis," in Rollo May, et. al., *Existence, op. cit.,* pp. 101-108.

Depression is slow-time. But as we know both metaphysically and psychologically, time is an experience of change. Given a stagnancy of change, time slows down in depression. As depressed teenagers aptly describe it, "Life's a drag." In treatment, as conflict-resolution and forgiveness allow the depressed person to "let go" of the past in favor of love perceived in the present, the clock speeds up to the pace of real time, love time.

The existentialists have beautifully captured the experience of time and how its perception is changed by anxiety, depression, mania, etc. What is suggested here is that when love is seen as the measure of reality, then the experience of real time is directly correlated with love time, and time-distortions are the products of and directly correlated with love distortions.

Henri Ellenberger provides not only a beautiful explication of existential time, he is even more eloquent in relation to our experience of space.[4] After tracking analyses of space from Descartes and Kant through Galileo and Einstein, he starts with the easily understood experience of space in agoraphobia, fear of open spaces, and claustrophobia, fear of closed spaces. Then, calling upon Binswagner, Husserl, and other existentialists, he gives us a lucid experiential description of how people "constrict" space, or "make themselves broad," of how space can seem near or far, great or small if we live in "oriented space," but "loses its consistency" in schizophrenia. Space can be "clear" or "dark" (Minkowski), and spatial experience changes with one's feeling tone or emotional pitch (Binswagner). Space experience involves all of our senses — not just sight, hearing and touch, but smell, balance, and maybe even taste.

Ellenberger's summary of existential space is beautiful. Yet, perhaps because his view of love is limited to the romantic "lover" experience, he does not arrive at a conclusion, a general principle, that can guide our understanding of the many ways that space can be experienced. Thus, he says, "Love, for instance, is

---

[4] *Ibid.*, pp. 108 -114.

'space-binding': the lover experiences himself close to the beloved in spite of the distance, because in the spatial modality of love, distance is transcended."[5] True enough — but as we've shown repeatedly, love must be understood as the far broader ontological, psychospiritual, essential, existential, and even physical ground of reality. All experience of space, like all experiences, period, can be truly understood only in a love context. By examining "love-in space" and "space-in-love," we can arrive at a general principle. (Let me say it before the critics: that does indeed sound like a "spacy" endeavor. But if we get too "far out" intellectually, we'll laugh. Laughter is one of love's most accurate tests of existential reality.)

As marasmus (failure-to-thrive) babies demonstrate, without love we perish. We just shrivel (lose space) and die.

As tiny tots, love (in the form of parents) is our only protection against threatening strangers and the overwhelming space of the world. Lost in a field or a crowd (apart from parent and love), children cry, terrified of space. Faced with a scary stranger, children hide behind love (Mama's skirts), limiting the space between threat and love. These common experiences already show that the love-space connection is far more than a romantic love phenomenon. These are rudimentary, prototypical experiences that are played out in a thousand other love-space ways throughout life.

In a mental hospital, a schizophrenic often can be identified as the one obviously managing space — shuffling slowly through a wide corridor, hugging the wall, limiting space between self and others. A second, terrified patient is lying in bed, curled in a tight fetal position, regressed in time, "shrinking space" to the size of a uterus, while protecting the small bit of space remaining in which the protection of love is remembered. A third patient stares blankly into space, seeing nothing, not "spaced out" but "spaced in," into a severely delimited interior space. Other patients

---

[5] *Ibid.*, p. 110.

are "lost" in a flight of ideas, or "lost" ten feet from their rooms. And in all these severe cases, just as with marasmus babies and frightened toddlers, the behaviors and symptoms, including spatial ones, are results of love-threats, love-deficits, love-losses. The space distortions can be understood only when we understand the love distortions. The principle is: space-life is a product of and directly correlated with love-life.

Life is love. Thus, an authentic love-life is essential to maintaining contact with reality, including the realities of space, time, materiality, how reality feels, looks, sounds and tastes, and remains balanced.

Causality, as experienced in our individual inner worlds, can correspond to reality only insofar as it is free of misperceived determinism and chance, and this is freedom that only love can imbue. With both love and hope "lost," the depressed person also loses faith in self as capable of determining, causing the future to be in any way subject to her choices, i.e., the person is not free because he cannot grasp love's inherent freedom.

At the opposite, equally unrealistic extreme, the manic person is operating on a regressed, childish form of pseudo-love — not loving, responsible freedom but irresponsible license, an infantile ignorance of cause-and-effect, "love" devoid of truth. Unbound by authentic love's true human limitations, every manic choice is magically "real," rosy, and boundlessly optimistic. In mania, every cause and every effect is influenced only by a "universal pseudo-love" which allows every choice to be "good," "right," and "loving."

Paranoia, understood in existential love terms, causes the person to impute motives to other people, "causes" of others' behavior which the paranoid person could never actually know — and none of those motives are loving. This is projection. The paranoid person has adjudicated every cause and every effect as unloving, hostile, and persecutory. Other people are not allowed the loving freedom to really mean what they say, because the paranoid has predetermined that everyone's motivations (causes) will be hurtful, unloving.

Existential materiality, our inner interpretation of the physical world, remains real, whole, and accurately perceived only insofar as love allows us to remain in touch with reality. When love is terribly damaged and threatened — as it is in children who grow up with physical, sexual, or emotional abuse — materiality sometimes can be lost altogether. As adults, these abused people often remember childhood times when they thought or wished they were "invisible," i.e., immaterial. These children magically "caused" themselves to be unseen and unreal because reality was too painful to remain within it. In emotionally deprived children, this same "invisible" experience is not chosen, caused by the child; they want to be seen, but the nil-love they receive from parents causes them to doubt that they are real, material.

The common defense mechanisms of denial and dissociation, often associated with the post-traumatic stress disorder that results from terrible abuse or witnessing horror, can be understood existentially as interior "tricks" designed to escape the material world altogether. Denial erases materiality as a whole. That part of reality which was so threatening is just "gone," vanished from the interior world. In dissociation, some of the material world and events are "split"; a real but terrifying event may be remembered, but all emotion connected with that event is split off so that, altogether, what materially happened is not experienced interiorly.

Finally, when psychosis is understood as near-total love-lessness, and love as "equaling" reality, existential love makes it a little easier to understand how schizophrenics can become convinced that the world has exploded, or, without love to keep reality glued together, how they can see walls, faces, or the whole earth as splintered, grotesque and upside-down. The principle is: love is materiality; without love, reality falls apart, and with it, time, space and causality disintegrate.

Until now, our focus has been on explaining the "existential" in love terms, and on showing how a purely "essentialist," objective, scientific view of the person can be damaging. Yet, an extreme existentialist approach can be just as nonsensical. We will have to struggle with a little more ontology if the subject-object cleavage is to be healed.

Existential analysts say they attempt to understand *Dasein*, which is interpreted as the person's uniqueness in "being-there," or "being-in-the-world," or "the existence of this particular being sitting opposite the psychotherapist."[6] With all due respect, that is impossible — i.e., if understanding the existence, the *subject*, i.e. self, is in any way separated from the person as *object*, viz., then existence and essence cannot *both* be understood. Just as observation and psychological testing of a person produces mere data, knowledge which is unreal, "factual" but not "truthful," it is just as abstract and untruthful to understand an individual's subjective existence as separate from his objective essence.

An "essence" is defined as "what a thing is in itself," or "that in a being by which it is what it is."[7] Thus, if I am trying to understand Henry, I need to understand (a) his "individual essence," i.e., his Henry-ness, and (b) his "generic essence,"[8] as one among many human beings who have the same nature, i.e., Henry as a thinking, feeling, loving, mortal creature, and (c) Henry's "existence," the specific acts and experiences that mark Henry's being and becoming as uniquely different from all others who share the same generic essence.

The proof that a *purely* existentialist understanding of Henry is impossible is that, without knowledge of his essence, I would have to ask some pretty silly questions of a "nature-less" creature — like, "Henry, do you ever eat, sleep, feel, think? Are you mortal; will you die someday?" Silly? Of course. But if no objective knowledge about Henry matters, if only subjective experience counts, as some pure existentialists imply, then no objective truths about Henry or about any human being could

---

6 Rollo May, "Contributions of Existential Psychotherapy," in Rollo May, et. al., *Existence, op. cit.*, p. 37.

7 Dulles, et. al., *op. cit.*, p. 22.

8 *Ibid.*, p. 32.

ever be taken for granted. Even sillier, if Henry said, "No, I never eat and never sleep, because I'm an angel," then with no generic essence, no objective truth, I could not say, "Henry, those are delusions." Granted, all this essentialist vs. existentialist discussion seems very abstract, but there are very practical consequences to any object-subject, scientific versus existential cleavage of Henry. Here are some quick examples.

A woman came for a first counseling session accompanied by her minister and three women from her church to support her strange, "supernatural" story. The woman would see "lights flash, like small lightning bolts," around various people. She interpreted these light flashes as spiritual signs that misfortune would befall the person who had been "struck," or that that person had a serious spiritual problem. Over several months, others in her church had become totally convinced she was correct. They had confirmed that injuries, sickness or even death did indeed befall some people soon after the woman said that she saw lights flashing around them. Or, if not a physical problem, every "light-flashed" person, when approached discreetly, acknowledged undergoing a recent spiritual struggle. The immediate problem was that the woman was having anxiety attacks because the lights were so foreboding, always a harbinger of bad news. In addition, others in the church were becoming anxious as word spread about the "prophet who saw spiritual lights." The minister wasn't sure if the origin of the lights was good or evil.

This was a case in which a lopsided emphasis on the subjective existential experience, and the exclusion of objective, scientific fact could have been very damaging. The pressure of the woman's convincing inner experience was supported by the zealous inner convictions of others in her church. When I insisted on checking out some possible sources of the lights other than spiritual ones, everyone was upset.

The "aura" or "lights" often associated with the onset of an epileptic seizure was my first suspicion. An electroencephalogram, however, was negative. Soon thereafter, though, the source of the "lights" was discovered: migraines. Not all, but some suffering these terrible headaches report a wide variety of accompanying symptoms, including seeing flashes of light.

In similar cases of anxiety, exclusive focus on the painful subjective experiences associated with heart palpitations could easily miss the objective culprit — a prolapsed mitral valve of the heart or a hyperactive thyroid. Existential treatment of only the subjective experience of depression can result in overlooking an objective cause, hypoglycemia. And a sole focus on the subjective aspects of sexual frigidity can result in blindness to more mundane, objective fact: the woman's husband doesn't bathe.

Yet, in the modern age of "scientific" psychology, and with our Western propensity for linear, boxy, abstract thought, when the existentialists decry the "cancer" of subject-object cleavage, and the objectizing of human beings by positivist scientists, I believe that they are ninety percent correct. Nowhere is this seen more clearly than in large public mental hospitals. In them, huge files are all too often filled with objective data about Henry and Mary, but no one on the staffs has more than a glimmer of subjective knowledge as to who the real Henry and Mary are as unique people. The result is that all the objective data is not just worthless paper, it is the vehicle for a damaging collective delusion, the shared false belief of the staff that "Of course we're helping Mary and Henry. See? All this paper, objective knowledge, is proof."

Once it is recognized that love and truth, paralleling subject and object, existence and essence, are indivisibly one, the schisms disappear. To love Henry is to know him, and to know him is to love him. To pretend to know Henry without loving him is to objectize him, make him an inanimate thing. The reverse is just as illusory: to pretend to love Mary without knowing her, both objectively and subjectively, is to love a phantom, a fiction, a meaningless file, and thus to not love at all. However, if I know-and-love Mary, my love-knowledge is one, just as Mary is one; as a result, any destructive cleavage of essence versus existence, object versus subject, psychology versus spirituality — becomes impossible.

Once the essential-existential unity of love-knowledge is affirmed, the age-old, bedeviling subject-object split is reconciled. The consequences for every philosophy, every school of psychology — every human discipline, in fact — are staggering. Our purposes here, though, are limited to psychology. Given subject-object unity, we can look at the practical consequences of love-thought for mental health — starting in the mental hospital with Henry.

If it is now accepted that we can only love the person we know, and know the person we love, that only love heals, and that healing occurs only when objectively- and subjectively-derived knowledge are fused into a subject-to-subject healing moment, it follows that every hospital resource, every professional discipline, every method of diagnosis and treatment must be crystallized so as to bring about a series of "healing events": intersubjective encounters during which Henry discovers his defenses melted, becomes vulnerable, and opens his heart and its wounds to a staff person who has both the objective and subjective knowledge needed to precisely target each wound and to then infuse healing love. More succinctly, love theory insists that mental hospital treatment would be more effective if the primary responsibility for love's healing of each patient were fixed in *one* staff member. Sound organizational theory insists that such a staffing pattern is simply logical because if everyone is responsible, no one is responsible.

Though healing love is always a subjective existential experience, love therapy may require many hours of very objective therapies before the time for existential healing can be reached — from objective data-gathering while obtaining developmental, medical and social histories to the use of very non-subjective approaches like cognitive therapy, behavior modification and assertiveness training. Those objective demands of love may receive priority in some cases. In most others, a mix of objective and subjective approaches is typical. There are, however, some emotional disorders that benefit most from "pure" existential love therapy. Here is an example.

Judy's Existential Uncertainty

A thirty-five year-old woman, a bright, attractive legal secretary, Judy had been in and out of counseling with me for four of the previous twelve years. An abusive marriage had consumed half of that time, but that was not her deepest problem. She was chronically depressed, mildly but persistently anorexic, and constantly anxious, hyperventilating several times a day. For fifteen years, she had clung to a job she hated because it was "secure," and because her employer seemed to be an approving father figure. She was one of six children, but she always had felt distant from the entire family, depersonalized, like she did not belong. In counseling, she had exhaustively uncovered the ambivalent, shallow form of love she had received from her parents, worked hard at grieving their lack of love and forgiving them. Yet, her depression continued unabated. She continued to present a charming, smiling, assured face to the world, and she continued to cling dependently to the therapist. Given love therapy, she had often said she "knew" that I loved her, and she had talked for many hours about the difference between parents' coldness and my warmth. Yes, she was "sure" of my love, but talking directly about the dependence, she could not understand why she could not let go of the therapist, nor why she remained almost as depressed, anorexic, and anxious as she had been ten years earlier.

In the following interview, Judy had been talking about how everything was so difficult, and how tough every decision was, and why, as a result, her life remained so miserable.

B. (Brennan Mullaney): You're generalizing again, Judy. Remember? Generalizing negativity triggers depression. Now, it's not *everything* going wrong, and it's not *every* decision that's so difficult, is it? Can you be more specific?

Judy: Well, I guess it's not everything wrong, but every decision is terrible, every single one, always…. Yesterday I stood in a store for fifteen minutes trying to decide if I should buy red or green Christmas candles. I just couldn't decide! It's always like that.

B.: Always? (Note: This sounded obsessive, but neither interviews nor psychological testing had ever revealed any obsessive-compulsive traits in Judy, so I was surprised.) What else is so hard to decide?

Judy: Everything! I go back and forth, yes and no, red or green, maybe or maybe not, on *everything*! I never know what I think. Up might be down — I'm never sure, of anything.

B.: (Still surprised, and trying to understand. Judy's indecisiveness seemed far beyond the level of either her depression or anxiety, both of which can interfere with decision-making. This seemed to be a totally separate disorder.) Wow, Judy, you've never told me that. Do you mean exactly what you said — that if you think yes, it might be no, "A" might be "B," right might be wrong?

Judy: Right. (Laughs) Or maybe wrong — about everything and everybody, but mostly me.

B.: So anything you think, anything you feel, you don't trust? You don't believe what you think? About *anything*?

Judy: Nothing... (tearing up) I guess that's why I keep coming to you... to make sure of what I'm feeling, of what I think. I'm never sure. You always make me feel better, but I'm still never sure about anything. I can hardly wait till I see you the next week.

B.: So all this time you've been sure of me, but somehow not sure. Judy, there have been dozens of times you've said you knew that I loved you. Do you know that? Do I love you?

Judy: ... Better than anything — yes....

B.: But...?

Judy: But... but you won't *always* love me. This will end someday.

B.: So my love for you isn't permanent; it's not real; you can't be sure of it?

Judy: (Harder tears now).... I'm not sure of *anything, nothing!*

B.: Oh, boy.... So what's real might be not real, right might be wrong, what you feel might not be what you feel.... Judy, if I quote Shakespeare, "To be, or not to be, that is the question," then what do you say?

Judy: (Tears slowing, thinking)... Maybe. To be or not to be *might* be the question... or to be might be not to be.

B : Oh, boy.... Let's try another one. Here is a first principle, a first statement about reality: "What is, is." React, Judy.

Judy: What is... maybe is — or maybe not....

B.: Wow. Try this: "A thing cannot be, and not be, at the same time." What do you say about that?

Judy: (Laughs) It can be for me! Anything can be, but it might not be true.... How would I know for sure?

Judy lived in constant, pervasive being-level uncertainty. The "losses" underlying her depression involved far more than the love-losses involving her parents, family, or even her own being. Her loss was being itself, reality in any form. In light of the love principle equating love and reality, counseling had to reach the deepest conceivable level, that of being itself. For Judy, though she "knew" and sometimes "felt" that at least the counselor loved her, it was as if love had never "clicked" as an intellectual-emotional whole; she "knew" but "did not know." Therapy then focused on enabling her to have her first subject-to-subject heart-deep experience of love as real, the event which can be called an "existential healing moment."

When "love" is added to the body of knowledge of existential therapies, insights emerge which cast both emotional disorders and counseling in a new and different light — this: underlying every serious and/or chronic emotional disorder is a hard core, a fixed existential *state of being*, which means that, in counseling, a loving healing moment must be reached if that destructive existential state is to be healed. The implications of these two concepts are huge. They are the subject of the next principle.

CHAPTER EIGHTEEN

Existential States of Love Disorders

Principle Eighteen: Love Heals Pathological States of Being

Serious and/or chronic mental and emotional disorders can be understood as pathological, existential states of being, fixed heart-mindsets which develop as adjustments to love wounds, distortions and deficits. These existential states form rigid cognitive-emotional-volitional (being-pervasive) false definitions of the self, others, and life itself. Located at the deepest perceptible "floor" of the psychospiritual heart, the existential state encompasses and thus colors and distorts every perception, emotion, thought and decision. For this reason, every symptom and cause of a disorder may be intensely treated without producing any marked change — because the existential *state* underlying the total being was not changed. In love therapy, accurate diagnosis requires discovery of the existential love-language that accurately describes a pathological-love state of being. Then, treatment requires subject-to-subject heart-level interpenetration of beings in which love can heal by "heart transplant," i.e. transformation of the pathological state into a state that truthfully reflects the unique love-reality of the person.

Explanations

• A pathological state of being is a fundamental, heart-level belief or conviction in which the totality of the person's being is

271

fixed in a lie, a distortion of truth which was originally designed to both protect and sustain love, and to evade the most destructive lie of all: "I-am-unlovable."

• The most persistently baffling question in mental health has been why are the disorders of some people chronic, intractable, and so impervious to even the best and most extensive treatment? In some cases, the answer is obviously that there is an unidentified organic problem. In many others, though, the answer is that the person is living with and in a sick existential *state*. By definition, a "state" is fixed, permanent; it does not move; it does not change.

• A pathological state of being may be viewed as an "I-am..." statement which defines personal identity (internal reality) at the being level, and thereby distorts and limits the perceived reality of others and life itself (external reality). For example, the pathological state of "Being-in-necessary-constant-dread-of-non-being" is one of the states typically found to underlie panic disorder. This state is a living lie because such dread is rarely ever "necessary," and because even when fearful events do occur, they do not cause annihilation, non-being, nothingness, the "worse-than-death" feelings that this state induces. Given the state, though, everything — self, others, world — is clouded, distorted and predetermined by the fear which is an integral and dominant part of the "I." Reality, therefore, both internal and external, is twisted by the state in various unreal ways because the person believes and therefore lives the lie.

• Each emotional and mental disorder can be more clearly understood when described in terms of the existential state that underlies it. Moreover, verbalizing the existential state can accurately express the single fundamental problem that underlies a multiple diagnosis and a variety of symptoms.

• An existential state of being both encompasses and determines the classic "modes of world" that characterize the existence of each person.

> The existential analysts distinguish three modes of world, that is, three simultaneous aspects of world

which characterize the existence of each one of us as being-in-the-world. First, *Umwelt* literally meaning "world around"; this is the biological world, generally called environment. There is, second, *Mitwelt,* literally the "with-world," the world of one's fellow men. The third is *Eigenwelt,* the "own-world," the mode of relationship to one's self.[1]

These three modes of being operate in complex dynamic interaction, but the single pathological state of being is a constant, an inexorable force that continually limits and skews all of reality, including the three modes of being-in-the-world. The "state" is the single underlying determinant of the ways that *mitwelt, umwelt* and *eigenwelt* exist and operate.

• The deepest, reachable "floor" of the heart that is formed by a pathological existential state is a false floor in that it cloaks and hides the deeper realities of personhood and authentic individual identity. "Knowing one's self" therefore becomes impossible. This false floor also acts as a barrier to aesthetic and spiritual sensibilities because it blocks the passageways to the interior mysteries that lie deeper in the heart.

• A pathological existential state is typically formed by multifarious love-related wounds and deficits. Healing consists of a corresponding number of "healing moments," intersubjective events during which love is integrated so as to infuse and fill each wound or love-deficit.

In actual counseling, when a person is finally enabled to put into words the pathological existential state that has dominated and twisted his identity, messed up relationships and caused oh-

---

[1] Rollo May, "Contributions of Existential Psychotherapy," *Existence, op. cit.,* p. 61.

so-much suffering, the discovery is met with a profound "Ohhh!" that expresses both the joy of liberation and the sad regret that the state ever had to be. Once discovered, the pathological state can be targeted and transformed, but in the beginning of therapy there is a hurdle to jump. Mention of that hurdle should perhaps preface this discussion.

Unavoidably, as we describe many of the existential states (below), many of the concepts are highly philosophical. What are ordinarily considered very abstract ideas must be brought down-to-earth. The person whose only "philosophy" has been "Live and let live," must learn to think in terms of "first principles," being, essence, existence, and logic. Ordinarily, this begins with a straightforward explanation: "You're talking about your deepest self, your very being, so you're talking about existentialism and ontology whether you realize it or not — so we need to discuss some philosophy so you can apply it to what you think and believe about yourself, and maybe rethink some of it at heart-level."

This discussion will be devoted to describing some of the more common mental and emotional disorders in terms of the pathological existential states which underlie them, define them, and determine their course. Be it "being-fixed-in-negativity," or "being-an-emotionless-thinker," or any of hundreds of other unique possibilities, each state may be viewed as the individual's "first principle of being."

Philosophers live by two adages: "Define your terms," and "Grant a man his first premise and he can prove anything." Grant me that "the moon causes madness" (as some actually believe), and I can prove that the sole mission of The National Institute of Mental Health should be to transport all mental patients to the moon so they can get to the root of their problem, or, that the role of NASA should be to cure all mental illness by blowing up the moon. Grant a child's first premise that he is "totally unlovable," and that child will "prove" that nothing that seems real is real because it is all unlovable. We'll call the child psychotic until someone can change his first principle, his state of being. Grant an incest victim her first premise, that she is defined as "an-un-lovable-nobody-except-for-sex," and she may turn to prostitution as a state of being in which she lives out her false first principle.

In each of the following states of being, though the word is sometimes not used, it can be presumed that obtaining or maintaining love was and is the original purpose and continuing goal of the state.

"Ontological Uncertainty"[2] (as seen in the case of Judy, in the last chapter) is a fixed state of being marked by the constant, deep inner conviction that any particular reality, defined as "what is," just might be "is not." The general result of this being-level disorder is an inability to firmly believe or trust anything that the self thinks, feels, or decides, and thus a similar inability to believe or trust reality as others present it. Though this deep uncertainty can result in many chronic disorders, including psychoses, some people can often function well vocationally and interpersonally, at least superficially, by "faking it," wearing a well-practiced mask of competence, cordiality, and ostensible agreement with what others say — while actually being sure of and believing almost nothing at heart level. The cost of this faked cordiality and amiability is repression of any emotion that would upset the precarious balance of external, "faked" certainty, and internal heart-level uncertainty. In turn, the repressed emotion may be manifested in depression, anxiety, or virtually any other disorder. Always, beneath the facade, a highly dependent personality is discovered — one who is constantly searching for affirmation of self and reality, loving affirmations which can allow certainty. The source of this profound uncertainty is invariably found to result from depersonalization in childhood: the person received a superficial "maybe" form of love from parents that disallowed the ability to affirm the inner reality of self, i.e., the capacity to

---

[2] The phrase "ontological uncertainty" is not mine; the concept was described in May, et. al., *Existence*. My contribution is the interpretation of ontological uncertainty as a fixed pathological state.

love the self and then be certain that being itself was ever "right," "good," or "true" enough to be loved and real.

The existential state of "being-fixed-in-negativity," is common in all depressions. It is a heart-and-mind-set that defines reality, self, others, past, present, future — being at every level — as wrong, bad, hopeless, negative. In mild depression, negativity may be present, but it is not "fixed" as a heart-deep conviction as it is in the existential set-in-concrete *state* that is seen in chronic depression. In milder negativity, the generalizations can often be reversed by discussion of specific negative items. When a negative state is reached, however, debate of item-by-item points is futile; healing must occur at the holistic heart-level. The difference between ontological uncertainty and "being-fixed-in-negativity" is that in the latter, reality, including the reality of self, is at least affirmed as real, even though it is interpreted as preponderantly negative.

"Being-fixed-in-past-time" is an existential state in which the person is essentially "living," not in the present, and with little or no thought of the future, but in times gone by — in past-time that receives constant rumination and the expenditures of all emotional energy. The fixed-in-past state must be differentiated from a regression. In a regression, the person returns to the present, whereas in an existential state, virtually every statement is in regards to the past, and any present reality is immediately related to the past. Nor is the fixed-in-past state the same as fixed or arrested emotional development, for in the latter, it is ordinarily not the total personality that is past-oriented.

"Being-as-anybody-wants-me-to-be" is an existential state marked by such extraordinarily low self-esteem and lack of heart-level identity that the person adapts and conforms his or her own personality to whomever he/she is with. With chameleonic facility, the person almost instantly changes the color of personality to reflect any person faced. People in this state cannot begin to answer the "Who am I" question. Rather, they wait for clues from others as to the kind of person preferred. This is a state of "being nobody" to a degree that is difficult to imagine. Following is an example.

Gretchen had grown up with three disturbed women, her mother and two aunts. All three "lived for" Gretchen. Even though Gretchen was married with three children, the trio would telephone her no less than fifteen times per day, and each day she would go out to lunch with one of them. They would dissect her every thought and feeling, doting on her, while at the same time smothering her. As a result, Gretchen was full of anxiety, and depressed, but most of all, "lost." When I asked if she knew who she was, she answered, "I'm nobody — except for who they (the trio) say I am." Were it possible for Gretchen to be any more enmeshed and consumed by her relatives, her identity would have become, "I am them."

"Being-in-necessary-constant-dread" is the being-level state that underlies many of the more severe and chronic anxiety and phobic disorders. Given that only love dispels fear (see Principle Eleven), and that anxiety is caused by threats to love, this state of constant dread can be pictured as a fixed threat that is falsely defined as true, and therefore is integrated into the ground of being at the deepest levels of the heart, thus causing the heart to be in constant dread of love's (being's) annihilation.

There are, of course, countless specific threats that are possible, so the wording of the state always needs to be expanded as therapy progresses and the object of dread becomes more clearly identified. For example, the state may be "*I-am*-in-dread-of-abandonment-by-anyone-I-love," or "*I-am*-in-dread-of-anyone-discovering-my-sin-which-defines-me-as-unlovable," or "*I-am*-in-dread-of-men-who-must-all-be-brutes-like-my-father." The individual heart-mindset that fixes the fear as a "necessary" and "constant" definition of self and being can be extremely precise and difficult to unearth. Indeed, especially in phobias, the actual object of dread may be disguised by a symbol associated with the actual threat. Most therapists are accustomed to helping the sufferer search for both the symbolic and actual threats that trigger anxiety.[3] Sometimes that is enough to relieve the problem, but certainly not always. In severe and recurrent anxiety disorders, counseling may trace the origins of the problem all the way back to preschool days, uncover the threat, its symbols, how the threat is connected to defense mechanisms, and minutely analyze the dynamics of the hidden fear that is producing the symptoms, and it might not be enough. The person's anxiety might well continue until the existential state that is *fixing* the fear as an integral part of the person's identity and being-in-the-world is also identified and changed.[4]

As therapy progresses, "being-in-necessary-constant-dread" invariably is expanded to name the bottom-line explanation of every anxiety, phobic, and panic disorder — a love threat. Thus, for example, states of dread that are more specifically identified as "dread-of-high-places-symbolizing-aloneness...," or "dread -of-open-places-representing-vulnerability-to-past-trauma...," and even "dread-of-heart-attack-and-death...," are invariably completed by words "...wherein-I-will-be-totally-unloved." The heart-level experiential equivalent of the last two words — "totally unloved" — might be described as "annihilation," "destruction,"

---

[3] *Ibid.*, p. 51. Here, Rollo May makes a distinction which helps to differentiate anxiety from fear: "While we are subject to anxiety, we are to that extent unable to conceive in imagination how existence would be 'outside' the anxiety.... Anxiety is ontological, fear is not. Fear can be studied as an affect among other affects, a reaction among other affects. But anxiety can be understood only as a threat to *"Dasein."* *Dasein* involves the individual's unique and total being, his being-in-the-world. In love therapy language, fear is "outside"; anxiety is "heart-deep."

[4] Most counselors help clients search for the underlying threat, a past experience, "old tape," that is causing anxiety or a phobia, but not all. Behavioral therapists treat the symptom directly by using a stimulus-response conditioning approach to "extinguish" or desensitize the fear. Nor do cognitive therapists search for repressed sources of the fear; they focus instead on here-and-now "automatic thinking" and "cognitive errors" that precipitate the fear. While love therapy may utilize either of these approaches to relieve symptoms, it would not stop there. If a symptom exists, it flows from a heart-deep wound, and that wound must be healed if full healing, wholing, is to occur. Symptom-relief and behavior change without heart-deep healing often means that expression of pain will pop up in another symptom.

or "being crushed to nothingness," or as "the agony of nonexistence." However phrased, the message of people returning from an encounter with the desolate depths of the worst anxiety all seem to be unanimous: "Without love, 'being' is not just an excruciating agony, it just doesn't exist." Without love, Shakespeare's "To be, or not to be," is not the question — because we don't even have the choice.

In actual therapy, arriving at the final encounter with the ultimate dread, lovelessness, first requires discovering some very unique, even odd, symbols, images and quirky meanings that individuals attach to their painful experiences. The following case illustrates just how unique the existential state can be.

Penny's Existential State

A thirty-two-year-old, single, very bright communications professional, Penny had suffered lifelong periods of alternating depression and panic attacks. She had grown up, she said, on the slum streets of New York City. Both her parents were alcoholic. Family life was tumultuous and poverty-stricken. At age twelve, she entered a mental hospital and saw her first psychiatrist — for depression and serious thoughts of suicide. She improved. Five years later, her father committed suicide. She survived that, but her sister became psychotic and her brother landed in prison. Life went on with her alcoholic mother — "hell on earth." Penny left home in her early twenties, but had been in therapy with five different therapists for a total of twelve years. She came to see me for panic attacks and depression that she had never escaped for very long.

In her fourth interview in love therapy, the question turned to why she always relapsed. Just the hint of disapproval and a tiny argument with a new boyfriend had thrown her into severe panic attacks during the previous week. With other therapists, she thought she had unraveled and worked through all the traumas, fears and losses suffered in her alcoholic, strife-ridden home. Yet,

the least upset (a spat with a boyfriend) had again thrown her
into a panic attack.

Penny: I became vulnerable again and I don't like it. I had feelings for him and I didn't realize it... till I thought I had hurt
his feelings. Then I panicked. I was terrified! My heart was
pounding and I couldn't breathe! It was horrible! Saturday,
I called him (the boyfriend) thirty times and couldn't reach
him. I was a mess. A mess! But why do I always go back?
Why do I always hit the bottom of the barrel? It was bad. You
could have scraped me off the bottom of the barrel — again!
Why? Over and over....

B. (Brennan Mullaney): This was three days ago, so you've had
time to think. What are you coming up with?

Penny: I did the cognitive stuff you taught me. You were right.
The thoughts in the back of my mind were all negative (quoting her hidden thoughts): "I screwed up everything, like
always," and "I'm just stupid," and telling myself I hadn't
learned anything in therapy, ever. You were right: I was
telling myself a bunch of lies.

B.: And did you catch yourself regressing?

Penny: Oh, yeah! In my mind, I took Jerry (the boyfriend), and
lumped him together with Dad (viz., his suicide), and then
I called Jerry thirty times and got no answer, and I thought
he might have killed himself. I see what I did now. I always
see it — later; I've had a lot of therapy, you know. But why,
why do I keep hitting the bottom of the barrel?

B.: Maybe we need to jump in and look at the bottom of that
barrel. That "bottom" you always go back to sounds like a
fixed state to me. (Here I explained the idea of pathological
existential states at some length, using "being-in-necessary-
constant-dread-of-love-loss" to describe the "bottom of the
barrel" of an anxiety state.)

Penny: Oh! Oh! That's it! Ooohhh! I just remembered! (Trembling.
Cries hard for a full two minutes.) When you were describing those states, you said the word "core," that these states

exist at the core of our being, and I remembered the big flat piece of metal that covers the hole that will suck me into it! Ooohhh.

B.: A hole…?

Penny: Nothingness! Ugly! Oh God! I'll be gone! (Bending double in her seat, covering her face, crying).… This was the same feeling I had when I saw, when I went in the mental hospital when I was twelve. That black hole, like a tornado; it's going to suck me into it! Oh, God! You talked about a state, the core of me, and I got the image of that flat piece of metal. I can't describe it.… There's a huge whirling black hole that's going to suck me into it, so I invented this big thick piece of round metal to cover the hole.…

B.: Go on.…

Penny: It's still there! The hole! It's always been there. But sometimes the piece of metal slips! There's the hole! (Even harder tears. Her whole body is trembling.)

B.: (Hugging her.) Will you let me be there with you? Try to listen to me, Penny. I think I understand what happened to you. That hole isn't real. There's no such thing as nothingness. It can't get you. It won't suck you into it because it's just an image. I think that hole was just a bunch of bad feelings, the image that little twelve-year-old Penny used to picture those bad feelings. But it's not real, Penny.

Penny: Oh, God, it *seems* so real! In the hospital, I didn't tell the psychiatrist about the hole because I thought they'd think I was crazy and never let me out of the hospital. I've been running and working my whole life to keep that hole covered with the metal plate. God! What *is* it? That hole?! It's horrible! Horrible!

B.: I'll tell you what I think it is in a second, but first we need to do something. First, tell me everybody in your life who loves you, even a little.

Penny: (Names two best friends, a "little love" from her brother and sister, and a few others.)

B.: So we agree that you are lovable, and that you couldn't be
totally unlovable?

Penny: No, I usually feel unlovable, but I know I'm not.

B.: But you feel unlovable because that's what the hole represented.
The opposite of love is nothingness — like that black hole,
a horrible empty pit — nonexistence. And that's what the
little twelve-year-old Penny had felt all her life, unloved and
unlovable — because both of her parents were sick and they
just couldn't love her the way she needed and deserved. But
now you know you're lovable, so you don't have to be afraid.
There is no hole.

Penny: That's why I was always afraid? — the hole.... No doubt
of that. But what is it? I felt unloved — that's what the hole
is?

B.: We'll have to search for words to express it, but your entire
being was fixed in a *state* of keeping that hole covered, keeping nothingness, unlovability, at bay. For the twelve-year-old
Penny, that was a powerful experience, powerful enough
to start you thinking of suicide. I think the hole was the
child's way of taking all the bad, sad feelings she couldn't
voice — feelings of bleak emptiness, hollowness, the black
hopelessness and the lovelessness of the family — and
expressing all of them the only way she could, congealed
into an image, the hole, the tornado. The image of the hole
is like a "picture" of the black depression, emptiness and
lovelessness you felt. Scary feelings; there's nothing scarier
than lovelessness, so you dealt with the hole the only way
you could: you imagined a metal plate covering up the hole.
Actually, it was a very creative solution, but not a real one.
It's like you tried to build your entire personality on top of
that metal plate.

Penny: Ohh, Lord! (Still shuddering) It seemed so *real*. I can still
see that hole — pitch black darkness. But it's not real, dammit! I've got to believe that.

B.: You do indeed. That powerful experience was the deepest
conviction of your life, the way you defined your very being.

If we translate the hole into words, it was like you defined yourself as, "*I am*, at heart level, an empty hole of unlovable nothingness." Now, that's a damn lie! That's not you. Who are you?

Penny: Lovable?

B.: (Laughs) Absolutely! Now all you have to do is start believing that.

This interview demonstrates both the common, and some very unique features of the pathological state of being we call anxiety or panic. In this case, the anxiety was closely linked to feelings of profound depression. Later, Penny described her state as "being-in-constant-mortal-terror-of-a-hole-of-loveless-nothingness."

Writers of every school of psychotherapy have struggled to find words to express the interior world of emotional disorders, which sometimes take on weird, surreal dimensions. With Penny's case, which is fairly prototypical, we can perhaps better understand why finding words for the interior experience is so difficult: facing lovelessness, which is existentially experienced as nothingness, utter unreality, nonexistence, the feelings produced are very real. The person experiences blatant interior contradictions: nothing feels like something; unreality feels real; a painfully palpable feeling is produced by nothing; non-being seems as real as or even more real than being. Defense mechanisms and symptoms continually express these contradictions, but the contradictions remain in force as an integral part of the state of being — being that is defined in both essential and existential ways as unloved and unlovable. Such contradictions, like anxiety itself, can be found underlying most disorders.

In the child Penny, who was not psychotic, one "hole" came to represent the nothingness of lovelessness. In one who is psychotic, there may be scores of "holes," sprinkled with bits and glimpses of reality tied together only by unreal symbols of love-as-a-wish. For example, while psychotic, one young woman was convinced that the rock singer, Prince, was her lover. Another, a middle-aged woman, though she works and functions well in daily life, lives with the delusion that the television evangelist, Pat Robertson, is in love with her. In these cases, both women found bits of convoluted "truths" to prove that they were loved by their symbols, Prince and Robertson, albeit from afar. For both women, their fantasy lovers had been integrated into their states of being — pitiful substitutes for the authentic love that was so terribly missing in both their lives.

Paranoia, as a fixed state of existential being, may be expressed as "being-loveless-and-thence-in-distrust-and-unwilling-ly-vulnerable-(unprotected-by-love)-in-a-world-defined-as-unloving-and-hostile." A delusion of persecution, like any false belief, is a distortion of truth. Love is truth, and trust is possible only as a function of love. Paranoia is well-known as a stubborn, intractable disorder, so it can readily be seen as a state of being, a fixed way of viewing life. Suffice to say, though, if a counselor focuses solely on trust issues, the delusional state will persist. However, when the rock-hard defenses of the paranoid person are melted by love, trust inevitably follows as the fundamental state of being changes.

Hypochondriasis, as a state of being, can be expressed as "being-in-constant-fear-of-the-pain-of-love-loss-with-that-heart-level-pain-fixed-obsessionally-in-pseudo-physical-illnesses." Hypochondriacs will often "doctor hop," so doctors and attention-getting sometimes become integral parts of the persons' states of being. In those cases, after the hyphenated phrase above, adding the words, "seeing-doctors-as-the-last-hope-for-love," may better express the state. No question, though, hypochondriacs are in pain; something is indeed always hurting them, but that pain is heart-level, the abiding presence of the agony of missing love.

These few examples must serve to illustrate that every disorder is grounded in an existential state, a "heart-mindset" which is formed in response to a wide variety of love wounds and deficits and all the sad ways that love can be twisted, rejected, slashed and ripped. In the examples given, hyphenated phrases attempt to express the "heart" of each disorder. I should hasten to add that an existential diagnosis can never be a pat formula. On the contrary, every individual's state of being includes utterly unique features which can only be discovered intersubjectively. Penny's state, for example, included a "metal plate" (defense) covering a "hole" (loveless nothingness). Similarly, a paranoid person may "fix" on a particular (innocent) person — perhaps a neighbor, Mr. Higgins — as the sole persecutor, spy and scoundrel whose imagined skullduggery is making the paranoid person's life miserable. In that case, "Mr. Higgins" would become an integral part of the deluded state of being of the paranoid person.

Let me hasten to add that reaching the existential depths of a person is by no means a word game. Be it a "metal plate" or "Mr. Higgins," "finding the right words" to express a disorder, by itself, heals nothing. Rather, finding the right words is important only because love must be "on target," precisely zeroed in on heart wounds.

As we continue to grapple with words to express the *experience* of healing love, it may be helpful to apply the existential approach to understanding how love is communicated and exists, "lives" in the patient-therapist relationship.

Heart Transplant

I have emphasized that love therapy requires heart-to-heart interpenetration of beings, subject-to-subject communion, the goal being "transformation" of the pathological state into a loving state which reflects the deep inner reality of the person. That treatment process, in severe cases, is tantamount to a "heart transplant."

Unlike a physical heart transplant which takes place in a few hours, psychospiritual heart transplant often requires years of work. The end result may be just as dramatic as a physical heart transplant in that the person is given new life to replace one that was near death, but psychospiritual transformation is the effect of many "healing moments," a thousand small steps. Until now, I have spoken of these moments only in the generic sense.

In fact, there are many types of healing moments which can be differentiated. Understanding of the existential states of being which underlie various disorders makes it easier to understand healing moments.

Healing moments are like "mini-states." As *experiences*, they are typically brief in duration, but each moment then "becomes absorbed" into the whole of the person and lives on as an integral part of the person's general state of being.

Like existential states, healing moment experiences can best be expressed with series of hyphenated words. If we are accurate in our attempts to "capture" love experiences, the following examples of healing moments will speak for themselves and require little explanation (even though every reader will surely not have had every experience). The notes that accompany the healing moments pertain to goals and expectations in therapy.

"Being-heart-to-heart" (intimate intersubjectivity) — These "moments" come and go in therapy. "Objective" discussion is always necessary, but on balance, speed in healing is directly proportionate to the amount of time spent heart-to-heart, intersubjectively.

"Being-infused-with-warmth" — This is the client's major emotional experience of the therapist's love, but this experience is actually far deeper than emotion; it is soul-stirring. Unlike a fleeting feeling, this experience brings about permanent, heart-level change. For some patients, this is a new or rare experience. Some are taken aback by it.

"Being-melted-and-made-open-(non-defensive)-by-the-dis-arming-mildness-of-undeniable-love" — Painfully "breaking" defenses with aggressive, direct interpretation is rarely necessary. The same interpretation can be given mildly, lovingly, with far better effect. Better still, powerful love, with no interpretation at all, will often allow defenses to be dropped. The first experience of this healing moment, that point in time when a person responds to the safety which love offers and then melts, lowers defenses, becomes open, trusts, and allows self to be reached and loved, is often remembered as the first real breakthrough.

"Being-surprised-to-tears-by-love's-spontaneous-gift" — Unexpected kindness can melt any of us, but for people who have received a paucity of love in their lives, or for those who always thought they had to "earn" love, the experience of the authentic gift of love with no "catches" can bring profuse tears. These tears are lovely signs of healing.

"Being-relieved-of-heart-level-pain-as-a-wound-is-infused-with love" — This is the quintessential healing moment of psychotherapy. Objective fact-finding, exploration and ventilation of feelings, correction of cognitive errors, assertiveness training and many other steps may be necessary preludes to this moment, but only love makes healing happen — and that is always mysterious. Because healing love is psychospiritual, we are forced to use images and metaphors in efforts to describe it. We may picture healing love as "spiritual flesh" being poured into a gaping, empty wound in the soul, filling and renewing the heart, vanishing the wound. In another case, we may imagine healing love as warm water being poured into icy pools in the heart, warming them. When a "dead" area of the heart is brought back to life, we may need to wax poetic by envisioning healing love as a "holy elixir" which causes resurrection from death. Beyond any words or images, though, love always remains an awe-inducing enigma — even, or perhaps especially, when it is we ourselves who are ministering the love.

"Becoming-physically-lighter-as-love-lifts-the-burden-of-wounds-borne-alone" — People typically report "tons" being lifted from their shoulders after unburdening heavy souls and being authentically loved. Many report feeling "light as a feather." (This physical effect of a healing moment is a mini-illustration of how love can heal psychosomatic and psychogenic physiological illnesses.)

"Becoming-clean-of-heart-as-forgiving-love-replaces-guilt" — This is the profound and universal healing moment that follows confession of great guilt and the experience of being forgiven and loved. It is not the therapist's forgiveness that is needed nor given.

Rather, the therapist's love guides the person to seek forgiveness from another person, from God, or from themselves. The "cleanness" that is experienced is often accompanied by the "lightness" mentioned above; guilt always lies "heavy" on the heart. Depression often fades after this healing moment.

"Being-tearfully-grateful-for-love" — This "mini-state" often is a precursor of other healing moments which are more specifically wound-related. For any of us, love is always a gift for which we are grateful. For people who have been love-starved for much of their lives, their gratitude is akin to that of a person dying of thirst in a desert who is given lifesaving water. Perspective is needed. People who experience such huge, tearful gratitude for love have typically falsely defined themselves as unlovable. Their tears can become an occasion for even more healing if the therapist's response is to the effect, "But you are a lovable creature, *easy* to love, so why should you be so surprised if I love you."

"Being-in-withness" (Communion) — "Withness" describes a mini-state-of-being which people who have always felt "utterly A-lone" have never experienced; they have never been able to let anybody "in." Though similar to the "heart-to-heart" experience, "withness" must precede heart-level communication. Faced with a person who has been defensive and alone for a lifetime, a counselor can "see" walls go up when the person's heart is approached. If the counselor responds to the walls warmly, saying, "Has anybody ever been truly with you — *with* you? Can you let me in? Let me *in*. Let me be *with* you," the person often will. As a first time experience, when defenses are lowered, tears often follow. This is a time people need and can accept being hugged.

"Becoming-transformed-by-the-presence-of-the-loving-other-becoming-integral-with-self" (healing by union-level identification) — In love, by definition, we always become "one with" those we love who love us. Normally, a child with loving parents is loved, loves, and that love creates, forms the child's personality. In therapy, severe love deficits vanish as the client is loved and becomes one with the therapist. This may be a long process, so the transformation may involve countless tiny formational healing moments. The cumulative effect of a thousand existential love experiences — a nod, a smile, a word, a hug, a tilt of the head — is that the loving presence of the therapist "abides" as a permanent, integral part of the client.

"Becoming-alive-to-self-and-senses-as-love-melts-defenses" — After being too-long preoccupied with workaday problems, most of us have had the happy experience of "waking up and smelling the roses," suddenly realizing that there are still clouds in the sky, trees to be seen, and air to breathe. Sometimes it takes a vacation to restore that sense of aliveness, but we are not so surprised when the full experience of being alive returns to us. In contrast, some people with emotional problems have virtually never had that experience. For them, defenses have not only kept the threat and pain of life out, they have kept life out, period. Severe defenses cause us to throw the baby out with the bath water. When love allows those defenses to be melted away, people with lifelong depression or anxiety are often utterly amazed to discover that the existential state of aliveness actually exists. With the discovery, senses awaken and the simplest life experience suddenly seems new. Wind on the skin, a child's laugh, a starry sky — all are experienced as if for the first time. Some describe this experience as being like rebirth.

"Becoming-present-to-self" — As the "becoming-alive" experience relates to the senses and the outside world (the *Umwelt*), the "becoming present" experience relates to the inner world of self (the *Eigenwelt*). Though most of us are very aware of our being, a person who has been splitting-off feelings for a lifetime (dissociating), or one who has been "stuffing" many emotions (repressing or denying), may be utterly surprised to discover, "I am!" One man compared this experience to hearing a teacher call roll: "It's like I faintly heard my name being called, over and over, thousands of times, and then it suddenly dawned on me, 'Hey, I'm here! I'm alive! Present!'"

The twelve healing moments described above are just a few

of the innumerable experiences, some subtle, some profound, which occur in the process of love's infusing and transforming a painful, pathological state of being into one which is symptom-free and love-centered. In the course of therapy, it is not always necessary or even possible to find words to express all the positive nuances of experience that go into healing. Sometimes, though, it is essential. Yet, we have had no means by which to identify these positive events. Hospital charts and office records typically say little more than "Patient feels better," or "Less anxiety today," or "Client reports depression lifted somewhat." It is noteworthy that Psychology has focused a mountain of attention on developing lists of hundreds of symptoms, scores of defense mechanisms, dictionaries and manuals full of pathological terms — all negative — while giving so little attention to the positive experiences of healing. Why is that? It is as if we thought that if we could identify and get rid of the negative that the positive would automatically follow. That is not so. Draining pus from a physical wound may *allow* healing, but it is not in itself healing. So, too, draining negative emotions from a heart wound (catharsis) may facilitate healing, but it is not in itself the positive experience that heals.

The lesson was clear for love therapy: counseling must be proactive, essentially positive. Identifying the negative (symptoms, painful memories, defenses, etc.) is important only insofar as it targets where love, a totally positive experience, is needed. More specifically, by naming the precise, positive healing moments which the client needs to experience in order to be healed, the therapist can then structure and guide the interview, and precisely tailor and target love so as to bring about each specific, positive experience, each healing moment.

When love pervades the whole atmosphere of counseling, clients will often begin a session by saying, "I'm better," without being able to say why. Identifying the precise healing moment can be an important step. Following is a typical example. This was a 40-year-old man suffering depression.

Brennan Mullaney: I'm glad you're better — but you can't say
why? Look, you must know by now that I'm kind of incor-
rigible: when you're down, or hurting, I want to know why;
when you're up, feeling better, I still want to know why.
When, how, what's better?

Client: I think it was after I saw you last week. You were late for
the appointment, and I was mad....

B: And...?

Client: And I *told* you I was mad. I almost yelled at you.... I
couldn't believe it. I got mad and let you know — told you....
When I was a kid, if I ever got mad at my father, he'd knock
my head off.... But you didn't even get mad.

B: Of course not. You had a perfect right to be mad. Like I said
last week, I was late because I was held up in traffic, but that
doesn't mean you didn't have a right to be angry. You did.

Client: Well, it was a first for me. I *never* get mad, at *any* body. I
think I've been squelching anger all my life.

This man's healing moment was a first-time experience of
"being-loved-(even)-when-I'm-angry." For the therapist, accepting the man's anger was not a conscious effort "to love and to
heal"; it seemed at the time to be a mere common courtesy: I was
late; he was angry; I accepted his anger as his perfect right, so I
apologized, and we went on — no big deal.

But it was a big deal to him! Love is always a big deal,
but staying conscious of how love is working requires what we
described earlier as a mind "set" on love, an effort to constantly
"think in love terms." Perhaps women know better than men that
love is mostly "the little things." Even a tiny common courtesy is
loving, and therefore might be healing. In counseling, as everywhere, every little bit counts.

Existential love therapy suggests the answer to the most
baffling and frustrating question about mental illness — "Why
are these disorders often so intractable, recurrent, and difficult
to change?" The answer, in a word, is that mental illness is a

state of existential being, a fixed heart-mindset which develops in response to love deficits, distortions, and damage. That state exists at the deepest reaches of the inner world we call subjectivity, the center of being. As such, a disorder cannot be touched nor affected by any "objective" means, no matter how "correct" those means may be. Thus, psychological testing, analysis, cognitive and behavioral therapies, educational programs, and other objective approaches may pave the way for healing, but actual healing occurs only in the context of the most nakedly human, heart-to-heart intersubjectivity, and then only if the love given is received. Only love heals.

Again, by no means do I mean to present love as some magic elixir that can perform some razzle-dazzle quick-fix on emotional disorders. On the contrary, if we realistically imagine a pathological state as being formed by a thousand heart wounds, we can "quantify" total healing as requiring a corresponding thousand healing moments. If anything, therefore, love therapy presents emotional disorders as far harder to heal than any of us want to admit, perhaps because they seem to demand more love than we think we have.

Do we dare ask if we have enough love to help the teeming millions who are suffering love disorders? Love, beyond all odds, beyond all reason sometimes, is inherently hopeful. As noted earlier, hope certainly does not lie in "more knowledge," for knowledge alone heals nothing. Nor does hope lie in "more professionals," for there will never be enough of them to provide anywhere near the vast quantity of love that is needed. Indeed, love is the only hope. Given that hard fact, all we need is a love revolution, that's all. This book, following the mad, mad, mad demands of love, has the audacity to call for that revolution. In later chapters, at least a peek, if not a vision, of how that revolution just might be possible will be offered.

The foregoing eighteen principles provide the theoretical foundation of love theory and love therapy. A principle is defined as "a fundamental, primary, or general truth, on which other truths depend." So how many more love principles are there? God only knows; maybe oodles.

Surely these eighteen principles have provided some inkling of just how all-encompassing and comprehensive a concept love is. But God alone is a comprehensive thinker, so only He could write love principles "correctly."

In the next part, many major mental and emotional disorders are reinterpreted and redefined in light of the love principles. In the process, examples are given as to how love therapy is practiced, and how many of the traditional therapy models and personality concepts are integrated into the love paradigm.

Throughout the book, the overall goal is to incarnate love, to bring it down to earth, not just in principle but in practice. Aye, there's the trick, to *practice* love. Who knows but that after wading though all the complexities of love, we'll discover that learning to love is just like mastering golf or the piano — "Practice, Practice, Practice" — and that love is all just play.

Part Three

LOVE THERAPY WITH THE MAJOR EMOTIONAL DISORDERS

People who do not intuit or respect the laws
of acceleration and momentum break bones;
those who do not grasp the principles of love
waste their lives and break their hearts.

Lewis, Amini and Lannon[1]

---

[1] Thomas Lewis, M.D., Fari Amini, M.D., Richard Lannon, M.D., *A General Theory of Love* (New York: Vintage Books, 2000), p. 13.

Chapter Nineteen

Utter Lovelessness: Death or Psychosis

> The deepest need of man, then, is to
> overcome his separateness, to leave the
> prison of his aloneness. The absolute
> failure to achieve this means insanity.
>
> *Erich Fromm*[1]

The deepest need of woman, man and child is to be loved and to love, and in so doing to overcome aloneness. The absolute absence of love means death, and the near-absolute absence of love means insanity.

The remainder of this introduction to love therapy has a few somewhat ambitious goals: to reinterpret the entire spectrum of mental and emotional disorders in the light of love's understanding of them; to persuasively show how all mental/emotional problems are love disorders; and to describe how love, and only love, can and does heal them.

As noted earlier, the concepts of quantity and even quality inevitably fail to fit with the mystery that love is. There is, though, a kind of "scale," albeit a rough one, which can be intuited as love therapy is practiced. This "Love Scale of Disorders," a simple, six-level chart that relates every disorder to one of six broad "quantities" of love, is shown in Chapter Twenty-One, and discussed more fully there. Here, we need to explain only that love at Zero

---

[1] Erich Fromm, *The Art of Loving* (New York: Harper & Row, 1956), p. 9.

Level produces death, and that in the next levels up, One and Two, the quantity of love is so minimal that psychosis results.

Zero Love Level: Marasmus Death and Suicide

The most negative extreme on the love scale, total absence of love in early infancy, provides absolute proof that life and love are the same thing, a perfect equation. Infants who are grossly deprived of minimum human warmth — cuddling, touching, and fondling, the rudimentary kinds of love essential for beginning life — though they are adequately fed and physically provided for, quickly shrivel, wrinkle, and die. These are the "marasmus" or "failure to thrive" babies described in Chapter One, the infants who died during the Spitz study.[2] Their deaths were induced by lovelessness.

Suicide

Though it is infinitely more complex than marasmus death, most suicides are also classified as Zero Level love disorders. Suicide occurs when neither love nor hope for love can be perceived, so nonlife, i.e., non-love, becomes intolerable. Excluded from the category are those suicides by people who are "apparently" rational and who destroy themselves for a motive they perceive as "good." Given love theory, this misperception would be called a deadly pseudo-love. These supposedly rational suicides, supported by such organizations as the Hemlock Society, are in fact tragic mistakes of logic and belief.

Other than the pseudo-rational type, all suicides are products of virtually absolute lovelessness. The love therapy interpretation makes it clear why it is not life that suicides want to escape, but the opposite. Life is love. Love cannot be destroyed

---

[2] René A. Spitz, *op.cit.*

by physical death, but physical life in the total absence of love is nonlife, death, an intolerable agony which the person feels must be escaped.

Though it may sound contradictory, suicide must be understood as an escape from living death through physical death. Given zero love, all of us would be marasmus babies or suicides.

The brevity of this explanation of suicide obviously cannot do justice to the multitudes of variables that surround self-destruction. Some suicides are accidents, pleas for help that backfire. Many are impetuous actions influenced by alcohol, drugs, or psychotic panic. A few are consequences of perverse sex games gone awry, while a few are tragic results of curious children "playing" suicide. Most, though, are best explained in terms of non-love. Deep depression, despair, self-hatred, anomie, and soul-wrenching agony — all the horrible feelings that lead to suicide — are understandable only in love terms, for love, after all, is our only hope.

Suicide is discussed here only in order to provide a needed perspective for understanding psychoses. In a later chapter focused on depression, suicide is discussed more extensively.

Love Levels One and Two — The Psychoses

The next level up on the love scale are the schizophrenic, bipolar, paranoid, and schizo-affective psychoses. Psychotics fill the hospitals, and more thousands roam the streets, muttering and hallucinating, and virtually that entire population is given standard ineffective treatment: stupefying doses of tranquilizers and a twenty-minute chat with a psychiatrist every three months to adjust medication. The barest fraction of them are given intensive psychotherapy. A few are given day treatment, i.e., socialization programs, but the greater truth is that *standard* treatment of psychosis is this: little help.

Why? There is broad agreement that no one has understood what psychosis really is. Thousands of experimental studies have amassed a mountain of descriptive facts, but little understanding. Hundreds of theories have been advanced, but virtually no knowledge that could bring real healing of psychoses. The latest popular theory is that psychosis reflects "chemical imbalances." The fact that Lithium sometimes helps dramatically with bipolar (manic depressive) psychosis may account for the increased popularity of the chemical explanation. Yet, psychotics still overflow the wards and roam the world, perhaps not hallucinating as much, but stuporous from psychotropic drugs.

In the face of all this failure to understand this most tragic of all human conditions, psychosis, I offer here a single explanation — gross love deprivation — and an overwhelming difficult prescription to fill: love in massive doses. Yes, it is a simple one word solution, but not at all simple to understand.

(Note: this discussion of psychoses must be prefaced by the forthright admission that my personal clinical experience with psychoses has been somewhat limited. In graduate school, I spent a year of field training on a ward of psychotic men in a V.A. hospital, and in social agencies, a number of psychotic clients were always a percentage of the caseload. Yet, of the thousands of people with hundreds of various disorders whom I have counseled in the past forty years, the least number have been psychotic. While I believe love therapy can be more successful than other approaches with these disorders, my small sample of clients and my limited experience with psychotics must be taken into account in evaluating this chapter. More than any other, this chapter is the most purely theoretical. It is based primarily on sheer logic of love theory, and must be evaluated in that light.)

Psychotics, unlike marasmus babies, do not physically die. They are given enough love to survive — but barely enough. The psychotic is so grossly deprived of love that the self remains unformed, fractured, splintered, "unrealized," and therefore unable to realize the reality of self, others, or the world. Without love to protect us, the world is a fearful place to be. Only love can protect me from storms and strangers, but more, only love can *form* me so that I am not a stranger to myself, another feared object in a stormy, terrifying world.

Love alone provides cohesion for the human personality. Love is the internal glue that keeps our personalities intact; drastically deprived of it, we collapse into shards. Faced with non-love, unprotected by love from outside, unformed by love inside, the psychotic withdraws from reality, takes flight, "goes to pieces." Thus, the most common identifying symptom in "simple" schizophrenia is "flight of ideas." The schizophrenic's ideas are fragmentary — pieces flying — but they accurately reflect the helter-skelter content of a self, unformed by love, that is full of memory-experiences which have no place to be grounded, rooted, integrated. Without love as a formational "substance" which is the self, life's experiences are like dandelion seeds blowing in the wind with no good earth upon which to land.

Inappropriate affect, another major identifying symptom of psychosis — silliness, flattened feelings, quickly alternating laughing and crying, mugging, and the like — are similar expressions of the absence of love's integrating guidance. All emotions are various expressions of love (per Principle Five), but in schizophrenia, love has been so seriously deficient that emotions are not ordered, not grounded. In this "loose" state, the emotions of the schizophrenic are prey to whatever willy-nilly stimulus happens by, be it a surge of adrenaline, a capricious memory, or an insignificant exterior happening.

Despite overwhelming odds, until we can find a way to instill massive doses of love into schizophrenics, thus "giving them a self," their emotions and thoughts will remain groundless.

The other schizophrenias are variations of the same theme: loveless people who are thus selfless.

The hebephrenic schizophrenics are those who assume identities of others because they are so substantially lacking a self — and simply need one. Thus, becoming Napoleon, the Virgin Mary, or Lincoln are pathetic efforts to be, not a selfless, unloved nobody, but "somebody," even if it has to be somebody else. Interestingly, the new persona assumed is typically somebody known to be especially great, good, and lovable.

The paranoid schizophrenic's delusions of persecution especially reflect the distrust and fear of people and the world, fear and distrust which only love can heal. But harkening back to Principle Eleven, only "love casts out fear... fear has to do with punishment."[3] The unprotected, loveless interior of the paranoid makes suspiciousness and expectation of punishment inevitable. Paranoid people with whom I have been allowed to intimately communicate, describe a degree of loneliness that normal people cannot imagine. It is not like solitude, nor being lonesome; it is that living nonexistence in a devastated wasteland which I previously described as "A-lone!" The delusions are, in fact, ways of reaching out for love. For example, a dominant paranoid feature, "ideas of reference," the false belief that "people are talking about me," perhaps even in television newscasts, are pitiful ways the unformed self uses to say, "I'm not nobody; I'm not so utterly A-lone; I'm somebody important enough for strangers and the T.V. to talk about." At the same time, with no love, the fearful expectation of punishment and persecution saturates the whole perception of the world.

The psychoses, a short step removed from marasmus death, ordinarily develop in the preschool ages, in the sense of beginning, but the lack of love, the aloneness, the separateness, usually can be seen to have pervaded childhood. These are the most severe disorders because the formational role of love in creating the self was so thoroughly absent that interior reality was never existent enough to receive, perceive or interpret outer reality. Reality, then — other people, the world, self — is utterly confusing. Inner and outer reality cannot be differentiated clearly. Fear, distrust, delusions, hallucinations and weirdness are inevitable when love is grossly deficient.

The defined limits of self, which therapists call "ego boundar-

---

[3] 1 John 4:17.

ies" are in fact "love's reality boundaries," a reality that is defined by love, felt as love, and integrated into the self as love. Only love defines reality, and the only reality of the personhood is the self that has been loved. The hard fact is that when therapists try to help psychotics *find* their ego (love) boundaries, they are asking them to find something that is substantially nonexistent. This is extremely analogous to asking a congenitally legless person to learn to walk, to find their legs. Yes, that sounds cruel, but that is precisely what is happening to psychotics, and it is just not fair because it is wholly unrealistic. People suffering from psychosis are "developmentally loveless" just as surely as others who are born with limbs that do not grow. Ego boundaries, love boundaries, indeed the self itself, must be given to the psychotic. They do not need therapy that is merely reconstructive; they need that which only love can provide, formation from the ground up. The formation they need requires not just a creative form of therapy, but a therapy that is creational.

Thinking back to Principle Seven on Reality, and then considering the ideas of psychosis as "congenital lovelessness,"[4] note that "congenital" and "Genesis" both relate to our beginnings. In the beginning, "Love created the heavens and the earth…" and people. Each and every one of us has our own unique Genesis. We are generated with love. In the beginning — for each of us who is fortunate enough to be sane — we were created by love. The genesis of self, of our own unique reality, is the genesis of love. Self-reality-love; it is all one package. We began, each of us, when love created us, and only to the extent that love created us. For believers, God began the creation, but He was and is dependent on us and our parents, all of humanity, to complete the creation, the loving genesis that He began in us. In the genesis of the psychotic, something went wrong; the creation was not complete enough for

---

[4] It may be noted that I alternately use the phrases "developmental lovelessness" and "congenital lovelessness." "Developmental" is more semantically accurate when applied to psychoses because the *absolute* absence of love, as is implied by the adjective "congenital," would produce a marasmus or still-born baby.

a reality of self to form. Congenital lovelessness resulted.

Genesis, the very creation of a self, is the only healing for psychosis. "Healing," though, is a great understatement of the need of psychotics. The self — not just ego boundaries, but the heart of a unique person — must be planned, nurtured, and formed, created. And there is only one way to do that — with massive doses of love.

How that much creative love can be mustered to be given to the massive population of people lost in psychoses is clearly a matter of not just change, but revolution, a wholesale reorientation of society. Is that a grandiose, utopian idea? I believe that is not the question at all. The question is not, "Will we ever get there?" (to a loving society). The question is not even, "Will we begin?" Rather, the question can only be *"Will I begin?* to love, in earnest, and put my whole heart into it?" Realistically, the only way to begin this revolution is the hard way — one by one by one, beginning with me. Paraphrasing a hymn, the revolution will begin when I say, "Let there be love (and peace) on earth, and let it begin with me."

The love revolution has begun.

Did I digress from the subject of psychosis? Not really, because the reason psychotics cannot find enough therapists with enough love to heal them is directly due to the stark raving madness of a generally dog-eat-dog society that damn well refuses to love. While I do not agree with many of the gloom-and-doom views expressed by R.D. Laing, he is a beautiful psychiatric iconoclast who sees the madness of the "normal" world very clearly.

> Humanity is estranged from its authentic possibilities. This basic vision prevents us from taking any unequivocal view of the sanity of common sense, or the madness of the so-called madman....
>
> The condition of alienation, of being asleep, of being unconscious, of being out of one's mind, is the condition of the normal man.

> Society highly values the normal man. It educates children to lose themselves and to become absurd, and thus be normal. Normal men have killed 1,000,000,000 of their fellow normal men in the last fifty years.[5]

The reason for psychotics going so often unhelped must be seen against the backdrop of massive social madness called alienation — the massive sheer craziness that Laing is very correct in lamenting. In stark contrast, however, my view of sanity and insanity is unequivocal, and the basic vision of love is quite clear, wholly unalienated, and incorrigibly hopeful.

At this juncture, it may be time to ask the most painful question of all: Is there any hope for the world's millions of psychotics? Even if we refuse to buckle under the weight of Laing's description of the world and "normal" people as all sick-sick-sick, and even if we hold out hope for normal people becoming more loving and thus more able to heal, is it in any way realistic to say that love is the ultimate hope for the world's psychotics? As a research hypothesis regarding the psychoses, love has lots of competition. Let's tackle it.

Causes of Psychosis: Organicity versus Lovelessness

Quickly, having made the bold assertion that lovelessness causes psychosis, let me leap to recognize that my exception of "organic" disorders may include a vast number of chemical, hormonal, or electrical brain disorders which in future years may be proven to be the causal factors of *some* psychoses. One need see only a few CT scans of the brains of chronic schizophrenic patients — pictures of cortical atrophy, gross ventricular enlargement, or a lymphoma of the corpus callosum, for example, and the fact that some schizophrenias are organically induced becomes

---

[5] R.D. Laing, *The Politics of Experience* (New York: Pantheon Books, 1967), pp. 12, 28.

indisputable. Neuroendocrine disorders, clearly shown by measures of CRF, ACTH, DST, or MHPG, also show that some other disorders may be hormonally or chemically induced.[6] Yet the fact that a chemical, hormonal, electrical, or even a structural anomaly of the brain can be shown, does not preclude the possibility that many of these physical disorders were originally caused by the psychogenic disorder that I call lovelessness. Remember! Marasmus babies sustain such horrible organic devastation, including brain damage, that death results — but the primary causal factor was that those babies were grossly deprived of love. In addition, we know that an enormous range of organic diseases, everything from skin to stomach to heart diseases, some of which do enough damage to cause death, are caused primarily by emotional disorders, viz., some type or degree of lovelessness. Is it not entirely reasonable to hypothesize that if disturbed emotions and love deprivation can cause a stomach to perforate or a heart to physically break causing death, that that same love dysfunction might just as easily cause the brain's serotonin system, dopamine transmission, or caudate nucleus to go physically awry, or even to deteriorate, causing a "nervous breakdown," a psychosis?

Clearly, this is a chicken-and-egg question which will be debated for decades to come. We will not resolve it here. For the present, all any of us can do is sift the research, boil it down, and finally act on what we *believe*. Surely there is not one answer. Multitudes of answers will come, and many will prove to be not either/or organicity versus lovelessness, but both/and.

Is Psychosis the Parents' Fault?

Lest the parents of patients suffering chronic psychoses be hurt unnecessarily, let me hasten to explain that even though the

---

[6] Nancy C. Andreasen, M.D., Ph.D., *The Broken Brain* (New York: Harper and Row, 1984). More detailed information regarding the terms used in my few paragraphs on organicity can be found here. This is an excellent overview of the physiology of the brain and of research regarding organic causes of mental disorders.

conclusion is unequivocal and definitive — lovelessness causes psychosis — this does not necessarily mean the parents of psychotic patients did not love their children. On the contrary, there is abundant evidence that the parents of many psychotic patients did indeed love them. Clearly, there are enough families in which all the children are emotionally sound, except for the one psychotic child, to prove that some parents are consistently loving and one child still becomes mentally ill. So what happened? What is the answer to the seeming contradiction between "lovelessness is the universal cause of psychosis" but "some parents of psychotics were loving"?

The answer to that riddle may lie in an experience we have all had to one degree or another: just because I am in fact loved does not necessarily mean that I receive and experience that love. The apparent contradiction of love existing, but not being perceived, and therefore not being received, happens all the time. It happens with adults, and children experience the contradiction frequently. Is there *any* parent who has not heard his or her pouting child say, "You just don't love me"? Indeed, there is good probability that every one of us has said or at least thought those words as children. And for the child, the words "Nobody loves me" are often felt and believed to be the truth. Granted, sometimes those words are just pouty ploys to get a cookie. Often, though, that pouting child really is convinced that he or she is unloved by Mama, Daddy, and the whole world.

For the psychotic suffering lovelessness, but one who in fact was loved, it is as if the love in his/her life acted like vaccinations do sometimes: the love was given, but for some mysterious reason, it just "didn't take"; parental love was given but not received by the child. Why a particular child did not receive the love that the parents are sure they felt and offered, might be extremely subtle: an older, demanding sibling constantly interfering with the love-communication process can "short circuit" the parents' love, usurp that love, or shunt it away from a younger child. A noisy, too busy, rambunctious home can be so distracting that love actually communicated is never heard.

It is also plausible that a child saying "Nobody loves me" could, for various reasons, become "stuck" with that idea. Freud spoke of a child becoming "fixated" at certain stages of development — oral, anal, Oedipal — but that is a rather superficial, analytical, "heartless" idea that has never adequately explained the mind-ripping and soul-shattering agony that can cause psychosis. For a young child to become "fixed," convinced, and self-defined as "unlovable," however, *does* explain how the whole interior psychic world of a child can be so thoroughly devastated that reality is "lost."

Again the question, "But *how* could the nobody-loves-me idea become so fixed?" is open to many subtle possibilities: a four-year-old who is feeling "Nobody loves me," simultaneously told by a "mean" six-year-old sibling, "Nobody loves you," could permanently absorb that idea if it happened often.

It is also plausible for the "Nobody-loves-me" idea to become fixed as a result of an accidental event coinciding with the child's magical wish. We know this can happen. A child feeling "Nobody loves me" is quite likely to also have companion thoughts like "I hate Mama/Daddy; I wish they'd die." While these thoughts are going on, if the parent is hurt in an accident, the child will too often feel that she/he caused the injury with the wish. This is the well-known capacity of the child for magical thinking; the "wish becomes the deed." In this case, though, the wished deed becoming a reality has a devastating effect; it "proves" to the child, "Nobody loves me — *because* I'm not worthy of love *because* I hurt people with my wishes." The result then is that the typically short-lived thought "Nobody loves me" becomes supra-reinforced, "proved," permanently fixed. Thenceforward, love can never be sufficiently received so as to provide love's "grounding" of reality (described earlier).

In fact, though, these possible reasons for some children becoming fixed with the "Nobody-loves-me" conviction, and eventually becoming psychotic, are hypotheses, theoretical possibilities, not proved. There is research that supports these possibilities, however. It has been statistically shown that low-income people suffer psychotic disorders more frequently and more severely than higher income groups. Any social worker who has visited many homes of the poor can testify to the kinds of disorder, discord, and distractions described above. It is entirely reasonable to deduce that this high distraction level would correlate with love's communication to the child being more frequently short-circuited or blocked in the homes of the poor.

We also know that when births of two or more children are spaced too closely in time, given the fact that there is only yea-amount of mother-love to go around, one child may be unintentionally given short shrift, and thence be relatively unloved.

The possibility of the child's "Nobody loves me" and "hateful" wishes coincidentally becoming reinforced by real events, is also supported by the statistics on crime rates in geographically poor areas. The chance of a child wishing a parent dead, and the death or injury becoming fact, is far higher among children of the poor — just as psychosis is higher.

Suffice to say here, while it is entirely reasonable to state that lovelessness induces psychosis and to then deduce the scores of possible ways that the fundamental love needed as grounding for reality is blocked, shunted or short-circuited, we need a great deal of research.

Parent-Induced Psychosis

The focus above was on the subtle ways that love can be blocked and psychosis can develop in the child of loving parents. The lovelessness is far easier to see in other families. We need not belabor this. As love providers, some parents are extremely disabled. Some children receive just enough love to avoid death as marasmus babies, but not nearly enough to provide grounding in reality, sanity. It requires no subtle understanding of love deficits to see the paucity of love in battered children or in the sexually abused or grossly neglected. Nor does the twisted mock-love of the schizophrenogenic mother[7] require a subtle investigation of damaged love; the lovelessness is blatant.

But psychosis-producing lovelessness sometimes exists in middle-and-upper-income families, hidden behind an All-American facade of ultra-sanity. Here are parents who appear totally well-balanced, express genuine concern for their psychotic son or daughter, say all the right things, and "just can't imagine" how he/she became so sick. Indeed, unless the therapist asks specifically about how the child was loved, the lovelessness that caused the psychosis can be easily missed. It is missed because therapists, too, may be subject to a peculiar bias that is especially prevalent in an All-American culture: we equate money with love. That bias causes a halo-effect. We presume that parents with money, people who are successful in business, who are outgoing, glib, and well-mannered, are automatically successful in loving children. In fact, a close investigation of precisely how the patient was loved may disclose quite the opposite, that is, that making money, climbing the social ladder, and becoming "successful" were accomplished at the total expense of love.

The social history obtained on every patient should in fact be a "love history." Specific questions about "warmth" and "closeness" in the home may reveal, for example that the successful, intelligent, well-spoken parents are, in private, very cold people who were never "close" to their children. Questions about "heart to heart" talks with children, or how "tenderness" was expressed, or about "hugging and kissing" or how they "tuned into the child's feelings" or how they "encouraged" or "soothed hurt feelings" — questions specifically focused on various aspects of loving — will sometimes uncover lovelessness where it is least expected. But the history-taking must be consciously focused on love or this vital diagnostic material will be missed.

The eighteen principles of love therapy are attempts to

---

[7] A "schizophrenogenic" mother, in brief, is one who induces psychosis in a child by virtue of her pathological ways of communicating and relating (or not relating) to the child. The mother then is the "genesis" of the child's schizophrenia.

capture the major aspects of loving that the history-taking on a psychotic patient should assess. Many other vital aspects are described throughout this work. It is perhaps Principle Two, describing human love, that is most helpful in diagnosing and understanding the *specific* type of lovelessness that a particular psychotic patient experiences. There, human love is described as an experience of "intersubjectivity, a communion of uniques in their uniqueness, an interpenetration of beings, a dynamic mutuality of subjective selves given, received, and shared in mysterious unity." The *absence* of these qualities is lovelessness, and it is precisely these qualities that cannot be found in the social, family, or developmental history of many peoples suffering psychosis. On the contrary, one finds the opposite: an absolute sense of "aloneness" and "separateness" (Fromm), a life with "no meaning" (Frankl), utter "powerlessness" (Adler), a gross sense of "inferiority" (Sullivan), an inability to assume "responsibility" for one's life (Glasser) and distorted "cognitive awareness" (Beck) — all of which are various descriptions of the devastating effects of lovelessness.

A paucity or an utter lack of "intersubjectivity," the experience of never experiencing a "communion of uniques" nor the "interpenetration of beings" — lovelessness — may be described by patients in language that is vague, strange. It is a language that is sometimes heard only with the heart.

In the love therapy process, a crucial difference from traditional therapies needs to be highlighted. That difference is a hard-to-explain form of aggressive, relentlessly real, insistent, repetitive, urgent, totally confident love that is so essential for getting through to, reaching, and finally penetrating the heart of a person who has been horribly damaged by vacuous non-love or violent anti-love. Perhaps the greatest of all misconceptions about love is that it is soft, placid, or in any way weak. Authentic love is powerful.

James McNamara, quoting Rollo May extensively, goes very far in describing the powerful love that love therapy demands of the therapist.

Traditionally, love and power have been viewed as opposites; the more power one shows, the less love; the
more love the less power. Love is seen as powerless
and power as loveless![8]

...To say that one can love and renounce power is to
fall into the trap of pseudo-innocence because it fails
to take into account the realistic difficulties of love
and the inevitable struggle between good and evil
which love itself entails.... [One] cannot love unless
one recognizes one has power...; the fallacy of this
juxtaposition of love and power comes from our seeing
love purely as an emotion and power solely as force of
compulsion. We need to see them both as ontological,
as states of being or processes.[9]

...love needs power if it is to be more than sentimentality, and... power needs love if it is not to slip into
manipulation [or]... cruelty.[10]

...Compassion ties love and power together.[11]

I would rather say that love is the compassionate use of
power, and the powerful use of compassion. McNamara and
May, though, beautifully define the way power serves love in love
therapy. That power is humble, but the power that love brings
will not remain a humble servant of love unless it remains God-
centered. McNamara goes on to say that "love and power can
come together in strength" when they "appreciate that, at the
heart of who they are as spirit, is the creative love of God... [for]
spiritual life begins with a focus on God's love and his action in
our lives here and now.'"[12]

---

[8] Rollo May, *Power and Innocence* (New York: Norton, 1972), p. 99.

[9] *Ibid.*, p.106.

[10] *Ibid.*, p. 250.

[11] James McNamara, *The Power of Compassion* (Ramsey, NJ: Paulist Press, 1983),
pp. 44-47.

[12] McNamara, *ibid.*, p. 45.

Allow me to pause here to recognize that McNamara has caused me to depart from my format — and I'm glad. I had intended to present love theory and therapy first, and to bring spirituality into the picture only in later chapters. But McNamara makes it clear that love and power "at heart" must be together in spirit as "the creative love of God." That is nowhere more obvious than in addressing psychosis, so allow me to state this without equivocation: trying to heal (not just medicate) psychoses without God is like trying to obtain light from a lamp with no bulb plugged into a dead outlet. Therefore, although most of spiritual healing will be discussed in a final chapter, God must be included in the remainder of this discussion of the psychoses.

The "spirit" of love that is powerful enough to reach a person who is lost in psychotic lovelessness is a far cry from a religiousy or preachy spirit. Yet, when that juncture is reached when a theretofore "unreachable" psychotic person is reached, the therapist and patient alike often can affirm that God surely sat in on that interview.

This powerful love is the heart of the methodology of love therapy. The therapist who best captures this spirit, and whom I will also call upon to speak for love therapy in relation to this vital infusion of love with power, is Karl Stern:

> God loves man with the madness of love and he tries man's love to the point of madness.... He really did sacrifice His only Son. It is a mad story, and those who get involved must be affected by divine madness. 'God is a devouring fire.'
>
> When it comes to the life of the spirit, our concept of normalcy breaks down because it is a concept of conformity, of the *juste milieu*.
>
> ...[In] a living relationship with God, there is a total abandoning, a foolish surrender — from man to God and God to man. The saints move outside the *juste milieu* and belong to what well-integrated bourgeois people call the 'lunatic fringe.'

Thus we see that clinical concepts which refer to reason in the practical things of everyday life lose their significance when we enter the life of the spirit. We have indicated in other places that psychiatry and psychoanalysis are unable to penetrate into the mystery of the Person.[13]

But love therapy can and does penetrate the mystery of the Person! Therein lies the crucial difference. The difference is fire!

The methodology (which I prefer to call a "way") of love therapy has little relationship to the *juste milieu* of the mainstream, secular mental health professions. Indeed, the mainstream might view love therapy as disrespectable, as beyond the fringe of "normalcy," or indeed, even as part of the lunatic fringe. The *juste milieu* of psychotherapy does not mix psychopathology and religion, and it certainly does not aggressively pursue psychotics beyond the fringe and into the heart of the mad mystery of God. The *juste milieu's* typical treatment of psychotics is mild, benign, accepting, and quietly benevolent. Stern calls mainstream therapy "bourgeois." I call it insipid. The fire, the power, the spirituality, and the God of love therapy may well rock the bourgeois boat of mainstream therapy. I should hope for controversy; there can be fire in that. Without fire, psychotics cannot be helped.

Yes, challenging words. My hope is that they will be read as not "plain" but divine madness, and light some fires. Surely other professionals must feel, as I have for so long, that "something is missing" in all the typical lukewarm mainstream therapies. Though they surely would not give themselves such an appellation, my firm conviction is that any effective therapist has been a love therapist all along. As proof, I would ask therapists to look back at their most difficult but ultimately successful cases, and to remember the consuming fire they shared with the hearts they

---

[13] Karl Stern, *The Third Revolution: A Study of Psychiatry and Religion* (New York: Doubleday, 1961), pp. 160, 161.

actually reached, penetrated, and healed. Will any counselors deny that the real secret of their success with their toughest cases has been their powerfully patient, gritty, determined and irresistible love?

If psychosis, developmental lovelessness, is to be healed, then the powerful blazing love of a blast furnace is the only effective treatment. Indeed, precisely because the psychoses involve the madness of virtual non-love, therapy must bring a powerful infusion of love that is a devouring fire and might well appear mad to the *juste milieu*. Love is always a risk. I know of no way that a therapist can undertake the risk of love therapy with a psychotic person without God. Similarly, to use any other form of therapy with a psychotic is a futile, destructive game. The continuing destructiveness of that game is evident in the millions of psychotics roaming vacant-eyed through the streets of the world.

In fairness to mental health professionals, the responsibility for the mentally ill cannot be shouldered by professionals alone. If all professionals gave every ounce of the love they possessed, it would not be nearly enough. Yet, as I affirmed earlier, professionals do not have a corner on the market on the capacity to love! Love is not a professional something; it is human and divine. Churches and benevolent organizations, volunteers in massive numbers, could turn the tide on mental illness. Indeed, that will require a revolution. This will surely not happen in my lifetime. Realistically, though, if one considers the evolutionary upward spiral of humankind toward what Teilhard de Chardin calls the Omega Point[14] (God, the Love Point), the love revolution will indeed come to pass.

Given the limits of one short chapter on a subject so terribly complex as psychoses, it need not be surprising if we have raised more questions than we've answered. I will be happy to have posed a correct question or two. It is said of Gertrude Stein (the poet of "A rose is a rose is a rose" fame) that as she lay dying

---

[14] Teilhard de Chardin, *The Phenomenon of Man* (New York: Harper & Row, 1959).

she suddenly sat up and said, "What's the answer? What's the answer!?... What's the question?" And then she died. When I heard that, my response was, "Both the answer and the question, Gertie, have something to do with love."

There is surely no satisfying way to conclude a chapter on such a mind-bogglingly complex subject as "Psychosis," but let me share this parting thought: the only thing that separates the insane from the sane is the reality of a thin quantity of love that the sane would be wise to treasure, to be grateful for, and to share.

CHAPTER TWENTY

Anxiety Disorders: Love Deficits

> Anxiety is... always a threat to the foundation, the center of my existence. Anxiety is experienced threat of imminent non-being.   *Rollo May*[1]
>
> Love has no room for fear.   *John 4:18*

With one vital exception, anxiety and fear are identical. The physical reactions are the same: a threat is perceived; the autonomic nervous system kicks into high gear; adrenaline flows; the heart beats faster; blood rushes from internal organs to extremities; muscles tense in preparation for fight or flight; breathing speeds up; eyes dilate; perspiration flows; and if the threat is severe, instant urination or defecation may occur. The one difference is that, with fear, the threat is present and seen here and now, whereas in anxiety the threat is vague, not seen, unknown.

Most approaches to therapy for anxiety center on helping the person discover the unknown source of the threat, and correctly so. Often, though, the source is obvious. Any adult who was a child abuse victim, for example, grew up in very real fear, and adapted to self, other people, and life itself as a victim. That person must be specifically helped to see that their victimization is in the past, over, and that the danger that was very real as a child no longer exists. Through a child-victim's eyes, if a parent is a

---

[1] Rollo May, "Contributions of Existential Psychotherapy," in Rollo May, Ernest Angel, Henri Ellenberger, Eds., *Existence* (New York: Basic Books, Inc., 1958), p. 50.

victimizer, then all adults might well be victimizers. These people must be specifically shown that not everybody is an abusing parent who is probably going to hurt them. They must be taught that life, though tough, is not abusive ordinarily and that their hearts need no longer remain shielded and shuddering.

Love therapy treats these identifiable causes of anxiety in much the same way as most therapies do. Whether it is the threat of physical abuse, verbal attack, loss of protection, abandonment, or rejection, if the threat can be specifically identified, concretely seen in light of reality, the shadowy specter of anxiety often vanishes.

Hearkening back to Principle Seven, though, reality and love are virtually synonymous terms, so it is more accurate to say that the inner darkness that hides unreal, phantom fears is banished by the light of love.

As shown in Principle Sixteen, the love therapy way may integrate transactional analysis, psychodrama, gestalt, art or cognitive therapies or any number of other methods in the treatment of anxiety disorders, each model serving a specific role in accomplishing one purpose: to allow love to effectively reach and heal the afflicted area of the heart that is causing the anxiety. That "afflicted area" can be best understood by picturing it in our imaginations, contrasting the heart affliction of anxiety with, for example, the wounds caused by rejection.

A son abruptly rejected by his mother, or a wife rejected by her husband, will often say, "Part of my heart was just ripped out," or "It was like a knife sliced right through my chest." The "picture" of rejection is uniformly one of a heart that is sliced, torn and bleeding.

In anxiety, the heart does not bleed, nor is it torn or sliced or ripped. Rather, we can picture the heart quaking, shrinking and cowering. Looking closer, one sees that the normal "protective layer" around the heart is missing in some areas, thus allowing threat to enter too easily. In those areas, there is no protective love to stop the threat.

It is helpful to visualize the healthy heart as it would be seen in Kirlian photography[2] emitting an aura of bright blue light, a glow that streaks outward in dancing shafts of lumination. That aura is like the love that protects our hearts. Understanding how love normally protects us is essential to understanding anxiety. (See Figure 4, Chapter Ten, the Psychospiritual Heart.)

Only love protects us from the thousands of dangers that the world presents. For the little child, love is embodied in the parents. Faced with a threatening stranger, the child hides behind love's skirts, Mama. The protection against goblins in a dark bedroom is love, Daddy. With age, that love in internalized; love is "taken to heart" and the child makes love his or her own. As the internalization of love progresses, so does the child's confidence in its protection. Dependence on the parents' love wanes, and the child progressively says, "I've got my own love to protect me now, so I can do more and more all by myself." Finally, as a young adult, when love has been fully integrated, healthy self-love and with it, self-protection, allow total independence. This maturity of love, and with it, protection from danger, can be envisioned as a heart with a solid, intact aura — love's "all-around" protection.

The heart's protective aura is somewhat analogous to the concept of "ego boundaries" that is widely accepted in psychotherapy. Here, they are called love boundaries; the aura is love. That aura in a healthy person is substantially under voluntary control. When a threat, perceived fear, is encountered, the aura of love defends the center of being and disallows fear entering the heart. On the other hand, the aura can be voluntarily opened to allow entry of whatever or whomever is perceived as good, nonthreatening, lovable.

In anxiety disorders, the heart's bright aura of protecting love can be pictured as having one or more areas in which the

---

[2] Kirlian photography is a process that allows the so-called Psi energy emitted by all organic things, an irregular, spiking halo, or aura, to become visible on an electrified plate. Please note that I am using this aura only as an analogy, a metaphor. The "heart" with its "aura," as I use the terms, are psychospiritual, immaterial. Aura, halo, ring of protection — by whatever name, the effort is to visualize the inner power that protects us from threat.

surrounding light is very dim or even missing altogether, dark, as if the aura has holes in it (cf., Figure 4, Chapter Ten). These dark areas, unprotected by love, allow the naked heart to be too vulnerable, open to any threat that might be posed, defenseless. In this unprotected state, an adult faced with the perception of danger will react exactly like a young child, feeling not big enough or strong enough to protect the self. Confronted with a threat, the threatened adult wants to hide behind Mama's protective skirts, but Mama is not there. Daddy's loving assurance that there is nothing to fear in the dark room would help, but Daddy is not there. Alone, with no protective love, we shake, we cringe, we run. Our eyes dilate and dart, searching the darkness for danger. Our stomachs churn, and as the fear penetrates the aura-less areas of our psychospiritual hearts, our physical hearts beat fast with palpitations. The fear looms larger and we hold our breaths, waiting in dread anticipation. Then comes hyperventilation. As clients describe the threat looming, it is not difficult to visualize their psychospiritual hearts trembling, racing, frantically looking for someplace to hide.

Rathus and Nevid[3] provide what they call a "concise" list of over forty bodily sensations and common thoughts and feelings that accompany anxiety — from chest pains, to lumps in the throat, to dizziness, and from feeling the room is closing in, to jumbled thoughts, nightmares, feelings of "going crazy," and feeling that death is imminent. Once it is understood that it is one's entire core of being, the psychospiritual heart that is reacting to threat, then the bewildering array of anxiety symptoms become more understandable. As the heart moves, every physical, psychological and spiritual aspect of being reacts accordingly.

Sometimes the perceived dangers "stack-up" and "roller-coaster." Quickly, any unpleasant situation becomes the most extreme negative possibility. Ellis calls this "catastrophizing."[4]

---

[3] Spencer A. Rathus, Ph.D. and Jeffrey S. Nevid, Ph.D., *BT Behavior Therapy* (New York: New American Library, 1977), pp. 7-9.

[4] Albert Ellis, *Reason and Emotion in Psychotherapy* (New York: Lyle Stuart, 1962).

As I described rollercoastering and catastrophizing to one anxious lady, she responded, "That's it! That's exactly what I do. I start with the least little worry and within minutes I've created a catastrophe — a plague of locusts!"

What is most obvious about all the possible symptoms of anxiety is that we have needed a simpler way of understanding it. In 1972, Spielberger[5] estimated that there had been over five thousand books and articles written about anxiety. Has the number tripled by now, or are a mere ten thousand attempts to understand anxiety enough to persuade us that an utterly new, simpler understanding is needed?

Only love casts out fear. Only love can ward off danger. Anxiety is experienced in the heart, in the central psychospiritual center of our beings. From there, once experienced, once the protective cover of love has been penetrated and the heart starts shaking, its effects can show up virtually any place in the body, and in a thousand irrational thoughts and feelings. But note! In terms of understanding, it doesn't much matter what the various physical, cognitive or emotional responses are. All that really matters is that the person's anxiety-wracked heart has a defective protective aura, a love deficit.

The understanding of anxiety as due to a love deficit, experienced at the psychospiritual center of being, the heart, dictates a subtantially new and fundamentally different approach than other therapies.

Neither the stimulus that precipitates the anxiety reactions, nor the welter of possible bodily, emotional or cognitive responses can be the primary target of treatment because they are not the source of the problem. Eliminating stimulus (S) and response (R) immediately eliminates behavior therapy as a primary treatment method (although it is helpful in secondary stages of treatment).

Similarly, whereas cognitive therapy would view "hidden,

5   C. Spielberger, Ed., *Anxiety: Current Trends in Theory and Research* (New York: Academic Press, 1972).

automatic," distorted thoughts and meanings as causes of anxiety, the love deficit shows that these cognitive errors are secondary symptoms of heart-level love damage.

Freud attributed anxiety to the threat of taboo sexual or aggressive id instincts breaking through unconscious defenses, or as simply due to dammed up sexual energy. In love theory, the "unconscious" is seen as a relatively superficial repository of memories, and the id "instincts" that are so important to psycho-analysis are shown to be, in adulthood, like the long-lost acorn that germinated the magnificent oak tree — utterly unimportant. Nevertheless, because Freud still has such a following among professionals, it seems necessary to debate the man. One brief argument will hopefully suffice: if taboo id instincts are important in explaining anxiety, it would be because the instincts threatened some "something" that all human beings believe to be far more valuable than the instincts themselves. Were this not so, if the instincts were the stronger value, they would automatically be ex-pressed and there would be no anxiety. But that does not happen in anxiety. It follows, therefore, that there must be "something" in the person that is a stronger, more basic motivation. Ergo, that "something," not the id instinct, is the fundamental drive and goal of human behavior. The "something" is, of course, love.

It is not my intent here, though, to refute other theories. Rather, my goal is to highlight the need for the new approach.

The crux of the treatment approach of love therapy to anxi-ety disorders can be expressed quite simply: (A) diagnose in love terms, i.e., find the exact area at the heart where the love deficit exists, the place where the protective aura of love is missing; (B) provide new love to supplant the missing love. This supplanta-tion of love can be done in three ways: (1) by the direct love of the therapist, love specifically designed and tailored to provide the kind of love that is missing; (2) by the therapist enlisting relative or volunteer resources to love the client under the direction of the therapist; (3) assisting clients to love themselves in new ways by "transplanting" love from another area of his or her heart to the area(s) where the love deficit exists.

Following is a case account of a man suffering severe anxiety. Note how other therapies are integrated. The actual "loving" cannot be captured in mere words.

Vincent

"Vinnie," age twenty-five, a computer programmer, had suffered anxiety attacks for as long as he could remember — trembling, hyperventilation, palpitations, feeling a tight band around his head, anxious thoughts of danger and death, stomach churning, and more, yet his big presenting problem was his temper. Always, he had suffered anxiety for as long as he could stand it, "Then I blow — I yell, holler, throw furniture, just go nuts!" After he had "blown" and chased a neighbor with a crowbar, he knew it was time to seek help.

Through Rogerian non-directive therapy, we quickly established that Vinnie's basic problems centered around his father, a demanding, "macho," harsh man whom Vinnie could never please. Worse than the impossible demands, he felt that his father simply ignored him.

The diagnosis "in love terms" was written in my notes as: "Significant love deficit from father left Vinnie feeling generally 'weak-hearted.' Protective love from mother was never fully absorbed nor believed because, throughout childhood, the mother's love was never targeted toward healing the hurt, fear, and feelings of worthlessness that stemmed from the father's non-love. Anxiety reactions result from the very real fact that the father's love was never 'there' to protect him. No traumatic heart wounds are evident, but Vinnie has an extremely thin protective aura over entire area of heart relating to the father. Plan: confirm likelihood that anxiety attacks and rage surfaces primarily in relation to authority/father figures. Provide Vinnie with a heart transplant."

A "heart transplant" sounds as if it would require years-long therapy and total re-parenting. Not so. The love therapy process zeroes in on the fundamental quality of parenthood that was deficient, the specific kind of love that was missing or damaged — the heart of the matter. The therapist's task is to concentrate and to administer love as intensely as humanly possible, with pace and timing such that the person is able to maximally receive the love. This concentration on and targeting of love issues typically allows healing to follow much more quickly.

The pace and timing of loving is an intuitive process that is purely a product of the therapist's own capacity. Jesus, who apparently knew how to "concentrate" love and how to deliver it with perfect effectiveness, could nonverbally convey to a perfect stranger, "I love you," and then say, "Come, follow me," and have his love immediately accepted. The timing for most of us might be just a bit slower. But note: if the therapist takes "a while" to be able to authentically express love, clients can be expected to take much longer to receive that love. Because of this, the therapist's love must always be "aggressive." Here, that word certainly does not mean "hostile," but by no means can the counselor's love be passive, timid or "implied." If love is going to heal, we can't be bashful about it, and it cannot be left in the closet. Healing love is transparently open; it blatantly "yearns" to heal, so it might be called "irresistible," "passionate," "transparent," or even "blazing." Remember, though: many people with emotional problems have been burnt by love, and others have barely known what love is. It should not be surprising if the therapist's love is met with distrust and, at first, even more anxiety.

For Vinnie, as with many people, love came as a shock, as shown in the following interchange:

Vinnie: Dad would come home from work and never even look at me. And if I tried to say something to him, it was like talking to a wall, and then he'd....

B. (Brennan Mullaney): Wait, Vinnie, let me stop you a second. All that pain, all those negative memories. You keep going over them, and over them, and over them, and it just kills me, because wallowing in the pain won't get you anywhere — and that's really starting to kill me.

Vinnie: (surprised) Kill you? How can it hurt you?

B.: It hurts me because it hurts you.

Vinnie: I don't see how... (trails off, puzzled).

B.: Ah, Vinnie, my lad, how long have I been with you, and you don't know me...? How long have you been coming in here, Vinnie?

Vinnie: I don't know, two, two and a half months. I think this is about the eighth or ninth session.

B.: Yeah, and they've been pretty intense meetings, haven't they? Do you think you know me yet?

Vinnie: Sure — kinda, well, I guess I do.

B.: Sure you know me. Now, how do you feel about me?

Vinnie: Fine, I mean, I — uh, I like you. I mean — you're okay.

B.: Okay? (smiles) Vinnie, I think maybe I'm more than that to you, but okay's okay.... Now, how do I feel about you?

Vinnie: Me? I think you.... I guess you like me....

B.: Like you. You mean like okay? (smiles)

Vinnie: (Embarrassed) Well? Damn, how do... I mean, how would you say it?

B: I say — I love you, Vinnie.

Vinnie: What?

B.: (Leaning far forward) I love you.

Vinnie: Oh (eyes brimming with tears). Damn.

B.: (After a full minute) Want to tell me what you're feeling?

Vinnie: Nobody in my life has ever said that to me (hard, sobbing tears).

B.: (Hugging him — waiting for tears to subside.) Whatcha thinking?

Vinnie: God, I don't know, a thousand things.... It's the best and worst feeling of my life all at one time.... I can't explain it.... It's weird. It scares the hell out of me.

B.: Maybe you mean I scare the hell out of you?

Vinnie: Yeah, you do.

B. Well, when I say I love you, I mean it. Just don't get me mixed up with your father. I'm just me. You don't have to be afraid with me, Vinnie. You're safe with me.

Vinnie: Oh, God! (More tears) I've never been safe.

B: And that's scary — and that's a big part of your anxiety. But now?

Vinnie: Whew! I donno, something's sure happening. I feel like the whole inside of my chest just... flip-flopped.

This exchange marked the initial "breakthrough love." As often occurs, Vinnie's anxiety episodes decreased by at least half immediately following this session. As is also typical, several subsequent interviews were largely centered on Vinnie's testing me to affirm and reaffirm that my love for him was real. Like everyone in therapy, he asked in dozens of ways, "Okay, you love me, but what's the catch?"

The presence of the therapist and the endurance of thetherapist's love need to be believed and integrated by the client. The obvious key to facilitating that belief is that the therapist's love must be unquestionably authentic. Love simply cannot be faked. Let alone being dishonest and unethical, a therapist who tries to feign lov will soon discover that it simply does not work. Clients know; then the phony love becomes counterproductive and damaging. But people also know — their hearts read — when the therapist's love is the real article, and the more intense and concentrated the love, the sooner they know it. They know intersubjectively. They enter communion (as described in Principle Two).

Love therapy is described as not a method but a "way" of healing. With anxiety-affected people (or any, for that matter) there is a way that the counselor's love can be made permanent. It is a very straightforward way.

Deliberate Communion

Principle Four describes love as a gift. By combining Principles Four and Two, the therapist simply offers the client a gift of intersubjectivity, communion, shared mutuality — love — and asks the client to accept it, absorb it. In day-to-day life, average people do not put love into words very often; non-verbal communication is the rule. Most of us are a little reticent, a little shy about expressing love. A love therapist must struggle directly to overcome that tendency, because people with emotional problems need love in more open and concentrated form and they need it faster. The following way makes use of imagery coupled with the attempt to put the intersubjectivity of love into plain words. This way of loving is used only after the breakthrough love experience has been accomplished, and after the major obstacles to the client's receiving love have been removed. The process is called "deliberate communion."

Client: I think I'm getting a lot better. It's the first time in my life that I ever really felt loved. You were right, I wasn't loving myself, but I didn't know that till it finally dawned on me that you really did love me.

Therapist: That's great. How about when you're not here, when you're not with me? Feel loved then?

Client: A lot more than before… but sometimes it's like I slip back to the old me. I get what you call that "A-lone" feeling and I feel my insides start shaking.

Therapist: Yeah, and it's that utterly a-lone feeling that causes the anxiety. Why don't we try to fix it so that you're never A-lone again? If I were with you all the time, do you think you'd get that feeling?

Client: Oh, no. It's like when the past starts creeping back on me, and… I don't know how that happens.

Therapist: The past creeps back, and those old scary experiences become stronger than the love experience with me. Know what I think? Maybe you need to take me with you.

Client: (laughs) Put you in my purse?

Therapist: Closer than that — in your heart. Let's do that. Why don't you close your eyes, and let's see if we can't get close. I want to try to get so close to you that I'm a permanent part of you, part of your heart, so that I'm with you in spirit all the time. Could you let me be that much to you?

Client: Sure!

Therapist: Okay, now we've talked a lot about love, but this time
I want you to very deliberately try to receive my love. We've
talked about your heart, the very center of your being. So try
now to picture yourself in your imagination, and then see
your heart exposed, vulnerable, wide open.... Now picture
me... and see my heart wide open.... Now I want to show
you how I love you, and I'd like for you to see the love happening, okay? Now, see the two of us in spirit, and I want
to give myself to you. See? I'm walking toward you to give
me to you, to be an actual part of you. See? I come toward
you, and I walk right into you. And now we're one! You're
part of me, and I'm part of you. We're standing inside each
other's shoes, and I can look out at the world and see it as
you see it, and hear what you hear. But look, our hearts are
together, so I can feel what you feel, and you can feel as I
feel. And that's what love is. Now, the question is, may I
stay with you, a part of you?... If you let me, I'll always be
part of you. If we're not physically together, I'll still be with
you, and you know me well now. You know I love you, and
that you're always safe with me. If threats come along that
can cause anxiety, think back to what I'd be saying about
those fears. You can call upon that love to keep you safe and
protected at any time. Remember, too, that love is a gift. You
can't earn it and you don't have to. I love you just as you are
— and I always will.

Love is an act of the will both in giving and receiving. Hence
the name "deliberate communion." As the client decides to accept the therapist's love, he or she decides to make the therapist's
person, and the protection, guidance, warmth and assurance that
the therapist represents, an integral part of the self. As this is accomplished, the love deficit is replaced and the protective aura of
love is restored on a permanent basis. Thereafter, as threats loom,
they are thwarted and anxiety typically drops substantially.

The "deliberate communion" process works in much the

same way and with much the same effect as ordinary loving parental presence. For example, my own mother and father have been dead for several years, but when a threatening situation arises, their "presence," and the protective love that they gave me is still very much alive in my inmost being. Faced with a threat, I find myself saying, "Dad would say..." such and such. Similarly, clients I meet after many years prove that the process works when they say, "I think of you every day almost," and "I can still hear you say..." such and such. Besides making my day, they provide the clinical evidence that permanent healing of anxiety, or any other disorder, is a product of communion. Authentic love never dies.

My clinical experience can be immediately affirmed by any experienced therapist who has had occasion to encounter former patients. Clients may not have ever known which school of therapy was utilized, but the enduring experiences they recount are the "caring," the "warmth," the "acceptance," the therapist's "being there" — love in its many forms expressed in as many shy and reticent ways.

Phobias

A phobia is an irrational fear. More precisely, using Beck's definition, a phobia is "fear of a situation, that by social consensus and the person's own intellectual appraisal when away from the situation, is disproportionate to the probability and degree of harm inherent in that situation."[6]

Animal, mineral or vegetable, anything or anyone, whether natural or supernatural, can become the object of a phobia: high places, low, open, or closed places, dogs, cats, lightning, ghosts, dirt, God, bugs, Dracula, strangers, or a specific person like Uncle George. These phobias have been given some outrageous scientific

---

[6] Aaron Beck, *Cognitive Therapy and the Emotional Disorders* (New York: New American Library, 1976), p. 159.

names like erythrophobia (fear of blushing), xenophobia (fear of strangers), ophidiophobia (snakes), and panphobia (fear of everything). I don't know the scientific name for a fear of tomatoes (nor do I want to learn), but a six-year-old boy that I saw was scared to death of them. That little boy had watched a camp movie, *Attack of the Killer Tomatoes*, which he called "really scary." It was about tomatoes becoming bigger than houses and rolling through the streets crushing people. Silly? Not to the terror stricken little boy. With some circuitous reasoning and the magical thinking of childhood, he believed that tomatoes could kill you, even though he also knew that they couldn't. Similarly, when away from the feared object, adults know that the fear is "silly," but faced with the closed place or bug or lightning or the airplane that induces the fear, they believe that what is actually silly is totally real. This contradiction between knowledge and belief, objective and subjective truth, is a hallmark of all phobias. The heart of the phobic person has been invaded by a lie that causes one to say, "I know what my head says, but don't confuse me with facts."

The treatment approach of love therapy to phobias is guided by three basic principles: "Love and truth are one"; "The truth will set you free"; and, as is applicable to all fears and anxieties, "Love casts out fear."

The two models of therapy that love therapy integrates most frequently are Carl Rogers' non-directive therapy and Aaron Beck's cognitive therapy. Here, relative to the dynamics of phobias, I defer to and strongly recommend Beck for a basic and valid interpretation of the heavy role that cognitive contradictions and ideational problems play in the development of phobias — but I would hasten to add that the core of the phobia is not cognitive.

The core of a phobia can be described as a "mistaken heart" that follows a breakdown of the protective aura that surrounds that heart and results in a "heart-centered," not a "head-centered," problem with fear. In other words, again, Beck is absolutely correct in his analysis of the contradictory ideas and automatic thinking that surround a phobia, but he did not go far enough in terms of identifying the core of the problem. More to the point, Beck is a beautiful therapist who utilizes his concepts of cognition, unquestionably helps people quite effectively, and then believes that the primary help he offered was cognitive — but he is mistaken. All the while Beck is administering cognitive therapy, along every ideational step, midst every automatic thought discovered, he is loving his patients. Again, changing thought patterns is often absolutely essential in the treatment of emotional disorders, but changing thinking, by itself, has never healed anybody. Love alone heals, and the focus of both the problem and its healing is the heart.

We need not reinvent the wheel by repeating all the cognitive contradictions surrounding phobias that Beck analyzes so lucidly. Rather, let me begin with his own case example and his explanation of the case, and then show how it is quite obvious that in addition to and beyond his cognitive help, Beck was providing heart-level healing by loving his patients.

The love that saturates Beck's cognitive approach is quite transparent in his treatment of a depressed man who had been in a hospital bed for a year and was afraid of walking. The transcript shows Beck "logically" questioning the patient about "why" he couldn't walk, and what he thought would happen if he tried. The patient tells Beck he's "crazy" for saying he can walk. Beck suggests they "test out" whether Beck is crazy or whether the patient actually can walk. Finally, Beck "bets" the patient that he can walk to a door that is five yards away. Quickly, the man discovers he can walk.

Clearly, this patient "changed his mind" (cognition) about walking, but as I read the events, the essential thing happening was that Beck was loving the guy. If we follow the transcript of this successful case, reading between the lines, Beck's love is clearly apparent. Following is Beck's case report line by line, interspersed with my interpretations (in italics) of what was happening in love terms.

Therapist: I'll bet you can walk from here to the door [about five yards].

Interpretation: "Betting" on the man is a strong vote of confidence,
a loving gift. Confidence is felt in the heart, not cognitively. The
thought, "Maybe I can walk after all," might have followed the
heart response, but it obviously did not come first.
Patient: What happens if I can't do it?
Therapist: I'll catch you.

Interpretation: "I'll be present with you; I'll be one with you: I'll
join with you in your suffering; I'll try with you; I'll support you
even physically; you won't be alone anymore; I'll be in communion
with you" — all these offers and promises of love are implicit in
the simple promise "I'll catch you."
Patient: I'm really too weak to do it.
Therapist: Suppose I hold your arm. [The patient then took a
few steps supported by the therapist. He continued to walk
beyond the prescribed five yards...].[7]

Interpretation: This is "hands-on" love if ever I saw it. In hospital
language, Beck is extending TLC (tender loving care). Is that not
love?

On the contrary, Beck would argue that he had set up "a
project in such a way that the patient's performance... test(ed)
the validity of his ideas. Thus the completion of the task will
contradict the patient's hypothesis that he is incapable of doing
it."[8] And indeed Beck accomplished exactly that. The patient who
had been bed-ridden for a year progressively walked farther and
farther, all around the hospital. How then can I argue with such
dramatic success?

Quite obviously I cannot and do not dispute the cognitive
elements of this case. On the contrary, I enthusiastically affirm
them. At the same time, as my love-related interpretations show,
this was not just a cognitive process. Love was the vehicle, the
totally surrounding context, the essential ambience that allowed

---

[7] *Ibid.*, pp. 284, 285.

[8] *Ibid.*, p. 283.

the cognitive events to be effective. In other words, this patient allowed Beck to help him change his distorted cognitive process only because and after the patient was quite sure that Beck loved him. The evidence of this can be borne out only by our own heart-level personal experience.

Consider: a cognitive response requires that the patient listen, but in matters of the heart, on subjects involving our inner-most thoughts and feelings, people simply do not listen and certainly do not hear people who do not love them. A therapist might deliver the most brilliant cognitive analysis, but if it is not presented with love, if the patient detects a scintilla of hostility or uncaring, the effect of that brilliance will be not even a spark.

But the obverse is also true: love must be wise; it must be targeted; it must be cognitive. The therapist who thinks he can simply love willy-nilly, gushing warm puppies, bouquets and valentines would be more effective in a gift shop for pets.

Clearly, both cognitive therapy and love therapy are needed in cases involving intractable symptoms. In everyday language, we might say that a hard head has a hard heart that must be melted. As noted in Principle Sixteen, the relationship of the two forms of therapy is one of interdependence.

Perhaps the one generally accepted truth about phobias is that the ostensible or presenting fear is an expression of a deeper, unexpressed fear (though not necessarily "unconscious"). Here, it must suffice to describe only two phobias which often appear together and then to show the several possibilities regarding unexpressed fears that the external symptoms are disguising.

Panic Disorder and Agoraphobia (Fear of Open Spaces)

Sadly, this fear of going anyplace outside the home too often has been going on for months or even years before the person comes for help. As might be expected, the longer the person has been in the house, the longer it takes to get him out.

Because agoraphobia is so often associated with the fear of panic attacks, I am discussing them under one heading.

The verbalized fears — of crowded places, streets, or open places — may be external expressions of any of the following more fundamental fears: fear of being lost and/or alone; fear of being seen or of being stared at; fear of having to talk to strangers, all forms of fear of social disapproval; or, fear of a panic attack.

Panic attacks are described by clients as "worse than death" experiences. The DSM-IV describes thirteen symptoms that may be associated with panic,[9] many of which can be seen in any form of anxiety — shortness of breath, dizziness, palpitations, trembling, numbness, fear of going crazy or of dying — but that symptom list does not accurately describe the extreme severity of the experience. As I have heard it consistently related, a panic attack is an experience of stark, brutal terror.

Organic problems like hypoglycemia and hyperthyroidism can cause identical symptoms of panic. When they are ruled out, the theories regarding the causes of panic are numerous. My clinical experience is that people who suffer panic attacks had been "expert" at denying fears and at suppressing anxieties over the course of many years. As a result, it is as if the anxiety accumulates, hidden behind strong defenses, building and building until the defenses break down and all the "piled up" anxieties suddenly explode in a flood of overwhelming, uncontrollable emotion — like filling a balloon to the breaking point.

The DSM-IV lists separation disorder ("school phobia") and sudden loss of social supports as predisposing factors in panic attacks.[10] The many cases I've seen have indicated that growing up in an alcoholic home is an even more typical predisposing factor. Children of alcoholics are taught the defense mechanism of denial as a way of life, and often experience panic attacks in later life when the anxieties accumulate and the wall of denial suddenly collapses.

---

[9] DSM-IV, *op. cit.*
[10] *Ibid.*

It is the fear of sustaining a panic attack that is a typical cause of agoraphobia. The person is afraid to be caught in a panic attack "outside" where they have no place to hide. While the person permits him- or herself to suffer agoraphobia, the far more excruciating fear — panic — can be avoided by hiding "safely" in the house.

The treatment of agoraphobia and/or panic is usually a long process of unraveling a multitude of fears, many of which began in childhood (as the predisposing separation anxiety indicates). As the fears are untangled in counseling, traced back to their origins and confronted, it is not at all unusual for clients to re-experience horror, terror, being "scared to death" while re-living traumatic events of childhood — and this terror is identical to that experienced in the adult panic attack. In extreme cases, as the original trauma is faced, the person may faint, or end up in the corner of the counseling office curled in a fetal position. Almost invariably, as people describe the original trauma-filled events that later produce panic, they were children facing terror alone. It is not coincidental that agoraphobics so often say they can leave the house and venture outside to the marketplace so long as they are not alone. Treatment of these disorders centers first on the "crying" need to supplant the original feeling and fact of being alone-with-horror with the experience of a loving presence. Techniques, when a person is cowering in terror, are meaningless. Someone "being there," the most rudimentary form of love, is all that matters to them in their agony. For the therapist, authentically "being there" requires the willingness to enter directly into the agony with the client, suffer there with them, and then love them enough to bring them out of the pain. This is therapy that transcends description. No method is involved, no technique, no model, no theory; in fact, this is one of the few times that the counselor does very little thinking of any kind. It is as if only the heart of the counselor matters, and as if only the heart is operational. Indeed, people in this kind of soul-wrenching pain need precisely that, someone who is "all heart."

"All heart" love does not mean gushy sentimentalism. Quite the contrary, it takes enormous strength to endure the feelings of helplessness that sweep over a counselor while trying to "be there" with someone who has withdrawn to God-only-knows what kind of hell, and is screaming in raw terror or mute and whimpering. It takes courage to continue trying to communicate courage to a terrified person when the therapist, too, is aghast and frightened by what is being witnessed.

Lynn's Agoraphobia

The dialogue that can be recorded of sessions in which traumatic events are abreacted (re-experienced) is minimal. Periods of silence, broken only by crying or unintelligible words from the client may extend for long minutes up to an hour. Following is a severely edited record. It is the case of a twenty-nine year old woman who had suffered agoraphobia and panic attacks for five years, and had been totally house-bound for two years. The child of an alcoholic father and a severely disturbed co-dependent mother, she had grown up in a constant atmosphere of turmoil and violence. The violent episode below was the core of the anxiety. The first half hour of the interview led up to the memory of the violence "exploding" into consciousness. Her name was Lynn. She was talking about a vague (repressed) glimpse of "something" that happened when she was eight or nine years old. Then she began spontaneously regressing.

Lynn: [Eyes clenched shut] Oh, God, I can't... can't. I don't want to. Nononono...[tears] No! OOOOOh, Brennan, I'm scared [trembling].
B. (Brennan Mullaney): I know, Lynn; it must have been terrible. But I'm right here with you if you want to remember it now.
Lynn: Oh, no, oh no [hiding face in her hands]. Oh God, oh no, I'll die, I'll die, I'll.... unnnngh. NOOOOOO!! [Screams —

long and ear-piercing. Jerks hard "away from" something she remembers, falls off the chair and scrambles on all fours across floor to the wall. Huddles with arms wrapped around knees.] Oh God, she's, he's, she's... OOOOhhh, bleeding... Oh he's cut... Oh! She's gonna die. Oh, it's on me, it's on me. Uhhhh, bloodbloodblood. Nono, look, it comes off. Oh me me me, they're cutting, cutting. Cut... There! Cut... I'LL KILL YOU! Cut – Bastard! Cuts.... oh God hide, hidehide-hidehide. They'll get Tommy [her little brother]. We'll run, we'll hide, Tommy... Oh, God, why are they doing this?... Whywhywhy... Oh Daddy, stop! Stop! Stop! OhmyGod, Mama! [screams repeatedly].

[All the above was said in a little girl voice. To this point I had said nothing. I had squatted on the floor next to her. When the second set of long screams came, I reached out to try to comfort her; she jumped away and slid along the wall back into a corner. There she sat rocking, wrapped in a fetal position. For the next five minutes, she sat whimpering, shaking uncontrollably.]

B.: You know I'm still with you, Lynn. I'm here, hon.

Lynn: You are?? [Said with real surprise — still in a little girl voice] Are they gonna die?

B.: No, no, hon. They'll be okay. [All I knew for sure at this point was that the event involved both parents and that someone had cut someone. However, I did know that both her parents were still alive; hence, my answer.]

Lynn: But they're not moving! Oh, there's blood all over. Tommy'n me'll hide. Don't worry, Tommy, we'll hide, don't worry.

B.: I'm still here with you, Lynn. Can you let me be with you?

Lynn: You are?? (same utter surprise)

B.: Can you let me in, Lynn? Let me be with you?

Lynn: [Flings herself at me, clutching her arms around my chest — a terrified child] I'm gonna die! They'll kill us.

B.: No, no, no, I'm with you now. It's over, Lynn; it's over. They won't hurt you. It'll be okay. See, I'm right here with you. It'll be alright.

Lynn: [Still clinging tightly to the therapist's chest, cries for
the next fifteen minutes — deep, wracking sobs, as if she
is breaking in two. Very gradually, while still crying, she
returns to present time, though occasionally regressing to
voice more fear. During these briefer regressions it became
clear that both her mother and father had stabbed and/
or slashed each other with kitchen knives. After this half
hour, Lynn still held tightly to the therapist for several more
minutes, gradually relaxing and finally seeming to be near
sleep.]

B.: Hey, gal, don't go to sleep on me. How you feeling?

Lynn: Sleepy.… I just want to stay here.

B.: [Laughs] Well, I'd like to let you sleep, but I'm getting a cramp
in my leg.

Lynn: [Smiles wanly. Stands. Straightens her clothes, hair] Lord,
I'm a mess… Oh, Brennan, look at you; did I cry that much?
[referring to therapist's shirt which was drenched]

B.: It'll dry. Let me call and change some appointments. Then
maybe we can talk about what happened.

Lynn: I feel weird… Good, but weird — like my whole insides
have been taken out. I feel like I could just float.

The story that emerged from Lynn was one that would
have emotionally crippled anyone. Her father had come home
staggering drunk and raising hell. An escalating verbal battle
between the parents led to the father punching his wife in the
face. Enraged, she tore after him with a butcher knife, racing
through the house, cutting him in several places on his back and
neck. After rampaging from room to room, a stand-off came in
the kitchen — a knife fight that witnessed each parent stabbing
and slashing the other midst screams, shouts, curses, and blood
being splattered all over the kitchen. Through all this, Lynn,
age nine, and her little brother Tommy, age five, cowered in terror in the corner of the room. At one point, blood splattered on
Lynn's arm. She wiped at it and discovered she wasn't cut, but it
seemed certain she would be. She was sure she was going to die.

Even then, though, she was trying to protect her little brother. She remembered thinking that they could escape and hide, but she was in the corner, and her parents were between her and the door, swinging the knives. Eventually, both parents collapsed in the kitchen floor from loss of blood and/or exhaustion. Until an older brother came in and called the police, Lynn stayed curled in the corner. Eventually, a policeman took her out of the corner and sat her and her little brother on the front porch while the emergency squad was administering aid and placing the parents in an ambulance.

Amazingly — testimony to the power of alcoholic denial — the incident was never, ever discussed nor even mentioned by anyone in the family. Lynn and her two brothers were placed with a paternal uncle and aunt while the parents were in the hospital. The uncle, too, was alcoholic. He and his co-dependent wife were also expert at denial, so they never discussed what had happened.

When the parents were released from the hospital and/or jail (Lynn did not know which), and the family was reunited, the incident was still never mentioned. Alcoholic and co-dependent denial had simply erased that terrible day from reality. Lynn, too, had been taught denial as the only way to cope with reality. It was as if the horror had never happened.

Interestingly, Lynn's agoraphobia, caused in turn by panic attacks, was in fact the opposite of a fear of open places. She was actually afraid of being caught away from a corner at home where she could safely hide when fear threatened. The threat was precipitated by the sound of any siren. She remembered the sirens screaming outside just as her father was trying to get up off the floor, knife still in hand. In later life, when she was away from home, the sound of a siren immediately catapulted her into a panic attack. The hidden thought accompanying the siren was, "Oh-oh, it's happening; hide; get back in the corner!"

The kind of love described in this intense abreacted (re-lived) experience, which I call "loving presence," or authentically "being there," is surely not much different than any therapist would demonstrate in situations like this. The problem has been that in the lexicon available in the respectable scientific world, there has been no name and thus little conscious awareness of what the therapist is actually doing during such events. In point of fact, though, the therapist can do nothing but be "human" in the most naked, exceptionally vulnerable way, and just be there. It is not the time to analyze or theorize, and certainly not the time to discuss stimuli and responses, nor meaning, power, complexes, parent-child roles, nor anything else. It is simply a time to be present.

The admission of the word "love" to the professional consciousness can be a great confidence-builder in general, but especially at times like the one described above. Sometimes, all a therapist can do is love — and that is all the client wants or needs.

Other Phobias

Freudian explanations of phobias as repressed sexual taboos are helpful in an extremely small percentage of cases. Maybe there was more sexual repression in Freud's early-1900s heyday. But skyrocketing illegitimacy and promiscuity statistics would seem to indicate that Americans are troubled precious little by sexual repression nowadays.

On the other hand, if the generally quoted statistics are true that one in three or four girls and one in seven boys are sexually molested in childhood, then all that trauma must indeed show up in an enormous number of anxiety disorders, including phobias. And that is indeed the case. Yet, Freud's writings are not just useless but misleading in these kinds of cases because we now recognize that sex has little or nothing to do with sex abuse. Sex abuse involves hostility, manipulation, power — and these, in turn, produce threat, anxiety.

Cogent explanations for the great majority of phobias are provided by behavior and cognitive therapists. For example, fears "taught" to children by their parents form one large category of phobias. Phobias resulting from trauma are the other. An example of each might be seen in a phobia of water. We might find that the patient's mother was deathly afraid of water, and taught that fear to her child, or we could find that the person almost drowned once and has been afraid of water ever since.

Our focus here is on understanding phobias in the fundamental sense. We need to show that all phobias, like all other disorders are, en fin, love disorders.

Let us take the hypothetical case of one of the most loving mothers in the world. She's perfect — with one exception; she has a phobia for heights, and she has unwittingly "taught" this phobia to her child. Today, there are three predominant theories regarding the fundamental cause of her phobia:

(1) Psychoanalysts would begin looking for a taboo sexual instinct in both mother and child, the taboo being the fundamental internal fear that is then displaced onto the external one, heights. Freud himself stretched his sexual theory to the point of absurdity. Would he have found the fear of height to represent the height of a phallic symbol, or the "high" that accompanies an orgasm? I do not mean to insult modern psychoanalysts who have already revised many Freudian concepts. I do intend to emphasize, however, that there is no fundamental psychoanalytic explanations of anything; i.e., there are many valid concepts, but the entire theoretical substructure is fundamentally fallacious.

(2) Behaviorists would suggest that the child is afraid of heights because of "conditioning." Thus, each time the frightening stimulus, a height, was presented, the mother's response, fear, became the stimulus for the child's fearful response to height. Over time, this stimulus-response pattern was increased by "reinforcement." Indeed, that explanation, as far as it goes, is perfectly reasonable and valid. The only problem with it, as we shall see below, is that it is not a fundamental explanation.

(3) Cognitive therapists would say that it is not the height that is feared at all, but the consequence of the height, fear of

falling, and further, that the problem lies not in the neural, "knee-jerk" stimulus-response mechanism, but in the cognition, in the hidden, automatic thoughts associated with heights. Here again, as far as it goes, this explanation is perfectly valid.

The need to go further than behavior or cognitive therapies in search of a fundamental explanation of phobias is demonstrated by a simple question: if the root cause of phobias is found in discrete thoughts, or in isolated stimulus-response mechanisms, why does the whole person respond to the threat? Behavioral and cognitive answers and methods, helpful as they are, do not resolve the basic "why" because behavior and cognition are obviously only parts of the whole person. These therapies accurately show how two major human faculties operate, but they do not relate the "pieces" of a person to the whole.

In response, behavioral, cognitive and other therapies can ask a very reasonable question: if we are treating only parts of people, how do you explain our successes? How do you explain that the whole person gets well in response to many types of what you call "partial" therapy?

My answer is that all successful therapists, whether they are consciously aware of it or not, are loving their clients, the whole persons; it is the therapists' love, not their methodologies, that is the actual healing agent. Affirmations of that answer can best be tested by counselors themselves examining their own hearts and re-examining the fundamental dynamic of every successful case. My bet is that they will discover that they "just naturally" loved those clients, and that they viewed that love as just part of their jobs that they took for granted. Contrariwise, there is another test that therapists can use: if they can find even one client whom they were "mean" to, actually callous or neglectful and uncaring toward, who still got well, they will disprove the love theory (and I'll eat my ever-loving hat).

CHAPTER TWENTY-ONE

Slashed and Decayed Hearts:
The Deeper Disorders

"Heart transplant" — what an inspired
visual symbol for psychotherapy!
Irvin Yalom, M.D.[1]

Which of us who has not been stretched on the torturer's rack would presume to speak as the final authority on the experience of being torn limb from limb? Who of us who has not experienced raw, naked terror for years on end can pretend to thoroughly understand the human spirit that has been savaged? Which of us who has not experienced unrelenting horror can offer a definitive understanding of how *angst*, trembling unto death, can gnaw its way through every fiber of brain and heart to produce a labyrinth of bizarre thought and excruciating emotions? And who is the person so wise who can say without a shade of doubt that every odd-acting patient who says that he or she saw a demon, is hallucinating, and that absolutely none of them could be reporting a fact? (This last-mentioned, most highly controversial possibility, is addressed directly in Chapter Twenty-Five.)

Terrible anxiety, stemming from deep love deficits, can produce feelings, thoughts and behavior that are utterly strange. In centuries past, these odd symptoms were universally seen

---

[1] Irvin D. Yalom, M.D., *Love's Executioner and Other Tales of Psychotherapy* (New York: Basic Books, Inc., 1989), p. 251.

as so impossibly mysterious that mental patients were simply chained, hidden away and forgotten. Over the decades, many of the symptoms that had been totally incomprehensible became better and better understood, so much so that many schools of psychotherapeutic thought began to expound the certainty that mental illness contains no mystery at all. To extremists of positivist science, "mysteries" of all human life and mental illness are merely "tough problems" that will someday be fully understood, so there is no such thing as mental illness that is spiritual in origin. That attitude in therapy is deadly. It results in therapists giving up when faced with bizarre symptoms, behavior that *could* be understood if the therapist had not disowned his or her own spiritual faculties.

This chapter focuses on some of the deeper levels of anxiety, and on the greater love deficits that produce severe emotional disorders. Obviously, neither love nor anxiety can be quantified, but if diagnosis is performed "in love terms," a rough "scale" can be discerned between the "amount" of the love deficiency and the intensity of anxiety. In turn, the deeper the anxiety, the more circuitous and varied the routes it takes to express itself in symptoms. This "scale," the broad levels used in love therapy to gauge love-needs and disorders, is shown below. A few of the deeper anxiety-related problems — obsessive-compulsive, psychosomatic, and hysterical disorders — are briefly discussed in terms of love theory.

The Love Scale

Love therapy does not use a detailed typology of emotional problems. Broad "levels" of disorders serve intersubjective, heart-level diagnosis quite well enough.

It is important to remember, per Principle Five, that there are a limited number of basic emotions — anger, guilt, fear, grief, joy, peace and a few more — and all are expressions of love, a reality that encompasses all emotion. By the same token, there are a limited number of disorders. The American Psychiatric Association's *Diagnostic and Statistical Manual of Mental Disorders* (DSM IV)[2] is a beautiful categorization of disorders, very reasoned, but there is nothing sacred about it. The DSM's categories are actually somewhat arbitrary. Instead of two-hundred-plus disorders, we could name twenty, or one thousand, just as reasonably.

In love therapy, the chosen number of categories to cover all functional mental and emotional disorders is six — from zero to five. These broad levels of disorder used in love therapy are shown on the Love Disorder Scale that follows. In posing these six levels, I am absolutely not suggesting that the DSM be discarded. Rather, I am saying that after therapists make the major decision as to which of the two hundred-plus categories of disorder their patients fit, the major task still remains: finding the "simple truth." Granted, that is rarely simple, but the six levels are a step in that direction. These levels facilitate diagnosis and prognosis by providing at least a broad gauge of the central questions: how much love damage has this person sustained, and how much love will be required to heal them? The greater benefit of the Love Disorder Scale is that it provides a simple way to keep the focus where it belongs, on love. Is it too simple? In a Shakespeare sonnet (No. 66), there is a phrase, "and simple truth miscall'd simplicity." Simple truth is its own defense, or it is surely not simple enough.

The Love Disorder Scale

Level Zero: Infant Marasmus Death and Suicide [Measure: love is non-existent or is perceived as such.]

Level One: Psychosis — severe and chronic schizophrenia or bipolar (manic-depressive) disorder. [Measure: near-total lovelessness experienced during infancy and/or preschool ages. Love damage may be beyond human means of healing, so spiritual

---

[2] DSM IV, *op. cit.*

love therapy is indicated in most cases (cf. Chapter Twenty-Five). "Heart transplant" — massive love infusion by family and volunteers, in addition to professional therapy, is essential if massive love deficit is to have reasonable hope for being achieved.]

Level Two: Psychosis, sporadic, acute and less severe, plus psychosis as a feature of depression. [Measure: gross love damage from early childhood, or severe trauma exacerbating milder childhood love damage.]

Level Three: Obsessive-compulsive disorder, character/personality disorders, non-psychotic paranoia. [Measure: severe love damage and/or deficit, usually with preschool etiology.]

Level Four: Emotional Disorders, non-psychotic affective disorders; non-psychotic depressions, phobias, psychosomatic, hysterical, sexual and anxiety disorders. [Measure: moderately severe love damage or deficit.]

Level Five: Milder anxiety, depression or behavior disorders of adults; adolescent adjustment and childhood behavior disorders. [Measure: moderate to slight love damage.]

In the following, several of the major disorders are reinterpreted and redefined in light of love theory. In each description, the goal is to show how a mind "set" on love, and "thinking in love terms," allows us to avoid becoming confused by the bewildering array of symptoms that accompany serious disorders, and to stay targeted on the heart of the problem wherein healing must take place.

Obsessive-Compulsive Disorder (OCD)

An obsession is a repetitive, irrational, anxiety-induced thought. Its counterpart in behavior is a compulsion — an irrational, repetitive, anxiety-induced act.

The classic compulsive symptom is repetitive hand-washing — upward of one hundred times per day sometimes — although the compulsion can take many forms: rituals of repeatedly folding back sheets and precisely lining up shoes at bedtime; perfection in housekeeping carried to outrageous lengths; checking and rechecking; hoarding; making endless lists; washing chairs before sitting in them; or scrubbing car keys before and after each use.

Obsessions can best be described as involuntary "broken record" thinking — like a phrase repeated over and over, or being internally "forced" to repeatedly count the panes in a French door, or being plagued with involuntary hostile thoughts. One lady I saw would count my words as I spoke, then divide by two, then by three, and then tell me the quotient. Needless to say, having your words counted can make a counselor a little punchy. The only way I could deal with it was by kidding her: "I know you're *counting* on me to help, but this is getting a little ridiculous," to which she would invariably respond, "I know, but you've got a sense of humor, so I'm *counting* on you *retaining* it." (Retention, hoarding, she was aware, was another symptom of her OCD.)

Other symptoms of obsessions are: fear that something terrible is going to happen; disgust and frequent focus on body secretions; excessive prayer (beyond expectations of one's religion); perverse sexual thoughts or images; repeated mental calculations; and intrusive words, sounds or music.[3]

Freud conneced this disorder to fixation at the anal stage of development, about age two. I have made clear that I radically dsagree with Freud's reductionist and animalistic view of people, but he was correct in saying that a battle with mother over toilet training is seen in these disorders, but only sometimes. By no means can Freud's toilet training and "anal" theories be considered universal explanations of OCD. The age that parents commonly call the "terrible twos," Erik Erikson calls the "age of mastery,"[4] the age when a child is discovering an independent self. Discovering mastery, the child naturally becomes "impossible,"

---

[3]   A more detailed list of common obsessive and compulsive symptoms, ranked in order of frequency of diagnosis, is reported in a study by the National Institute of Mental Health, "AOCD survey," Ciba-Geigy Corp., *Journal of the American Medical Association* (1995).

a rambunctious delight who says "No!" to virtually everything. Erikson's broad view of the child's development of mastery is far more realistic than Freud's narrow, closed-sphincter idea, and the concept of mastery is indeed helpful in understanding OCD. Surprisingly, Erikson did not pursue it in his explanation of compulsions; rather, he virtually parroted Freud,[5] sadly giving credence to "pregenitality," the infantile sexual explanation for human behavior. By revivifying the concept of the child's development of mastery, however, re-forming it, so to speak, by understanding it in love terms, I believe we can arrive at a more accurate understanding of obsessive-compulsive disorders.

The love therapy theory of OCD views what is happening to the self, the independence, and the confidence of the child at ages two to four, and explains the disorder as stemming from hostility- or fear-induced domination and spirit-killing over-control of the primary care-giver, usually Mama (but Daddy can sometimes figure just as prominently into the pain). Some of these toddlers receive, not mother love, but "smother love," which is not love. At the same time, the father, the one whom one might expect to "empower" the child, impart "strength," and thus applaud the child's newfound *mastery* of self and the world, is either absent physically or emotionally, or proves himself unable to even protect, much less empower the child. The child at age two wants to say "Yes" to her/his own beginning self, and thus says "No" to everything else. Some mothers show the little one who's boss, thoroughly squelch and control the child to make him/her good, and then perfect — but nothing is good enough for some of these mothers. The child is therefore afraid, but turning to father does no good; he is not capable of providing the child with the authen-

---

[4] Erik Erikson, *Childhood and Society* (New York: W.W. Norton, 1950, 1963), pp. 74 and 89 show Erikson's charts of human development, which he unfortunately includes in a chapter entitled, "The Theory of Infantile Sexuality," which, in light of love theory, is an oxymoron. Erikson's valuable concept of the child's developing "mastery" was lost in Freudian sophistry, and thus must be retrieved and "re-formed."

[5] *Ibid.*, p. 60.

tic love that intrinsically contains the love-power that imparts protection, strength, and mastery. Thus, the fullness of authentic, person-respecting love comes from neither parent. Result: the child is both afraid and brimming over with anger, anger that will eventually become a lifelong drive for mastery — power, control, control, and more control, all of it magical. OCD is magical mastery, a fixated search for the love that inherently contains the power to abolish anxiety, the hidden fear of being controlled and then overpowered, annihilated. Only love protects us. When mother and father have consistently controlled and dominated a child, is it so surprising that that child will view all persons as parental representatives and then be afraid of everyone, trust no one, "open up" to no one? It is not the child's anal sphincter that is so uptight and closed in OCD; it is the child's heart that is closed. And is it so surprising that a child who is rendered so heart-empty by love's withdrawal would be a retainer, a hoarder? It is not "things" that people with OCD hoard; it is the remnants of love that those things represent that are saved. And if a child is rendered defenseless, i.e., loveless, is it so surprising that the child should begin to build defenses against threat using the only powers available, magical ones?

Looking back at the list of common OCD symptoms, above, the involuntary, repetitive thoughts and actions are explained in love theory as fixation at the preschool level of loving, that is, "getting stuck" at the age when a child should learn that love provides real protection against fear, and that love is not magical. The thoughts and actions of the obsessive-compulsive are "magical," "wishful," straight out of the land of "Let's pretend" that is so real in childhood. For the child, "the wish becomes the deed." Jumping over cracks in the sidewalk while saying, "Step on a crack and break your mother's back," a child's favorite way of fulfilling a hostile wish magically and benignly, becomes a way of life for the obsessive-compulsive.

With all due respect to Freud's anality and Erikson's "age of mastery", which contain some partial truths, obsessive-compulsives have a severe love disorder. The love that their mothers did not give them has to be replaced. First, though, the distorted love that they were given — smothering over-control and rigid domination, spirit-killing distortions that these clients have a perfect right to be angry about — has to be brought out and drained off. The obsessive-compulsive is still a two- or three-year-old trying to say "NO! NO! NO!" and just once get away with it. The problem is they have been trying to exert this angry *control* magically and indirectly. Their rage is extreme, so extreme that they are scared to death of it. As a result, the repressed anger/fear shows up as terrific anxiety which has to be drained away, temporarily allayed by the magical obsessions and compulsions.

Love therapy begins by encouraging the angry "NO!" to be brought out openly and directly, and then showing the person that there is nothing to fear, that all their controls are unnecessary, and they have every right to be angry at their parents. As the anger is brought out, the successive "NO's!" become more successful. The counselor does not punish nor control them; confidence then grows, and with it the real self. In a word, the person gets some "spirit." The controlled, uptight, stingy, perfectionistic, anxiety-driven non-person is replaced by one who is more masterful, confident, and free. As the freedom is given to express rather than control, decide without fear of reprisal, act instead of wishing, the therapist sees the childish half-person change into a spirited, confident, real one.

Eventually, though, as therapy progresses, the *source* of the anger, fear, control, perfectionism and magical thinking has to be confronted. The love-hate conflict that has so long existed in relation to the parents has to be not just understood, but resolved. And this is where love must be brought directly to bear on open, gaping, painful wounds in order to heal them. Being angry and fighting back at mother or father, even though it is being successful, even though the client is more confident, and a freer, more genuine person, is not enough. The session finally comes when the person sees that all his anger and fear and controlling devices have a common source. Suddenly, the anger is seen clearly to be shooting up, like explosions from a volcano, out of gaping wounds that slice deep into the bowels of the soul. And then the tears come, like boiling lava, and the counselor embraces and tries to comfort a heart-broken child who suddenly realizes that the mother's love, albeit present, was always wrapped in demands, always linked to excessive control, never given without extreme conditions.

Quickly, lest this focus on the mother of the obsessive-compulsive seem hyper-critical, I should note a peculiar, sad irony about the mothers of obsessive-compulsives — this: these mothers *try* far harder than the average woman to be good mothers. They keep their children better groomed; they oversee children's schoolwork more diligently; they are stricter with discipline; and, in short, they exert far more effort than most to control their children's development into "perfect" young citizens. In fact, these mothers are generally perfectionists. Why? Because they are very likely to have some significant obsessive-compulsive traits themselves. No, I do not have research evidence of that, but consider: in the limited number of cases of OCD that I've seen in the past few years, every single case has more than one member of the family with a similar diagnosis. In one case, a mother with one daughter and three sons all had OCD. In another, six siblings, all adults in their forties and fifties, *all* had significant levels of OCD. And these are not unusual cases; they seem to be typical of OCD.

As I looked back over my OCD caseload, I did find a few cases in which no OCD among family members was evident. When I looked further into those cases, though, I discovered they *all* were families in which the general anxiety level of the home was sky-high (and recall that the bottom-line force behind OCD is anxiety).

In the last chapter, most anxiety disorders were described in terms of a love deficit, a defect in the *outer* protective covering of love that protects the heart. But on the Love Disorder Scale, note that obsessive-compulsive disorder is at Level Three, a level deeper. Obsessive-compulsives have sustained not just an "outer" protective deficit, but damage to the core of the heart. In treatment, that large missing part of the heart has to be constructed, created. In many respects, though it may sound dramatic, this treatment is extremely analogous to a partial heart transplant. In the person with OCD, it is as if "love's right ventricle" is missing and has to be constructed. The heart donor is the therapist — and in tougher cases, God.

Mind-Body Love Disorders

Ulcers, asthma, colitis, hypertension, skin disorders, headache and migraines are just a few of the body problems often attributed to a "mind" origin, but arthritis, cancer, coronaries and the common cold are also studied in mind-body terms. These are often psychosomatic disorders, illnesses that are very real, certainly not "imaginary," but their origins are psychogenic, i.e., they start in the mind and emotions. Love theory offers a new view of these mind-body disorders.

Conversion reaction, once called "hysteria," is a body dysfunction that is not caused by any organic disease nor by any physiological impairment. Paralysis, blindness, choking, pain, weakness, breathing problems or even heart attacks and epilepsy can be experienced by people who are shown to have no physical problem whatsoever. These disorders, too, must be discussed in the context of the mind-body problems.

Though not usually studied in the same context as psychosomatic and hysterical disorders, the mind-body problem is also important in understanding some of the bizarre behaviors and physical sensations and delusions seen in psychoses.

For operational purposes, several of the theories of hysteria contain enough truth to enable therapists to provide effective help in most cases of conversion reaction. When a patient comes in blind, or with a paralyzed leg or hand, and no organic cause can be found, one of several theories is usually effective in removing the dramatic symptom. A psychoanalytic theory, that the symptom is a symbolic representation of a taboo drive or idea, may be found to be true. For example, a girl with a paralyzed arm may be discovered to have an unconscious forbidden desire to hit her sister with that arm. In another symptom, an unconscious sexual wish may actually be found to be converted into a hysterical symptomatic reaction. Or, Charcot's 1890 theory[6] (re-introduced in recent years by Beck[7]) that the hysterical symptom resulted from a "pathogenic idea," may prove true. For example, a soldier believed a bullet had severed a nerve in his leg and then developed "stocking" anesthesia (numbness that "stopped" at a defined point on his leg, like a stocking, and did not follow nerve pathways). When shown that the nerve was fine, his anesthesia vanished.[8]

The mind-body problem posed by psychosomatic disorders has barely begun to be solved. The number of migraines, skin, intestinal and other psychogenic disorders appearing in doctors' offices is ample testimony that the mind-body problem has barely begun to be unraveled. Similarly, if we had a deeper grasp on how the psychotic's delusions of body odors and missing limbs came about, we might be able to provide something more effective than drugs.

For centuries, the "mind-body" problem has been debated medically, philosophically, theologically, and psychologically. Philosophers begin with "matter" versus "form," or "existence" versus "essence" as they debate the concept of "reality," and before human reality is even discussed, there is disagreement. Some of these arguments become patently absurd. "Idealism," for example, may argue that *nothing* is material, that life is all a dream. At the same time, materialism argues that only the concrete is real, that even ideas are products of the material.

These philosophical debates are not just academic exercises.

---

6 J.M. Charcot, *Hemorrhagie et Ramollissement du Cerveau Metallotherapie et Hypnotisme. Electrotherapie* (Bureau du Progres Medical, 1890).

7 Aaron T. Beck, M.D., *Cognitive Therapy and the Emotional Disorders, op. cit.*, p. 209.

8 J.M. Charcot, *op. cit.*

Read any article on psychosomatic disorders, hysteria or conversion reaction and philosophical assumptions are always present, at least implicitly. One theorist will lean heavily toward the body side of the problem, another will put weight on the mind, while a third tries to show a parallel. The problem has been that no one has shown, nor even asked, what the link is, what the connection or means of communication is, between mind and body. Bluntly stated, the problem in solving the mind-body question is that it is the wrong question. As asked, the question presumes that an answer somehow can be found *within* mind or body or some combination of the two. But that is not so.

Heart Language

Love theory applied to the mind-body problem produces a very new set of answers that provide new hope for understanding mental and emotional disorders. The heart, empowered by love, is the link, the multi-channeled center that connects the body and the many psychospiritual functions of the heart which we ordinarily call the "mind."

A preview of love therapy's answers to the mind-body problem has already been shown. From the outset, we have referred to the "heart" as the psychospiritual center of the human being. As shown in Chapter Three, Figures 1 and 2, the heart is the total encompassing "structure" that contains, directs and coordinates all the secondary functions usually referred to as "mind." Though "psychospiritual" is an adequate central concept, in order to address the mind-body question more graphically, we can expand our definition: in love therapy, the heart is the *somatopsychospiritual* center of the soul, the central structure from which love directs and coordinates body, mind and spiritual functions in order to maintain unity, the oneness of the human person.

This definition is abstract, certainly, but we need to recall that "mind" is no less an abstraction. Even if the mind is defined in purely biologic terms as "all the functions of the brain," those "functions" remain abstract. Similarly, if the mind's "structure" or "functions" are spoken of as consciousness, unconscious, id, ego, superego, cognition, emotions, intuitions, conscience, sensory perception, stimulus-response center or "mindons," we still remain firmly planted in the realm of abstraction. Therefore, rather than spend a zillion words and more abstractions in defense of the heart definition, it seems wiser to allow love, always vulnerable, to be its own naked, self-evident defense.

Given that the definition of the heart is accepted, we can show how the definition is applicable to psychotherapy. The definition, in essence, provides a much deeper and more holistic way of understanding and thus of interacting with the person. Note that the heart maintains the *unity* of the person. This cannot be overstated. That unity, the integrity that the heart provides, means that a thought never exists alone, nor does an emotion or physical sensation or spiritual sense; when one faculty speaks, they all speak; when one faculty acts or responds, they all act and respond. The mind is never disembodied, nor is the body ever mindless; both speak together, or not at all, as directed and maintained as one by the heart. In psychotherapy, therefore, effectiveness increases in direct proportion to the therapist's ability and the client's capacity to speak and understand the language of the heart.

We can immediately recognize that communicating at the level of the heart is extraordinarily difficult. For any of us, the rarity of the times in our lives when we have spoken with absolute openness and intimacy, in an authentic "heart to heart" way, are always considered treasured moments. The risk of lowering defenses and allowing the heart to speak openly is monumentally more difficult for the person with emotional problems who has *never* done it. But that is precisely the goal of love therapy.

The language of the heart requires that the therapist speak and understand that language. Though plain, day-to-day words are used, when the heart's *unity* of body-mind-spirit-heart are kept in the forefront of consciousness, some very new understandings, new forms of conceptualization begin to emerge that immediately allow the linkages, the bridges between psyche and soma, thought and deed, feeling and fact, symptom and cause, to be discovered. In a later chapter, this kind of understanding is discussed in terms of Eastern, Oriental, more holistic thought processes, as compared to our Western, more linear, cause-effect, dualistic thinking. Here, as we try to convey the general ideas, we should note that the "style" of the therapeutic thought process (though not much of the content) is analogous to that used by existential analysts and phenomenologists. Just as they, for example, try to attune their thoughts and feelings to the client's own sense of his or her "being-in-the-world," and to the client's "mid-, inner-, or outer-world," the love therapist develops even more varied ways to use language to express the complex interaction of several human faculties that are all operating as one.

The following series of short statements are intended to provide an overview, a quick, intuitive "feel" for the language and dynamics of the heart.

◆ The language of the heart is cognitive-emotive-somatic-spiritual.

◆ Rather than the therapist listening to identify discrete feelings and thoughts, it is much closer to the heart, and thus much more helpful to the client, to listen to "thought-feelings" or "felt-thoughts," and then to reflect back to the client in those terms.

◆ A "conflict" cannot be adequately defined as "a mental struggle that arises from the simultaneous operation of opposing impulses, drives, external (environmental) or internal demands."[9] Similarly, while "approach-approach" and "approach-avoidance" conflicts do indeed exist, the human struggle is typically demeaned or not at all understood if it is seen in "mind" or "psychic" terms. A conflict that is powerful enough to cause disturbance is typically far more profound, a matter of the deeper recesses of the heart. A sex-drive-versus-thought conflict, for example, invari-

---

[9] *American Psychiatric Association's Psychiatric Glossary, op. cit.,* p. 22.

ably disguises deeper needs for love that can find resolution only at the deeper levels of the heart where body, thought, will, and conscience come together.

◆ The link, the bridge to understanding the "mind-body" conflicts that cause conversion reactions (e.g., paralysis in the absence of a physical cause) or psychosomatic disorders (e.g., hatred-induced ulcers) is formed by the heart. It is there, at heart level, that the underlying causes of these disorders must be found.

◆ When heart level is reached, it is often discovered that the body is making one statement, the mind (conscious and unconscious) two more statements, and the heart a fourth and much more conclusive statement. For example (though greatly oversimplified), the body of an ulcer patient may be saying, "The guilt I feel for my hatred, and the hatred itself, are eating my guts out, but pain is easier to deal with than hatred." The conscious mind is saying, "I love everybody; I don't hate anybody." The unconscious is saying, "I hate my boss, my father, and myself." But the conclusive, more truthful and more intractable statement is made by the heart: "I hate, damn betcha, and I'll keep on hating because I need to do so in order to preserve my integrity; to let go of the hatred would require forgiveness, but I believe in my heart that to forgive would mean admitting that those who hurt me by rejecting me were correct, and that would mean that I am just as my enemies said, unlovable. That is an unbearable thought; hatred is the only alternative." Ironically, at heart level, hatred's misbegotten goal is to preserve love; that is the heart of the conflict.

◆ Four concepts revealed in the heart statement above bear special mention. First, note that the central illness, hatred, is clung to by the heart as a matter of integrity, unity within itself. Secondly, note the curious intra-heart conflict: holding on to hatred in order to prove that one is lovable; that, irony of ironies, even hatred is motivated by love. Thirdly, this is a classic affirmation of the love therapy principle, "Unforgiveness blocks healing." Fourthly, healing in this case, involving forgiveness and repentance of hatred, will involve the spiritual depths of the heart, far deeper than the unconscious.

◆ After the cognitive therapy approach is exhausted, and every hidden and automatic thought is found, asking the question, "Now, listen deep within yourself and tell me, what does your heart say?" typically produces even more profound answers — *raison de coeur*. The same is true of every other method of therapy. Few of them conceptualize anything deeper than the unconscious, so they miss the entire realm of spirituality and all the more profound conclusions of the heart.

◆ A therapist does not just barge into a heart. Emotionally damaged hearts are fearful, distrustful and well-defended. Only love casts out fear, so love is the price of admission to the heart. The language of the heart is love. From the hurting client, the therapist might hear fearful love, distrusting love, torn, hopeless, abandoned, lost or confused love.

◆ An angry heart produces a totally angry being. This is seen in some depressions: neither angry emotions nor thoughts are expressed. Rather, spiritual anger, anger at God, or anger stemming from frustration over the inability to find spiritual meaning in life, unexpressed, is aimed back at the self, producing depression.

The feelings of emptiness, separateness and aloneness encountered in many forms of emotional disorder, are always direct statements of the naked heart. When there is enough client-therapist trust established that an empty heart is admitted, it is always a direct, (albeit nonverbal) plaintive plea, "Please! Love me!" In turn, there is only one effective therapeutic response: intense love given in massive doses. Virtually any other response reveals a therapist who is personally timid or grudging or defensive in relation to love. To ask what the client "thinks" or "feels" about such emptiness simply will cause the person to wallow needlessly in pain. Certainly the emptiness has its effects, but those can be explored later. One does not stop in the middle of a heart transplant to banter about how the emptiness in the chest feels.

Shattered and Terrified Hearts

She was age five when it happened, age nineteen when she could finally talk about it. Following is an account of a young woman in the midst of an abreaction, a vivid "re-living" of a traumatic event that occurred years before. She was very much regressed as she spoke.

Client: [In tears, in a little girl voice] I tried! I tried and tried and tried! Oh. Ohhhhh! (working, twisting her pointed finger "down") It won't come out.... Umphh, gotta get it. Ohhhh.

[Later, when her adult voice had returned, she explained what she was doing with her finger.]

Client: Oh I tried so hard. I thought I could make her come back to life. But she was dead, wasn't she? [She said this as if realizing it for the first time].... They had a big fight, screaming at each other. Then Daddy pulled a gun out of his jacket pocket and shot Mama. He ran out and slammed the door, and Mom looked at me, and then she fell, and she was bleeding. I was thinking I just had to stop the blood, and I had to get the bullet out, so I stuck my finger in the hole in Mama's chest.... I was all alone! (tears)

Words fail. How could any mere words ever describe what such trauma does to the whole interior being of a little girl subjected to shock and horror like this? If for no other reason, the "heart" must be recognized in the professional lexicon. Words like "unconscious," "repression" and "defense mechanisms" not only allow professional defensive distance from the pain, they are "heartless" words that demean human suffering.

A twenty-five-year-old man had been homosexually abused by a priest from age eleven to fourteen when he pulled away from the relationship. In a severe depression by age fifteen, he mustered his courage and finally decided he had to tell someone. Without relating what had happened, he asked his father whom he could go to for counseling. The father recommended another priest, a family friend. Unbelievably, the second priest tried to convince the boy that he was homosexual, and again sexually abused him.

My first contact with this young man was when he came for marriage counseling. His wife could not tolerate his withdrawal into silence and frequent rages. When, after his many years of secrecy and shame, the man could tell me what had happened, his agony was frightening. Again, words fail. If it is possible that the psychospiritual heart can be ripped in two, or explode in a shower of gore, that is what I saw this poor man undergo. And with that ripping and exploding of the heart came undeserved shame that could cause mountains to hide, and hatred that would melt the hardest steel.

Megan's Conversion Reaction

Following is an entirely different form of traumatic heart damage — the case of a twenty-eight-year-old woman who suffered conversion reaction, hysterical paralysis of the legs, from the hips down. The paralysis had been sporadic over a ten to twelve year period, and ranged from total immobility on two past occasions, to various degrees of partial paralysis. She was a waitress, very poor, so when the paralysis had hit her in the past, she had gone to a city general hospital where she was given tranquilizers, brief counseling, and sent on her way.

She had hobbled slowly into my office. I'll call her Megan. In the following interview, she had been talking about the last night she had spent with her alcoholic and very disturbed mother. Megan was ten years old. The lights were out in the house, apparently because her mother had not paid the electric bill. Megan had done "something" wrong, and her mother was cursing and raging. As Megan talked, regression could be heard in her voice as she began reliving (abreacting) something horrible that had happened.

Megan: I remember running to the bedroom in the back of the house, and I hid way back in a dark corner behind a big chair. ... (Then shifting abruptly into a little girl's voice, whispering) Hide! Hide! She just has one candle; maybe she won't see me....

B. (Brennan Mullaney): So it was dark...?

Megan: [Grabbing her chest] Oh, it hurts. Uh! I think I'm having a heart attack... Oh-my-God! I'm scared, I'm scared!... Oh, no, my legs. Oh, they're getting numb again. [Puts both hands over her head and bends over in the chair.] Oh, oh, oh God, help me. Oh, she's — [stops abruptly].

B.: She....

Megan: No-no-no, I don't want to see it.

B.: It's okay, Megan, I'm right here with you. Whatever that old bad memory is, it's hurting you. I'll stay with you. If you want to remember, it'll be okay.

Megan: Oh-my-God, oh Jesus. She's gonna kill me. She's gonna kill me.

B.: No, no, Megan, I'll be with you.

Megan: Shhh. Shhhhhhh. She'll hear. [Whispering] She's comin'. Oh, don't let her find me. [Pulls her legs up on her chair, crouches in a ball, with head on knees, arms over head, hiding].

B.: Who, Megan? Who's after you?

Megan: Mom! Oh God, those scissors are sharp. [Whispering] Where is she? Shhh, shhh, shhh, don't breathe. Don't move. Don't move. Don't move... She's in the hall. Shhh. Don't move...

B.: [Whispers] What's your Mom doing, Megan?

Megan: [Whispers] She's gonna kill me. Shhh. She's gonna cut my heart out. She will! She's crazy! Oh, shhh, shhh. Don't move.

Five minutes passed during which Megan remained tightly curled in a ball on the chair in my office, her arms wrapped tightly around her legs or over her head. Her whole body trembled.

When she peeked out of her curled ball, her eyes were wide with
sheer terror. For half of this time, I could not reach her at all. After
repeated assurances that I was with her, that she was safe, she
returned to the present — but now her legs were totally paralyzed.
She could not move them at all, and could feel nothing in them.

B.: How long had you stayed in hiding?

Megan: [voice still tremulous] All night. The sun started coming
    in the window and it scared me, because then I knew she
    could see me.

B.: You had stayed curled up with your legs wrapped to your
    chest all night long?

Megan: Yes [tears]. And I had peed in my pants.

B.: Hon, as terrified as you were, it's no wonder. Anybody would.
    But Megan, think back. You finally had to move. When you
    tried to move, what did you feel?

Megan: I couldn't! It scared me.... I remember trying to stand up,
    and I couldn't get up [tears].

B.: Just like now.

Megan: Yes...

B. Megan, if you had been curled up all night long with your legs
    in one knotted position, you had probably cut off a lot of the
    blood supply, and you might have been pinching nerves so
    that your legs *went to sleep*. Did you ever sit in one position
    for a long time and have a foot go to sleep, get "needles and
    pins" in it? Maybe that's what happened to your legs. Think
    back to that morning. Did the feeling gradually come back
    into your legs?

Megan: Yeah, it took a while... and they hurt.

B.: Right now how do your legs feel?

Megan: Numb... but they hurt.

B.: [Smiling] Think you can let the feeling come all the way back
    now without being afraid that your mother will find you?

Megan: [Surprised] Ohh? Is that what it was?!... Ohhh? I'll be
    darn [Looking at her legs, smiling but shocked]. Oh, would
    you look at that. Can you believe that? I'll be darn. Would
    you look at that?

B.: What?

Megan: [Smiling] All the feeling started, like, *jumping* back into my legs. Ohhh, I get it now. It was all because of that one night. That's why my legs get paralyzed! I'll be darn!

Megan's mother had stalked the ten-year-old through the pitch dark house for hours, candle in one hand, scissors in the other, screaming and cursing, threatening to cut her heart out. Whether drunk or insane, Megan never determined, but she knew that the threats were indeed earnest. Her mother had cut her once before. When her mother came again and again into the back bedroom where Megan was hiding, the glint of the scissors and the wild shine of her mother's eyes were indelibly engraved on her memory.

Words fail. The most chilling tale of Edgar Allan Poe or the worst horror movie pale to fairy tales in comparison to the real life terror that this little girl underwent. There are lines in Coleridge's *Rime of the Ancient Mariner* which offer a hint:

> Like one, that on a lonesome road
> Doth walk in fear and dread…
> Because he knows, a fearful fiend
> Doth close behind him tread.[10]

But Coleridge is describing mere dread. Discussing Megan's trauma, even the word "horror" is weak. What mere words can describe what happens to the heart of a little girl whose mother is the "fiend" determined to kill her? Could anything be worse?

When feeling returned to her legs and she could finally walk, Megan crept out the back door, ran to a neighbor's house, and told them what had happened. She recalled the police taking her to a children's shelter. Her last memory of her mother was in Juvenile Court (apparently in a custody hearing). She remem-

---

[10] Samuel Taylor Coleridge, "The Rime of the Ancient Mariner," in *World Masterpieces*, Vol. 2 (New York: W.W. Norton & Company, Inc., 1956), p. 1600.

bered her mother yelling at the Judge, "No! I don't want her!" and then pointing at Megan and screaming, "That little bastard has ruined my life! I don't give a *damn* what you do with her, but I don't want her!"

Megan's father, also an alcoholic, placed her with his sister in another state. Her mother was never mentioned, nor did Megan ever ask what had happened to her.

Parents terminate their rights and place children in adoptive or foster homes every day, usually for reasons beyond their control. It is rare that a parent volubly, maliciously rejects a child to the child's face. As Megan's case unfolded, it was that rejection, experienced as a "heart attack," that always preceded the leg paralysis. (Previously, I had mistakenly interpreted her "heart attacks" as palpitations, one of the common symptoms of anxiety. Given the vicious rejection by her mother, it became clear that Megan's psychospiritual heart was "broken" that day in Court, and that that pain was experienced in her physical heart.)

If these three cases seem incomprehensibly cruel, experienced therapists will affirm that traumatic and inhuman events can become even more brutal, utterly unfathomable. Even the most compassionate and solidly grounded counselor must have a "threshold of incomprehensibility," the point when it becomes no longer possible to absorb more horror and suffering, no longer possible to sympathize, empathize or even analyze, and the therapist just "blanks out" the pain, denies it, intellectualizes it, or in some way escapes it in much the same manner as the person did who underwent the suffering.

T.S. Eliot, describing our response to horror, says "Human kind cannot bear very much reality."[11] It is perhaps for this reason that so many approaches to psychotherapy are so "scientific," so analytic, so "heady," so apparently bloodless and even heartless. Most therapists are exceptionally warm, compassionate, loving

---

[11] T.S. Eliot, "Murder in the Cathedral," in *World Masterpieces*, Vol. 2 (New York: W.W. Norton and Company, Inc., 1956), p. 2233.

people, so why have therapy models seemed so coldly intellec-tualized? Understandable defensiveness against a steady diet of daily horror may be one reason. The other is the intense focus on the "mind," the thinking apparatus. Hopefully love therapy's offer of the "heart" as central focus can restore some heart to the profession. But this can happen only if professionals will admit that they, too, need love in big daily doses. Only a powerful love can face horror without cringing. Dealing with horror on a daily basis means that therapists need far more love than the average person.

In the last chapter and this one, we have traced anxiety from the slight tremor caused by the slightest love deficit that leaves the heart unprotected, to the more severe anxieties related to severe heart damage. We have tracked anxiety through obsessive-compulsive disorder, hysterical and psychosomatic disorders and on to existential *angst* and the nebulous anxieties associated with spiritual realities. Note that all these anxieties are experienced intra-heart.

In the next chapter, we'll try to understand what happens when the anxiety and internal pain spill out, into violence.

CHAPTER TWENTY-TWO

Pathological Loves:
From Twisted to Murderous

Man has no choice but to love. For when he
does not, he finds his alternatives lie in
loneliness, destruction, and despair.

Leo Buscaglia[1]

It is precisely because love is so fundamental — so absolutely
necessary, so universally sought, so uniquely satisfying, so singularly motivating, so incomparably and deeply felt, so essentially a
matter of happiness or unhappiness, life or death — that love can
become so bewildering, so sick, so tragic, so generally screwed up.
It must remain clear as we dive still deeper into some of the sad,
twisted, and sometimes sickening ways that love can be patho-
logically contorted, that authentic love is, as it was described in
the eighteen love principles, all good — freeing, respectful, trust-
worthy, beautiful, and, in a word, Godly. So, when we talk about
"sick love" or "murderous love" or "jealous love" or "perverted
love," we must constantly remind ourselves that we are not talking about authentic love. Nor can authentic love be blamed for
the multitudes of ways it is bamboozled, sliced, slandered, and
murdered. The atom was used to make a bomb that destroyed
masses of people, and steel is molded into bullets that kill, but no
one says the atom and steel are bad, nor would anyone say that the

---

[1] Leo Buscaglia, *Love* (New York: Ballantine Books, 1972), p. 168.

atom *is* a bomb or that steel is the same as a bullet. Sadly, though, love is a victim often blamed for its own abuses.

Yet, diagnostically, as we try to understand ourselves or others, if we can see precisely how love is twisted or confused, it tells us exactly what the problem is. Sometimes, though, we have to slog deep into the boondocks or way out into left field to find just how far from home (truth) love has gotten. Here are some examples.

Love Twisted into Violence

Client: I just don't understand it. I just went crazy, totally berserk. I started busting up the furniture, and yelling and hollering. She (his wife) just wouldn't listen! So I started throwing tables, chairs, pictures — anything that would fit I threw out the window. She wouldn't listen!
Therapist: What were you trying to tell her?
Client: That I *loved* her!… She just wouldn't believe it.… Neither did the cops. They hauled me off.

Authentic love can be intense, the feelings it can arouse can even be described in poetic terms as overwhelming, passionate, or wild. But never violent. Love and violence are utterly antithetical. In the case above, the violent furniture mover was having a childish temper tantrum. That had always gotten him his way when he was a child; his mother always appeased him. But it was not appeasement he really wanted. It was authentic love. That, we learned, he received very little of. As a result, he had remained a child, having tantrums with his wife.

Jealousy, Possessive Pseudo-Love

Client: I just loved him too much, I guess. I just couldn't stand it if he even *talked* to another woman, and he always did. I

kept thinking he was fooling around on me. So I bugged the
phone and started following him.
Therapist: That's not called love; it's called jealousy.
Client: Hell, that's what he said. That's why he left. But can't you
understand either? I just loved him!

Jealousy has no relation to the person who is the object of the
jealousy. It speaks, rather, to the inability to trust and the feelings
of inadequacy of the person who is jealous. This is not to say, of
course, that a woman whose husband is being unfaithful will feel
nothing. Given evidence of infidelity, she surely will feel suspicion, and if the evidence is confirmed she will feel hurt, rejected,
crushed. But actual betrayed trust and the inability to trust that
causes irrational suspicion, jealousy, are utterly different.

Principle Six describes trust as "an indispensable precondition and an integral dynamic of love." Love and trust are existentially an integer, one, so in reality there is only "love-trust" or
"trust-love." Trust can exist alone as a mental abstraction, but in
the living of it, as a dynamic act, trust cannot come into being nor
remain alive apart from the act of loving.

In this light, irrational suspicion, jealousy and paranoia are
expressions of non-love, the inability and/or refusal of the so-
called lover to actually risk loving. The suspicion has absolutely
nothing to do with the supposed beloved, who is in fact not loved
to the precise degree that suspicion exists.

The person who is jealous and paranoid, rather than loving
or being loved, is operating on an internal message, "He (she)
doesn't love me; maybe nobody can; I'm afraid I'm unlovable;
ohhh, no-love is terrifying; I need absolute *proof* that I'm loved."

There is no proof. Love, trust, faith and hope, even as psychological realities, exist in the realm of the spirit, in mystery.
Trust can never be proven, nor can any other element of the love
quadruplex be proven. If you trust me a thousand times, I could
betray you the very next time. Trust is always a risk, as are hope,
faith and love. The risk of love obviously cannot be taken lightly;

we are, after all, gambling with our most precious possession, the core of our beings, our hearts. Clearly, love requires wisdom; it is only the heart that is wise enough to weigh the risk. Once that risk is taken, though, once authentic love is given, trust is given with it; once that is done, jealousy is impossible.

Principle Ten insists that love must be balanced. In fact, there are many love-balances in every relationship, but especially in marriage. The basic balance may be expressed this way: God's love can be unrequited; He can love and love and love and require nothing in return; in a marriage, though, if I'm going to love and keep loving, then I've just got to be loved in return. When there is a gross imbalance, when the love is pseudo-, then tragedies like the following are encountered.

Battered Wife Syndrome

Sophia had been married for thirty-five years, and for that many years she had been systematically beaten bloody by her husband. She came in to the counseling office with a blackened and cut eye, patches of hair missing from her scalp, and bruises all over her body. As is the case almost invariably, Sophia said she had endured her suffering for all those years because of "love."

Many women suffering the syndrome of symptoms associated with long-term battering present a distinctive countenance and tone of voice. At first glance, they appear depressed, but there is a unique quality to their depression. Talking to them is like talking to a vast empty room; you can almost hear your own voice echoing back. Days and weeks after they have been beaten, it is as if they are still in shock, and able to absorb only a fraction of what they hear. Ask them what they're feeling and the most typical responses are "Nothing" or "Numb."

Their spirits are broken.

The battered wife has a self-concept, self-esteem, and self-confidence that are frequently minus-zero. They see themselves as "nobody," "nothing" *without their husbands*; with him, they are still minus-zero and becoming less every day.

Here is a principle I present to all battered wives, and to any others who are caught in the web of pathological relationships: *The only way to "adjust" to a sick individual, family or situation, is by getting sick.* The only way to "adjust" to a totally domineering, threatening, abusive husband is by becoming totally submissive, obsequiously subservient, a "zero person." Obviously, the quotation marks around "adjust" say that the only way to sanely, authentically adjust to a battering bully is to *stop* adjusting to him, leave him, have him jailed, and refuse to reunite until he has received successful treatment. In such extreme abuse cases, this is the first priority of treatment, a matter of life and death.

Wife-battering is like alcoholism, a progressive disorder. The battering *invariably* gets worse with time — more frequent and severe beatings until the woman is sometimes killed. The wife is caught in an especially tricky, manipulative kind of pseudo-love.

A frequent pattern of the abusive cycle is this: enraged, the husband beats his wife, but then returns within a short time, overwhelmed with grief, swearing his undying love, and vowing to never, ever, ever lay a finger on her again — "because I love you." One of the common "tricks" that makes it so difficult for his wife to escape the vicious cycle is that the husband is oh-so-sincere and so extra-loving when he swears his contrition. The other trick is that after swearing his love, the wife-beater inevitably adds a disclaimer: "You know I love you, and I'd *never* hurt you. It's just that you make me so mad sometimes that I can't help it." (In other words, the battering was her responsibility.) And, again inevitably, she feels guilty — as if it were her own fault she got beaten. So she agrees to try again, and feeling responsible for his behavior, becomes even more subservient, more determined to not make him angry... and then she is beaten again... and again.

The picture of the heart of the battered wife is one of hollow emptiness, interrupted only by a few spots of pseudo-love. Her spirit is trashed. In fact, though, the twisted version of love these couples represent is difficult to untangle. These men are absolute masters of post-abuse *protestations* of love, pseudo-love in its most insidious form — totally empty protests that perpetuate the wife's empty, defeated, lifeless heart, a broken spirit. The wives feel so much like nothing that even he seems "better than nothing," which is why they defy all reason and continue to stay.

Healing the Victimization Syndrome: Love Empowers

Physical or sexual child abuse victims, rape and incest victims, emotional deprivation victims, racism victims, child divorce victims, domineering and spirit-killing parent victims, adult-child alcoholic home victims, crime victims, even unemployment, poverty, and war victims all share a configuration of common symptoms, a definite pattern of feelings, false beliefs and behavior which can only be called the "victimization syndrome." Many people seen in counseling suffer the victimization disorder to one degree or another. In the following interpretation, the victim's symptoms and feelings, and how we can begin to change them, can be seen.

Therapist: I think I understand enough now to see how all those bad experiences (abuse, deprivation, rape, etc.) have hurt you, and I also see something more fundamental, a thread of damage that we can break immediately. It's a sweeping attitude toward life and a destructive belief about yourself that you can start changing right now.

Let me tell you, just point-blank, the bad news and the good news of your life — bad news first. Ready? Okay, the bad news is that you really were hurt as a child (or when you were abused, raped, deprived, etc.). You were made to feel pain and all the bad feelings we talked about. You were neglected, humiliated, beaten down, damaged. So here's the bad news of your life: you were indeed a *victim*. You were truly victimized and there was nothing you could do about it. There's no sense in denying it; it happened and it was awful.

Now the question is — what do victims feel? It sounds overly simple, but they *feel* like victims; they act like victims, and they think like victims. It's like this [therapist takes off reading glasses]. It's like you put on "victim glasses" and begin to see the world and everybody in it through victim eyes. We talk about some people putting on rose-colored glasses and they see everything as rosy. But what does a victim see?

If I am a victim, then anybody and everybody else just might be a *victimizer*. If my parents victimized me, people who were supposed to love and protect me, then who can I possibly trust? (That statement can be customized to name the victimizer who betrayed trust and love.) So anybody *might* be a victimizer, so I have to stay on guard, defensive, avoiding threat, waiting to be hurt, distrustful of everybody. And that leaves me alone, unable to really get close to anybody.

What else do victims feel? As a victim, you were *powerless.* You were indeed. As an abused child (or rape victim, etc.), you felt weak; there was nothing you could do. You felt small, defenseless, overwhelmed by power that everybody but you had.

Then, as a victim, you felt shame, and guilty, like you must have done something wrong or you wouldn't have been so victimized. That's false guilt.

Victims also are full of fear, full of anxiety. They think, "When will the victimization happen again!?" As a victim, you never knew when you were going to face threat, so you stay scared. You see threat everywhere. So victims stay anxiety-ridden.

Victims, feeling powerless, feeling that they can't change *anything,* begin to feel hopeless, even despairing, depressed. After all, the view through victim glasses is not rosy; it's dark, grim. So victims, feeling powerless to change anything, continue to feel hopeless in relation to *ever* being happy.

Now, we have to face this, the bad news of your life. You were indeed a victim, and you did indeed have all these victim feelings, and the sad truth is that it did you some damage. But the worst damage might not have been what happened in the past. The worst damage might be that you've taken on an *identity* as "victim." You've still got the victim glasses on, and you've led your life as a victim — feeling, thinking, and acting like a victim, right up to the present.

And that, my friend, is the bad news of your life. [I usually pause here to confirm that the person has indeed taken on a victim identity. Then....]

Now, are you ready for the good news? This may come as a shock. The good news is that, in fact, in reality, in the present, you are *not* a victim. In reality, as we sit here, you are no more a victim than I am. If you still feel like a victim, it's only because you've still got the victim glasses on. But all you have to do is take them off. So take them off, right now, right this second. You're *not* a victim! You're not powerless any more. You have the power to change the way you see yourself, the world, and other people. Look, I'm not a victim and neither are you. Is anybody really trying to victimize you right now? Get this: *nobody* can victimize you anymore unless you let them. But you won't let them. You have the power now to stop them.

Do you know why it's a crime and a sin to victimize other people? It's not just the physical pain. The real crime of victimization is that it *makes* people feel ways they don't want to feel — fearful, powerless, distrustful, defensive, weak, shameful and guilty. But you are no longer a victim! Look, I'm not a victim, and nobody on earth can make me feel like a victim. Granted, somebody can rob me, bloody my nose, beat me up, scare me, even kill me, but they *can't* make me keep feelings I don't want. God made you the master of your own soul and your own feelings, and you have the exclusive power over which feelings you keep, reject, or change. Why? Because you're as strong as anybody else. Yes, your power was taken away and you need to get your power back, but the reality is that you're not a victim anymore.

That little speech covers a lot of internal territory in many disorders. Sometimes several sessions are involved in working out the many ramifications. Thereafter, throughout the course of therapy, people will catch themselves in an "old tape" feeling or thought and say, "That's victim thinking, isn't it? I can change that."

Love empowers. Recall that the word "courage" is derived from the French *cœur*, heart. "Encouragement" in therapy with the many people suffering the victimization syndrome means literal "enheartenment": into the fearful, vacant chambers of the victim's heart, the therapist infuses courage, more heart, the power to overcome a lifetime of powerlessness. Only the power of love has the capacity to authentically empower at the deepest level of being.

In victims, we again see the need for heart transplant.

Rage — With and Without Hatred

Victims sometimes become victimizers. Thus, when I meet a mother who has abused a child, it is a very good bet that I'll discover she herself was abused. Love breeds love, but rage breeds rage. It is important, à la Glasser's reality therapy principle of responsibility,[2] that human beings, no matter how upset, full of rage or psychotic they may be, always must be held accountable for their behavior. Allowing a person to "cop out" on responsibility because they were "too sick" and "couldn't help it" is to forsake the capacity to love, to abdicate freedom, to repudiate love's essential power to distinguish good from evil and to choose

---

[2] Glasser, *op. cit.*

the good. Acceding to irresponsibility is the death knell of love and the harbinger of hopelessness, violence and murder. Evils like the raging desire for violence, though powerful, are never mandatory. The abusing mother, or any of us who hurt others, always have a choice.

Rage can be experienced without being allowed to be acted out. When that is done, the act of suffering rage can be an act of love. But when we judge, when we blame others for our rage in order to deny personal responsibility, that is called hatred, and hatred allows rage to be irresponsible, conscienceless, out of control. Judgment breeds hatred breeds violence breeds abuse in all its forms, including murder.

Murder and Suicide

There is but a butterfly's breath of difference between homicide and suicide. Because both the killing of another and the killing of self are seen as ultimate acts of hostility, the choice of one or the other is often finally determined only by some capricious turn of fate. Some accept as gospel that the two acts are virtually identical. We will distinguish here several forms of both suicide and homicide. One form is the murder-suicide "toss-up," an event which seems to fuse the idea of killing self or others into one thought: just kill.

A classic example of the "toss-up" murder-suicide was cited in a study of suicide among police: "...the case of a policeman who waited for hours to kill the sergeant he hated. When the sergeant failed to appear, the patrolman killed himself."[3] We need not look far for more examples. Every day, we read in the news of another case of a husband-wife, mother-children, or whole family murder-suicide.

Two other "types" of murder are those involved in two types of paranoia. In one type, the paranoid "fixes" his delusion of per-

---

[3] Paul Friedman, "Suicide among Police: A Study of Ninety-Three Suicides Among New York Policemen, 1934-1940," in Edwin S. Schneidman, *ibid.*, p. 428.

secution upon one innocent person as the sole source of misery. One tragic example is enough: a young psychiatrist was shot and killed by a paranoid schizophrenic. The only precipitating factor that could be discovered was that the psychiatrist wanted the man to re-enter the hospital.

Another paranoid type involves jealousy. The all-too-frequent story of the ex-husband (most typically) killing his estranged wife is an example.

But the types that horrify us most are the mass-murderers and serial killers. Many years have passed, but my city (Louisville) is still in shock over a mass killing in a printing plant. An ex-employee armed with automatic weapons wandered through the plant shooting everyone in sight, and then killed himself. Elsewhere, a man opened up with an automatic weapon in a McDonald's restaurant, killing children, adults, anyone he could see. And in a Texas tower, a sniper perched for hours with a rifle, killing, killing, killing.

The notorious Ted Bundy, who gave the appearance of a perfectly respectable, clean-cut young man, was executed. By some accounts, he had raped and murdered over one hundred little girls and young women. Gacy, Zodiac, Son of Sam, Manson, the Hillside Stranglers, Jeffrey Dahmer, the BTK (Bind-Torture-Kill) monster — the list of serial killers and/or our detection of them is growing.

Then we must add the skyrocketing number of drug-related murders that is terrifying whole cities, not to mention the steady number of robbery and other crime-related murders.

When we allow ourselves to become conscious of the violent death that seems to surround us, all of us are overwhelmed. We can try to comfort ourselves that the police are out there protecting us, but they, too, are overwhelmed; the police suicide rate is about double the rate of the general population. Mental health professionals, too, are overwhelmed; the suicide rate of psychiatrists is six times that of the general population. All of us look at the carnage and shake our heads in shock, totally unable to comprehend: how can human beings do things like that?

Here again the hard facts loom large: many theories of personality provide partial explanations, but all the existing theories combined, when we stand facing the savagery, the heinousness, the inhumanity of multiple murder, leave us still shaking our heads, unable to comprehend. Love theory offers a deeper, more comprehensive view of such acts, and within its framework we can arrive at a better understanding, a simpler, less abstract way of grasping the enormous complexities. We obviously cannot unravel here all the twists and tangles of murderous minds. Perhaps, though, we can take a step closer to the "heart of the matter" of murder or, it would be better to say, the heartlessness of it.

Willard Gaylin discusses a case that we can use as a prototype of "twisted love" as a cause of murder. We can then show how all homicide begins with love-damage.

> Richard Herrin, using a claw hammer, had battered to death his "beloved," Bonnie Garland, while she lay sleeping.... [She] had survived the night and was found gasping, drowning in her own blood. Richard was informed by the priest to whom he had turned himself in that Bonnie was still alive. Richard responded, "She can't be alive. When I hit her, her head burst open like a ripe watermelon." What kind of person says a thing like that? What kind of person even thinks that way?
>
> ...in Richard's defense, his lawyer made a great issue of the fact that this was a tragic example of love betrayed. Richard had never loved before; in losing Bonnie, he was losing the only love of his life. It is my conviction, however, that Richard never "loved" Bonnie — not in the sense of fusion or attachment which is the necessary condition of love. What Bonnie betrayed was not Richard's love, but his sense of manhood. He felt humiliated more than bereft. He saw Bonnie's rejection as exposing to a mocking world his own self-image

of inadequacy. Bonnie was not only Richard's evidence of his lovability, but a bulwark of his own shallow and vulnerable sense of potency, both sexual and other.[4]

Yes! If now we could just crawl inside Richard, we could perhaps begin to answer Gaylin's questions more thoroughly: what kind of man could talk about the head of his "beloved" as a "watermelon" he had just burst? "What kind of person even *thinks* that way?" Gaylin, an extraordinary psychoanalyst, provides a very non-Freudian understanding of the case: Richard never "loved" Bonnie. Understanding Richard is rather a matter of tracking his flagging feelings of manhood, humiliation, inadequacy, and impotency. Comprehending the incomprehensible Richard is also a matter of understanding what Bonnie represented in relation to his "lovability."

Undoubtedly, what Bonnie discovered about Richard that prompted her rejection is precisely what Richard eventually proved, that he did not love her at all, and, further, that he was blocked in both loving and receiving authentic love.

As love theory "measures" development along the Love Scale (Chapter Twenty-One), we can be sure that he had received enough early love in his life to ensure survival (Level One love); he had not been a failure-to-thrive baby who died for lack of love. Nor is there evidence that he was psychotic (Level Two), so he also *had* received enough early love to place him in basic contact with reality. We must presume, though, that he fell in Level Three, seriously emotionally disturbed, but able to make rational choices between right and wrong. We are talking, therefore, about love that is so horribly twisted that what Richard perceived as "love" one day could be killed the next.

One key in understanding Richard's crime is volition, choice. Was Richard free not to kill? Yes. How do we know?

---

[4] Willard Gaylin, M.D., *Rediscovering Love* (New York: Penguin House, 1987), p. 168.

Inherent in the act of murder are feelings, thoughts, and psychospiritual convictions (at least temporarily held) of all the following seven factors: (1) rage; (2) devaluation of human life; (3) consequent depersonalization of the person killed to the level of an inanimate "thing"; (4) infantile and/or grandiose conviction that the self is the "center of the universe"; (5) disbelief in God or any Higher Power; (6) arrogation of omnipotence to self, i.e., all rights, all power, like God, including the right to give and terminate life; and (7) a voluntary decision to misuse the power of existing love in order to obtain or retain pseudo-love by any means. In turn, a pseudo-love can be virtually *any* tangible or symbolic intra-psychic representation of authentic love — power, money, public adulation, sexual gratification, sexual power (potency), drugs, retention of a defense that represents love (such as Bonnie represented for Richard), food, status, or retention of an idea that represents love as a defense against unlovability.

The paragraph above is loaded with meaning and will require closer examination. First, though, it must be clear that once love is twisted, contorted, mutilated, it must become a pseudo-love and that can be virtually *anything*, tangible or intangible, real or psychic. It is only in this light that Richard's murder, or any other, can be understood. *Murder always has a pseudo-love as its object.*

We read of proof of the murderous power of pseudo-love every day and wonder, "How can any human being stoop so low to do something like that?" One wino kills another fighting over fifteen cents. Two brothers argue over a pork chop; one kills the other by cramming the meat down his throat. And every day during these drug-infested years, one junkie kills another in a fight over a ten-dollar rock of crack cocaine. Once authentic love is lost, once the fundamental grounding in reality has crumbled and pseudo-loves have been chosen as substitutes, all of life can be worth no more than fifteen cents, a pork chop, or a vial of crack. Only in this light can the humanly incomprehensible be understood: that fifteen cents, that pork chop, is "love," is life, and is therefore all that matters.

Looking back now at the seven feelings/mental convictions inherent in murder, it can be seen that the seventh, the *decision* to obtain or retain a pseudo-love, was made possible by the preceding six components; yet, only the decision can be said to actually account for the act of killing. Though the previous six may cause mental or emotional illness, they, by themselves, can never cause murder.

Rage, the first requisite for murder, is experienced by many people and it is present in many disorders. By itself, there is nothing murderous about it. Frustrated infants kick, scream, and turn purple with rage, and thousands of depressed people are eventually discovered to be brimming with rage — but they don't kill. A decision is required.

Yet, some may argue that rage is not even required for murder, as evidenced by professional hit-men who murder in emotionless cold blood. In most cases, if a murder is cold-blooded, the rage is surely present, but repressed. There are, though, murders that are motivated by sheer evil. (The study of evil and the possibility of evil spirits being real and instigating murder are beyond the purview of this book, but for the record, I have witnessed such events. One such case is discussed in Chapter Twenty-Five.)

The devaluation of life and the depersonalization of the person to the status of an inanimate "thing" are rather self-evident. This kind of depersonalization is seen in many disorders. In satyriasis (male sexual addiction), for example, the Don Juan literally sees women as sex *objects,* non-personal "things" whose only meaning or purpose is to gratify his sexual desires. In treatment, as he is gradually challenged to see women as persons, he finds himself unable to exploit them. Again, though, people devalue and depersonalize others every day without resorting to murder. Other conditions must be present.

The self as "center of the universe," the God-like possession of omnipotence, and the absolute right to determine life and death that are inherent in that self, once these attributes are assumed, bring the possibility of murder ever closer. Yet, there are many people who are extraordinarily grandiose, including some who are convinced that they are God, who never decide to kill.

Earlier, discussing suffering, I highlighted the fact that it is the unwillingness to endure one's own suffering and the displacement of that pain onto others that is a precondition of evil. That unwillingness is a choice that seems, except in cases of organic brain damage, always available. As Scott Peck notes, "Evil people, refusing to acknowledge their own failures, naturally desire to project their evil onto others."[5] Others, courageous people, true saints perhaps, make the opposite choice: "Indeed, there is some reason to suspect that in certain cases psychosis is chosen as a preferable alternative to evil."[6]

Exactly! It is, in fact, very reasonable to state firmly that in any case of psychosis in which rage is involved — which is many, many cases — the break from reality was *always* chosen as a courageous defense against the evil of murder. Though this seems to romanticize psychotic people as heroic, there is some evidence of this heroism. Note, for example, how often people on the *verge* of psychosis seem to "just make it" to the hospital before completely decompensating, dropping their last defense, and raging murderously, mad — openly expressing murderous rage only when it is safe to do so, in the hospital where they will be restrained. The high numbers of rage events seen in the admitting office and in the first days of hospitalization (though not at home) do not seem coincidental. It is as if the person thinks, "I'm so full of rage I want to kill somebody! I'm either going to kill somebody or go insane because I can't stay facing reality and not kill. But I don't really want to kill anybody, so I'll just have to lose my mind instead." It may be that a psychosis is a final, brave, pitiful gift of love.

The murderer, though, is a coward. Most are not psychotic. Many, in fact, like the monster Bundy, who quite lucidly carried out his own legal defense, seem totally sane, and motivated solely

---

[5] Scott Peck, M.D., *People of the Lie, op. cit.*, p. 62.
[6] *Ibid.*, p. 264.

by evil, the freely chosen violation of love. Cold, rational murderers have not "lost their minds"; they have "lost their hearts to evil."

The heart of the matter in understanding homicide lies here, in the question of how the major, deciding portion of the entire deepest center of a human being can become, not merely emotionally disturbed, but freely given over to evil. What this essentially means was discussed in relation to the seven inherent feelings, thoughts, and/or psychospiritual convictions that are essential requisites for the act of murder. We need to review those seven components.

Evil is always presented in the guise of love, as a pseudo-love, a seductive lie, and as the seventh step to murder is described, the decision to kill is always on behalf of gaining or retaining a pseudo-love. The pseudo-love can be a million dollars, sex with a diseased prostitute, the retention of corrupt political power, status in the role of "boss" in a hobo camp, or preservation of a grandiose delusion. They are all the same; in comparison to the value of human life, all pseudo-loves are trifles.

The essence of murder is the choice of the trifling pseudo-love. But how is it possible for murderers to make that choice? Who can even *think* like that?

One who kills is "playing God" in the most real sense of the word. The murderer, by definition, is grandiose in the extreme, omnipotent. In legal terms, the evidence of the invariable presence of that omnipotent grandiosity is *prima facie*. And again, the evidence that disbelief in God, lost faith, is an invariable precondition of murder is also *prima facie*. One who authentically believes in God simply does not conceive of the possibility of replacing Him or of usurping His exclusive power in relation to life and death.

Against this backdrop of rage, lost faith, omnipotence, and pseudo-love, one can begin to understand how the murderer can think and act so inhumanly. Granted, it is not easy to see because all these murderous preconditions take place deep in the heart. It is there, hidden in the darkness of lost faith, that the monster,

Raging Evil, lies in wait, living only in a lie. The lie is that the pseudo-loves will suffice, or that they will somehow be transformed into authentic love and authentic life. And within that lie is contained another lie, that the pseudo-love *is* life, whereas, in fact, it is death — the only real death, lovelessness.

Here we must stop because the next line of inquiry must be: "But how can we understand evil?" The answer is quite simple: we cannot. Evil can be brilliant in its pose and eloquent in its delivery, but it is the antithesis of truth, totally pseudo, lie within lie, and therefore inevitably inane, incomprehensible, and utterly, utterly insane.

CHAPTER TWENTY-THREE

Depression: Love's Life Lost

When in disgrace with fortune and men's eyes
I all alone beweep my outcast state...
And look upon myself and curse my fate...

Shakespeare[1]

Love is consolation in desolation.

Miguel de Unamuno[2]

Simple truth, the simpler it is, always seems to be hidden midst more and more perplexing mazes of complexity. Given that love is accepted as the fundamental goal and drive of life, however, we now can move swiftly in cutting through that complexity to arrive at a better understanding of depression. I will begin with a conclusion, boldly stated.

Depression always begins with the loss of a love (or pseudo-love), and thus, initially, feels exactly like grief; unlike grief, though, which is a normal, necessary, and time-delimited emotion, a reaction, depression results when the love loss is compounded by internal actions, decisions and judgments which produce either hatred (bitterness, desires for revenge, unforgiveness), or guilt or false guilt (self-abnegation, self-hatred, self-punishment); when the judgmentalism-induced hatred or guilt (or both) are superim-

---

[1] William Shakespeare, "Sonnet 29," *Shakespeare. The Complete Works* (New York: Harcourt, Brace, 1958), p. 1600.

[2] Miguel de Unamuno, *Tragic Sense of Life* (New York: Dover, 1954), p. 132.

posed on and mixed with the love-loss, the effect is to keep that loss fixed in the heart so that it is experienced as an eternal and infernal trap, a dark, empty hole of unending grief — Hell.

That statement is shamelessly suspect in its simplicity. Should I blush? No, I believe we need just such boldness in the face of depression! We must turn the tables on the complexity of emotional disorders. By boldly stating the conclusion first, we can test whether the multitude of questions about depression can always be answered in terms of a very simple concept: *love-loss* compounded by judgmentalism imposed upon others and/ or self.

Varieties of Depression: The Common Elements

There are a dozen or so different ways that depression has to be diagnosed — the level of it, which ranges from the vegetative psychotic to the chronic neurotic, to the reactive type, to the normal everyday blues; whether it is an agitated depression, i.e., mixed with anxiety; whether it is cyclic, alternating with periods of euphoria, mania (bipolar); whether it is grief-related, i.e., realistic, and therefore very normal and necessary.

The symptom picture of depression can be very complex: sadness, heavy crying or the opposite (inability to cry because of flattened, frozen, or deadened affect), withdrawal, negative feelings about self, the future, the world, and life itself, hopelessness, inactivity, inability to "try" because "nothing will work out," self-abnegation, self-hatred, self-criticism, escape-avoidance, a sense of meaninglessness, *anomie*, feelings of worthlessness, emptiness, separateness, aloneness, sleep disturbance, loss of appetite, loss of sex drive, self-rejection, self-condemnation, deep internal pain, a sense of powerlessness, a sense of being overwhelmed, inability to enjoy anything, despair of achieving goals, rumination and imagery involving death, extreme sense of guilt, regret, self-punishment, feelings of abandonment, broken-hearted feelings, confusion, "inability" to think, feelings that thoughts are "stuck" in a meaningless cycle, and the most dangerous symptoms — thoughts, desires and planning for suicide.

No one person suffering depression has all these symptoms, thankfully, but complexity is present even in milder cases. Immediately, therefore, though we can assert that the bottom-line cause invariably will involve the simple dynamic of love-loss, this does not mean that treatment, reaching that bottom-line, is going to be a simple process. The perfect cure for depression is not "Cheer up!" nor is it "Just love!" Rather, as we try to understand ourselves or another person who is depressed, we can expect to find that the vast array of symptoms are all expressions of the central problem of depression: lessened ability to love or be loved. It is precisely that inability, that loss, that is so complexly expressed as depression.

The reason that grief and depression are so often compared is not only because of the similarity of symptoms — sadness, tears, feelings of abandonment, emptiness, loss of appetite and sex drive, etc. — but because they are identical in terms of their beginnings, with a loss that is near and dear. In grief involving the death of a loved one, the loss is obvious. When these same feelings are experienced following a divorce, or after rejection in a love affair or by a friend, it is often called "depression," but incorrectly so. The inevitable feeling following the departure from our lives of someone we love, the experience of loss, whether the one lost is dead or alive, is called grief — a totally normal and necessary part of life. When our stomachs are empty, they growl; when our hearts are empty, they grieve.

Grief, it might be noted, is totally centered on reality. My mother died; I wept. My father died; I wept. Lazarus died; Jesus wept. But normal grief does not cause us to keep on weeping, withdrawing, and being sad indefinitely. Normal grief fades with time; its duration is limited. How long is normal? Any study cited, I believe, may be misleading because grief is proportionate to the loss. Grief of a spouse for dead spouse, child for parent, friend for friend, etc. — every relationship is different, and the grief fades gradually; it does not just abruptly stop. Most "close" relationships require grieving at least several months. If the sharpest edge of hard grief has not begun to at least soften after a year or two, I'd wonder if grief alone is at work. However, a parent losing a child under tragic circumstances may grieve much longer, perhaps years. Even the parent-for-child grief should be time-limited, however. If the child died tragically, particularly under violent circumstances, the parent's grief may become mixed with anger, even rage. If that rage is not acknowledged and it is turned inward upon the self, then grief can become mixed with depression. All depression begins with grief, the normal, inescapable response to love loss, but then the grief becomes mixed with, and entrenched by, disordered emotions and internal acts — hatred, bitterness, real or false guilt, and unforgiveness.

Loss of Heart

Given the understanding that all a person truly is, is the totality of her or his loves (Principle Eight), depression and all of its accompanying symptoms become more understandable: depression is the response to real or perceived loss of love, the innermost reality of being, or heart, which occurs when that loss is interpreted as, or is actually, due to one's own violation of love, a violation that remains unforgiven. When the violation was caused by another person, that is, when that person injured or neglected the one who is depressed, it is still the depressed person's own love-violation — hatred, the desire for revenge, and unforgiveness toward the injuring party — that is the precipitating cause of the depression.

The consequence of love-loss coupled with an unforgiven love-violation is a myriad of emotional, physical, and spiritual symptoms — guilt, self-hatred, self-punishment, sadness, over-generalized negativity, withdrawal, hopelessness, etc. — all of which are expressions of the depressed person's relative depth of belief that love, and thus self and life itself, are permanently lost. Indeed, while unforgiveness remains in place, that is an accurate self-appraisal. As Love Principle Fourteen states unequivocally, unforgiveness blocks healing, stops it "dead" in its tracks. Until forgiveness is given, love remains effectively blocked, and thus the hurt/loss remains unhealed.

The love therapy explanation of depression centers on three major concepts: (1) loss (always interpreted as love-loss, i.e., self-loss); (2) violated love (with consequent guilt attributed to either self or others); and (3) unforgiveness (and consequent blockage of the healing love that can replace, "refill" the loss that the heart has sustained). This therapy focuses emphatically on forgiveness, for it is the first and absolutely indispensable step toward healing. We can show why this is so, and further explain the basic dynamics above, by contrasting depression with grief, anxiety, and rage reactions.

In grief, the loss is centered on reality. A loved one dies or leaves my life, and my heart, my very self, sustains a void. That person, one of the integral loves that made up my very being, is gone. A love is indeed "lost." But the pain of that loss, if it is a "clean" loss, i.e., not encumbered by mixed anger and resentment and the desire for revenge, fades with time. How does it fade? There are two ways.

First, in the case of a loved one dying, while recovering from "missing" the actual physical presence of the person, and remembering the departed in oh-so-many ways, we are actually remembering the ways the departed person loved us. Gradually, it dawns on us that *love never dies.* The person we loved is indeed dead and gone, but in the truest sense, in some spiritual way that defies explanation, the essence of that person, the love that he or she gave me, is still very much alive! Eventually, then, we discover that the painful void in our hearts is becoming less and less painful. Grief leaves. Why? Because love heals. How? We discover that the self-same love that we *thought* we lost when the person died, as we remember it, is filling the void right back up. In comparison to depression, which can hang on for decades, grief heals relatively quickly because, unblocked by anger and venom, love, which never dies, always restores itself. Love heals grief.

In anxiety, as shown earlier, there is fear of the loss of love, and indeed there may have been love missing that caused the heart to feel so unprotected. The focus of anxiety is on an outside threat to love. The focus of depression, however, is internal, and the loss of love is perceived to have already happened, and there is blame, anger, guilt, and unforgiveness attributed to the loss.

It is also helpful to compare depression with overt rage. Two people may experience exactly the same kind of injury to the heart — a severe insult, for example. One person becomes enraged, but never becomes depressed. The other becomes depressed and never demonstrates the slightest anger. The difference lies in the depressive interpreting the insulting injury as a loss of heart, so the anger becomes entrenched, self-directed, whereas the raging person, experiencing the same loss, "throws fits" and continues spitting anger for a while, but never becomes depressed. (A third person receiving the identical insulting injury may react with depression over long periods interrupted by sporadic outbursts of rage.)

It should be noted that neither the depression nor rage will begin to abate until forgiveness and/or self-forgiveness is achieved.

These examples demonstrate that it is certainly not injuries nor losses alone which cause depression. It is, rather, the *addition* to the loss of the factors of resentment, hatred, venom — the *moral judgment* of the person causing the injury (including self) — that is the first culprit. When that judgment is stubbornly held, it is called unforgiveness. We need to show how the major dynamics of depression — repressed unforgiving anger, repressed unforgiven guilt, negativity, meaninglessness, and lost hope — are all expressions of lost-love-plus-judgmentalism and unforgiveness.

Earlier, discussing the Loving Anger Principle, I lauded the biblical admonition, "Be angry, but sin not," as sound guidance that can help people deal with the pernicious kinds of anger that are components of so many emotional problems. That admonition is especially applicable in depression, so it bears reviewing.

There are two clauses in the sentence: First, "Be angry...,"
which is to say, "Of *course* you're going to get angry sometimes.
Of course, you'll be frustrated sometimes, so *be* angry. Naturally,
being human midst other fallible humans, you'll be hurt sometimes, so have at it, be angry." But secondly, "sin not," which is to
say, "Don't hurt anybody with your anger, including yourself. You
have an absolute right to be angry when you are treated unjustly
and hurt, but you have absolutely no right to hurt *anyone* no matter how badly they have hurt you. Nor do you have any right to
hurt yourself. So be angry... but then immediately begin trying
to forgive. Be angry; go on and get the anger out of your system;
get mad as hell! But then *let that anger go.*"

Unfortunately, the person who is depressed hears *neither*
clause of the "Be angry but sin not" admonition, at least not
consciously. Oh, the anger is there all right, in spades, but at the
beginning of therapy, if the person is asked point-blank if she or
he is angry, the answer is usually in the negative. This stuffed
anger, along with guilt and feelings of powerlessness, are the
active agents and proximate causes of the feelings of depression. The anger expresses itself in the form of self-hatred, self-
abnegation, self-condemnation. Note again that these all involve
moral judgments. Though the depressed person initially is totally
out of touch with the anger, we can hear it plainly. Like children
bickering and name-calling, the anger is heard in the typical *self
put-downs* of the depressed: "I'm no good"; "I feel worthless";
"I'm just stupid! — ugly — hopeless"; "I'm just a weakling — a
nerd — a sicko"; "I hate my guts!"; "I wish I'd die"; "I'm dead."
One depressed man whom I asked to describe himself may have
spoken for all depressed self-deprecators: "I'm snail slime." Talk
about put-downs! And that is precisely what the self-directed
anger accomplishes: the person puts the self down — feeling as
low, nasty, and worthless as snail slime.

The repressed anger works in complex and variable ways
with several other concomitants of depression — powerlessness,
guilt, fear, and a typically hypersensitive conscience. Understand-

ing what anger is, we can see how it is linked to the accompanying elements of depression. Alfred Adler, whose central concept of personality was the will to *power*, is quoted by Albert Ellis in the following discussion of anger:

> It is probably true, as Adler states... that anger is an affect which is the veritable epitome of the striving for power and domination. Not that the angry person *consciously* craves to be godlike and indomitable; but... we had better believe that virtually every time we become irate, we at least temporarily believe that someone else *should* not be acting in a certain manner or that the world *ought* not to be the way it indubitably is. But to demand or dictate that people or things *must* be the way we want them to be is to be grandiose: since only God, obviously, has that power; and these days, even he is having one devil of a time exercising it.[3, 4]

It must be noted first that both Ellis and Adler made a mistake; they are not describing "authentic" anger, for real anger is a good thing, a necessary expression of love in response to real injustice, without which we would all be forced to live as victims (per Love Principle Twelve). Given that big caveat, the distortion of anger that they describe is very accurate. With that understanding, note immediately the curious and suspect apparent contradictions between what anger and depression express: anger of the type described by Adler is a craving "to be godlike and indomitable"; yet, the depressed feel not godlike but wormlike, and far from feeling indomitable, they feel the opposite — weak, powerless, hopelessly dominated by life. Normal anger speaks of *others'* injustice, of what *someone else* should or must do; the depressed

---

[3]   Albert Ellis, Ph.D., *Humanistic Psychotherapy* (New York: McGraw-Hill, 1974), p. 116.

[4]   Alfred Adler, *Understanding Human Nature* (New York: Garden City Publishing, 1927).

are only full of recriminations about what "I" should or ought to have done. Not only is this typical denial and contradiction of anger that the depressed person presents suspect, it is simply untrue. Beneath the sad surface, depressed people *typically* are mad as hell, sometimes raging with anger — but that anger and hatred of others has been effectively flip-flopped, directed back at the self.

Note also in the Ellis quote on anger that he underlines the words "should," "ought," and "must." Thus, we can conclude: *depressed anger is a moral indictment that invariably follows a moral judgment of what someone else, or I, should or ought to have done.*

In the light of depressed anger as a moral statement of right and wrong, it logically follows that guilt and anger are inseparable bedfellows. Moral judgment of others is a right that human beings simply do not possess; that is a right that belongs only to God. So when Ellis describes anger as a "godlike" craving, he is incorrect in regards normal anger, but absolutely correct if he is speaking only of the kind of judgmental anger that accompanies depression. The judgmentally angry person in so many words is saying, "I'm hurt and by God you're guilty as hell because you are no damn good! I'm God, and I can read the depths of your secret heart, so I know your intentions were pure evil; I, the eternal Judge, have spoken."

That pitiful judge is then stuck with the finality of his/her own hateful condemnation. Judgmental anger imputes motives and condemns the offending person; normal anger, in contrast, may vociferously object to the hurtful action, but spares the personhood of the sinner. This inseparable anger-guilt connection automatically tells us when we have been judgmental, used anger unfairly. Immediately after expressing anger unfairly, we feel guilty. How often do we find ourselves feeling ashamed and saying "I'm sorry" immediately following a tirade?

Curiously, even though the depressed person beats up on himself as one guilty enough to deserve punishment, and flagellates the self with such fury that one might suspect there is a wee bit of anger present, there is very typically no conscious

anger at all, and the guilt felt is vague, amorphous. In fact, all
feelings are prohibited except one, feeling "dead."

Love's Healing of Depression

In the early process of love therapy with depressed people,
many of the dynamics and feelings described above are addressed
very forthrightly. The paragraphs below are compressed versions
of the interpretations I give to depressed people. These interpretations are presented, in a word, lovingly, but I should immediately
note that this love is in no way syrupy or weak. On the contrary,
especially with the depressed, it is important that the compassionate element of love not be misinterpreted as pity and thus
reinforce the destructive self-pity that is already present.

Reading between the lines, so to speak, most of the dynamics
and feelings described above can be seen reflected in the following interpretations, which are usually given early in the treatment
process for depression:

Therapist: Depression is always connected with anger, guilt and
fear in some combination. Let me show you how it works.
Let's suppose some stranger walks in the door and, for no
reason, walks over and punches you in the nose. What's
your immediate reaction?
[Most people recognize that they would be angry. Men often
can say, "I'd punch 'em back." Some women will say "I'd
cry," but given some encouragement to "forget the lady-like
business," they, too, will admit anger and the immediate gut
reaction: punch back. Then I continue.]
Therapist: When we get hurt, with a bloody nose, or deeper, in
our hearts, one way of expressing that hurt is anger, punching back. But let me show you what happens in depression.
[Demonstrating] See my fist? My fist is the anger, and I
start to swing with it, putting energy behind it. Halfway
through the punch, something stops my fist: it's either guilt

or fear. Heart level, I say to myself, "Oh, I *shouldn't* feel that; I *shouldn't* hurt anybody, and guilt stops my fist in mid-air." Or else I say to myself, "Oh I'd better not punch back, or I'll be hurt worse," and then fear stops the punch. But look what happens then! That fist can't just stay hanging in mid-air. The fist is our feelings, and they're dynamic, alive! Feelings don't stop just because we are too afraid or too guilty to express them. Those feelings have just *got* to go somewhere. So look what happens: watch my fist. The fist doesn't just stop in mid-air and relax. In depression, (demonstrating) it's like the fist makes a circle and comes back and starts banging me on the top of the head. The anger boomerangs, comes back and drives me right down into the ground where everything looks black and hopeless. Do you see? Anger turned inside-out, anger that is repressed and turned back on myself might cause depression.

But sometimes, it's not anger. Sometimes it's guilt that is the culprit — either real guilt stemming from some big fat sin, or false guilt, the result of somebody laying a guilt-trip on me, putting me down and convincing me I deserved it. If we feel guilt, if we can't obtain forgiveness from someone and/or can't forgive ourselves, we sometimes think we need self-punishment, so we start that fist banging on our own heads again, driving us down. And then we feel down, down, down — depressed.

People in depression, I believe, are typically the most hyper-moral people on earth. They've got rights-and-wrongs coming out their ears. Often, when they say they feel "bad," they mean morally bad. When they say they feel "low," it's morally. "Down" means "fallen," morally low. And like fallen angels, they feel like they're "down," in Hell. All of their feelings, then, are viewed in moral terms, and that mistaken notion has to be aggressively changed. If my basic interpretation of feelings fails to start feelings pouring, I offer a second interpretation; it starts with a question.

Therapist: Do you know the one word in the English language
that irks me the most? It's "should." People say "I should
feel" this, "I should feel" that, and it drives me nuts. There's
no such thing as "should-feel"; we just feel! But for some
people, it's like life is one great big Should. When it comes to
feelings, I say "Damn Should." You know, there once was a
woman, a psychoanalyst, who spoke of Should as a disease
that people get. Let me describe the disease and ask if you
think you have it.
The disease is called the "Tyranny of Should." For the people
who have it, life rarely includes "I want..." or "I will..." or
"I'd like to..." *Everything* they think, do and feel is in terms
of "I should... I ought to... I must... or I've got to... " Duty,
responsibility, and the Shoulds totally dominate and saturate
their lives. "Should" is a tyrant with a big club always ready
to bop you on the noggin for the slightest 'bad' thought or
feeling. Should is a vicious king who keeps people in prison,
or even kills them for the least angry or lusty or selfish
thought. And if you ever commit a real sin, oh, God help
you; the tyrannical Should will triple-murder you for that.
Now, question, have you got the Should disease?

A person who admits to having the Tyranny of Should[5] automatically can be assumed to be carrying a load of guilt a mile
high, including guilt over being angry. Typically, ninety percent
of it is false guilt, i.e., feelings of guilt despite being innocent,
sinless. Sometimes, this stacked-up guilt, alone, accounts for the
depression, and the depression sometimes lifts virtually overnight
when the person gains sudden insight, kicks the tyrant Should
in the tail and exclaims, "My God! It *is* false guilt; I'm not guilty
after all." Only when a person can "damn the shoulds" can they
understand that we just feel what we feel, and then give them-

---

[5] Karen Horney, *Neurosis and Human Growth: The Struggle Toward Self-Realization*
(New York: Norton, 1950).

selves permission to recognize their anger and guilt. For some, only then can changing depression begin.

Anger is surfaced through expression; guilt is surfaced by confession. Once they are surfaced, the real question is, what do we do with them? *Doing* something with the anger and guilt of depression is where love is the *only* way, and this is where love therapy's understanding of depression is distinctive.

I have people express anger by beating on a chair in my office, or beating up pillows at home. I usually say, "Get the anger out any way you can, but safely. Go driving alone and scream your head off. Go howl at the moon! But that self-directed anger of yours is like a rotten tooth; it's got to come out. Once it's out, we'll figure out what to do with it." The love therapy way of surfacing anger is not much different than most therapies.

The love therapy way of surfacing guilt may be different from other therapies. It is at once aggressive, lovingly confrontational, and defense-disarming. The actual interpretation I give probably describes it better than an analysis would:

Therapist: When we talked about "shoulds" and guilt, and depression and guilt, you nodded your head like you understood. So let's talk about guilt. Let me tell you something I see with many people I see. The name of the game in counseling is trust, right? So I say, "Trust me." I don't use the word "trust" cheaply; it's tough for all of us sometime. So I say, "Okay, test me; see if I can be trusted." Test me, test me, test me to see if you can tell me something awful that will shock me. Do you know the last time I was shocked? Maybe a century ago. Guilt? Friend, I've heard them all! Now let me tell you what I see: people come in here one time, ten times, ten months, and finally, *finally* they trust me; they know I'll love them regardless of what brand of skunk they've been. Then they finally tell me *that one thing* in their life, that one really bad 'something' they did, or that was done to them, that they could never, ever tell *anybody*. It's not just guilt;

it's worse, more like *shame*. It's so, so bad that it just burns inside, and we spend half our lives trying to hide it even from ourselves. It's shame, just shame. Now do you know what would help? Save us a lot of time? While I was talking, describing that shame, it would really help if you'd just tell me. Trust me. Just dump the thing you were thinking about, that big secret shame of yours. Just put it right here on the floor. Right now. Dump.

And bingo! Out it comes, the big secret of their lives, the big secret that is the core of their depression. Sometimes, though, the person hesitates, silent; I get aggressive. "That! That guilt you're thinking about right this second! Dump it!" Some people will hold back until the next session or much later, but eventually, if the shame is there, they will come back to take advantage of my aggressively loving offer to serve as their dump. I have come to believe that there are a huge number of people, maybe a majority, who are carrying around one or two secret old sins and burning shames that are so depressing and so desperately in need of confession.

Once the guilt and anger are out, expressed, what we do with them is crucial. This must be clear: anger and guilt and depression cannot be healed; only wounds can be healed. Anger, guilt, and depression are *expressions* of woundedness, but they are not the wounds. As shown earlier, there is only one place where we can be really hurt, wounded — where we love, in our hearts.

This may be a surprising statement, but anger and guilt are such inseparable bedfellows that they might well be considered the same emotion, like two sides of the same coin. The common coin is hurt, a wound in the heart, a way that love has been violated, betrayed, damaged. In depression, as in many disorders, anger often is discovered to be guilt flipped inside-out. So, too, when it is unmasked, anger often is revealed as a masquerade for guilt.

Anger, translated into words, always says, "You've hurt me, whom I love," or "You've hurt someone I love, which is the same as hurting me." Guilt, translated, says, "I've hurt you, not loved you, and in doing so, I've hurt my own love."

We can also arrive at two other translations of the anger-guilt connection: "You've hurt you, whom I love, and that makes me angry," and "I've hurt me, not loved me, and that makes me both angry and guilty." Any of these translations can begin the process leading to depression.

Intellectually, abstractly, we are accustomed to thinking of guilt and anger as totally separate feelings. Existentially, though, as we live and breathe them, they are frequent companions which are, at heart level, inseparable. Both emotions are often experienced any time love is hurt.

Once the emotions are surfaced, we can see why anger and guilt can be very helpful emotions: all we have to do is track them back to where they came from, hurt love, and they tell us precisely where and what kind of healing our damaged hearts need.

Principle Thirteen stated that guilt flows as a natural consequence of violated love. The guilt that feeds depression can be true or false, self-induced by a real sin, my own love-violation, or falsely and unjustly induced by someone else.

Depression Induced by False Guilt

There are, in my experience, three types of family backgrounds of depressed people in which false guilt seems to be absolutely invariable.

First, and in greatest numbers, are children who grow up in alcoholic homes; they are invariably laden with mountains of false guilt. The alcoholic maintains his or her disorder by two major defense mechanisms: denial, and displacement of responsibility onto others. Children in these homes are denied childhood. They are made into "little adults," responsible for all duties, all unhappiness, and all the sins of the alcoholic, including the drinking itself ("You kids *drive* me to drink!"). People growing up in the midst of the blame-game played by the alcoholic typically feel guilty just for *being*. Their depression is often mixed with anxiety stemming from the very real fear that they lived with, but their false guilt makes them responsible even for causing their own fear.

The second large group of people suffering depression induced by false guilt are those suffering the victimization syndrome. Overt victims of rape, physical and sexual abuse, or of emotional abuse, whether child or adult, have had false guilt crammed into their hearts as an integral concomitant of the abuse. But there are insidious forms of victimization-caused depression that are not so readily diagnosed. These are the cases in which the person was a victim of emotional neglect and deprivation. A social history which reveals parents who were socially hyperactive and ultra-successful in business can sometimes be a clue that depression stemmed from emotional deprivation, love deficits. These are literally the "poor little rich kids" who had everything money could buy, but were simply not loved enough. Similar covert victimization is seen in children caught in bitter divorces. As pawns in the parental war, they are indeed victims — precisely what their depressions silently scream.

The third group of people depressed due to false guilt are similar to children caught in divorce wars. These are adults who, at an early age, lost a parent in death, and then become "victimized by omission" — the omission being that no one took the time or had the sense to explain to the child why a parent died. The death is then interpreted by the child as punishment for "being bad," or even that the child did something wrong that actually caused the parent to die.

While the three categories of victimization/false guilt above are the backdrops in a great many depressions, false guilt comes in many forms.

A nine-year-old girl I saw in a child guidance clinic was brought in by her alarmed and angry parents after the little girl climbed out an attic window onto the roof of the house, naked as a jaybird, and began dancing, singing and yelling to all the neighbors. (Note: I did not laugh as I was told about the little naked dancer — not until the father described running all over the roof trying to catch her.)

As the picture emerged in counseling, this little girl was the most emotionally healthy member of the family. She was also the scapegoat; all four other members of the family agreed that *everything* was her fault. These four members had difficulty describing and coming to grips with their own problems. But Little Miss Naked had no problem at all in explaining exactly why she had put on what she called her "show": "They always made me feel bad. They said everything I did was wrong! All of 'em! But I could never figure out what I was doing that was so bad. Did you ever feel bad and not know why? So — I just decided that if I had to feel bad, I'd do something real to feel bad about."

This little girl exemplified the perfectly appropriate way to respond to false guilt — with *anger* openly expressed. Her openness was a naked way of saying, "You call me guilty?! Well, I'll show you!" Her nakedness was an angry proclamation of perfect innocence, like Adam and Eve in the garden before they sinned and then discovered that they were naked.

Interestingly, this little girl chose exactly the right method to ensure that her disturbed family got help. Somehow she knew that her mother was extremely puritanical and guilt-ridden, and that "public guilt" was terrible. As the family fought, screaming at each other, the mother was forever admonishing, "What will the neighbors think!?" On the roof, the girl sang to the world, "This house is crazy!" Fittingly, when I assured the girl that she was guilty of very few of the accusations her family laid on her, she said, "I think I knew that. I just had to show 'em."

Traumatic Guilt Causing Depression

There is, though, guilt that is very real, and huge. Terrible sin, the gross violation of the sacred love that resides within us, has many psychological repercussions, but it is fundamentally a spiritual problem. More directly, a-spiritual therapy, psychology alone, is absolutely useless in cases of self-induced, traumatic guilt. Not only is the "therapy" ineffective, it is harmful because it prevents the person from finding effective spiritual help.

Human beings are capable of falling to almost unbelievable depths of degradation. We are capable of utterly defiling, mutilating, and deranging our own souls. Later, when authentic remorse comes, for one who is literally broken by sorrow to hear from a therapist, "Just let the guilt go," is sometimes a crass insult to the depths of the human spirit. It is also a clear-cut signal that the therapist has only the shallowest understanding of what guilt really is. Monstrous, inhuman acts produce monsters — guilt that cannibalizes human hearts. Consider these five cases:

Case One — A depressed woman contemplates suicide. She finally tells you that while addicted to crack cocaine, she sold her one-year-old baby girl for sex use — one dollar per man.

Case Two — He was homosexually raped at age eleven by three eighteen-year-olds. The rapists bragged, telling everyone in the slum where he lived that he was "queer." Other boys followed the leaders and often coerced him into sexual service during the following year. By age twelve, when he entered the school lunchroom, everyone stood up and cheered him as the "President of the Queers' Club." Twenty-five years later, he was paranoid, depressed and suicidal. He was not homosexual at all, but fear of being called "queer" and being publicly humiliated had caused him to hide his face in shame all his life. When asked what the guilt and shame had done to him, he said, "It's like I've got no skin."

Case Three — A forty-year-old woman who had been depressed for nearly twenty years, hospitalized on four occasions, in counseling for years with several therapists, finally shared her secret. As a young woman, she had gone to Hollywood with dreams of becoming a star. Instead, she was pulled into pornography. After forsaking "stardom," she returned home with one indelibly engraved memory: she had performed sexually with a pig.

Case Four — His depression had been diagnosed as merely

"reactive" to his wife's death by suicide. After five years of counseling with three different therapists, he was hospitalized and given electroshock. Still he told no one. When I met him, he said the depression was even worse. His secret: the day before she committed suicide, his wife had caught him in bed with another woman, her sister.

Case Five — A thirty-year-old woman, recently married, was severely depressed, suffering panic attacks, and contemplating divorce even though she loved her husband dearly. She was too guilty to face him, much less have a sex life. She hated sex, and had never had orgasms, not with her husband nor anyone else. She finally shared the source of her guilt: before marriage, she had been sexually promiscuous. How promiscuous? Very. How "very"? Her best estimate was that she had had sex with three thousand men. (Much later, we would discover that this woman had been an incest victim, and that all the sex had been "acting out," i.e., irrational sexual "drivenness" as opposed to freely chosen acts.) She described the memories of three thousand men as "forever pounding into me, pounding into my brain like nails."

Can we say to these people "Simply let go of the guilt," or "Just forgive yourself"? In the face of such guilt, is there a therapist who has the audacity to say, "I forgive you"? Who can forgive guilt at such depths? Who but God? When our sin is like scarlet, who can say, "Your sin is forgiven. You are clean again"? No one. Facing gargantuan, traumatic guilt, the normal human response is to cringe, and to cry out like T.S. Eliot's Chorus (quoted in Chapter Thirteen). If we could be the Chorus for the sad guilty people in the cases above, perhaps we would cry:

> We are defiled!
> The baby's blood dries purple around every orifice of its little body. Who will wash the blood that stains our souls?
> Rape and public humiliation have skinned his soul. Scour the skin! Scrub the flesh! Hide the soul!

Animal semen dries on a woman's legs. Who will wash us, wash us, wash us! Wash the bone! Scour the soul!

A wife is lowered into the grave, and the spirit of the husband who believes he murdered her goes right into the grave with her. The universe wails! Who will resurrect us from living death?

Thousands of memories of men pounding into her thighs will not stop pounding in her brain. Burn the brain! Slay the mind!

In the face of heinous, humanity-staining sin, our guilt consumes us! Shame sears our souls, wrenches our guts, scalds our hearts, strips our skins, shatters our beings! Oh, hide us! Hide us! Ban the light! Bolt the doors! Draw the shades! Darkness. Darkness! More darkness! In the black night of the soul, guilt cannot expose our corruption. In the living death of mortal terror, we wait, hiding from eternal damnation, not truly alive but at least still mortal.

When we begin to fathom the darkness that is sought as a shield against exposure of horrific guilt, are the hopelessness, the withdrawal and the black thoughts of depression really so surprising? When we see that guilt can produce not just self-punishment but a form of modified self-execution, living-death, are not the slowed bodily functions and "dead" emotions seen in depression more understandable?

In depressions brought on by authentic guilt that is huge (as opposed to false guilt), the obvious first task of the therapist is to obtain the confession, exposing the very guilt that the patient's entire life is devoted to hiding. Sadly, that crucial step is all too often not accomplished. Too often, the guilt symptom is fed, masked beneath antidepressants, tranquilizers, or shock treatment. I wish I were wrong on this point, but in a clinical sample of over forty years, I have encountered too many depressed people, each of whom had been in and out of hospitals and in counseling with several therapists, who had never "opened up" and confessed the huge guilt for which their depressions were precisely designed to hide.

The tougher question is, though, given horrendous guilt such as it is described above, how is it resolved? My answer may not be popular with those who deny spiritual reality, but this is a hard fact that needs to be faced squarely: when authentic guilt reaches the destructive and suicidal levels seen in deep depression, it may well be beyond human capacity to absolve. Professionals can help "resolve" guilt, but when a person is facing unspeakable sin, resolution is impossible without absolution, and that is the province of God alone. When the sin is so great that it befouls humanity, when it is "inhuman," it may well be a sin that the greatest human understanding, human compassion, human forgiveness, and human love are simply not enough to heal. It is precisely this that deeply depressed people know better than anyone else. They hide their dark secrets from all humanity for years, and try their best to hide their secrets even from themselves. Who can forgive that which seems to be humanly unforgivable — who but God?

Without Love, All Is Negative, and That Is Depressing

Depression, like all emotional disorders, to the degree that they exist, can be described as the relative inability to love or to receive love. The effect of this disability in depression can be seen most clearly when we examine what we say and feel when we experience depression's opposites — happiness, joy, elation, optimism, confidence, self-esteem, lust for life. What do we say after a sweet success? I loved it! What do we say after a superb meal? I loved it! What do we feel when we have self-esteem? I love me! When we are most in touch with other people (not withdrawn)? I love you! And so it goes. The drive and goal of all life and all behavior is love, so when love is going well, we acknowledge it. We love it!

Depression is the opposite. Rather than expressing and feeling love, we experience the opposite: negativity, the absence of love in the present and the expected absence of love in the future.

Love is the Yes of life. Love is the I Want, I Can, and the I Will of life. Love is the Faith and the Hope of the present, and Love is the future.

But in depression, love has been lost someplace in the past, hidden and blocked by bitterness and hurt. As a result, life becomes one big NO.

This tendency of depressed people to see themselves and life itself as ubiquitously negative has long been recognized. Their tendency is to *generalize* and exaggerate the negativity. If I'm depressed, and the morning newspaper delivery is late, the whole day is bad. I don't just make a mistake; nothing I do is right, nothing I've ever done is right, and nothing I ever will do will be right. If the boss corrects me, I'm not just corrected, I'm despised, hated. If I'm complimented, the compliment is negated. If I'm loved, that too is negated.

This negativity is seated deep in the heart, but it is expressed in thought, word, and deed. At the thought level, Beck thoroughly captures the pervasiveness of depressed negativity:

> Pessimism sweeps like a tidal wave into the thought content of depressed patients...
>
> Depressed patients have a special penchant for expecting future adversities and experiencing them as though they were happening in the present or had already occurred.
>
> The predictions of depressed patients tend to be overgeneralized and extreme.... If a patient feels miserable now, it means he will always feel miserable. The absolute, global pessimism is expressed in such statements as "things won't ever work out for me"; "life is meaningless"...
>
> Pessimism... permeates every wish and every task

> ... he is hypersensitive to stimuli suggesting loss and
> is blind to stimuli representing gain... he is facile in
> recalling unpleasant experiences, but may "draw a
> blank" when questioned about positive experiences.[6]

Beck is very accurate in his descriptions of the thought distortions that accompany disorders, but cognitive therapy does not explain how these disordered thoughts originate. The evidence of this is seen in my earlier descriptions of the heart-level effects of authentic and ravaging guilt. One does not merely think oneself into such abysmal depths of despair, nor does one merely think one's way out. Rather, the negative thoughts must be seen as *symptoms* of what the negative heart is silently saying, feeling and suffering. Viktor Frankl sums up the important but limited role of thought in the development of emotional disorders very concisely, "All this is not to deny that ideas are still conditioned psychologically, biologically, and sociologically. 'Conditioned' but not 'caused'."[7] My summary is a bit more concise: thoughts do not suffer; hearts suffer.

Lovelessness Is Meaninglessness, and That Is Depressing

In severe depression, it is common to hear people say, "I get confused; I just don't know what life means anymore." "Everything looks black. I don't see any sense in anything." "Nothing, I see nothingness. I am nobody, nothing. Life is nothing." "I just see emptiness everywhere. I'm empty. Life is empty. Sometimes I think I don't even exist."

The source of the meaninglessness that is so frequently seen in depression lies in the loss and/or blockage of love, which is effectively the same as loss of self, and thus the loss of any interior

---

[6] Aaron Beck, M.D., *Cognitive Therapy and Emotional Disorders* (New York: New American Library, 1976), pp. 116-119.

[7] Viktor E. Frankl, M.D., *The Doctor of the Soul. From Psychotherapy to Logotherapy* (New York: Vintage Random House, 1986), p. 16.

reality into which meaning could be grounded. There are many ways that this love break-down can be expressed. As shown in the chapter on psychoses, utter lovelessness leads to an utter loss of contact with reality. A "nervous break-down" is a relatively total "love break-down." Life is love; with love lost, sealed away, not only is the meaning of life lost, life itself is lost. If it is true, as the Basic Love Principle says, that love is the universal drive and goal of life, it follows logically that when love is felt to be lost, then life must necessarily become goal-less, meaningless, empty, depressing. If "meaning" is defined in terms of what has significance or import, then it follows that when love cannot be found, nothing else can be significant enough to be called meaningful.

In depression, the perception of lost love means lost meaning, which in turn means, "So why try to work for something meaningless," which then "logically" produces apathy.

Viktor Frankl's logotherapy is centered in meaning, "*logos.*" Indeed, in the treatment of depression and all other disorders, love therapy integrates logotherapy repeatedly. Frankl was one of the first, and he is still one of the few therapists who boldly acknowledges the essentiality of the spiritual in treatment. He put it plainly:

> What is still missing is a form of psychotherapy which gets underneath affect-dynamics, which sees beneath the psychic malaise of the neurotic his spiritual struggles. We are concerned with *psychotherapy in spiritual terms.*
>
> It helps us little to know that the patient's despair has developed psychologically in this or that fashion. No matter that we may be able to disclose the inferiority feelings which were the psychic origins of his spiritual distress; no matter that we may "trace" the patient's pessimistic view of life back to certain complexes, and even convince him that his pessimism springs from these and these alone — in reality we are only talking around the patient's problem.

A doctor should not prescribe a tranquilizer cure for
the despair of a man who is grappling with spiritual
problems. Rather, with the tools of 'psychotherapy
in spiritual terms' he will be able to give the patient
spiritual support, to provide him with some spiritual
anchorage.[8]

While moderate depression might be found to be primarily
psychological in origin and respond to treatment at that level,
deeper depressions *invariably* have a spiritual component and
typically that spiritual dynamic is by far the more important.
When the depressed person says that she or he has lost the meaning of life, they are usually talking about the spiritual meanings
that flow from love and the faith and hope that only love can
engender.

Lost Love, Then Lost Faith and Hope, Then Depression

Faith is built upon reason. Spiritual realities and matters of
faith are never *proved* in the scientific sense. Rather, if we believe
something spiritual, it is because we have accepted that it is
reasonable to believe. We build truth upon truth upon truth, but
eventually faith requires a leap. Thus, in presenting love therapy,
I have moved gradually from psychological to spiritual, starting
with love as a self-evident reality which is known experientially,
and moving gradually toward the Love who is God. Viktor Frankl,
though, makes a direct leap, so I turn to him to present the case
for expanding psychotherapy to include spiritual reality:

It is self-evident that belief in a super-meaning —
whether as a metaphysical concept or in the religious
sense of Providence — is of the foremost psychothera-

---

[8] *Ibid.*, pp. 11, 13, 14.

peutic and psychohygienic importance. As a genuine
faith springing from inner strength, such a belief adds
immeasurably to human vitality. To such a faith there
is, ultimately, nothing that is meaningless.[9]

Yes, Viktor, forsooth! Verily!

But just as it is true that perfect faith could never be stumped
for meaning, and could "move mountains" if necessary to discover meaning, when love-loss turns to depression, then faith and
thus meaning at all levels — in self, humanity and God — are
also lost. That this is true is entirely evident in the depressive
mood, negativity and *de facto* disbelief in just about everything.
Contradictorily, at the exterior level of consciousness, many depressed people still voice a belief in God; it's just themselves and
the world they don't believe in, they say. Combining love therapy
and a cognitive therapy approach to finding "hidden thoughts,"
we can go much deeper than consciousness to discover what the
person is secretly saying in their hearts — as in the following
interaction:

Therapist: So you were always pretty religious. Believe in God?
Client: Sure… that's probably the only thing I do believe.
Therapist: So do you believe God loves you?
Client: Sure; God loves everybody.
Therapist: Yes — but does God love *you*, you personally?
Client: Me?… I'm not sure.
Therapist: Wouldn't it be good to find out for sure? Can you be
        quiet for a minute and look deep down inside you? Look
        into your heart and tell me, do you believe in God?
Client: No. No! [Crying]
Therapist: Can you tell me what are the tears saying?
Client: That I *want* to believe in God.… I don't want to not believe.
        I just can't!

---

[9] *Ibid.*, p. 33.

Therapist: What do you think God thinks about the fact that you can't believe in Him? [Note that this question implicitly assumes belief, affirming the positive position that the person stated in the beginning.]

Client: I think He hates me.

Therapist: I thought you said you didn't believe in God.

Client: I do and I don't.

Therapist: How can you do both — believe and not believe?

Client: Oh, damn!... My head says I believe, but my heart says I don't.... or maybe it's the other way around.

Therapist: Good! That's very honest. Now all we have to figure out is what you honest-to-God believe — get your head and your heart on the same wavelength, talking to each other.

What is demonstrated above is a classic *psychospiritual* conflict of the kind almost invariably found in severe depressions. With strongly avowed believers, the psychological-spiritual conflict sometimes is all the more profound. It is with professed atheists and agnostics that the conflict becomes of paramount importance in lifting the depression. The process is usually the opposite of that described in the dialogue above. The atheist starts with a well-reasoned disbelief in God and then may discover to his amazement that, at the heart level, belief in God is equally profound. Resolving the conflict with an atheist requires the utmost respect. As a love therapist, I make no bones about my personal belief in God as a fundamental reality, but love absolutely demands that if a depressed atheist resolves a conflicting heart and consciousness by concluding that there is no God, that conclusion must be respected. Faith, after all, is a gift, and to even think of coercing someone into accepting a gift would be unloving.

"There are in the end three things that last: faith, hope, and love, and the greatest of these is love."[10] Make no mistake, that is a psychological statement. Granted, it is also a spiritual state-

---

[10] 1 Corinthians 13:13.

ment, but human beings do not live as purely spiritual beings. As a matter of fact, we cannot thoroughly grasp what the word "spiritual" even means. When Paul made the statement, he was speaking psychospiritually.

Why is love greater than faith or hope? Because it is not just more essential to life, it is the very substance of life. Properly considered, it is life. Without love, there can be no faith, there can be no hope, there can be no life — and this explains precisely what is happening in depression. Love is lost and with it, faith and hope. Then suicide.

Total Lovelessness, Lost Hope and Suicide

Is there anyone who can doubt that deliberate suicide is a spiritual decision? Even the atheist, still denying God, before pulling the trigger or swallowing the pills, facing imminent death, must ask a final question and make a decision: will I face God or nothingness after death? That decision is not just a product of the person's psychology; it is a spiritual bet.

Hope is the faith that love never dies and that love never fails, and that the future, therefore, will inevitably bring love. Hope's object is always love. Contrariwise, without love to hope for, there is only hopelessness. Despair, spiritual hopelessness, reaches the absolute level of suicide only when love is perceived as totally lost. We can view this as absolute truth: love causes hope; hope does not cause love. It is only the reaction to love's loss that breeds hopelessness. Love is life. Without love, life is no more. It is this intolerable state, living death, absolute loveless-ness, which immediately precedes suicide. In all human respects, psychologically and spiritually, most suicides are "dead" before they kill themselves.

Accidental suicides, viz., "gestures" gone awry, and so-called "rational" suicides based on the delusional and tacky logic promoted by the Hemlock Society are obvious exceptions to the classic picture of loveless-hopelessness described above. Indeed, there are other suicidal scenarios, but to promote an idea that "motives behind suicide are as varied as the number of people who solve their problems in this way"[11] is a meaningless generalization, an intellectual cop-out which — irony of ironies — would cause us to despair of ever understanding suicide. People are individuals, yes, but there are only so many motives for killing a flea and just so many for self-murder. There are, in fact, only two categories of suicide properly considered: the classic category of loveless-hopelessness, described above, and a category I shall call "sophistic-intellectual."

The gesture-gone-awry accidental death should not be considered suicide *per se*; the intent of self-murder was not present. Just as we do not call accidental death by shooting a homicide, but rather, "involuntary manslaughter," the accidental self-caused death is not suicide. Similarly, the drunken teenager who kills himself playing Russian roulette, and the accidental hangings that occur during perverted sex-play, lack the suicidal intent. However, like the Hemlock Society member's self-murder based on sophistic, spurious reasoning, there is a category of suicides that stems, not from emotional disorders, but from tragically illogical reasoning, plain bad ideas.

The sophistic-intellectual suicides are those stemming from any of the several fallacious conclusions which justify and promote self-murder. They are of two types. In one, erroneous conclusions are often enmeshed in a tangle of long-winded philosophic meanderings. In the other, a single hyped-up idea, wrapped in pseudo-idealistic hoopla, leads people who are otherwise sane to buy into a glamorized but deadly idea that suicide can be noble.

M.D. Faber, in a study of the very different ideas of suicide that were held in Shakespeare's time, provides a good overview of the sophistic-intellectually motivated forms of self murder:

---

[11] Louis Dublin and Bessie Bunzel, *To Be Or Not To Be* (New York, 1933), p. 4.

...the religiously or politically motivated suicide might be labeled what Durkheim called 'altruistic suicide.' The fact is that altruistic self-murder was universally admired in Shakespeare's England. Whether one destroyed himself for the sake of his friend, his master, his spouse, his nation, or his faith, he was sure to be extolled. [Faber also discusses the "suicide of chastity," as in *The Rape of Lucrece,* the honor suicide, and (God forbid!) the so-called love-suicide.][12]

Behind each of these irrational motives for suicide were well-worn and illogical philosophies, but the people who actually did themselves in were often just duped, ignorant victims who were sold a loudly bandied slogan: "Death before dishonor," "Death for the Emperor," or "Death for 'freedom.'" Today, young Iraqis are persuaded by their fanatic politico-religious leaders to drive suicidal car-bombs. Praise and eternal glory are promised to the self-killed "martyrs" of the "holy war." In World War II, young Japanese Kamikaze pilots dove to their deaths, crashing their planes into ships for the sake of Emperor and ancestors.

But if there is a tragedy of tragedies relative to suicide, it is the "suicide for love." We do not know the exact rationale behind the suicide pacts of teenagers who, thwarted by parents or for some other reason, decide to "die for love." We can only surmise that their notion of love was twisted, not unlike the heroine of John Webster's *The Devil's Law Case* (ca. 1617):

Standing over the bodies of two young gentlemen who have just displayed their eagerness to bleed for her love, Jolenta... remarks: 'Well, these are perfect lovers.' And when she is asked why they are perfect lovers, she

---

[12] M.D. Faber, "Shakespeare's Suicides: Some Historic, Dramatic and Psychological Reflections," in Edwin S. Schneidman, Ed., *Essays in Self Destruction* (New York: Science House, Inc., 1967), pp. 33, 34.

replies [that] '...none love perfectly indeed,/ But those that hang or drown themselves for love.'[13]

Jolenta lived in Elizabethan times, so our tendency may be to look back smugly and say that her oh-so-obviously-mistaken idea of love was "tragic but stupid," and in this modern age, we know better. But do we? Do we?! If we do, then how do we explain the large number of teenage suicides each year in this country, many, many of which were surely caused by the young people simply never being taught what authentic love really *is?* Ask any professional who sees suicidal teenagers how many are love-sick and heart-broken, and then ask how many of those kids possess even the slightest intellectual (much less heart-level) understanding of what authentic love is all about. *Love needs to be taught in schools as a matter of life and death, both.* We will always have the suicide cases flowing from the agony and tragedy of severe emotional problems, but I firmly believe that thousands of lives could be saved each year if only the most rudimentary intellectual understanding of authentic love were taught in the schools and through the public media.

Most of us would agree that the loss of love, whether through death, rejection, or deprivation, brings with it the greatest suffering that life can present. In the foregoing pages, though never stated directly, the message has been that love loss need not lead to depression. When a lost love is faced forthrightly, it is called grief, and grief in time naturally fades. It is only when that grief is mixed with unnatural emotions, decisions that are unworthy of us, like the choice to be judgmental, to live in bitterness, hatred, and resentment, that depression develops.

---

[13] *Ibid.*, p. 34.

Healing Depression

We began this discussion by risking simplicity, briefly redefining depression in love terms. Risking simplicity again, the following brief paragraph describes the process and major steps typically seen in love therapy's healing of depression.

When a person gains heart-level understanding that their depression began with love-loss, the first major step toward healing has been taken. When the depressed person recognizes that he/she has caused, or at least allowed, his natural grief reaction to the loss of love to become befouled and complicated by unnatural, unbecoming hatred- or guilt-inducing judgments — damning others and/or condemning self — depression is moved another giant step toward healing. However, it is only when the depressed person has been empowered to overcome inertia and assume responsibility for the judgmentalism, hatred and/or guilt and begin heart-level forgiveness and self-forgiveness that the heavy yoke of depression actually begins to lift. To forgive is to begin to love again and thence to live again. Finally, though, it is only when the depressed one has forgiven enough to disentangle and let go of the guilt and hatred, and then to forthrightly grieve the love-loss, that true healing happens. Then the day comes when the person discovers that he/she has turned the tables on depression, that life and attention are now focused not on the love lost (negativity), but on the life-giving love which is still possessed. The love loss has been honestly and directly grieved and accepted, or the lost love has been replaced.

The foregoing nutshell description of healing depression is intended, as always, to capture the heart of the matter. There are, though, other major factors in healing depression that need reinterpretation. Again, the key to healing depression or any other disorder is to think "in love terms."

The Powerlessness Factor in Depression

"I can't…" "I'm just stuck in a black hole…" "There's nothing I can do…" "I'm just weak…" "I'm too tired to do anything…" "I failed at everything I tried, so I gave up trying…" "I just feel helpless." These are typical expressions of the overwhelming feelings of powerlessness that accompany depression. Responding to these feelings, the person oft times just goes to bed and stays there as long as possible (hypersomnia), and/or becomes withdrawn, lethargic, slowly dragging through life, "dead" tired all the time, feeling trapped in helplessness. That sense of powerlessness must be one of the first targets of counseling.

As shown earlier, love is the only authentic power, so the question is, *how* does love empower? Please do not expect a glib answer, for that question plumbs to the depths of the relationship between love and all energy and the multitude of powers of the soul which allow us to be human. In Principle Seven, relating love to reality in general, love was described as the central power of the atom and of every cell, the most elementary of elementary energies and forces, and the very stuff of life itself. If we can zero in and relate to that energy and power at the atomic and cellular level, it will help us understand how one person can love, and thereby plant power, in another.

The depressed person feels isolated, A-lone, and loveless. In that state of lovelessness, when he says that he cannot help himself, that he is powerless, he is telling the truth. Cut off from love, we are truly powerless. Given that realization, the formula for overcoming depressed powerlessness becomes obvious: the power must come from someone else. Simply put, the depressed person must be loved, and thereby empowered. The power of a counselor, relative, or friend, must be infused into the depressed person in the form of a gift, love. Having voiced this, let me recognize that this "giving" approach of love therapy flies in the face of most therapeutic models which take a more laissez-faire, "client-centered" approach, typified by such therapist interpretations as,

"I can't do it for you; I can only help you help yourself," and "The answers must come from within you," and the proverbial, "Well, what do you think?" To the contrary, I am clearly saying that if the love-infused power does not come from someone other than the client, that depressed person is going to remain trapped in powerlessness.

How does one person build power in another? As I described my own experience of loving (Chapter Two), I said that I left myself and entered you. I stand in your shoes, and look out at the world through your eyes, see as you see, feel as you feel... When I love you, I offer myself as a gift, and I enter you bearing gifts, including my strength. As I become intersubjectively one with you, I make you part of myself, and ask you to do likewise, making me part of yourself. As I love you, though you may be afraid and distrustful for awhile because you have been hurt, you cannot fail to realize the presence of my love. Nor, if my love is authentic, will you be able to resist it for very long, for love is all that any of us really want. As you trust more, open up and become more receptive to me, and then make me your own, you will begin reciprocating love. Then you will make a remarkable discovery: as you are infused with love and feel what I feel, you find yourself feeling stronger. As you accept me as a part of yourself, my feelings become yours, and among those feelings, an intrinsic component of love, is power. Thus do you gain the power to begin overcoming the powerlessness in which your depression has had you ensnared. Love is a gift and with it, power is a gift. Once given, the power is yours, mine no longer. It is therefore your own power that will overcome depression. And when that happens, you will surely begin reaching out to help others in the same way as I helped you.

Authentic power is love, which is never actualized nor realized until it is given away.

Lost Love, Hope, Meaning And Life — Suicidal Depression

Hope, in two little words, is future love. In love therapy terms, hope is an inseparable component of love's quadruplex integer: love-faith-hope-trust. Although we can intellectually discuss any of the four as a separate entity, existentially, i.e., in actual day-to-day living, not one of the four ever exists without the other three. Thus, to say that I love you but don't trust you is a contradiction in terms. In real life, if I love you, and/or myself, I am to that same degree placing faith, trust and hope in us. (Cf., Principle Six.)

In any level of depression, the quadruplex breaks down. The love-loss that initiated the depressive spiral downhill intrinsically caused a corresponding degree of faith-loss, trust-loss, and hope-loss. When near-total lovelessness is experienced, a correspondingly devastating loss is experienced of faith, trust, hope, and with all those losses, the experience of the depressed person is utter and agonizing emptiness, stark inner desolation, soul-burning nothingness, intolerable meaninglessness, and thence lifelessness, death. Life is love. With a perception of total lovelessness, the opposite of love is experienced — annihilation, an excruciating "living death," which is the immediate precursor of suicide. This is an intolerable state, one that the suicidal person feels is far worse than any real death could ever be. In this perspective, the suicidal person presents a curious paradox: it is not his life that he wishes to kill; it is the death that he is already experiencing.

As the concept of love's quadruplex is related to the traditional treatment approaches to suicidal-level depression, perhaps the first suggestion to counselors, not just therapists and hospital staff, but volunteers on suicide hot-lines, police, and emergency response teams, is that the temptation to address the stereotyped major problem presented by suicidal people, hopelessness, should be resisted. Granted, that is the most blatant and frequently voiced symptom of those intent on suicide, and it is certainly real, but it is not the heart of the problem. We can sum up the suicidal situation in a theorem: imparting hope without love is utterly impossible, but to infuse love is automatically to infuse hope.

Facing an imminent suicide, hope must be considered the last priority, after love, after trust, and after faith. Consider: hope relates to the future. If I am suicidal, I have already reached a firm conclusion that I cannot tolerate another minute of the *present* life, much less the future. My excruciating suffering is *now*; that suffering I believe in, nothing else. Nor do I trust myself nor anyone else; I am feeling that all have failed to love me in the past, so why should I trust? Neither hope, nor faith, nor trust are the priorities for the suicidal one. His immediate suffering is due to his experience of utter lovelessness, and it is that which must receive priority. But how? How does one transmit life-saving love to someone intent on ending an "agony of living death" with real death?

Let us suppose that a man named Jake, who has been in the very depths of depression, is now sitting on the ledge of a sky-scraper, threatening to jump, and you are the only person there to talk to him. High above the street, you lean out a window to talk to him. What do you say?

When we stop to really think about it, when we are facing someone like Jake who is facing suicide and death, the idea of using any kind of "psychology" on him is a day late. One who is nearing suicide has lost all hope, faith and trust in himself and in anything human, including psychology. All that remains of life is spiritual — spiritual questions, a spiritual crisis, and a final spiritual decision, to jump or not to jump into death. There is, I believe, only one idea that can prevent suicide when it reaches this critical stage: "Love never dies." If that is true, then it is reason-able to believe that somewhere down inside Jake, in some hidden corner of his soul, some remnant of living love still remains. It is that scrap, that tiny shard of love that can save Jake's life — if you can just reach it.

I believe the key to preventing an imminent suicide is to quickly enable the person to "remember love" in one of three ways: (1) Remember the person(s) who most loves you now, or who loved you best in the past; (2) Remember the time when you most loved yourself; or (3) Remember the time that you knew that God loved you (which is also now). It is only love that can prevent Jake from jumping, and it is precisely that slaughtered love, which he is convinced he has lost, which has brought him to this building ledge. If, though, you can keep him talking, and persuade him to focus on the love experiences of the past, he will not jump while his focus is on love. Love heals. That love is sometimes buried in the garbage of hell, but if you can jog Jake's memory to recall past loves, a remarkable thing will happen: love will become alive again; it will be resurrected, revivified, and when that happens, the other three elements of the quadruplex of love — faith, trust, and hope — also return to life. With a bare twinkling of love's light shining, hope can live again, and it then becomes possible for you to persuade Jake that love never dies, that he can find it again, and that he is really not quite as dead as he feels.

There are, of course, no scripts, no magic words which can be recited that will ensure that Jake will not jump. The three themes named above are simply concepts which must be translated into language of the heart. If you dare speak to Jake of love, you can be quite certain that he will know if you speak from the heart.

I hope we agree that there will never be scientific experiments on alternative methodological approaches to suicide carried out on skyscraper ledges. This approach to preventing suicide is the one I use in an office setting. It has worked to this degree: I have never had a client commit suicide. I agree, that is flimsy data. There are, though, two little experiments which anyone can perform to indirectly test love as a suicide preventative. Experiment One: for the next fifteen seconds, do not think of the word "aardvark." You couldn't do it, could you? The point is: do not tell Jake not to jump; that is the sure way to keep his attention fixed on jumping. Instead, focus him on love. Experiment Two: (this test is best carried out when you are feeling a little blue.) While you are feeling down, think back to the time in your life when you were most loved. Remember the person(s) who loved you. Remember how you felt. Remember the warmth of the love. Stay with that feeling. Now, *while* you are recalling love, answer this question: where are the blue feelings you were having? Gone, aren't they. That is precisely the way it can work with Jake.

Finally, if, as you envisioned yourself talking to Jake, and thought of talking at heart level about remembering love, I should hope you reached a spiritual level that led you to spontaneous prayer, asking God to guide your words, and asking Him to help Jake. Poised to jump, feeling utterly loveless and in agony, Jake is at the spiritual climax of his life. His spiritual senses are acutely sensitive. If you did not silently pray, Jake surely knew it and concluded that you didn't love enough, and he might have said that you, like everybody else, didn't really give a damn about him. But if you prayed, Jake surely felt the love.

Chapter Twenty-Four

The New Sexual Revolution: Love

...the sexuality of the woman in love
is tinged with mysticism.

Simone de Beauvoir[1]

Platonic love is not love without sex. It is
love that finds in the body and in human
relationships a route toward eternity.

Thomas Moore[2]

One of the funniest things about love is that it always seems to be brand new and sparkling, full of surprises.

So here we are in the twenty-first century, some fifty or sixty years since the beginning of the so-called "sexual revolution," and young people claim to know everything that could ever be known about sex. More teenagers are progressively having more sex at younger and younger ages, and they are very comfortable talking about sex. Before the "revolution" the common debate was whether it was wise to kiss on the first date; now it is whether to have sex on the first date and whether to use condoms. Their sexual sophistication has been enhanced by sex-saturated movies and Madison Avenue ad men pandering to hormones following the brilliant discovery that "sex sells." Television talk shows explore every conceivable form of kinky sex, and the politically

---

[1] Simone de Beauvoir, *The Second Sex* (New York: Bantam Books, 1961), p. 610.
[2] Thomas Moore, *The Care of the Soul* (New York: Harper Perennial, 1994), p. 81.

correct audience response is, "This is America, so freedom is paramount; if somebody wants to have sex with their pet moose, that's fine."

Then, in the midst all that boisterously ballyhooed and brazenly blazoned promotions of SEX-SEX-SEX, comes a surprise: it is just a tiny whisper, but it is the voice that is heard clearly by every human heart, a voice saying, "Pssst, hey, the real sexual revolution hasn't begun yet, but it's time; the revolution starts with a new idea: great sex, authentic sex, is something spiritual, a product of love."

In order to begin an authentic sexual revolution, it is necessary that we expose the modern-day so-called sexual revolution for what it is: phony, the direct product of the cockamamie ideas of a coke-head, Sigmund Freud. Late in this chapter, we will provide evidence that shows how Freud's cocaine addiction led directly to a worldwide, wrong-headed view of sex. First though, let us begin proactively, by sharing love theory's view of what real sexuality is not and is.

Authentic sex can be confused and abused, distorted into two or more pieces of meat flopping in a variety of contortions, incorporating all sorts of implements, not just whips, dildoes and inflatable sex dolls, but "implements" called animals and children. Authentic sex, rightly called love-making, can be so twisted and perverted that it becomes hate-making, or anxiety-spilling, a vehicle for violence, self-punishment, infantile escapism, or just plain perverted, boring evil. Such distortions have nothing to do with bona fide sexuality; they are varieties of lust. Lust is not sex. In fact, once authentic loving sex is experienced, one readily understands that lust is not the least bit sexy.

Lust? Perversion? Why, those are not even professional words, are they? In love therapy they are.

The Sick Sexual Revolution: Are Perversions Passé?

In the psychiatric lexicon, the word "perversion" is not used. Instead, exhibitionism, pedophilia, sexual sadism and other forms of distorted sexuality are called "paraphilias." That is an interesting word — one that is roundly rejected in love therapy because it leads to the destructive misunderstanding of the meaning of love.

"Paraphilia" is derived from two Greek words. *Para-* means "at the side of, alongside." It can also mean "by," "to one side," "amiss," or "beyond." In the Greek, *philia* has been used classically to mean "fraternal love." Literally, then, a "paraphilia" might mean anything from "alongside love" (implying equality between love and perversion) to "amiss love." In any case, a paraphilia inescapably implies that any form of deviant sexual behavior is some kind of "love" — and that is simply not true. On the contrary, these disfigurements of sexuality are primarily designed to avoid authentic love, or to twist, punish or destroy love altogether. The same objection obviously applies to all other sexual "-philia" words, including "coprophilia" (feces) and "necrophilia" (dead bodies).

If truth is to be served, the word "perversion" is perfectly appropriate to describe sexual deviances. "Perversion" is derived from the Latin *pervertere*, meaning "to overthrow, corrupt." Indeed, that is what happens when these sexual malignancies take over a personality: the human capacity for love and authentic sexuality are overthrown, turned upside-down, corrupted.

The word "paraphilia," in my opinion, is a professional cop-out, a way of avoiding the uncomfortable necessity of calling lust, "lust," depravity, "depravity," and perversion, "perversion." In love therapy, the word "paraphilia" is rejected, not just as professionalese but as destructive gobbledygook. Instead, each of the sexual deviancies is called a "perversion disorder."

But so what? Why all this semantic fuss over one word? Because it is just such seemingly innocuous psychobabbling and dilutions of the meaning of both the word "love" and "sex" that have fed the present-day destructive sexual revolution that is killing both love and authentic sex.

Consider: according to the DSM IV, a paraphilia is considered a disorder only if the aberrant sexual behavior meets two criteria: (a) the behavior goes on for at least six months, and (b) "the fantasies, sexual urges or behavior cause significant distress or impairment in social, occupational or other important areas of functioning."[3] This clearly implies that a masochist who happily submits herself to beatings and humiliation, a man who daily smears himself with feces (coprophilia), a sadist who has a willing recipient for his cruelty, and a window peeper who is never caught, so long as they are not in "significant distress," and function okay in daily life, are *not* considered to have a diagnosable condition. In other words, according to official psychiatric criteria, these non-distressed perverts are considered normal.

Of course, the psychiatric community's intent was to define mental and emotional disorders, which are usually defined by distress. It is also argued that mental health practitioners cannot dictate morality, that we are not cops, and not clergy, nor are we the guardians of public mores. It is not the therapist's role, it is argued, to pass judgment on consenting adults' sexual behavior, however kinky, nor can therapists help persons who are "comfortable" with their sexual weirdness and refuse help. True enough. But the question is, "Has there been a cause-effect relationship between professional refusal to name perversions as a disorder, and its minimized, diluted, distress-only definition of sexual deviancy, and the rapid escalation of the so-called sexual revolution into a licentious, promiscuous, if-it-feels-good-do-it, VD-ravaged, amoral society?"

My answer is yes. Yet, the problem is much deeper, much more pervasive, and much older than the use of the word "paraphilia," and much older than this generation of mental health practitioners. It is an insidious and pernicious attitude that was

---

[3]   D.S.M. IV, *op. cit.*, pp. 523-532.

planted in the mind of Mental Health about a century ago, and since then has infected the whole of society.

Origins of the Sick Sexual Revolution: Freud's Cocaine Habit

Wholesale misunderstanding of what sexuality fundamentally is has been rampant since the advent of Freud's deification of the sexual instinct, and the subsequent deification of Freud himself. For over a century now, the fundamental drive that Freud named the "id" and the core of personality structure that he proclaimed the "unconscious," have continued to dominate professional thinking. The presentation of the love principles includes a new fundamental drive, a new personality structure, and a new view of personhood, including sexuality. However, if the truth about love and authentic sexuality are to be understood and accepted, Freud's fallacies and fabricated pseudo-scientific theories must be exposed for what they are — lies, just plain baloney.

In recent years, the baseless foundation and baseness of Freudian theory have sustained increasing criticism, but Freud has weathered it. After decades of adulation, that is perhaps not so surprising. But belief in Freud and his psychoanalytic credo have created a "pseudo-sexual revolution" which must be ended so that truth can be seen. Here, the effort will be to expose the great harm that Freud has done and then to apply a *coup de grâce* to his thought and pernicious influence. Lest that sound surprisingly unloving, I should preface my forthright attack by stating that it is not my intent to judge Freud's moral culpability. It is my intent to slaughter his cancerous influence on minds and morality, ending that influence where it began, on sexuality.

For a psychoanalyst, one who is trained to be an official Freudian disciple, to forthrightly recognize the damage which psychoanalytic theory has rendered for humankind, as Dr. Willard Gaylin does, is a truly heroic step. Though he mistakenly defends Freud on one vital point, Gaylin succinctly describes the Freudian fallacies and tragedies.

Given the fact that our daily experience is saturated with problems of love and loving, one would assume that the concept of love would be the center of psychoanalytic theory. This is far from the case. In an unanticipated development, psychoanalytic theory created a loveless world. Psychoanalysis enshrined the sex drive, the libido, as the primal factor governing human activity.

The unpredictable result of this strange set of priorities was not just the reduction of love, but also, ironically, the trivialization of sex....

...the only empirical results of that illegitimate offspring of Freudian philosophy, the sexual revolution, seems to be the spread of two new sexually transmitted diseases, genital herpes and AIDS; an extraordinary rise in the incidence of cancer of the cervix, and a disastrous epidemic of teenage pregnancies. For the abandonment of love, Freud holds some of the responsibility; for the trivialization of sex, he must not be blamed.[4]

For a follower of the Freudian credo, that is a truly extraordinary statement. It would have been most fitting for a psychoanalyst to apply the final *coup de grâce* to the major tenets of the psychoanalytic belief system. Gaylin's statement, though, powerful as it is, is an understatement; his last-minute defense of Freud is indefensible. To admit that Freud is responsible for the "abandonment of love," but then say that he "must not be blamed" for the trivialization of sex and all its consequent evils is a clear contradiction of the law of cause and effect. It is like saying that Hitler should not be blamed for millions of deaths and atrocities because "all he did was issue some proclamations." Freud's "abandonment of love" was far worse than if Alexander Fleming

---

[4]　Willard Gaylin, M.D., *Rediscovering Love* (New York: Penguin Books, 1984), pp. 10-11.

had deliberately abandoned penicillin, tossing it away as "just a mold," and then devoted his life to germ warfare. The truth is that Freud trashed love, and then transformed it into a virulent, mutant distortion of sex.

In Gaylin's perfectly truthful words, Freud's followers "enshrined the sexual drive, the libido, as the primal factor governing human behavior" and thereby "created a loveless world." The enshrined sex drive was god. Love was then reduced, trivialized as a sexual byproduct, and the actual God was debunked as "the father image projected [onto] the sky."[5] The "enshrining" of sex and the designation of sex as the "Prime Cause" (instead of God, i.e., Love) can only be called a religion.

Once Freud deposed God, despiritualized life, reduced love to the defense mechanism (sublimation) and ensconced an animalized, instinct-driven version of loveless sex as the meaning of life, the so-called "sexual revolution" was inevitable. But the sexual revolution is simply one symptom of the loveless world that Freud did so much to create. Should anyone doubt that we are now facing a truly sick society, we need only scan the last three decades.

In 1985, the Education Commission of the States, a body of business, education and political leaders set up to advise the States on education, published these findings:

> Drug and alcohol abuse among young people is 60 times higher than in 1960.
>
> Teenage homicide is up 'an astounding 232 percent for whites' and 16 percent for non-whites since 1950, while suicide is up more than 150 percent.... A teenager commits suicide every 90 minutes.
>
> Teenage pregnancy is up 109 percent among whites and 10 percent among non-whites since 1960, with a

---

[5] Sigmund Freud, *The Future of An Illusion* [1927] (Garden City, NY: Doubleday, 1957).

million teens becoming pregnant each year.

The national dropout rate averaged 26 percent and was as high as 40 percent in some cities.

And overall, at least 15 percent of American teenagers between 16 and 19 are unlikely to become productive adults because they are disconnected from society as a result of drug abuse, delinquency, pregnancy, unemployment, and dropping out of school.[6,7,8]

Those sickening statistics, alone, provide evidence of a sick society, and those figures are only for the teenage population. Worse still, those figures are over two decades old, and the destructive trend has continued. In fact, the most recent statistics can only be called shocking. In 2008, a study published by the U.S. Center for Disease Control and Prevention (Dr. Sara Feldman) showed that the overall STD rate among girls fourteen to eighteen during 2003-04 was twenty-six percent. The teens were tested for four infections: human papillomavirus, chlamydia, trichomoniasis and genital herpes. These girls were not tested for gonorrhea or syphilis, so the figure showing one in four teen girls has an STD is a conservative figure.[9] Thus, by even the roughest measure, the clinical picture is inescapable: the social structure of the United States, along with its traditional moral, familial and religious foundations, is crumbling like a sand castle in the waves.

And the sickness of this society, by the greatest single measure, is attributable to the loveless world created by the insidious

---

6   Education Commission of the United States, 1985, in *The Courier Journal*, Louisville, Kentucky, November 2, 1985, p. 1.

7   The dropout rate gradually declined between 1972 and 2004, from 15 percent to a low of 10 percent in 2004. (Child Trend Data Bank. childtrenddatabank.org)

8   More recent statistics show that the teen birthrate (age 15-19) is at its lowest level in 30 years, down 36 percent since its peak in 1991. Good news also is the fact that teenage abortions dropped 50 percent since their peak in 1988. (U.S. Pregnancy Statistics, Guttmacher Institute, Wall Street, New York, N.Y. September, 2006). Yes, the figures are still high. Yet, perhaps we are seeing the first signs of reversing the effects of Freud's pernicious heritage.

9   Lindsey Tanner, Associated Press, "Study: 1 in 4 teen girls has an STD," *The Courier Journal*, Louisville, Kentucky, March 12, 2008, p. A3

effects of Freudian thought. No, Freud did not do all the damage, but his thought dominated the minds of the professional leaders whom the public trusted as "doctors of the soul." When those doctors were convinced by Freud that the "soul" was actually a "libido," a sex-driven animal instinct, true believers were created and all hell broke loose. Loving souls shriveled as the experts successfully proselytized the world, teaching that loveless sex was the essence of life.

Only since the mid-1980s have the facts about Freud the man, and the truth behind his bizarre theories, begun to emerge.

It is now clear that Freud was a chronic cocaine addict. Inevitably, some are still shocked, if not incredulous, but the evidence of Freud's drug abuse is convincingly documented in E.M. Thornton's *Freud and Cocaine: the Freudian Fallacy*.[10] Given an understanding of cocaine's typical effects, the origins of Freudian thought become transparently clear: Freud's repudiation of God was a direct product of his own messianic obsession and delusions of omnipotence, his circular and reductionistic reasoning, and his fanciful, bizarre and hypersexualized theories were all the direct product of a toxically drugged brain. The evidence is entirely convincing that the most devastatingly influential concepts of the twentieth century, ideas which were "the rage" of the psychiatric, literary and even the political intelligentsia, the thoughts which have ravaged both love and authentic sexuality to produce a host of progressively loveless societies, were the progeny of a spaced-out, sexed-up, drug-sick mind.

Not only does Thornton document the overwhelming circumstantial evidence of Freud's drug abuse throughout his career, she uses modern knowledge of the distinctive sexual, emotional, and intellectual effects of cocaine in order to show how each of the major Freudian theories indubitably was produced by that drug. Theory by theory, Thornton exposes Freud's "science" as an irrational collection of cocaine-derived concoctions.

---

[10] E.M. Thornton, *Freud and Cocaine, The Freudian Fallacy* (Worchester, Great Britain: Billing and Sons, 1983).

Freud's early experiments with cocaine and his own
use of the newly synthesized drug as a medication
in the years 1884 and 1887 are known from his early
papers and appear in all his biographies.... This book
presents evidence that Freud resumed his use of cocaine in the latter half of 1892.[11]

Thornton does provide this evidence, and it is entirely convincing. She then interprets Freud's theories in light of cocaine's
effects.

The first significant fact... is that cocaine... effects...
greatly increase sexual excitation as occurred with
Freud... but with prolonged use... cocaine has an anti-
aphrodisiac effect....[12]

Freud's abrupt conversion to the sexual hypothesis... was caused by cocaine. It was cocaine too which
induced the early cessation of the sexual activity in
both Freud and Fleiss which they called the "male
menopause."[13]

The second significant finding is that cocaine...
induces in its victims a peculiar messianic obsession....[14]

These two traits in combination, his own greatly
increased libido and his messianic obsession with
sexuality, must inevitably cast doubt on the validity
of Freud's theories. The unavoidable conclusion is that
they were the products of his cocaine usage and had no
basis in fact. And with this realization, how preposter-
ous and pathological now appear the theories that have
been accepted as truth for so many decades. That they

---

[11] *Ibid.,* p. 1.

[12] *Ibid.,* p. 4.

[13] *Ibid.,* p. 188.

[14] *Ibid.,* p. 4.

retained their hold on so many people of intellect and ability for years is one of the strangest aspects of the Freud story.[15]

When Gaylin, like so many professionals, says that Freud should "not be blamed" for the trivialization of sex, one can only become angry at their continuing perpetration of a glaring untruth. Thornton exposes Freud's grand design and his heart's desire.

> Another draft, that of February 8, 1893, calls for the complete overthrow of established sexual morality. "Free sexual intercourse between young males and respectable girls" was urgently necessary [Freud] said. If this were not implemented, society was "doomed to fall a victim to incurable neuroses which reduce the enjoyment of life to a minimum, destroy the marriage relation and bring hereditary ruin to the whole coming generation."[16]

This sick, amoral version of a "sexual revolution" *was* Freud's original conception, and one of the great pities of the twentieth century is that the societal "neuroses," "minimum enjoyment of life," "destroyed marriage relation," and "hereditary ruin" that Freud foresaw if his idea of "free sexual intercourse" were *not* socially accepted and promulgated, is precisely what is occurring because it *was*. What is even more astounding and ironic is that he was able to so effectively hoodwink so many millions of our most brilliant minds. It is as if Freud stole their hearts and common sense right out from under their noses — (noses, by the way, which the coke-snorting Freud pronounced to be a major sex organ).

Given the Freudian cocaine connection, it is perhaps more

---

[15] *Ibid.*, p. 5.
[16] *Ibid.*, pp. 189-190.

understandable why, in presenting love theory, I felt it so necessary to start from ground zero, re-thinking everything about human beings and reality itself, laboriously building a personality
theory principle by principle. It was necessary because, strange as
it seems, Psychology has never had a valid comprehensive theory
upon which to build. In the Introduction, I recounted my constant
opposition to Freudian ideas in graduate school. I did not know
then, nor did my teachers know, that the Church of Freud is built
on, not quicksand, but deep, soft "snow," cocaine.

But enough now. Enough. As is said so often in therapy, the
name of the game is not blame. It is, rather, to see the truth, to
identify the problem, and then to do something about it. So after
we quit laughing-crying over the Freudian farce, what is the truth
which we now face?

The truth is that the "loveless world" which we now inhabit,
though horribly damaged, is *not* entirely loveless at all. Indeed,
love sometimes seems like a lovely perennial flower: the more
manure we throw on it, the more beautiful it becomes when it
survives the winter and rises from the ground the following
spring. Such is our hope for the twenty-first century. It is not too
late. By enshrining sex as god, Freud said that love was dead.
Similarly, Nietzsche, affirming power as god, could say "God is
dead." That does not make it so. Love and God are both still very
much alive, and so is authentic, loving sexuality. All three are
waiting — shyly, politely, whispering softly together as lovers
do — waiting for the din of the pseudo-sexual revolution to die,
waiting to be invited.

Authentic Sexual Love

In Principle Two, I experientially described the supra-rational,
mysterious act of human love. We spoke of heart-knowledge and
-fusion, and of the continuum of love that stretches from down-to-
earth, incarnated love straight back to the Source of all Love, God
Himself. It is only in the context of this mysterious understanding

that we can even begin to comprehend the mystery of authentic sexual love.

Sex a mystery? I was talking about that mystery once in a marriage counseling session. George, the husband, interrupted, saying, "Wait a minute. You're getting way out. I don't see any big mystery about sex. What's so complicated? You just do it." His wife turned to me angrily and said, "See? What did I tell you? That's why we need counseling. George thinks he solved the whole mystery of sex when he figured out which end of his penis went *in*!"

Granted, there was a wee bit of exaggeration in this wife's angry protest, but the laughter that ensued started this couple on the road to mystery. The question became, "If real sex is more than getting the right end of a penis into a vagina, then how much more?" Let's start with the minimum requirements for an authentic sexual encounter, the experience of real love making. Actually, those basic requirements were already described — in Principle Six, "The Five Acts in Every Authentic Love."

Rather than page back to that chapter, let's do a very quick and terse review of Principle Six. Any human relationship that purports to be in any way loving, be it a marriage, a sibling or parent-child relationship, or a friendship, is characterized by five marks or developmental stages, five fundamental ingredients that mark the relationship as "authentic" — as opposed to an abusive, utilitarian, dishonest or phony relationship, and as opposed to a beginning or immature relationship. Those five marks or stages are:

1. Knowledge. The first tiny step that begins a relationship is simply learning more and more about the person. As real love reaches fruition, that knowledge becomes, beyond thorough, "heart-level."
2. Giving and receiving. Love is always a gift (remember Principle Four?). To "relate" means to offer the gift of one's self to the other and to correspondingly receive the self of the other into oneself. This interdependence is the beginning of two people becoming "one."

3. Faith, trust, hope and love (the quadruplex integer, the inseparable qualities of authentic love) develop and grow, meaning.
    a. Faith, transcending knowledge, reaches the stage where I can leap to say, "I believe in you, just as you are."
    b. Trust comes. Given faith in you, I find myself deciding to become more and more open and vulnerable to you, emotionally naked and willingly defenseless, because I am sure you will never willingly hurt me.
    c. Hope becomes permanent. Given faith and trust, I become progressively certain that my faith and trust in you, and our relationship will be here tomorrow and tomorrow — even unto death and beyond.
    d. Finally, given the foundation blocks of faith, trust and hope, and given the deep knowledge I have gained of you, the first level of authentic love develops.
4. Commitment. In any deeper authentic relationship, the time comes to promise that this affiliation will be permanent. This commitment may be legal and declared, as in a marriage, or it may be unspoken but nonverbally declared (just "known" at gut level) as in many friendships.
5. Bonding. All the above steps do not *fully* describe an authentic love relationship, especially as we try to capture the essence of marriage. The fulfillment of a love relationship brings oneness — two people in some mysterious way have become one. The image of bonding bears repeating: in an authentic love bond, two glasses of water, one colored blue, the other yellow, are poured together to create green; once done, we never can go back to yellow and blue. That's a bond.

In love theory and therapy, those five stages or ingredients are considered bare bones minimum for an authentically loving sexual relationship. Moreover, if those five aspects of authentic love have not been reached, we would say that authentic sex would not be possible. More explicitly, sex without authentic

love is not sex. But if it is not sex, what is it? Sex without the fullness of authentic love is called either lust or perversion, and in
love therapy, they qualify as diagnosable disorders. I'll describe
those disorders below. First though, let me acknowledge that
love therapy, when it involves marriage or sexual counseling, is
setting a much higher standard for defining healthy sexuality
than most mainstream therapies demand. So too, love therapy's
methods aim higher.

Mainstream psychotherapists and sex therapists offer an
array of helpful approaches to couples having marital and/or
sexual difficulties. They may focus on relaxation techniques to
reduce "performance anxiety," the most common culprit in sexual
dysfunction. They may suggest touching exercises, "pleasuring,"
as a means of reducing threat.[17] They may give sexual anatomy
education. If a physical problem is suspected, they may involve
consultation with a gynecologist or urologist. Certainly they
will inquire into the dynamics of the couple's relationship. They
may help one partner or the other discover feelings and past
experiences, or even repressed trauma, that are interfering with
the present relationship and adequate sexual functioning. All
these approaches are good and necessary. Love therapy does all
these. What has long been needed, though, is an accurate psychospiritual definition of sexual love. The physiological goings-on of
sex have been exhaustively researched by Masters and Johnson[18]
and many others. Hundreds of books have so meticulously and
energetically described sexual positions, gyrations and gymnas-
tics that sex begins to sound like an Olympic event. Sexual aids
now come in so many flavors that we expect Betty Crocker to
come out with a sexual cookbook. And all this has been in pursuit
of "adequate sexual functioning." However, there is a huge dif-

---

[17] An overview of a wide variety of direct sexual therapy approaches is offered in
Helen Finger Kaplan, M.D., Ph.D., *The New Sex Therapy* (New York: Time Books,
Random House, 1974).

[18] William H. Masters, M.D. and Virginia E. Johnson, *Human Sexual Inadequacy*
(Boston: Little, Brown, 1970).

ference between the way traditional therapies and love therapy define that term. Love therapy seeks infinitely more. That seeking of "more" is based on the belief that it is a rare person who can settle for merely "adequate" sex. Don't we all want great sex? Surely. The goal in sex, as in all quarters of our lives, is the same: we want fulfillment. And what is that? Answering that question we arrive at a definition which recognizes that authentic loving sexuality cannot be separated from spirituality.

In love therapy, "sexual fulfillment" is defined as the joyful celebration of a man and a woman committed and united in love through one of the highest and holiest demonstrations of their love, the bond of sexual intercourse — two in one flesh, two in one spirit, two in one heart, melted together, united and fused into the love of God — a physical union that is experienced primarily in their united hearts, hearts overflowing with so much love that it erupts, beyond orgasm, into the spasmodic surges of spiritual ecstasy. By "beyond orgasm" is meant that, in the climax of the experience, two fused beings transcend their bodies to arrive at a state that at times may approach a mystical encounter. At minimum, even for people who deem themselves "not religious," an authentic, loving sexual event will contain a quality of extreme goodness and purity which, if not called spiritual, will evoke heart-level warmth with an utter lack of guilt, shame or regret, and a conviction that the experience is "right" and fulfilling at the deepest reaches of the heart.

Some may read that definition of sexual fulfillment and be baffled or incredulous for one of two reasons. The first group may say, "But what about sex of a deeply committed and loving married couple who sometimes just frolic in sexual play, doing it on the proverbial chandelier? Is that not authentic sexuality?" Love therapy's answer is, "Absolutely — and more power to them!" — so long as that couple is united in a love bond as described above. There is absolutely no contradiction between spiritual experience and authentic sexual experience. In fact, sometimes, the most intensely spiritual experiences can be the greatest sexual fun.

A second common reason for not understanding love therapy's sexual fulfillment definition stems from the misconception that "holy" people, people who pray, are almost by definition, not very sexual. Nothing could be further from the truth. The clincher that a spiritually-based sex life is a realistic standard would come if a scientific study asked married couples about their spiritual experiences during love-making. In this regard, we have two reports.

First, it is the clinical experience of love therapy that the *majority* of couples in authentic loving marriages report at least occasional spiritual experiences during love-making. Granted, most couples do not use words like "transcendence" to describe their spiritual experiences, nor are they wont to say God was right there in bed with them. Most people, to their credit, are entirely too humble to even consider that possibility. More accurately, many have been misled into believing that ordinary people never experience God in *any* setting, much less in bed. However, given support and challenged to "hang words" on their best sexual experiences, many will use the words like "bliss" and "heaven" and then say it was "almost like" God touched them. Given more support, people often surprise themselves when they think back on "great" sex and then recognize that it was a God experience.

This clinical experience is admittedly flimsy evidence for those who love hard numbers. There is better research evidence that supports the love therapy view that sexual fulfillment is largely determined by spirituality:

> In one recent study of young adults, in only about one third of marriages did both husband and wife say their sexual fulfillment was excellent. When both husband and wife had strong positive religious images and when both prayed every day, then three quarters said the sexual fulfillment was excellent.... This particular study focused on marriages in which at least one partner was Catholic. In other words, despite

the negativism of Catholic sexual teaching, ordinary normal people were able to relate intense religion to intense intimacy.[19]

One study, in scientific circles, rarely "proves" much. The study above was limited to Catholics, so the scientific question will be, "Is Methodist, Buddhist or Jewish sexual love very different than Catholic?" There is no precise study that answers that question. However, a telephone survey of nearly fifteen hundred adults revealed that a solid eighty percent of Americans believe in God. Of these, sixty-nine percent "know God exists and I have no doubts about it," and twelve percent said, "While I have my doubts, I feel that I do believe in God."[20] This would suggest that a great majority of people do believe in God to some degree, and that they enjoy sexual fulfillment to that same degree. (Clearly, much more scientific study would be needed to verify that suggestion.)

These few little studies, viewed together, strongly support the love therapy definition and description of sexual fulfillment as universally applicable. Do they prove it? No. I should hope only to show that while at first glance the love therapy view of sex may seem to be utopian, there is more than my own clinical evidence to suggest that it comes closer to the truth than do traditional descriptions of "sexual adequacy."

The New Love-Centered Sexual Revolution, Starting in Church

In historical perspective, in the context of the heritage and socially acceptable attitudes that surrounded them, it is clear that the responsibility for neglecting God's role in sexual love has

---

[19] Fr. Andrew Greeley, "Religion and Sex are Inseparable," *A Piece of My Mind… On Just About Everything* (Garden City, NY: Doubleday and Company, 1983), p. 99.

[20] Media General-Associated Press, Associated Press report cited in *The Courier Journal* (Louisville, Kentucky), January 2, 1985.

not been primarily that of therapists. The culprits have been the churches. Given the leadership of the church, however brave the therapists, they usually bent to the popular, two-tiered religious view that God was "way up there somewhere" while we were "down here," and if He ever came down, it was only to "holy" people who were, by definition, asexual. In decades past, never, never could it be conceived that God might actually like sex and choose to participate in the juicy rhythms of intercourse, adding His own ecstatic surges.

No one has summed up this damnable ages-long error of the churches more succinctly than the priest-sociologist, Fr. Andrew Greeley. He addresses only his own Catholic Church, but he might well have been speaking of the recent history of most churches:

> … a gorgeous Irish redhead in her forties said… "Most of us know that sex is essential in keeping the glow in marriage…. Why doesn't the church provide us with motivation?"
>
> The greatest failure of the church… is the nonrecognition of the spiritual and ascetic dimensions of sex.
>
> And I don't mean the spirituality of not having sex or not enjoying it much when you have it. After a while, that takes no spiritual motivation at all. I mean the spirituality of celebrating sex and keeping love alive with it. That failure, in centuries to come, will rank with the Galileo Caper.[21]

The Church's "caper" could not be described more honestly unless Greeley's statement were proclaimed by the Pope to be an understatement — which it is. Immediately, though, this criticism of churches' past arch-conservative and erroneous teaching about sex must be placed in perspective. Today, most churches must be lauded as the last protectors against a pernicious, libertarian view of sexuality that is eroding the social and moral fabric of the

---

[21] Greeley, *op. cit.*, p. 87.

world. Skyrocketing venereal diseases, illegitimacy, and divorce rates are only hints of the depth of the moral disintegration that is occurring. Historically, the sexual behavior pendulum has swung to and fro, from Roman orgies to archconservative Victorian prudery and back to present-day explosion of porn, promiscuity and divorce. But throughout all these eras, there has been a constant: people have been searching for authentic love (Principle One). The simple answer to all sexual problems is "love," but the complex question is, "How can nations-full and a world full of people, each of whom is powerfully pushed to express love sexually, be taught to love — love first — or to abstain?" If the sex education courses in the schools were changed to "love education," that would be a solid beginning. If states required pre-marriage evaluations and straightforward instruction in love, the divorce rate would plummet. But the first change must be among university intellectual leadership. As simple an idea as "Love" being taught as a basic course in Psychology, Nursing, Psychiatry, Social Work, Occupational Therapy and all the helping professions would do wonders. We have had the so-called sexual revolution. Could we now have a love revolution? Is it conceivable, as Greeley's red-haired parishioner asked, that the churches could lead the way?

The thesis of this section has been that the key to healthy sexuality, and especially to great sex, is to elevate it spiritually. Focus on God and prayer by married couples is also the best therapeutic approach to sexual dysfunctions in some cases. By emphasizing this much-neglected aspect of sexuality, however, I certainly do not mean to disparage or discourage the use of other proved-effective sex therapy methods. Love therapy often includes behavioral approaches — the Semans technique for premature ejaculation, for example, or various touching and pleasuring instructions as means of overcoming fears and inhibitions — and let us not forget Viagra for erectile dysfunction. Nor can the multitude of possible physiological causes of sexual dysfunction be neglected. Thus, while love therapy recognizes that authentic sex has God in its midst, I would be quick to discourage the misuse of God by a misguided attempt to substitute a disembodied flight to heavenly prayer when, in fact, some down-to-earth pleasuring of a vagina or penis is the appropriate treatment. Nor should my focus on the ultimate joys of sexuality that can be found spiritually be misconstrued as discouraging couples from sometimes having plain fun with sex. On the contrary, when love and sex and God are well integrated, we discover that even love-making while hanging from that proverbial chandelier can be a God experience.

Sexual Love Disorders

The enormous variety of sexual disorders cannot all be addressed here. Nor is the treatment of sexual disorders in love therapy radically different from other therapies. Rather, what I hope to show, through brief examples, is how the fundamental understanding that the therapist conveys to the client about the love-sex connection can hasten recovery.

At the risk of belaboring what some may feel is obvious, it is imperative that physiological causes of sexual dysfunction be totally ruled out before psychotherapy or sex therapy is undertaken. Every year, more and more physical links to problems like impotence and frigidity are being discovered. In an article on "Sex and Type 2 Diabetes,"[22] Gambert lists twenty-three "diseases associated with impotence and/or reduced libido" — a list ranging from endocrine problems like hypo- and hyperthyroidism or Addison's disease to metabolic diseases like diabetes, to neurological, vascular and genital disorders to the effects of surgery and chronic illness. Add to the list the effects of various drugs and the fact that virtually any physical illness affects sexuality.

Following is a rather typical example of how a physical problem can be misinterpreted as a love problem.

---

[22] Steven R. Gambert, M.D., "Sex and Type 2 Diabetes," in *Medical Aspects of Human Sexuality*, May, 1990 (New York: Cahners), p. 22.

Diane and Vic

Diane, age 37, came for counseling "secretly." She did not want her husband to know that she was seeing me; she just wanted to know how she could make him love her again. "I know Vic must be having an affair. He doesn't want anything to do with me anymore (sexually)." Vic could not keep an erection. Diane interpreted this as a clear sign that "I can't even turn him on anymore!"

When I finally could persuade Diane to talk to Vic and let me see him, the first five minutes of the interview revealed that Vic was being treated for hypertension. Some antihypertensive drugs, including Vic's, will often produce impotence. A call to his physician suggesting a change in prescription quickly improved Vic's potency. The medication's side effects masqueraded as a love problem.

In other cases, vaginal dryness and painful intercourse may indeed signal a love disorder — heart-deep hurt that makes sexual arousal impossible — but the lack of lubrication might have a simpler explanation like too little foreplay.

Authentic sex is an expression of love, but sex may also become the outlet for ventilation of any of the many forms of damaged love — anxiety, hatred, grief, flight from reality, guilt, anger, or murderous rage — or any of the many responses to a wounded interior love-life. Sex, authentically speaking, is indeed love-making, but it can also be fear-flight, grief-spilling, rage-venting, anxiety-salving, or guilt-punishing. In keeping with Principle One, all human acts, including sexual acts, are driven by, or in pursuit of, love. And in keeping with Principle Five, all emotions, including those experienced sexually, are pursuits of or expressions of love. That love may be twisted, hornswoggled, disguised or perverted, but once the tale is untangled in therapy, it is always a love story.

The following brief case histories, viewed together, provide an overview of how the truth of the love principles is borne out in practice.

Gracie

Gracie was a single, attractive, twenty-four-year-old secretary masturbating upward of ten times a day, before, during and after work — even on buses. She came into counseling because she was a "sex fiend," she confessed. At first, she could report no other painful emotions — no conflicts, no big anxieties, no other symptoms of any kind — and she presented her childhood as "perfectly normal." Her only problem, she insisted, was that she was obsessed with sex.

And indeed, that was the diagnosis. Gracie was obsessive-compulsive, and sex was the primary medium of expression of her disorder. She was obsessed in her thoughts about sex, and here masturbation was the primary compulsive expression.

In counseling, as we explored running battles with her controlling mother and passive-aggressive father, Gracie started experiencing extreme anxiety. As the anxiety appeared openly, the masturbation waned. Finally she realized that sex was a "tranquilizer and an escape" from the pain and anxiety caused by being too little loved by her parents and self-identified as unlovable. Soon, the masturbation stopped, sex as an obsessional defense waned, and Gracie centered in on her heartfelt pain and fears.

Deacon Hugh

This forty-year-old minister came into counseling with severe anxiety after walking out of an "adult book store" (a sex shop) and running smack into a married couple from his church. Pornography, he admitted, was a sporadic obsession that he has always had to "pray away," but no, he had no idea of *why* he was so obsessed.

In the second interview, he admitted that his "real" problem was that he had always been afraid he was homosexual — but it was quickly discovered that Hugh was afraid of anything resembling sexuality, homo- or hetero-.

Through "healing of memories" (a form of healing prayer which we'll discuss in Chapter Twenty-Five), Hugh discovered that his mother had sexually terrorized him. A prudish, pseudo-religious, man-hating woman, she had constantly threatened to "cut it off" if she saw the little boy touching himself. When he finally braved a meeting with an older sister, she confirmed that Hugh's prayer-retrieved memories were true. The sister recalled seeing his mother give Hugh a bath when he was three years old. When it came to washing his genitals, she threw the washcloth between his legs, saying, "You wash that nasty thing."

Painfully, Hugh realized that the enormous sexual fear and false guilt were not the root problems. Rather, it was the near-total rejection by his mother — the love that never was.

Tina

This twenty-five-year-old woman came into counseling contemplating divorce because she was non-orgasmic and felt that she could not sexually please her husband. Moreover, she felt unworthy of him. When trust was established, Tina admitted having been promiscuous before marriage. How promiscuous? She didn't know, but laughed when I guessed, "Fifty." Her best conservative estimate was that she had had sex with over three thousand men. And she had never had an orgasm.

Counseling with Tina revealed a woman who as a child would have been quickly diagnosed as "battered child syndrome." Her father had regularly beaten her bloody with fists, twice with a bull whip. He locked her in the farm's pitch black underground smoke house with no food for days at a time. Once, in a drunken rage, he chased her through a nearby woods shooting at her with a deer rifle.

Tina suspected she had been sexually abused, but she wasn't sure. The family was "dirt poor," so six children and the parents slept on two beds and on the floor. She remembered sleeping in her parents' bed, and at about age six trying to "play asleep" while they had intercourse. Time and again during therapy she would get "flashes" of her father doing "something" to her in bed, but she would immediately fall apart, cry, shake uncontrollably and refuse to pursue the memory.

After two months Tina could admit that she hated all men, especially the three thousand she had slept with, all whom were "just like Daddy." Her husband, though, was "different — at least I think he is."

It took a year, but eventually Tina recalled the sexual abuse, and the source of her rampant promiscuity became clear. The only time her father had ever said he "loved" her was while he was sexually abusing her. As a result, Tina's entire existential state of being falsely identified her as, "I-am-loved-and-lovable-only-as-a-sex-object." (See Principle Eighteen.) Tina had virtually no boundaries. When I asked if she had ever said "No" to any man, she said "No." When I asked if it had ever occurred to her that she could say "No" she said "No." Tina's views of both sex and love were as tortuously twisted as a handful of spider webs.

Eventually, though, she began trying to forgive her father. Toward the end of the second year, every session centered on her "testing" of her trust and love for her husband. In this context, I eventually interpreted to her that human love is always a risk, and that trust and love, just like faith, always require a "leap" (cf., Principle Six).

Shortly thereafter, Tina came into my office dancing, twirling around, and singing a new song: "Tra-la-la, I had an orgasm! I had an orgasm!" Asked how it happened, she said, "I trusted him. I loved him! I did just like you said, I leaped! And no sooner did I trust him than I had an orgasm — first *ever*. Wow! What a leap!"

Lust Disorder

In love therapy, lust is sometimes considered an emotional disorder, sometimes a major one. At least if the client is "uncomfortable," therapists usually recognize extreme perversions — bestiality, pedophilia, necrophilia, exhibitionism, etc. — as disorders; yet, they rarely consider consciously and freely chosen lust as a direct cause of the disorder. Instead, fixated early development or unconscious drives are the usual therapeutic focus. Perhaps unintentionally, textbooks often teach therapists to equate healthy sexuality with the mere ability to have an orgasm, or as being emotionally "comfortable" with sex, no matter how weird or kinky it might be.

The very idea of talking about lust as a disorder, and of interpreting this to a patient may be viewed as a professional sacrilege. For professional therapists, there are a few nearly universal agreements: a therapist must maintain a non-judgmental attitude, must not impose his or her own moral values, and must meet the client where he/she is. When these basic precepts are synthesized, the single highest value that the counseling professions are seen to promote is "client self-determination" or "freedom" above all else. That sounds very American, but the problem is this: freedom which is not guided, disciplined, enlightened and constantly elevated by love quickly descends to license, anarchy, out-of-control craziness.

Obviously, the question as to which is the highest value — freedom or love — has ramifications in every phase of psychotherapy. Here, we need to show a general correlation: authentic sex is to authentic, love-guided freedom as sick sex (lust) is to sick freedom (license).

Lust is depersonalized, despiritualized, dehumanized, immature, self-fracturing, sensate activity that is not just unloving but anti-loving. Lust is a solitary activity no matter how many people are involved; others involved in the lustful activity are seen as objects, things, not persons. Etiology, the cause of Lust Disorder, is often partially traceable to fixated childhood personality development, but this is rarely the singular cause. More typically, the cause is a free choice, a refusal to love, not an inability. Once chosen, lust can become an addiction — insatiable drivenness. Satisfaction, fulfillment, and peace are sought solely in pleasurable sexual sensations — which never satisfy. More intense sensations are then sought, which still fail to bring peace. Thence, more and more intense sensations are pursued until the person is a slave, driven by senseless sensuality.

The understanding of lust is particularly important in the treatment of sexual disorders such a pedophilia, fetishes, exhibitionism, addiction to pornography, bestiality, satyriasis, nymphomania, and sexual sadomasochism, all of which have important lust components. This is not to deny that these perversions sometimes, often even, have some repressed childhood roots. However, it is a fact that the repudiation of that choice of lust is the most important factor in the person's overcoming the perversion and discovering what real sex is all about.

How are people helped to repudiate and forsake lust? Though greatly oversimplified, the answer lies in helping them rediscover the depths of their beings, their psychospiritual hearts. Lust causes us to live more and more intensely at skin level, to become lost in superficial sensation, and then to abandon the more valuable depths of the self. In therapy, as the cold emptiness and shallowness of lust is exposed, the voice of the heart will eventually emerge to be heard, often crying, yearning for love. Then the counselor's interpretation might be, "Do you understand yourself now? All that time you were so lost in the frenzy of lust, you were actually looking for love — but as the country song says, 'lookin' for love in all the wrong places.' Now, maybe you can look for what you've always wanted, not lust, but love. And where do you look for that? Not in your skin; in your heart."

Homosexuality and Gender Dysfunctions — Love Disorders?

As this is being written, scientific and ideological wars are being fought over a thousand questions about homosexuality, transsexuality, and the wide spectrum of gender identity disorders and sexual identity "choices." That word is placed in quotes in order to highlight one of the central issues: whether people who engage in same-sex activities are exercising free choice? Or are they acting out behavior that has been predetermined by genetic, intrauterine, hormonal, familial, cultural or other factors that would be considered pathological (including the newest theory, that homosexuality is caused by a virus or bacteria). Looking for causes of homosexuality, science has invoked an X chromosome marker named Xq28 and a factor in the hypothalamic nucleus called INAH3. Researchers have concluded that male homosexuals often have a domineering mother and a weak, remote or hostile father.[23] Lesbians were found to have unmet same-sex love needs as children.[24] Male homosexuals were found to lack bonding with a father or any male role model.[25] Such studies number perhaps into the hundreds. Yet, position papers of the American Psychiatric Association have reported that there are no replicated scientific studies supporting any specific biological etiology (cause or origin) for homosexuality, and that no specific psychosocial or family dynamic cause for homosexuality has been identified, including histories of childhood sexual abuse. That association has taken a position opposing all "reparative" treatments aimed at changing sexual orientation.[26] The American Psychological Association has taken a similar position. A professional organization taking a very different view is the Catholic Medical Association. That group offers the most extensive review of research available anywhere on the subject and concludes that homosexuals are "not born that way," and that homosexuality is "not genetically predetermined" and "not unchangeable."[27]

But there is far more to the debate than is indicated by all the scientific studies and position papers, and that is the political

[23] A. Bell *et al*, *Sexual Preference: Its Development in Men and Women* (Bloomington, IN: Indiana University Press, 1981), pp. 41-62, 117-134.

[24] E. Moberly, *Theology*, 1980, p. 83.

[25] M. Hallett, *Nucleus*, January 1994, pp. 14-19.

[26] American Psychiatric Association Board of Trustees, *COPP Position Statement on Attempts to Change Sexual Orientation (Reparative or Conversion Therapies)*, March 2000, Approved by Assembly May 2000.

[27] Catholic Medical Association, *Homosexuality and Hope Statement*. See online: www.cathmed.org.

heat that is generated by the gay liberation sector. That political lobby would argue that even asking the question as to whether homosexuality is "normal" is a sign that the questioner is biased, a homophobe, or perhaps a stupid Nazi. And at the other extreme are the gay bashers who portray homosexuality as a contagious disease.

So let me be clear: I absolutely dread writing this section of the book. It is a clear no-win-no-win dilemma. Why? Because there are deeply entrenched "sides" to this issue, and I readily admit the need to be loved, so I don't want to be rejected by either side. So what shall I do? Stick my neck out and have it chopped off by one side or the other? Or shall I chicken out and pretend the issue doesn't exist, or that it is somehow irrelevant to a book about love? Only this is clear: there is no proven scientific evidence regarding the etiology of homosexuality and transsexuality. Thus, there is only opinion, anecdotal evidence, and belief that can be presented. But even recognizing all the unknowns, love therapy's view is somewhat different than all that has been written. Here it is.

In the Introduction, I stated that all emotional disorders could be reinterpreted and better understood in light of the love principles. I have concluded that homosexuality, with very few exceptions, is an emotional disorder, a love disorder.

In 1973, following the pressure of gay parades, hot rhetoric, the demands of homosexual marchers and a coterie of homosexual psychiatric professionals, it seems clear that "political correctness" induced the American Psychiatric Association to remove "Homosexuality" from its official list of mental and emotional disorders, the DSM. Thus, one day homosexuality was a disorder, the next day it was not — as determined by the political winds and a vote. Truth is not discovered by popularity contests, debates, nor by votes. It is my position that the most loving thing that the mental health community could do to help homosexuals is to re-recognize the disorder(s) and return it to the DSM — but *not* the way it was written in 1973. First, homosexuality needs to be better understood. Here, of necessity, we are limited to the most elementary, bare-bones beginning of a new understanding of this exceptionally complex set of disorders. (Note the plural, disorders.)

Succinctly put, the most common error committed in everyday language and in professional reporting is in categorizing "Homosexuality" as one thing. It is not one thing. In fact, homosexuality is a group of several love disorders that are all loosely connected by two common symptoms: same-sex sexual attraction and behavior, and/or opposite-sex fear and avoidance. Just as succinctly I can say: homosexuality is not "normal"; it does not reflect authentic love; it is a product of several types of painful and deceptive pseudo-loves in which the sufferer is trapped.

Love therapy identifies (at least) seven types of homosexual love disorder. With case examples of each, the seven are:

1. *Sexual Abuse-Induced Homosexuality* — The most common cause of homosexuality is same-sex sexual abuse at a very early age. The effect of the sexual abuse is akin to "imprinting." Sexual behavior and experiences in early childhood (before age seven) becomes deeply ingrained in the psyche. The well-known statistics showing that one in four girls and one in seven boys are sexually abused is, not research proof, but strong evidence to support the assertion that sex abuse is a prime cause of homosexuality. It is just one group of a vast array of emotional and sexual disorders that are caused by sex abuse.

Case example: Herb was sexually abused by an uncle from age four through age twelve. In addition, his alcoholic father told him he had always wanted Herb to be a girl. His mother, also an alcoholic, ignored him. For Herb, from the earliest age, the only attention (love) he ever got was sexual, from men, when he acted like a girl. It seemed to Herb that he was "born" homosexual. In therapy, he recognized that it began at age four. That was when he began pursuing love in the only way he had been taught, with men, sexually.

2. *The Fixated-and-Acting-Out Homosexual (or Heterosexual)* — Akin to imprinting, any sexual act that is strongly linked with

"love" at a very early age may become "fixed" at an unconscious heart level and then cause irrational, automatic "acting-out" as an adult.

A heterosexual case: Rose received her first kiss at age sixteen, whereupon, without a second thought, she instantly slid down the surprised boy's chest and initiated oral sex. She did the same as an adult with every man she dated, and then with her husband. Only in therapy did she discover that her automatic sexual response was not "normal." Rose was "acting-out." A kiss caused her to regress, and then to automatically "re-enact" an early-age "love"-linked behavior. Why? Rose had been sexually abused. She had been French kissed and induced to perform oral sex at age four by her teenage brother. As a neglected, love-starved child in a terribly dysfunctional family, she was all too prone to confuse sexual abuse with "love." Here, the point is that had Rose been a boy, she would have become "homosexual." Given a backdrop of love deprivation, any sexual act may become misidentified and love-linked at the unconscious heart level.

3. *Genital-Phobic Pseudo-Homosexuality* — This type of homosexuality is marked by aversion for the opposite sex, or more specifically, by phobic-intensity terror of the genitals of the opposite sex. A sex drive is powerful; if it cannot go one way, it may go the other, as if by default.

Case example: Deanne, age twenty-one, first presented herself as depressed and as a confirmed, practicing lesbian. After about four months in therapy, she revealed a secret she had never told anyone: she had been brutally raped by two older teenaged boys when she was barely twelve, and raped again at age sixteen. The result: terrible fear of penises. By default, then, because men were objects of such dread, she concluded she must be a lesbian. After less than two years of working through the fears and hatred caused by the rapes, Deanne, at first to her own great surprise, began having sexual dreams of a heterosexual nature. Soon thereafter, she concluded that she was unquestionably heterosexual and that her depression was totally gone. Two months later, she began dating a young man, and then terminated therapy. A few more months she telephoned to tell me she had become engaged. I was tickled to death for her.

4. *Homosexuality-As-Pursuit-of-Love-of-the-Same-Sex-Parent* — There is evidence that boys growing up in a single-parent home, absent a father or father-figure, are statistically more likely to become homosexual. The same mechanism surely applies to both sexes. When the same-sex parent is emotionally absent, utterly unloving, the effect on sexual orientation is surely the same. Why, though, do not all children of single parents become homosexual? Because the offspring of some divorced parents retain a relationship with both parents, or receive authentic love from a same-sex relative or surrogate parent and role model.

Case example: Sandy's mother was cool and aloof, but benign, whereas her father was brutally abusive. Men became "the enemy," but at least the threat from women was benign. Thus, her lesbianism was an endless search for love from the many mother-substitutes she slept with.

5. *The Asexual Pseudo-Homosexual* — These are cases that can certainly be diagnosed as Gender Identity Disorder, but they run much deeper than confusion over identity. These cases are marked by utter rejection of *any* sexual identity and of all things sexual.

Case example: Trudy operationally labeled herself a "sometimes" lesbian, but she simply would not declare herself in terms of sexual identity. When I asked if she identified as "female," she said "No." When I said, "So you identify yourself as male," she said "No." When I then asked, "So Trudy, what do you call yourself?" she answered, "It. I'm an 'it.'" Trudy hated sex in all forms, refused identification with either gender, and was confused by both sexuality and gender. Why then did she practice female-female sex? Trudy's mother was a paranoid schizophrenic, and her stoic, withdrawn father was rarely home. Thus, Trudy was grossly love-deprived. Her only memory of "being loved" was of her mother giving her a bath; there, she received a "gentle touch" that was somehow sexual, and as close to "love" as she ever reached.

6. *The Gender-Confused Homosexual* — Again, these cases clearly involve Gender Identify Disorder, but that diagnosis radically understates the depth of the distortion that has occurred to these persons, such distortion of identity that it produces a virtual mockery of a human being.

Case example: Sam described himself as a "flaming fairy," and acted the part — swishing, lisping, and hip-wiggling with an exaggerated limp wrist. And no wonder. From his earliest memory till age ten, Sam's severely disturbed mother would push her little boy's penis up inside him and tell him he was a girl. She dressed him as a girl, and told him if he wanted Mama to love him, he'd walk, talk, and play like a girl.

7. *The Genetic Homosexual* — The Gay Liberation political rhetoric would have the public believe that all homosexuals are "born that way" so homosexuality is "normal." Is it possible that some homosexuality is a product of a genetic, gestational, hormonal, or some other physiological error? Surely it is. Yet, here, I place it last on the list of types of homosexuality because reason indicates that genes play a role in an almost infinitesimally small percentage of cases. If a genetic brain anomaly can account for the condition, a reasonable analogy can be drawn. We know that a genetic XY chromosomal mix-up causes hermaphroditism (the condition of being born with both vagina and penis). But that is an extraordinarily rare disorder. There is absolutely no evidence, nor any reason to believe, that genetically caused homosexuality is any more statistically probable than hermaphroditism.

The foregoing seven types of homosexuality — let me leap to acknowledge — are by no means proposed as some sacrosanct scientific typology. Rather, my intent is to present a first-blush introduction to the idea that homosexuality is not any kind of "one" thing, not a single disorder and not a single personality type. Until the 1960s, the word "neurotic" was used to describe a vast array of disorders that have since been identified by perhaps fifty names. Who knows but that "homosexuality" is just as equally an abused label.

Beyond the hot political winds and hate-mongering that have attended the issue, there is a vital point that must not be lost: on both "sides" of the issue of homosexuality, all the arguments are about love. Both sides — gay marchers and gay liberators on one side, gay bashers and homophobes on the other — are in pursuit of and protecting "love." Consider the irony of what is really being said: the homosexual crowd is actually arguing, "We need love! We have a right to love! Our love is normal!" Simultaneously, the anti-gay crowd is chanting, "You're not normal! Your abnormal love is threatening our normal love! We need love!" It bears repeating here: love casts out fear. Given an authentic loving sexual revolution, the issues surrounding "homosexuality," so-called, can be discussed without judgmentalism and condemnation born of fear and defensiveness.

The New Sexual Love Revolution

The evidence has been presented here that since the days of Freud, much of the world has suffered from a collective sexual disorder, a delusion first introduced by a cocaine addict. That delusion, briefly expressed, is the absolutely crazy idea that real sex can be experienced apart from authentic love. That notion is not just insane, it is deadly — and that statement is not just rhetorical hyperbole. Thousands of people are dying — of cervical cancer, AIDS, and yes, people still die of venereal diseases — simply because they are operating under the delusion that lust has something to do with sex, and because no one has given them the first bit of authentic sex education. They just don't get it:

THE ONLY REAL SEX IS AUTHENTICALLY LOVING
AND THE GREATEST SEX IS GOD-CENTERED

With those banner headlines, the new sexual revolution is introduced and heralded. Viva Le Revolution! Viva Great Sex! Viva Love!

CHAPTER TWENTY-FIVE

Sacred Psychology and Down-to-Earth Love

The people perish for lack of vision.[1]

I call you to bring in focus a broader vision
than individual healing....
Write, practice, and *live* new and
sacred psychologies.

Prophecy to Sally Lynch[2]

(Note: A "prophecy" within charismatic Christian circles, is not necessarily a prediction of the future; rather, it is a message from God delivered through whomever He chooses. As always, we are free to believe the message or not.)

"New and sacred psychologies" — now there is a vision for you! In this sophisticated, secularized world, who would have the temerity to broach the holy Berlin Wall separating Science and Church by using such an oil-and-water phrase as "sacred psychologies"? Who would bastardize the scientific purity that Psychology has so long sought by coupling it with such an immeasurable word as "sacred"? Well, maybe God would. In my timidity, I thought I was being too bold when I faced scientific Psychology and used the word "psychospiritual." When I read

---

[1] Proverbs 29:18

[2] Prophecy given to Sally Lynch, Co-Director, Association of Christian Therapists, at the 1982 International Conference. For those who believe in prophecy, Lynch would be recognized as the scribe, God as the author.

the "calling" above, God's plain speaking made it clear: God *abides* in the human person; it is wholly appropriate, therefore, that Sacred Psychology take its place right alongside Sacred Theology in the hierarchy of sciences, just beneath Sacred Writ. When we approach the inner sanctuary of the human person, the heart of his or her psychology, we are treading on sacred ground. Intuitively perhaps, we all seem to recognize that holy ground when we near it; in our most intimate moments with one another, we whisper — just as we do in church. Psychology, properly understood, is sacred. Sacred Psychology provides both the mandate and conceptual foundation for a revolution in the mental health system. This may be a startling new idea, though, so perhaps we should try to define it.

Sacred Psychology is the study of the human "psyché" in its original meaning as "spirit" or "soul," which includes both mind and heart. This study is inherently "sacred" by virtue of its subject, which includes God, Supreme Love, who abides in the person as a dynamic life principle, *le point vierge,* and by virtue of the nature of the psyche which is intrinsically spiritual in nature, and in its natural state, holy.

Conceptually, it was the gift of the simple phrase, "Sacred Psychology," which helped to round out and coalesce love therapy into a cohesive whole, and to fully distinguish it from other models while simultaneously allowing their inclusion in love therapy's comprehensive scope. It is, though, a surprising phrase, and its ramifications are staggering. If my reasoning is correct, then by virtue of one tiny word, "sacred," the field of Psychology and every model of psychotherapy are revolutionized.

Consider: if the sacred aspect of Psychology is acknowledged as fundamental and necessary truth, then it must be integrated into the entire thought process and every concept that has ever emerged throughout the history of this discipline. When that is done, we are impelled to ask some questions which rock our intellectual foundations. As an example, consider a subject that is a fundamental area of psychological study: cognition, "thought."

Is there any way in which thought can be considered inherently sacred? Of course, and the first level of proof is this: we do not know what a thought actually is. All efforts to explain human thought have proved woefully inadequate. Studies have linked ideation to the frontal lobe of the brain, and speech to the Broca area. Much has been learned about the brain's neurons, synapses, and the electrochemical operation of neurotransmitters, but after thousands of studies, we still do not understand what a thought actually *is*, nor can we even say for sure where the mind is. Indeed, the more we study thought, the more mysterious it becomes. Surely the frontal lobe of the brain is involved in thought, as are synapses, the connections between the brain's neurons. Neuroscientists look for the chemicals and electrical potentials that allow the synapses to work. But let us suppose that the scientists discover every minute fact that can be learned about the electrochemical operation of synapses, and the billions of possible interconnections between synapses. Will that tell us what a thought is? Not at all. In addition, there are studies which seem to show that the "mind," so called, is something that involves the entire body.[3] In other words, the more we study cognition, the more we encounter mystery. Now, once we acknowledge that mystery is mystery (not just an unknown), we have encountered the realm of spirituality, and it is then simply logical to recognize the sacred dimension of thought.

Of course, there is a critical choice involved as to whether one wishes to call the puzzles involving thought a permanent

---

[3] Cf. Andreasen, *The Broken Brain, op. cit.* Here is a very readable overview of what science has learned about the relationship of thought to the entire body. The far more convincing evidence that thought is not simply a brain function is experiential. People who have experienced past trauma, physical or sexual abuse for example, will often have "body memories," i.e., the memory seems to be hidden and "lodged" in the part of the body that was abused, but not in consciousness. While discussing a trauma from the past, they may feel acute pain in the part of the body that was afflicted years before. More generally, the human experience of the psychospiritual heart indicates that for all of us, our deeper and rarer thoughts do not "reside" in the brain. Of course, "heart-thought," as described in love therapy, is ultimately related to the mystery that will forever surround, underlie and spiritually "explain" what a human being actually is. The study of the brain will profit us, yes, but the study of mystery will profit us far more.

mystery, or simply unknowns which science will someday unravel. History and *evidence*, however, are on the side of mystery.
All the thousands of scientific studies done in pursuit of the
origins of thought have left us completely stumped. Logic says,
therefore, that thought is a mystery, something that is spiritual
in nature, sacred.

Positively speaking, though, if we were to consider thought
sacred, where would it lead us? Ah, here is where we encounter
the riches of the heart, for thought, when it is done well, when
its fullest capacity is exercised, leads inevitably and unerringly
to the psychospiritual heart. Once there, we arrive at the depths
of human capacity which all of Psychology has touched barely if
at all: the capacity to "think with one's heart." This has been the
exciting special focus of love therapy, to at least begin to map the
labyrinthine ways of the heart.

"Thinking with one's heart" is one of the deepest levels of
subjectivity (next to mystic contemplation, which is deepest),
and one of the highest human capacities. It is the attribute which
most clearly defines the wonderful meaning of being human.
Perhaps the clearest way to distinguish "heart thought" from
ordinary thought (like making a grocery list, working an algebra
problem, or assessing symptoms) is that heart-level thought is a
profound *experience* involving the total being, an experience of
encountering the love-infused truth that is the purest and most
accurate reflection of one's deep inner being, an experience which
is typically unforgettable. This experience is emotional, yes, but
it is far beyond emotion; it is an actual experience of the heart's
movement, a quickening of the deepest spiritual realm of one's
personal being. Again, to distinguish, heart-level thought is far
more than a profound intellectual insight (which might be very
abstract, impersonal); when thought is centered in and flows from
the heart, it induces a permanent change in the very foundations
of personhood, in the very "spirit" of the person.

Though it is extremely difficult to describe, I dare say most
people have experienced heart-level thought at some point in
their lives — but certainly not everyone. Thus, in almost every

love therapy case, I find myself asking, "You've told me what you think, but what is your heart saying?" With some, the question is more basic: "Do you know where your heart is?" Indeed, it can be accepted as axiomatic that the more severe the emotional problem, the further removed is the person from the riches of the heart. In many ways, that is precisely the challenge of the art called psychotherapy, to find creative ways to help people remove the obstacles that have prevented them from discovering the secrets and treasures of their own hearts.

In the love therapy diagrams of personality structure (Figures 1 and 2 in Chapter Three), thought is reflected as "Consciousness," which is shown as an integral function of the psychospiritual heart which emanates from the tiny point of Light that exists in the furthermost reaches of every heart, *le point vierge*, the Life Force, Supreme Love. *This* is the source of our heart-level sacredness, the Love in us which cannot be defiled no matter how deranged, sick, or perverse our minds, hearts, emotions and behavior become. And it is this same Holy Center of humanity which reasonably mandates that any study of the human psyche be called Sacred Psychology.

Crossing the Psychospiritual Bridge

If the authenticity of love is to be served, as the title of this book promises, this final chapter must address healing Love as God, or more precisely, how God heals emotional problems. God, after all, must be the ultimate meaning of "authenticity" as well as "love." When daring to speak of love in spiritual terms, though, I am acutely aware that it is incumbent of me to bring love out of the heavens and down to earth. So let me emphasize that the spirituality I speak of here is not the schmaltzy kind that drips piety. On the contrary, administering psychospiritual love therapy often demands getting your hands dirty and sometimes takes just plain guts. That will be apparent in a case example below. First, though, let me offer a little history that will show the intellectual linkage between psyché and spirit.

Given our Western mode of thought, it is far more difficult for us than it is for those who live in Oriental and Eastern countries to think of "psychology" and "spirituality" in the same breath. We tend to compartmentalize and to fit all our thinking into tidy boxes. Yet, it is a basic contention of love therapy that our psychology and our spirituality are inseparably one. It was for that very reason that I began to use the word "psychospiritual," and then to try to express what that meant in everyday Western language. Let me tell you: it's tough. It would be easy to write a psychology of love, and just as easy to write a spiritual book on love. Putting the two together is not so easy, which is surely why there have been a relatively few therapists, or clergy, who have attempted to cross the psychospiritual divide.

Though love therapy is not the first model of counseling that has attempted to bridge the chasm between psychology and spirituality, it is, I believe, the first to show that love *is* the bridge between these two so-called dimensions of reality. That bridge, I will show, is a very, very short one. Though we are accustomed to speak of psychology and spirituality as two different worlds, the logic of love theory shows: love is truth, and vice versa; truth is one; love is one; love and truth together form a oneness in which the human being can be unified, wholed, and healed.

Though they did not focus in so decisively on love as the bridge, other models of therapy have clearly spanned the psychological-spiritual moat. The Existential Metapsychiatry of Thomas Hora[4, 5] and Bernard Tyrrell's Christotherapy[6, 7] are two examples. Starting with those two, I must recognize, albeit briefly, the writers who have left the materialistic-scientific mold, and ventured onto the bridge I call "psychospiritual."

---

[4] Thomas Hora, M.D., *Existential Metapsychiatry* (New York: Seabury Press, 1977).

[5] Thomas Hora, M.D., *Dialogues in Metapsychiatry* (New York: Seabury Press, 1977).

[6] Bernard J. Tyrrell, S.J., *Christotherapy* (New York: Seabury Press, 1975).

[7] Bernard J. Tyrrell, S.J., *Christotherapy II* (New York: Seabury Press, 1982).

Christotherapy, in Tyrrell's words, "means the therapy or healing that comes through Christ," and more specifically, "the healing through enlightenment that Christ offers as the truth-value that sets us free."[8] Immediately, Christians will recognize the semantic identity between Christotherapy and love therapy. For Christians, Christ is God, and God is love. Christ and Love, therefore, are synonyms; so to say Christotherapy is to say love therapy. Beyond the similarity of names (if I may be permitted to speak from my own religious belief system) I believe I am not being presumptuous when I say that both models flow from the same Spirit. I also believe that the same Spirit Who led Tyrrell to call his model a "holy science," leads me to equate spiritual love therapy with "sacred psychology."

Yet, while sharing the same Spirit, love therapy and Christo-therapy are very different. In one sense, they may be compared by analogy to deductive versus inductive reasoning. Tyrrell starts with Christ and spiritual reality, and moves "down" to his psychology. I start with love and psychology and gradually move "up" to spirituality, Love, capital "L," God. It is my hope that in presenting love first, as a self-evident concept, that it will find acceptance both among and beyond those who call themselves Christian. Love therapy, I believe, is as usable by Buddhists, Hebrews, Sikhs and agnostics as it is by Christians, precisely because love precedes and is greater than faith. Christotherapists would be the first to agree that of the three, faith, hope, and love, "the greatest of these is love."[9] They would also agree that the first and only commandment Jesus gave was, not to have faith, but love — to love God above all things and the neighbor as one's self.

The existential therapists have had a profound influence on the development of love therapy, as two of the eighteen love principles, on existential love therapy, testify. Though Rollo May, Martin Heidegger, Sören Kierkegaard, and others have heavily contributed, it was Dr. Thomas Hora's Existential Metapsychiatry

---

[8]   Bernard Tyrrell, *Christotherapy, op. cit.*, p. 1.

[9]   1 Corinthians 13:13.

which has provided the validation needed for two of the most crucial, and perhaps most controversial principles of love therapy, the equation of love and truth (Principle Nine), and the equation of love and reality (Principle Seven).

Once we enter the form of prayer called contemplation, searching Silence for God, there are times when we return from the "trip" with insights that make the phrase "mind-boggling" seem mundane. After several such "journeys," perhaps thirty years ago, I began to see that love and truth were one, identical, simply two ways of seeing or saying the same thing. But given the insight, it seemed so abstruse, so "far out" in fact, that I frankly wondered if I weren't a little nuts, so I shelved the idea. Unfortunately, I had not read Hora at that time. By 1959, he had described a "loving form of cognition" in which love and understanding come together, fuse, in the same way as Love and Intelligence are one in God.[10] It was only after I read Hora that I gleefully decided I was not nuts after all, and then dared push the envelope to its logical conclusion, "Love is Truth."

In a similar way, much later (1977), Hora asked a question that very few therapists ever ask, "What is what really is?"[11] (Granted, his wording is a head-scratcher.) My answer to that question differs from Hora's in a very substantial way. My answer, "Love is reality" (because all that essentially is, in the positive, ontological sense, is love), may be difficult to grasp at first, but it is far less "spiritual" than Hora's. Hora, in fact, becomes too spiritual for me. He seems to echo the Zen view that the real world is a world of appearances which one can transcend entirely so as to totally enter the spiritual world of the divine. While I deny that, because I believe that material reality is as real as rain, I am simultaneously eternally grateful to Hora for his eloquent and convincing arguments that spiritual reality is more real than rain

---

[10] Thomas Hora, "Epistemological Aspects of Existence and Psychotherapy," *Journal of Individual Psychology*, 15 (November, 1959).

[11] Thomas Hora, *Dialogues in Metapsychiatry, op. cit.*, p. 11.

and thus must be afforded its rightful place in any Psychology that presents itself as realistic.

Morton Kelsey,[12] Roberto Assagioli,[13] and Carl Jung[14, 15] are three others to whom I owe special gratitude for their opening of the psychospiritual horizons.

Crossing the psychospiritual divide means that love therapy is both an art and a science, but a "science" in its original meaning: *scientia*, in Latin, means "to know," and the original meaning included "discerning" and "distinguishing." Science has always "cut" some whole (as, for example, in cutting up the atom, or distinguishing genus from species). Until the last few centuries, science had always understood the "whole" to include Philosophy and the "Queen of Science," Theology, the study of God, the study of Love, capital "L." The sciences were understood to exist in a hierarchy, with Theology and Philosophy at the top. In this sense, high science was the study of Love (God), and the lesser sciences — physics, chemistry, psychology, etc. — were devoted to the cutting of various pieces of the whole, mere facets of the entire diamond of Love.

Love therapy, though it is not a theology nor an ontology, logically begins with these original high sciences, and only then deduces its psychology. Avoiding the mysteries of love, the decidedly spiritual nature of it, is to avoid ourselves. Utilizing all the natural sciences, love therapy goes further and plunges onward into the spiritual dimensions of life. Thus, love therapy is a psychospiritual science.

---

[12] Morton Kelsey, *Christianity As Psychology* (Minneapolis, MN: Augsburg, 1986). Kelsey is a prolific writer, and all his works cross the psychospiritual divide. This particular book was especially helpful in helping me articulate the "open universe" theory of love.

[13] Roberto Assagioli, *Psychosynthesis* (New York: Viking Press, 1971).

[14] Carl Jung, *Collected Works*, vol. II (Princeton, NJ: Princeton University Press, 1978). The works of Jung are so voluminous that I seriously doubt that many professionals have read all that he offers. At least I have not. The reference below may be a better starting point for many.

[15] Anthony Stow, Ed., *The Essential Jung* (Princeton, NJ : Princeton University Press, 1983).

The full range of spiritual love therapy methods are beyond the scope of this book. Some of those methods are given "honorable mention" in the Afterword, but they are grounded in my own personal religious belief system, so it would be unfair to impose them on people of other religions. There are, though, approaches to spiritual love therapy that are universally applicable, methods of healing that are spiritual in the generic sense, not defined by the dogma of any particular religion. They do presume, however, that the client believes in a spiritual dimension of life and in One God, by whatever name.

The first of these forms of spiritual inner healing requires no special spiritual gifts to administer — just great love. My great hope is that this is an approach that mental health professionals will find helpful with some of their toughest cases.

Surrender

Any counselor who has been around for a while has been confronted with a person who can only be described as "broken" and in total interior agony. These are people who have sustained such wrenching internal damage that they may even want to die, and they can find no way out of their gut- and soul-ripping suffering. These are also the cases in which the counselor can find no stop-gap palliatives, no quick-fixes, *nothing* that can be said or done to relieve the pain, so the counselor, too, is feeling helpless as can be. In times past, these are the people for whom I would immediately recommend hospitalization and/or heavy medication. Sometimes I still do. There is, however, another approach, a spiritual intervention to encourage the person to surrender their lives, including their agony and seemingly insurmountable problems, to God.

Sometimes the worst crisis, a time of utter helplessness in the face of inner torment and turmoil, can become an opportunity. Sometimes, just when a crushed and suffering person is ready to "give up," commit suicide, or retreat into the unfeeling darkness of depression or psychosis, and though it may "sound" very frightening, the exactly correct path to follow is to do just that: "give up," admit their powerlessness, and surrender to God.

"Healing through surrender" is an *absolutely* spiritual event. Though I would prefer to be wrong, so little is written about it in secular therapy terms, it must be considered another of the scientifically taboo spiritual topics. Yet, in churches, and on the television evangelist programs, one hears reports every day of people in devastating, "hopeless," emotional, addictive, and interpersonal crises being almost instantly healed after they surrendered their lives to God.

So what's happening? Are all these thousands of reported miracles phony? When people stand up in a small-town fundamentalist chapel, or at a huge national Catholic Charismatic conference, or telephone in to Evangelist Pat Robertson's "700 Club," and report that they "surrendered their lives to Jesus" and were instantly healed of a ten-year drug addiction, or were instantly lifted out of a chronic depression, or that they are joyously happy today whereas yesterday they had a gun to their heads, or that a sexual, emotional, or even a psychotic disorder abruptly disappeared after they surrendered, are they all lying? Did they all abruptly switch into a manic "high"? Are they all victims of mass hypnosis? Are all these people bribed to make outlandish claims? Are they all manifesting some bizarre psychic reaction that is easily explained professionally as "magical thinking" or as an abrupt "reaction formation"[16] or as a spontaneous remission that will be scientifically understood someday?

Clinical experience indicates that the great majority of these people are telling it exactly as it happened: they surrendered their lives to God, and God healed them. Granted, a few may be subject to a weird "head trip" of some sort that allows human explanation,

---

[16] "Reaction formation" is a defense mechanism which allows us to literally flip our emotions and impulses inside-out. Love, for example, can become hate, and vice versa, or moral righteousness may disguise repressed desires to be a big sinner. The defense is usually signaled by the feeling in the counselor, "This person doth protest too much."

but that minority should not deter us from forthright attempts to capitalize on God's goodness.

Other than spiritual writers and professional Christian therapists, a very few mainstream mental health professionals have discussed spiritual surrender. Thomas Hora, though, an existential analyst, describes the surrender process in the context of therapy. He talks about the "fragmentation, disorganization, isolation, and unauthenticity of a human being" and then says:

> In such cases it may lead to existential crises of various degrees. It is at such critical points of anxiety and despair where man, having reached the limits of his endurance, becomes ready to surrender himself to God in the spirit of *Fiat voluntas Tua,* or seek psychotherapy in a serious and accepting way.[17]

Hora obviously understands how spiritual surrender works, but as I have read and re-read the sentences above, he seems to place surrender, the "Fiat..." ("Thy will be done") and "seeking psychotherapy" on an either/or basis, as if they were equals. While it is true that we often need both God and therapy, these are not co-equal alternatives.

In another paragraph, Hora beautifully affirms the reality of spiritual surrender, but we need to read him carefully:

> In situations of existential crisis, man often becomes open to meet his God and fellow man, and commit himself to dialogic existence. This is the point where suddenly existence and religion become authentic and directly meaningful in an experiential sense. The reality of God is grasped in a direct phenomenological-empirical way with the "inward eye." As Meister Eckhardt said: "I see God with the same eye as God sees me."[18]

---

[17] Thomas Hora, "Epistemological Aspects of Existence and Psychotherapy," *Journal of Individual Psychology,* 15 (November, 1959).

[18] Thomas Hora, *Dialogues in Metapsychiatry, op. cit.,* p. 11.

The crisis allowing openness to meet God, the sudden meaningfulness of existence and religion, and the direct phe-nomeno- logical-empirical grasp of the reality of God — all are beautifully accurate descriptions of what happens in surrender. However, Meister Eckhardt speaks as a full-fledged mystic, as one who has attained what theologians call the "unitive stage" of spiritual development. Benedict Groeschel's book on the psy-chology of spiritual development contains a lucid description of the "unitive way" that makes these lofty reaches of spirituality "almost" understandable even to us non-mystics.[19] Briefly, at the height of spiritual contemplation, a mystic "becomes one" with God, but that extraordinary state must be clearly differentiated from the first authentic encounter with God that is associated with a first surrender. In this sense, Hora's paragraph needs an explanatory footnote: comparing the beginner's surrender and God-encounter with Meister Eckhardt's, is like comparing a T-ball Little Leaguer with Babe Ruth. Otherwise, Hora is exactly correct in describing how a person who is in the depths of emotional pain and despair can suddenly experience a dramatic positive change following surrender to God.

The following case provides glimpses of both the effects of surrender and of the technique, the "how," in therapeutic dialogue, a suffering client can be led to surrender. (We need to remember, though, that *whatever* we do or say, the subject here is God, and He doesn't manipulate very easily. Thus, we cannot think of surrender as a mere "method." When, how, and if God responds to a person's surrender is God's choice. If the time for surrender is right, and Therapist "A" guides Client "B" to sur-render, it is because God moved both "A" and "B.")

A serious caution also must preface the following case his-tory. When a person is in sheer agony and seriously thinking of

---

[19] Benedict J. Groeschel, *Spiritual Passages: The Psychology of Spiritual Development* (New York: Crossroad, 1984), pp. 160-188.

suicide, a careful "risk assessment"[20] is absolutely essential, no *matter* how fervently the counselor or the client might pray. "Feelings," including "spiritual feelings" should never be the criterion as to whether a person is a danger to themselves or others. Prayer is no substitute when the use of a brain is in order (and vice versa). In the following interview, though it is not described, a careful risk assessment both preceded and followed the discussion and the prayer of surrender. Only following the concluding discussion did I decide not to hospitalize Shannon. As it happened, she didn't even need medication.

Shannon's Surrender

What can a therapist say to someone who has in fact been broken at a soul-deep level and has lost almost everything? Shannon had already lost almost everything before the "killing" blows came, one worse than the next, in quick succession.

She was age thirty-four, a lab technician, mother of two small children, with a fine husband who loved her, but her husband could not make up for all the trauma and losses.

Shannon had been sexually abused by her stepfather from age seven to seventeen when she left home. The constellation of shame, fear, rage, sexual dysfunction and devastated self-esteem that typically accompanies incest were all present in her. In addition, though, after four months in therapy, while talking with an aunt about the family, Shannon accidentally discovered that the man she had always known as her birth father (the first of her mother's three husbands) was not her real father at all. When

---

[20] "Risk assessment" is the professional interview process aimed at making the best judgment that a person who has given some indication of suicide will, or will not, make a serious attempt at self-destruction. Suicidal ideation, "thinking about" suicide is an indication that assessment is needed, but when the person describes an actual plan that includes time, place, method, and most importantly, firm intent, then the professional will determine that hospitalization is immediately required in order to protect the person from themselves.

she met with her mother to ask about her paternity, Shannon summoned her courage and tried to share with her mother the fact of the incest inflicted by her stepfather. Her mother blew up, and blatantly rejected her rather than confront the truth of the incest.

Confronting abuse and openly declaring the fact of incest, when done in timely fashion, can be healing steps, but these confrontations came long before Shannon was ready for them, and long before any therapist would have wished. Trying to pick up the pieces in therapy, Shannon could not accept my interpretation that the defense mechanism of denial, alone, could account for her mother's rejection. Her mother had been just "too mean, vicious." Talking about that meanness, Shannon suddenly was flooded with long-repressed memories of physical and emotional abuse throughout childhood by her mother.

For the next three months, Shannon repeatedly called her sisters, seeking solace, seeking a relationship, and urgently trying to confirm that her memories of the sexual abuse by her stepfather, and physical abuse by her mother, were "real." Her sisters reluctantly admitted that they too were sexually abused by the stepfather, but they refused to discuss it. They just wanted to forget it, and to do as their mother demanded, "let sleeping dogs lie." Besides, "Those memories," her mother said, "never happened," so they proved that Shannon was "crazy." Finally, the mother and two sisters made a joint telephone call to Shannon. In succession, each told her she was a troublemaker for wanting to dig up the past, and that none of them wanted anything to do with her again, ever.

Devastated, Shannon continued therapy, now shattered by the rejections, ripped by the incest and new memories of physical abuse, and in deep mourning over the discovery that she had "no father." As if that were not enough for one person to endure, her aunt, actually trying to help Shannon piece together her disjointed family history, mentioned that her mother had gotten her second divorce after having had Shannon's father arrested for "some kind of" child abuse. That triggered another "piece of a memory" in

Shannon, which she insisted on pursuing. A day later, she recovered another traumatic memory: at age six, she had been raped by another of her stepfathers, her mother's second husband.

That same day, now virtually falling apart, but certain that her mother would surely respond to her desperation, Shannon went to her in tears, hoping beyond hope, again reaching out. When she told her mother about the rape, the mother *laughed*, saying it was all in her imagination. In the same encounter, the mother actually *mocked* Shannon for "being a baby" and needing a father, and offered to go out and "buy" her a father.

I met with Shannon that night on an emergency basis. Her eyes were almost swollen shut from crying. Faced with years of sexual, physical and emotional abuse, multiple rejections, losses and shameful cruelties, I looked upon the heaving shoulders of a woman who was bent double, writhing in interior agony, convulsing with tears... and I simply did not know what to say or do. In hindsight I can say that humanity can indeed be so cruelly befouled that there are no human answers, but at the time all I could do was suffer Shannon's pain with her, and feel utterly, utterly helpless.

The following is condensed from a three hour interview which started with questions as to whether Shannon was acutely suicidal and needed immediate hospitalization. My first efforts, using basic crisis intervention approaches, were to little avail; she continued to "fall apart." With the basic love therapy question ever in mind, "What does love demand?" my interior experience was one of "being led" more and more toward a spiritual answer. That required no spiritual genius to see, however. It should be clear in the following dialogue that there is no "psychology" on earth that would ever have been able to help this woman. Her crisis reached the greatest depths of her soul.

Shannon: [Holding her midsection with both arms, crying, groaning as if her entire interior were breaking apart] Ohhhhhhh, I want to die. Oh, Brennan, I just want to die.... Why can't I be dead? I've got to die. Why? Why?! How could they do it?

Oh, God, I can't live. They've just torn the heart right out of me. Oh, God, what have they done to me? Ohh. [Vomits — we stop to clean her up.]

Shannon: [Face and eyes even more swollen, still crying] Oh, Brennan, it's like somebody just cut the whole insides right out of me. I've just got to die. It's got to end. I can't take any more. How could they *all* do this to me? Dad, gone — Mom, gone — sisters, gone — raped by one stepfather, sexually abused by another one, disowned by the one I always thought was my real father — beaten and battered my whole childhood. I remember it all now — treated like a dog — and they tell me it's all my fault, or that none of it ever happened, that I'm crazy. Oh, *God*, what did I do to deserve all this?! They've killed me. There's nothing left. Ohhh… They've murdered me… [Therapist holds her, hugs her.]

B. (Brennan Mullaney): [While holding her — suddenly aware, in some spiritual way, of the direction that had to be pursued.] Shannon, you know I'd do anything in this world to take away all that pain… but you know I've always been honest with you, so I've got to tell you the truth — and I think you already know: that with all that pain, all those rejections, all that loss, all the cruelty, wounds that are as deep as yours, it might well be that there are no human answers. You feel helpless, powerless; so do I. You ask why, and find no answers; neither can I. But Shannon, there's another way. You've got a strong spiritual sense; I've seen it. You believe in God; you've told me of lots of times you've prayed. So, Shannon, if there is no human love that is strong enough to heal all those wounds, if there are really no human solutions, if we really are helpless, powerless, then where do we turn?

Shannon: [Removes her hands from her face, tries to stop crying.] God?

B: Sure.

Shannon: God?? Ohh, I don't know.… I just want to die. [Harder tears.]

B.: Shannon, this is one of those times in life when it gets down to what do you really believe — not just what have you *said* you believed, but what do you honest-to-God believe. Shannon, do you believe in God?

[Discussion focused on her "heart-level beliefs." After she affirmed that despite her pain she "honest-to-God believed in God," discernment told me that it was a time for a leap in faith for both of us.]

B.: Shannon, I'm going to tell you something that will sound strange. Can you listen? [She is still crying.] It's important that you understand me.... God does wonderful things with people sometimes. I've seen God bring people who thought they were dead back to life. God is good, Shannon. He's so good that if we let Him, He can bring the greatest good out of the worst evil. If we can open ourselves and let Him come into our pain, if we can let Him, God can bring us back to life when we think and feel like we're dead. What I'm talking about is called "surrender." In surrender, we give our lives to God whole and entire, the good and the bad, all that we are, and we just trust Him to do with us as He sees fit. We say, "Lord, here I am; take me; I give you my life; thy will be done."

Shannon: [Has stopped crying; sits quietly thinking] Boy, this is weird. I don't really understand what you're saying — but I do, maybe I do understand.... I got the strangest feeling while you were saying that.

B.: Well, we're talking about something that is absolutely spiritual.

Shannon: [Actually smiles] I guess that was the feeling. It was like something, like, jumped inside of me. It almost tickled.

B. [Laughs] That's good! There's a name for that: sometimes when we touch a chord of pure truth, it's like our spirits leap, or like God within us moves. We say our spirits "quicken."

[A long conversation followed about God's love, God as a good Father who can be trusted, about death and resurrection, and whether spiritual realities are indeed "real."]

Shannon: God is the father I never had? [tears] Ohhh, how can He love me? I'm nothing. Brennan, I still just want to die. I really do.

B.: Shall I say it bluntly, Shannon? Maybe it's time to do just that. Maybe what your whole hurting heart is saying, that great parts of you have indeed been killed, is true, and that it's time to face that terrible truth and go on and let your old self die — but give your life to God, surrender both your life and your death to God, and trust that He'll resurrect you, and give you a new life.

Shannon: That sounds…

B.: Crazy?

Shannon: [Laughs nervously] Yeah, crazy! And scary! .… How do you know that, if you die, that God… How does God bring you back to life?

B.: I can't explain that; I don't know. I just know that He does.

Shannon: How do you know?

B.: Because he's done it for me. I've been dead, too, Shannon, and God brought me back to life.

Shannon: [Smiles] You?!

B.: Sure, me. Whatdayathink, that you've got this crazy counselor who runs around recommending to people that they die and just stay dead? I wouldn't suggest it, Shannon, if I hadn't been there. Just like you, I've been killed — rejected, slandered and betrayed by people I loved dearly, killed — and God resurrected me. But only when I got it through my hard head that I had to surrender.

Shannon: [Still smiling] Boy, this is so weird, but it makes sense somehow… You really did that — died, and God brought you back?

B.: Just like you're saying you want to die, and feel like you've been killed, that's exactly the way it was with me. It's a long story, but basically, starting with a series of misunderstandings, I was maligned and rejected and felt like my guts had been ripped out, like I'd been sliced open and my heart had been jerked out by the roots. My wife and kids and some friends loved me, I knew, but they couldn't help. I stayed effectively killed for four years — till I finally gave up, surrendered. Then, God, very abruptly, within a week, removed all the pain and lifted me back to life.

Shannon: And God will do that for me? He can even wipe out all the pain I've got?

B.: Shannon, you've never known a *good* father, or a good mother, but God — shall we say She or He — God is both to you, and God loves you. I *know* God will help. My only suggestion is that you give God your entire life, all that you are. Give him the rejections, the losses, the sex abuse, the rape, the beatings — all the suffering — but give Him the good parts of you, too. Give Him your talents, that bright head and pretty face, your family, even your dreams and every desire.

Shannon: Everything?!

B.: *Every*thing. I know that's scary to think about, so quick story: as a young guy, I remember talking to an old Trappist monk in a monastery — Father Gregory. I told him I had been try-ing to surrender my life to God, and he asked why. I said that all I wanted was a real, experiential encounter with God. He said, "Son, you're asking too much." I got mad, re-ally angry. I almost yelled at him, "How can an encounter with God be asking too much?!" He said, "Young man, God doesn't want you to surrender; He wants you to *unconditionally* surrender."

Shannon: Oh, boy — I don't know if I can do that.

B.: [Laughs] Take heart, lass. Do you know what that monk finally told me? — After I got so angry, and after I reluctantly agreed that *unconditional* surrender had to be the right idea, he stopped me as I was leaving, and smiled real big and said, "By the way, maybe I should tell you this: I've been in this monastery for thirty-five years trying to unconditionally surrender; I still haven't yet, but we'll keep trying."

Shannon: Now I'm confused. I don't want to live thirty-five min-utes like I'm feeling, much less thirty-five years.

B.: I know, Shannon. The monk's story was just to give you a *feel* for surrender. We're not bargaining with God, but on our part, all we can do is try honestly to give our entire beings to Him. God will always love you just as you are. But it seems like the more emptiness we present, the more love He can give us to fill us back up. If you've got big emptiness, that's more room for God's love. The deeper the wounds, the more love God can provide to heal them.

Shannon: [Smiles wanly] God might have a hard time figuring out which one of my wounds to start with.... And empty: I feel like there's nothing inside me but a garbage heap... and oh, God, it hurts. [Tears.]

Before she left the office, we prayed, and Shannon did indeed surrender. The words of the prayer are not so important, nor can I describe "how" one surrenders except to say that it is an act that transcends "giving up" (as in despair) so as to become simply "giving." What is given to God is the self — and that, by any name, is an act of love.

The despair-transcending act of surrender is so ironic, so contradictory, that we are tempted to say it is impossible. Here was Shannon, so broken, so devastated, so empty, so rejected and bereft of love and full of sheer agony that she was experiencing utter lovelessness, death. She actually had nothing to give. Yet, seemingly out of nowhere, she found the capacity to give her empty self to God. This "impossible love," though it seemed to be something that Shannon was doing, was in fact done for her and in her, by God. That is the only possible "explanation." It is one of those mysteries mentioned in the New Testament: when we think we are taking the initiative to love God, it is because God has first loved us.[21]

The effects of surrender are so mysterious, so clinically "impossible," so absolutely astounding, that our sense of reality is jarred. In Shannon's case — and this is typical — within less than ten minutes of the prayer, she reported that the empty agony

---

[21] 1 John 4:10.

she had felt was "more than half gone." She called the next day to report that she had continued praying, and that the pain was "almost gone." Within a week, the pain was gone altogether. In its place she described a feeling of incredible peace (peace that surpasses understanding). Beyond that sense of peace was the impossible-to-describe "feeling" of the living presence of God.

As Shannon described it: "It's uncanny. I can remember all the damage, all the wounds — the sex abuse, the rejections, the beatings, the rape, all of it — but the memories just don't hurt anymore. It's like they just don't matter. All that matters is God. He loves me so *deeply*."

In religious circles, Shannon's surrender would be described as leaving her on a "spiritual high." Typically, this "high" is like a spiritual honeymoon. Gradually (over perhaps a year), the elation fades, and the person comes back down to earth. Then the person may need help understanding the remarkable spiritual journey which has taken them from abysmal depths to sublime heights, a journey that resulted in impossibly rapid healing.

This is not to say, however, that the person is *totally* healed and needs no more counseling. Rather, in surrender, God, ever the good Father, seems to pick us up and carry us over the thorniest part of the path. While He's carrying us, we feel like we're up, in mid-air, spiritually sailing, and we think we'll never have another problem as long as we live. But then He puts us back down on our path and says, "I've carried you over the roughest part of the road, but now you must walk. Go ahead. You can do it." Once given that vote of confidence, we never forget. Even if we seem to be slaughtered again, once we have experienced resurrection, we can never forget for very long where real life is.

So it went with Shannon. After surviving the crisis, and spiritually sailing, she stopped therapy after another month — "feeling great!" Nine months later, she resumed therapy, realizing that she still had a lot of old emotional wounds to work through. This time it was different, though. One by one, she waded through the traumas in her life — the incest, the rape, the rejections, the beatings and verbal abuse — experiencing pain with each event, crying hard, and working hard at trying to understand and to forgive her sick family. Healing progressed rapidly. After about two years, we returned to where we began, discussing surrender, but in a new way — not as a first huge leap of faith, but as a day-to-day effort. For Shannon, surrender boiled down to a simple formula: staying open to the love of her new Father.

Spiritual surrender, it should be noted, is in no way confined to a particular religious belief. Shannon's God was Christian, but the Jews in the Old Testament surrendered to Yahweh and were healed, and there is no reason to believe that Jewish surrender and healing is not continuing. Native Americans, Hindus, Buddhists, whatever the belief system, there is no reason to believe that if a person surrenders to God in good faith, that God will not respond. Surely God is not such a stickler for doctrines and dogmas as we are.

The Sacred Psychology of a Loving Death

Life is a blink. The end of this book draws near, like death, just a few flips of the page away for even the youngest of us, so let's keep dancing.

The unexamined death is not worth dying. Oh, Groan! That play on the old saw about the unexamined life is intended to set the tone for a loving view of death, which is this: a groan it might be, but death is a laugh. The old Irish wake expresses perfectly the healthy, seemingly contradictory mixture of feelings about death that the world needs to rediscover: stand the coffin and the corpse in the corner of the parlor, and while some cry, mourning, others stand around laughing, Guinness in hand, toasting the departed, recounting tales and celebrating his or her life, and guessing about the reunion party going on in Heaven as the departed rejoins long-gone relatives and they all dance jigs with God.

Death is a time to party, a time for joy — yes, *joy* and jokes in the midst of loss and mourning. If both crying and laughing seem contradictory, who says death, or life, has to be simple? It sounds like a contradiction because that is precisely the way it is: death is not death. How can that be? Harken back to Principle One: human beings live for love, because life, after all the floss and flotsam are removed, is only love — and love never dies. There is no death, therefore. When we accurately examine our lives, we discover that all we are worth, all we essentially are, is the sum total of our loves (Principle Eight). Faith, trust and hope are integral parts of our love (Principle Six), so it seems logical to believe that our hope lies in eternal life.

Sacred Psychology, the study of the heart and soul, presents a view of the human being that is inherently grounded in life-after-life, and which interprets "death" so-called, as merely a doorway, a passage, a new and exciting chapter of living and loving. Make no mistake, though, this sacred view has very practical application. It is less about Afterlife than it is about finding and keeping perspective midst the slings and arrows of daily life. Indeed, in the most practical sense, some people with emotional disorders, and perhaps any of us at some point, can be helped only with Sacred Psychology.

When Rollo May describes anxiety as the threat of "imminent nonbeing,"[22] and Sören Kierkegaard describes anxiety as "trembling unto death,"[23] they are not using literary hyperbole, they are describing the horrible experience of living-death. And when severely depressed patients describe themselves as feeling "dead," and suicidal people say they would "rather die" than live, we are not just challenged, we are forced to come up with a *singular* meaning of "life and death" that makes so much sense that it reaches the very depths of the soul, the precise place where severely disturbed people are suffering. It is not enough to spout the frayed-cuff clichés that traditional Psychology has offered, like "Death is a part of life," or "You're not afraid of death; you're

---

[22] Rollo May, "Contributions of Existential Psychotherapy," in Rollo May, et. al., Eds., *Existence, op. cit.*, p. 50.

[23] Sören Kierkegaard, *Fear and Trembling* (Princeton University Press, 1941, Doubleday, 1953).

afraid of life." Every person who is in the midst of a worse-than-death panic attack, and everyone wanting to kill themselves has heard those sayings, which, albeit true enough, are too superficial to help much.

Facing horrendous anxiety or suicidal-level depression, the task of Sacred Psychology is to find ways to quickly plumb deeply to reach the love which has sustained mortal injury at the core of being, i.e., the very depths of the soul, the furthest reaches of the heart wherein disorders are almost purely spiritual. It is precisely at this juncture, where psychology meets spirituality, and the search for a bridge between the two begins, that love therapy reaches its heart. Let me confess that many years of effort have allowed me to barely touch the rich depths of Sacred Psychology, but there is one bold truth that has been consistently borne out in practice, a fascinating truth which must be stated without equivocation and with too-little explanation: *When the depths of the hearts of people who are suffering soul-searing anxiety and life-abolishing depression is reached, the mortal agony discovered there invariably centers on their inability to believe, or simply never understanding, that God loves them.*

That bold statement challenges individual belief, and belief by definition has no proof, so rather than try to defend the statement with intellectual argument, let me simply affirm that the statement flows out of clinical experience with many cases. Those cases involved suicide attempts, psychotic depression, and a panoply of the most savage anxiety disorders. These were people facing existential *angst*, despair, and *anomie*. These were people who were utterly lost, bewildered and torn apart, people who were scouring their souls for "an answer." Granted, no single answer exists, but if there is one that comes close, it is this simple assurance: "God loves you."

Almost always, at some point in love therapy, the psychological-spiritual bridge is spanned with this soul-deep question: "Do you believe that God loves you?" Surely, no attempt is ever made to impose values or beliefs, so when atheists dismiss the question out of hand, that view must be respected. For the huge majority of people, however, the responses to the question are often profound, and sometimes usher in an immediate breakthrough, an abrupt diminution of symptoms. But it is not the *question* that brings a "saving grace" to those who seem so hopelessly lost; it is grace itself, God — not God as an abstract idea, nor God as some general awareness that the person develops, but the living God zeroing in very precisely on a very specific pathological dynamic of the person's soul which had been unreachable in therapy. Following is an example.

Willie Facing Death

Willie, age fifty-five, had cheated death three times. Suffering severe diabetes, on kidney dialysis for years, he had lost toes to the disease, was losing his sight, and could barely dodder along with two canes. His insulin had become harder and harder to control. A heart attack and three insulin comas had not killed him, but three times in the previous two years his wife had been approached by doctors with the question as to whether they should use aggressive treatment and life supports, or allow him to die. Yet, Willie had refused to even read a Living Will document; he was afraid of death, he said, and just didn't want to talk about it.

A year earlier, Willie had been referred for counseling for major depression. He had been sleeping all day, withdrawn, and his doctor was sure the depression could not be attributed entirely to the physical problems. That proved true. As I obtained a history in the first interview, it was clear that depression had dominated Willie's life since childhood.

Willie's wife and two daughters came for counseling. Not all, but many of their issues related to Willie, whom they described as constantly withdrawn and negative. When he was not withdrawn in his home office, he was teaching his children that "Everything that goes up comes down, so never get your hopes up. Expect something to go wrong, because it always does." With counseling, the daughters had been able to see how that learned negativity had caused their own depressions, and they had rapidly improved. But not Willie. Improvement in his depression had been marginal at best.

In counseling, Willie had been able to clearly trace his depression to its origins. His mother had always given preferential treatment to his older sister, so much so that one of his favorite "jokes" was, "My sister was an only child." That left him feeling basically unloved, hopeless, sad, sour on life and negative on everything. "Something will go wrong" was his constant theme, and no therapy approach — not cognitive therapy, logotherapy, nor any variation of love therapy — had budged Willie's negative, doomsday view of life.

Then Willie landed in the hospital again and had a fourth brush with death — and still refused to even look at a Living Will form. When he returned home and came for counseling, I brought up the subject. Unbeknownst to me, this would provide an opening for God to step in. The Living Will discussion moved us into the Sacred Psychology arena.

Willie: Hell, yes, I'm afraid of death. Aren't you?

B. (Brennan Mullaney): Not really... What do you think happens when you die?

Willie: I don't *know*! That's why I'm afraid of dying!

B.: Well, none of us *know*, Willie, so we're forced to believe something about death. Now, you've told me you believe in God; that's not knowledge, that's belief. So do you believe God comes into the picture when we die?

Willie: Sure... but I'm afraid I might go to Hell.

B: (People who voice a fear of Hell sometimes have a big secret sin, some old, hidden guilt that they have not resolved. Such guilt can also cause depression, so I explored that possibility at length. My hunch was wrong. That was not Willie's problem. I continued...) Well, I don't get it, Willie. There are no old sins you're hiding, so why would you be afraid you'd go to Hell? Willie, you're a man who's just full of goodness, so why wouldn't you go to Heaven when you die?... Willie, do you believe that God loves you?

Willie: I guess... Sure, God loves everybody.

B: Yeah... but does God love you, you personally?

Willie: (Tearing up) I... I'm not sure. If I think I'm going to go to Heaven, something might go wrong...

B.: Go wrong?... Like what?

Willie: Hell, I don't know — something always goes wrong.

B.: Oh, damn, Willie, there you go again: "Something always goes wrong" — even with God?!

Willie: (Crying) I can't hope. I just can't hope. If I think God loves me, if I think I'll go to Heaven, God might pull the rug out from under me at the last minute.

B.: (Sitting next to him, arm around him) Ah Willie, Willie, Willie, if somebody really loves you, they *don't* pull the rug out from under you. God would never do that.

Willie: (Midst wrenching tears) My mother always did.

B.: Ah, Willie — God *loves* you. And God is not like your mother. He doesn't promise love, and at the last minute not deliver. He doesn't demand perfection like your mother did. He loves you, Willie — just as you are. He always has loved you and He always will.

Willie: Damn, I wish I could believe that.

B.: You will, Willie, I promise.

Cut off from love by his mother, Willie could never believe that anyone could love him, not even God. Reviewing the course of interviews with Willie, there was no great surprise here. The love problem with his mother, his consequent definition of himself as unlovable, and his lifelong negativity, withdrawal and depression, had all been apparent within a few interviews. But that knowledge had not enabled me to help Willie. His depression had remained intractable — until the question "Do you believe God loves you?" was posed. Why does that particular question so often allow a breakthrough, as it did with Willie? Because answers to questions about God's love can be found only in the deepest reaches of one's heart, in a dimension of our being which is beyond the psychological, a spiritual realm of being that is centermost in all of us.

After a few more weeks of struggle, Willie *experienced* God's love. (I will not attempt to describe that experience; I cannot.) Then he could open up to the love of his family, and his depression lifted. But Willie's struggle, though more difficult than most, was not so different than all of us face.

The psychological and spiritual dimensions of love form one piece, one "psychospiritual fabric." For any of us, this life's loves and the next life's Love, God, must come together in an integrated heart if we are to even begin to fulfill our potential for wholeness and happiness. As one fabric, which provides heart-level psychospiritual integrity, love faces death and overcomes it, transcends it perhaps. Even now, as we live in down-to-earth love, love's fullness allows us simultaneously to live happily in the here-and-now, and to live "beyond life," spiritually, which also happens to be beyond death. The Irish have it right: when we can face our own deaths squarely, and laugh, then we are free to live.

More Spiritual Healing Approaches

Just as there are many methods of psychological healing that must be excluded by virtue of the limits of one book — hypnosis, E.M.D.R.,[24] group and milieu therapy, for example — so too there are methods of spiritual healing that must be omitted. Among those psychospiritual approaches are healing of memories,[25, 26]

---

[24] Francine Shapiro, *Eye Movement Desensitization and Reprocessing* (New York: Guilford Press, 1995).

[25] Matthew Linn, S.J. and Dennis Linn, S.J., *Healing of Memories* (New York: Paulist Press, 1974).

[26] Ruth Carter Stapleton, *The Experience of Inner Healing* (Waco, TX: Word Books, 1977).

healing through lamentation,[27] and healing of the heart,[28] all of which I typically incorporate into authentic love therapy in my daily practice. There is one more approach to healing, clearly the most controversial, which I consider to be an integral part of love therapy. It is not a method that everyone, whether professional or lay person, should practice. It can be dangerous. At the risk of causing some to debunk the entirety of authentic love therapy because of it, conscience demands that I include at least one case example of a spiritual healing approach which can help some suffering people when all traditional methods of therapy and all medications have failed.

Deliverance

In the lexicon of the Catholic Church, "deliverance" is minor exorcism — emphasize "minor" — as opposed to major exorcism. The distinction is this: exorcism is a rarely used ritual that is administered to persons who are deemed to be "possessed" by evil spirits, whereas deliverance is given to people who are *not* fully possessed but are instead "oppressed." Exorcism can be administered only by a priest appointed by a bishop after a thorough investigation in which possession is proved. In contrast, prayers of deliverance can be provided by any Christian — although prudence and common sense dictate that it be provided by persons with experience in the field, people who typically have spiritual gifts[29] that can guide the process. Francis MacNutt, a leader in

---

[27] Robert Faricy, S.J., *Praying For Inner Healing* (New York: Paulist Press, 1979), pp. 17-30.

[28] Fr. Michael Scanlan, *Inner Healing* (New York: Paulist Press, 1974), pp. 51-55.

[29] These are the "gifts of the Holy Spirit" mentioned in 1 Corinthians 12:4-11. Among the gifts are wisdom, healing, discernment, prophecy, and speaking in tongues. Discernment is of special import in the ministry of deliverance. "Inner healing" is the gift of healing as especially applied to mental and emotional illnesses. That gift is always called upon following deliverance — to heal the wounds that have been exposed and cleaned out (of evil spirits). In love therapy, such gifts are judiciously integrated into the practice of counseling, inner healing and deliverance, the three of which are a "package deal," and practiced individually very rarely.

the field of spiritual healing and deliverance,[30] describes evil spirits as entering a wound in the person's soul and becoming wedged there, and thus preventing healing. The image I use is more graphic.

Evil spirits are real. They directly cause some cases of mental illness and emotional disorder, but more typically, they exacerbate problems, prevent them from being healed, and cause a problem that might have been acute to become chronic and intractable. Evil spirits, demons, enter at a point of vulnerability — an emotional wound, a trauma, someone's sin (it may not be the oppressed person's sin, but someone else's, as a result of a curse, for example) — and there they remain, infecting and filling the internal wound, like pus, and thereby preventing healing. Deliverance is the process by which the pus is driven out, and the wound cleansed so that it then can be healed. The Deliverer is not the therapist or the one who prays; it is Jesus.

Briefly, my experience with deliverance began in 1976 when I became involved in the Catholic Charismatic movement. My own spiritual shake-ups during that period is too long a story, so it must suffice here to say that until that time I could only be described as a hard-nosed science-minded professional with a well-formed "show-me" attitude. I was directing a social agency at the time, and that included supervising a professional counseling staff. During those days I was already teaching "love" as the fundamental concept necessary for good therapy, but never, *never* in my born days would I have believed that evil spirits were real, and moreover, that they were the real cause of a significant number (perhaps five to ten percent) of emotional problems. I was *shown*.

In the past thirty-plus years, I have been involved in perhaps two hundred deliverances. I now lead a six-person deliverance team, and in the past have been a member of two other deliverance

---

[30] Francis MacNutt, *Deliverance from Evil Spirits* (Grand Rapids, MI: Chosen Books, 1995).

groups. There is much to learn about deliverance[31-34] for those who feel called to it, but the process is simple to describe: we pray; we identify demons by name through spiritual discernment, and then we pray to cast each evil spirit out: "You evil spirit named (Rage, or Lust, or Jealousy, or Death, and the like) — get out! In the name of Jesus Christ, I cast you out. You must leave now and go straight to Jesus for Him to dispose of as He sees fit." Given that command, though there is sometimes resistance and struggle, one by one the evil spirits leave; the pus is cleaned out. Very typically, then, the person becomes amenable to healing and ordinary counseling treatment progresses very rapidly thereafter. It is not at all uncommon for people who had been completely stuck in chronic pathological patterns for many years to make dramatic improvements following deliverance. Not always, but very often, deliverance works when all else has failed.

Space constraints allow only one case example — but it was a dandy.

Automatic Writing — The Deception of Delores

If there ever was a candidate for "Mrs. Average American Housewife," it was Delores. Just over forty, attractive, bright, quick to laugh, outgoing, lots of friends, solid husband, three fine children, nice house, no big problems whatsoever — until Hell quietly moseyed in and turned her life into a nightmare. Hell could "mosey in" because Delores naively had left the door of her soul wide open for demons to sneak through.

---

[31] Michael Scanlan and Randall Cirner, *Deliverance from Evil Spirits* (Ann Arbor, MI: Servant, 1980).

[32] Matthew and Dennis Linn, Eds., *Deliverance Prayer* (New York: Paulist Press, 1981).

[33] Robert L. McDonald, M.D., "The Role of Memory Healing and Deliverance in the Treatment of Schizophrenia," *Journal of Christian Healing*, 5:1 (1983), pp. 41-51.

[34] James Friesen, "Treatment for Multiple Personality Disorder: Integrating Alter Personalities and Casting Out Spirits," *Journal of Christian Healing*, 11:3 (Fall, 1989), pp. 4-16.

Delores came to the first interview with two women friends and her husband who had called me on a Sunday and persuaded me to come to the office on an emergency basis. The women were there to "swear to" the bizarre tales they knew Delores would tell, and to swear that she was not "crazy" — unless they all were. All three women had participated actively in the "phenomena" that began six months previously. The upshot of their message, delivered at me rapid-fire, was that Delores was hearing voices, not sleeping at all, shaking uncontrollably sometimes, and spoke of strange powers and weird events. But I should not interpret the auditory hallucinations and delusions as hallucinations and delusions, they said, but as "something else." What? They didn't know, but they had heard I had dealt with cases like this. I hadn't.

Delores had seen a psychiatrist a few days earlier who had listened to her story, concluded she was *not* mentally ill, but said he was not equipped to deal with the "supernatural" phenomena he felt she was experiencing. He referred her to the Catholic Archdiocesan Chancery Office, who referred her to a Charismatic priest, who in turn, referred her to me.

Seven months earlier, "just for fun," Delores and two of the women waiting in the reception room had attended a Parapsychology course given as a part of the Adult Education sequence of a public high school. It was a survey course covering the entire range of "psychic" phenomena — clairvoyance, telekinesis and other E.S.P. abilities, as well as poltergeists, pyramid power, "spirit guides," psychic surgery, ouija boards, palm reading, Tarot cards and séances. Interestingly, about the only occult subject not discussed in the class was "demons."

"The instructor demonstrated psychic phenomena," Delores said, "like telling things about people by holding an object belonging to them. With me, I felt he told many things he could not possibly have known about me.

"Then some people came to the class and demonstrated 'table-tipping.' Three of us put our hands on top of the table. It lifted all the way off the ground. It tapped once for "no" and twice for "yes" when we asked questions. The table moved all over the room."

With that convincing beginning, Delores began studying the paranormal in earnest, experimenting with the psychic and occult methods that she read about.

At the same time — this needs to be emphasized — Delores, who had always been an extremely religious woman, continued to attend Catholic Mass about three times per week as she had for years. She was totally unaware that there might be a contradiction between her faith and her "psychic" dabbling. In fact, her naiveté was so profound that she was convinced her newfound occult knowledge would greatly enhance her spiritual life. Her two friends shared that view.

Then she discovered automatic writing. Within four months, her life became a nightmare.

The "voices," which Delores described as just as audible as my own, had grown progressively out of the automatic writing. In the end, the voices had become so horrifying and threatening, she had tried to stop them by renouncing the automatic writing and all the occult studies she had made. She had destroyed most of her writings, but had found about twenty pages on the day I first saw her. Her friends had brought some samples of it.

A page of the automatic writing showed strings of words run together across the page, not separated, so it looked like one long word stretching from margin to margin. I had a difficult time reading it, so Delores translated it for me. This came from about the tenth page.

> I am your Manny, your Master Guide that has been with you from birth. You knew you were the one that Manny loved is why you feel good about him. You knew that the one called Greede was not the one you thought him to be but he tried to make you think he was God but he was not and will never be.

In evaluating Delores, the telling fact that her "hallucinations" were not psychotic symptoms was that she had none of the other symptoms typically associated with a psychosis. Her demeanor, speech, reasoning ability and affect were all very appropriate. There was nothing to indicate flight of ideas, mood swings, flattened or inappropriate affect, nor any other psychotic indicator. The "voices" she reported simply did not fit with the rest of the personality I observed. In addition, the social history I obtained showed absolutely nothing to indicate any kind of earlier emotional disturbance. In fact, other than the abrupt onset of the voices two months previously, Delores was the picture of mental and emotional stability.

Moving conservatively, I referred Delores to an internist, a neurologist and a second psychiatrist for evaluation. A full physical, plus neurological and psychiatric evaluations all showed "nothing significant." The internist and neurologist both refused to conclude anything regarding the voices. The psychiatrist wrote, "This woman is not mentally ill. She appears to be possessed." (Note: The psychiatrist was correct in concluding there was no mental illness, but his word "possession" was technically incorrect, an overstatement. Delores was extremely *oppressed*. She was demonically infected, but the infection did not involve her entire being, as is the case in full-scale possession. Rather, only select faculties, parts of her being, were infected.)

Only when all other possibilities were ruled out did I allow myself to finally conclude what I had been nearly certain of from the outset — that the automatic writing and the voices were demonically produced, and that Delores needed deliverance.

As a matter of fact, Delores needed four deliverances. Her "spirit guides,"[35] demons by any other name, were deeply entrenched and especially deceptive and tricky.[36] In eighty percent of cases, one deliverance session lasting about two hours does the trick. Demons involving the occult are always the toughest to expel, for two reasons: first, the person ordinarily "invited" the demons to enter; the demons then think they have a "right" to

---

[35] John Ankerberg and John Weldon, *The Facts on Spirit Guides* (Eugene, OR: Harvest House Publishers, 1988).

[36] Raphael Gasson, *The Challenging Counterfeit* (Plainfield, NJ: Logos Books, 1966).

be there, so they stake out a homestead; secondly, occult demons seem to be higher in the hierarchy of evil spirits, and thus more powerful.

As my deliverance cases were typically performed, I had seen very few outward manifestations of the demonic.[37] With Delores, though, ten seconds after beginning the preliminary deliverance prayer, she was vomiting, and within five minutes a deep, harsh, unearthly voice, clearly not her own, was coming out of her mouth. (Yes, eerie. And for the record, to coin a professional phrase, it gave me the heebie-jeebies.)

After each deliverance session, Delores would report a dramatic decrease in the voices. Both the number of various voices that she heard, and the audibility decreased sixty percent after the first deliverance, eighty percent after the second, and another ten percent after each of the last two. Within three weeks, the voices were entirely dispelled. For the next six weeks, Delores experienced a few very brief episodes of faint "whispers." Although these whispers could have been temptations designed to cause her to believe she had not been delivered, they seemed more likely to be attributable to aftershocks of fear, like mild hysterical reactions. After all, she had been truly traumatized by the whole weird experience. Too, deliverance is like spiritual major surgery sometimes. Recuperation is necessary, and aftercare.

---

[37] Demonic manifestations often seem totally unbelievable even to those who are direct eyewitnesses to them. During a deliverance, I have seen a man's eyes turn as blood-red as a fire engine while he cursed me and snarled and spit exactly like an angry cat. I have seen a man in the midst of deliverance perspiring so much that the sweat literally puddled on the floor beneath his chair. That man uttered a growl that can only be described as unearthly. I have seen a woman's face grotesquely twist so that the corner of her mouth was virtually touching the corner of her eye — as if her face were made of wet clay and an unseen hand reached out and squashed it. I have seen the eyes of several people turn into ugly black empty pits during deliverance, and then watched as the beautiful color of life returned when the deliverance was completed. But those experiences seem tame compared to a case reported by a fellow member of the Association of Christian Therapists: Allan Weilert, M.T.S., "Deliverance Ministry: Some Practical Guidelines," *The Journal of Christian Healing*, 17: 1 & 2 (1995), pp. 23-29. There, he reports praying for a woman who "lifted up off the floor and floated in mid-air for awhile."

Delores' recuperation progressed nicely. After twenty years, there have been no recurrences of the "voices." A major goal in her life now is to warn others of the horrible consequences that dabbling with the occult can produce. Embarrassing as the story is for her now — "I feel like a fool" — she wanted the rest of the story, following, told.

It was the content of Delores' automatic writing, and the insidious way it crept into her life and nearly took total control, that provides valuable lessons about the occult, yes, but especially about the brilliant and elaborate schemes that Satan can hatch to intellectually poison hearts, rip minds apart, and pull them away from God and from themselves.

The central ideas contained in Delores' automatic writing, though they may sound farfetched or even ludicrous when seen in the clear light of day, were presented slowly, backed by an elaborate system of finely tuned but specious logic and elaborate "holy" explanations. Condensed, following are the major "truths" that were "revealed" through hundreds of pages of the automatic writing:

There are three great mistakes, omissions, in the modern version of the Bible, and Delores' automatically written book, dictated by the "spirit guides" was intended to "correct" them. She was commanded to write a new, "corrected" Bible.

The first omission was "reincarnation." Reincarnation, her "spirit guides" told her, had been taken out of the Bible in the early centuries after Christ because at that time the Church was young and struggling and the Fathers of the Church thought that if people knew about reincarnation, the Church would lose its power to rule the people. Now was the time, the spirits said, for people to learn that they would return to earth again and again. Belief in reincarnation would help bring peace to the world.

The second deletion that early churchmen made in the Bible concerned the power of the Holy Spirit. The evil spirits, mixing truth with lies and lots of "holy" words, offered tremendous power. We people of today have no idea of the fantastic power we have within us if only we "believe" that we have it, said the spirits. In fact, we can have anything we want — riches, prestige, authority — if only we will believe in the "power" of belief. Only in retrospect did Delores learn that the "power" they were talking about would not have been from the Holy Spirit but from Satan.

The third and greatest truth omitted from the Bible, the demons argued, is that our present God is not the first God. They said that the first God was someone named Mary Jude. The one we call God created man, and Mary Jude created woman. Mary Jude is the mother of God, and she existed *before* God. Mary Jude thought the world would be more accepting of a "male" God. Therefore, because she loved her son so much, she did not let him know of her existence.

When her "new Bible" was completed, Delores was told, an ancient manuscript would be found in the Middle East which would lend authenticity to all she had written. Then the world would believe in and adore Mary Jude as the one, true, first God.

Thus spoke the "spirit guides," demons all, liars all, as are all who speak or appear to anyone, be they spiritualists, channelers, fortune tellers, or duped dabblers in the occult.

Perhaps the saddest realization that flows from Delores' story is that, had it succeeded, you can bet that a dozen sects would have sprung up within no time devoted to the worship of the god of God, the "mother" of God, a new golden calf, Mary Jude. It is sad that so much of humanity, so desperate for love, can be so easily misled. Decades ago, a psychiatrist used hypnosis to regress a woman back to a supposed "previous lifetime" and Bridey Murphy,[38] so-called, emerged. Thousands of believers in reincarnation were born. A bearded swami came to the United States, Bhagwan Shree Rajneesh, who preached "love" and a fan-dangled religion, bought dozens of Rolls Royces, bought the whole

---

[38] Morey Bernstein, *The Search for Bridey Murphy* (Doubleday, 1956).

town of Antelope, Oregon, and duped thousands of people into following him. Reverend Sun Moon preached "love" and brainwashed young people to sell flowers for him and find the devil in everyone but the Moonies. And surely the Reverend Jim Jones, before inducing the mass suicide of nine hundred-thirteen people in Guyana, preached a diabolized, deceptive version of "love."

The deception of Delores was accomplished by an appeal to "love" — as are all great deceptions. If there were but one lesson to be learned from her story, it is perhaps this: even demons preach "love." Thus, John warns, "Beloved, do not trust every spirit, but put the spirits to the test to see if they belong to God, because many false prophets have appeared in the world."[39] The various ways that spirits can be tested is beyond our scope here. It must suffice to point to this great test: "Judge by the fruits."[40]

The fruits of authentic love are joy, peace, patience — unerring and enduring goodness.

Love Is Always Balanced

Now that authentic love theory and therapy have been explicated from both psychological and spiritual dimensions, and the combination, the psychospiritual, only a few cautions and perhaps some of the writer's secret dreams remain to be disclosed. The cautions and the dreams have much in common.

While I strongly insist that spiritual approach to healing is often necessary, I am just as strongly opposed to what I call "angelism," the tendency to over-spiritualize every aspect of human behavior. In that light, I thoroughly discourage those who say to the angry, cursing, fire-spitting delinquent, "Kid, if you'd just pray and give your life to Jesus, you'd quit being so bad." That's damaging. Jesus Himself would never place such guilt-trip on

---

[39] 1 John 4:1-3.
[40] Matthew 7:16.

a youngster. Similarly, the holy crowd who sees a demon under every rock and interprets all emotional disorders as an attack of Satan are doing a huge disservice to those they believe they are helping.

Flipping the coin, opposite the sin of angelism is the corollary wrong of "scientism." Included in this ultra-scientific group are not just the atheistic-materialists who hold that there is no such thing as spiritual reality; there are many well-meaning psychotherapists who have labored under the tradition-entrenched belief that professionalism forbids their intruding into spiritual realms that are the sacrosanct territory of priests, rabbis and ministers. Facing a patient voicing spiritual suffering, too many therapists automatically squirm and then refer by default to the clergy, not trusting their own good spiritual instincts.

Balance is the indispensable guide for any effective therapy and that means "thinking in love terms," always. Love that is non-spiritual is not authentic love. Love that is disembodied and hyper-spiritual is not authentic love. Balance is measured with a finely tuned gauge that is found in the depths of every person's heart.

It is of course my great dream that other mental health practitioners and theorists will see the benefit of adapting love theory so as to complete and enhance the effectiveness of the many hundreds of other treatment models and techniques. The motivation for doing just that, I believe, will be discovered in the same place that balance is found, by listening to the whispers of the heart, the voice that insists that love and truth are one and the same.

Returning now to Principle One of this work, let me recall that every single thing that any of us do is motivated by the need and purpose of loving or being loved. Obviously, writing books is included in those needs and purposes, as is reading them. With that fundamental backdrop, please now recall the love principle that describes Conscience as that tiny voice of the heart that insists on one undiluted rule for living our lives: loving everyone, always.

And given that admonition, you will also remember Péguy's great truth, "The only way to love a person is as he is."[41] So, given those reminders, I would reach out to each of you, asking that you accept this parting, heartfelt proclamation: "God loves you, every one — just as you are. And so do I."

---

[41] Péguy, *op. cit.*

Do You Believe?

This addendum to the *Authentic Love* work was necessitated by a pickle that I faced throughout the writing, a damned-if-I-do-or-don't dilemma. That struggle was between the two forces I spoke of often — the scientific, ultra-professional sector on the one hand, and the spiritual, healing-thru-prayer believers, on the other. As I scan back over what I've written, it is apparent to me that one group may say I got "too spiritual," while the other may say that I was "too scientific" and gave the spiritual dimension short shrift. The information presented in the main body of the book can be accepted as a basic framework of authentic love theory and therapy. That information, let's say, is the core work, and professionally I will stand there.

In this Afterword, though, let me spell out a little more fully how much more spiritual love therapy can become. I will do that by presenting the very best, most effective instrument of spiritual inner healing that I have ever discovered. In order to do that, I first need to provide a full personal disclosure, a confession if you will.

My own religious foundation is as a Roman Catholic, and as a charismatic. A "charism" simply means a "gift," or more precisely, a spiritual gift. Thus, about thirty years ago, I underwent a spiritual process that resulted in my receiving several "gifts of the Holy Spirit." One of these was the gift of prophecy.

A Healing Prophecy

In the final passage of this book, some readers will experience rapid healing of deep emotional wounds. That bold prediction is not a prophecy so much as it is the product of concrete experience of what has happened to many people when as they read what I believe to be the God-given healing message that follows, titled "Do You Believe?" Many people have reported being touched and healed at some deep level while reading it, so it seems to have passed the test that must be applied to any event that purports to be of spiritual origin — "Judge by the fruits."[1] The chance that the prophecy might help others is the first reason for reproducing it here. It is shown at the conclusion of *Authentic Love* because it seemed fitting to save the best till last. This prophecy contains the best expression and "final word" on inner healing and love that I can offer.

A brief introduction is needed. When I received this prophecy, on Thanksgiving night, 1981, it came out of the proverbial blue. I was internally *impelled* to write it. Throughout a Charismatic prayer meeting and for an hour afterward, three words, *"Do you believe?"* kept thrusting themselves into my consciousness like a rampant obsession. The words seemed to come out of nowhere. Every few minutes, the words, which made no sense at all to me, kept popping into my head: *"Do you believe?"* Then, a few minutes later, again apropos of nothing, the words repeated... *"Do you believe?"*... On and on. It was driving me nuts! The therapist in me started asking, "Mullaney, what have you got to be obsessed about?" Driving home, the question still kept popping into my head even more insistently. *"Do you believe?"* Finally, actually feeling exasperated, I acceded to the impulsion, sat down at the kitchen table and began writing, with no idea from one word to the next, of what I was writing about. After several lines, it became apparent that these were the kinds of statements someone

---

[1]   Matthew 7:16-20.

like Jesus would express, which mystified me even more. These were certainly not my thoughts. I wasn't even thinking! The words poured out, but I had no idea of where they were headed. I felt like a scribe, a stenographer recording an unseen speaker. Finally, I wrote the words, "I am…" and waited for the next words to come. "Am what?" The "dictation" had abruptly stopped in what seemed to be mid-sentence. Only then did I read back over the message. Unlike my own writing, which is typically labored and full of alterations, this was written in a rapid flow without the first correction (exactly as it appears below). The message was about inner healing, about what the Lord is doing when we are emotionally hurt. I was deeply moved by the words, but still uneasy about the way the message ended. The start of the last line, "I am…" seemed to be dangling, unfinished. Then, for a reason I did not understand at all, I was prompted to capitalize those last two words and to move them to the right, so I printed, "I AM" at the right of the last line. Only then did it hit me. "My God! That's a signature!" (The ancient Hebrew word for God was "Yahweh," which translates, "I Am Who Am.")

As I noted in the Introduction, there seems to be no graceful way to begin a book titled *Authentic Love*. Reaching a conclusion about love is even gawkier. Love leaves us too much in awe, tongue-tied, mumbling.

Following is a message about healing. The speaker, I believe, is Jesus, but of course I can't prove that. If there are readers who prefer to believe the speaker is God the Father, or Allah, or Waken Tanka, or Higher Power, I'm sure that is okay with the author. The only thing that would not be okay would be to attribute the words to me. I will acknowledge being the one who recorded the words, but I adamantly deny being the author.

And so *Authentic Love* ends with this message. It seems entirely fitting, and far more graceful, to let God have the last word on healing and love. After all, He Is.

DO YOU BELIEVE?

Do you believe that I love you?
Do you believe?
I love you.
Do you believe the Lord — your God?
If you believe, then you must allow my love
        to flow over you,
and through you —
even into the marrow of your bones.
If you really believe that I love you,
you must open your wounds to my gaze,
and then let me have those wounds.
Beyond your anger, beyond your hatred,
        beyond your grief,
your turmoil, beyond your tears —
all expressions of your woundedness —
I have seen each and every hurt you have ever received.
When you were rejected, I was there.
When you were insulted, I was there.
When your love was shattered, I was there.
When you were betrayed, I was there.
When you were lonely, dying in your solitude,
        I was there.
And when you were dead, unloved and suffering,
        I was there,
loving you, giving you new life, my life.
For it has all been done before you, you know —
I died in order that you might live.
So please, accept my life, the life I have given you,
the life I have given for you.
When I died, I took with me your wounds.
They entered the grave with me.
And when I rose from the dead,
        I left your wounds behind.

I have conquered death, and with it,
each and every one of your wounds.
Forgive those who have hurt you,
    and then I will heal you.
Do you believe me?
Do you believe I love you?
Where love is, there am I.
Where love is, there can be no wounds unhealed.
Where love is, I am healing
[Iam...>>>   I AM

Index

love, pseudo- 22, 30, 31, 36, 43, 57, 70, 71, 72, 87, 88, 89, 90, 91, 92, 93, 94, 95, 150, 194, 252, 262, 298, 368, 371, 380, 381, 383, 384, 385, 452
love, psychological 5
love, puppy 80
love, quadruplex 15, 25, 72, 140, 369, 419, 421
love, romantic 72, 76, 261
love, self-sacrificial 22
love, teaching in schools 6
love, theological 97
love, theory 3, 5, 6, 7, 12, 31, 43, 45, 48, 49, 56, 58, 59, 69, 73, 75, 108, 125, 163, 198, 207, 208, 229, 267, 293, 298, 300, 313, 322, 342, 344, 346, 349, 352, 354, 378, 379, 424, 434, 436, 462, 495, 496, 499
love therapy 5, 13, 389, 394, 397, 408, 409, 410, 416, 417, 419, 424, 425, 437, 438, 439, 440, 442, 443, 447, 451, 458, 460, 461, 462, 463, 464, 465, 472, 481, 483, 486, 499
love therapy, a way, not a method 223

love therapy, existential 210, 226, 231, 251, 254, 268, 291, 463
love, threatened 70, 130, 149
love, tough 170, 171, 172
love, types of 26, 71
love while sleeping 45, 378
love-centered eclecticism 223, 229, 231, 232
love-faith-trust-hope 21. See quadruplex integer
love-filled universe. See Figure 3
love-knowledge 266, 267
love-life inventory 258
Love-Reality Principle 99
love-thought 251, 258, 267
love-time, of causality 253
love-time, of materiality 253
love-time, of space 253
love-time, of time 259
"love-time" versus "clock time" 259
lovelessness 9, 11, 42, 44, 137, 145, 148, 156, 157, 172, 205, 263, 279, 282, 283, 297, 298, 303, 304, 305, 306, 307, 309, 310, 311, 313, 345, 384, 408, 412, 417, 419, 420, 477
loving 349, 369
loving, internal experience of 55, 208
Luke 63
Luke, suicide attempt 63
Luke, unreciprocated love 63
lust 72, 405, 424, 425, 437, 447, 448, 449, 456, 488
lymphocyte 10
Lynn. See agoraphobia

M

Mandala Therapy xvii
mania 24, 140, 253, 260, 262, 386
manic depressive 300
marasmus babies 3, 7, 8, 41, 262, 299, 300, 306, 309
marriage 42
marriage, authentic 42, 63, 81
marriage, test for authentic 82
Mary Jude 494. See automatic writing
Mary Lou 211
Mary Lou and Mamie. See love heals
mass murderer 179
Massignon 119
Masters and Johnson 437
May, Rollo 58, 224, 254, 255, 259, 264, 273, 278, 311, 312, 317, 463, 480
McKinney, W. 10